Digital Token Valuation

Roberto Moro-Visconti · Andrea Cesaretti

Digital Token Valuation

Cryptocurrencies, NFTs, Decentralized Finance, and Blockchains

Roberto Moro-Visconti
Catholic University of the Sacred Heart
Milan, Italy

Andrea Cesaretti
Rimini, Italy

ISBN 978-3-031-42970-5   ISBN 978-3-031-42971-2 (eBook)
https://doi.org/10.1007/978-3-031-42971-2

© The Editor(s) (if applicable) and The Author(s), under exclusive license to Springer Nature Switzerland AG 2023

This work is subject to copyright. All rights are solely and exclusively licensed by the Publisher, whether the whole or part of the material is concerned, specifically the rights of translation, reprinting, reuse of illustrations, recitation, broadcasting, reproduction on microfilms or in any other physical way, and transmission or information storage and retrieval, electronic adaptation, computer software, or by similar or dissimilar methodology now known or hereafter developed.
The use of general descriptive names, registered names, trademarks, service marks, etc. in this publication does not imply, even in the absence of a specific statement, that such names are exempt from the relevant protective laws and regulations and therefore free for general use.
The publisher, the authors, and the editors are safe to assume that the advice and information in this book are believed to be true and accurate at the date of publication. Neither the publisher nor the authors or the editors give a warranty, expressed or implied, with respect to the material contained herein or for any errors or omissions that may have been made. The publisher remains neutral with regard to jurisdictional claims in published maps and institutional affiliations.

This Palgrave Macmillan imprint is published by the registered company Springer Nature Switzerland AG
The registered company address is: Gewerbestrasse 11, 6330 Cham, Switzerland

Paper in this product is recyclable.

Contents

1	**Introduction**	1
2	**Asset Class Taxonomy and General Valuation Approaches**	27
	2.1 Purpose of the Firm Evaluation	27
	2.2 Back-to-the Earth: Functional Analysis and Business Planning as a Prerequisite for Valuation	31
	2.3 Are Cryptocurrencies an Asset Class?	35
	2.4 General Valuation Approaches	37
	The Balance Sheet-Based Approach	38
	Monetary Equity	45
	2.5 The Income Approach	47
	Estimated Normalized Income	48
	Choice of the Capitalization Rate	51
	Choice of the Capitalization Formula	51
	2.6 The Value Added	53
	Use Value and Exchange Value	55
	Practical Example—The Value-Added Cake	56
	Cash is King: The Superiority of the Financial Approach	58
	Empirical Approaches	68
	2.7 Terminal Value	74
	References	79

3	**The Scalable Valuation of Digital Intangibles**		81
	3.1	*The Intangible Roadmap*	81
	3.2	*Accounting for Intellectual Property as a Prerequisite for Valuation*	83
		Intangible Assets and Capitalized Costs	86
		Valuation Drivers, Overcoming the Accounting Puzzle	87
	3.3	*Intangible Assets Valuation According to IVS 210*	90
	3.4	*Financial Evaluation*	93
		"With or Without" Incremental Valuation	95
	3.5	*Value Co-creation and Economic Marginality*	100
	3.6	*The Valuation of Scalable Digital Platforms*	102
	3.7	*Sliding Doors: Network-Bridging Multisided Platforms*	104
	References		106
4	**Cryptocurrencies and Non-Fungible Tokens**		107
	4.1	*Taxonomy and Features*	107
	4.2	*Taxonomy of the Main Cryptocurrencies, With Some Evaluation Hints*	114
		Backed Stablecoins—More on Value and Key Features	120
		Crypto-Collateralized Stablecoins—More on Value and Key Features	121
		Algorithmic Stablecoins—More on Value and Key Features	122
	4.3	*Crypto Risk*	124
	4.4	*Impact of the SWOT Analysis on the Valuation of Cryptocurrencies*	127
	4.5	*The Impact of Cryptocurrency Volatility on Market Value*	130
	4.6	*Non-Fungible Tokens (NFT): Main Features*	133
	4.7	*NFT Valuation*	136
	References		138
5	**Digital Art and Non-Fungible Tokens**		141
	5.1	*Digital Art*	141
	5.2	*Timestamps*	146
	5.3	*Evaluation Approaches*	147

5.4	Interactive Art (Participatory or Relational) and Value Co-Creation	152
5.5	Copyright Framework and Valuation	153
	Exploitation and Copyright Protection	155
	From Copyright to Copyleft and Creative Commons	159
5.6	Reproducibility of Works, Real Options, and Digital Scalability	160
	The Secondary Market	162
	Non-Fungible Tokens (NFT)	163
References		166

6 Blockchains, Internet of Value, and Smart Transactions — 167
6.1	Blockchains: Definition and Main Features	167
6.2	Disrupting Traditional Business Models	172
6.3	Internet of Value	176
6.4	The Legal Nature of Public or Private Blockchains as a Prerequisite for Valuation	184
6.5	Valuation Patterns	189
6.6	Blockchains and Cryptocurrencies	193
References		196

7 The Metaverse — 199
7.1	The Metaverse: Definition and Business Applications	199
7.2	Scale-Free Networks and the Metaverse Topology	203
7.3	Scalability and the Network Effect	205
7.4	Multilayer Networks	212
7.5	Sliding Doors: Network-Bridging Multisided Platforms	216
7.6	From the Internet to the Metaverse	219
7.7	Synchronizing the Physical and Virtual: the Avatar Bridging Node	223
7.8	A Holistic Ecosystem: From Physical Reality to the Internet and the Metaverse	225
7.9	From Business Modeling to Economic Valuation	230
7.10	Crypto-Backed Metaverse	235
7.11	Metaverse and Decentralized Finance	237
7.12	Metaverse, Blockchains, and Cryptocurrencies	238
References		239

8	**Networking Digital Platforms and Virtual Marketplaces**		**241**
	8.1 Definition and Features		241
	8.2 Legal Aspects		251
	8.3 Networked Governance Around Digital Platforms		253
	8.4 Digital (Smart) Supply Chains		259
	8.5 The Assumptions of Evaluation, Between Digital Scalability and Network Theory		263
	8.6 A Theoretical Background for the Economic Valuation		264
	8.7 Open Source Platforms		268
	8.8 Proprietary (Commercial) Platforms		270
	8.9 Adaptation of the General Valuation Approaches		274
	8.10 Specific Valuation Approaches		277
	8.11 The Valuation of Virtual Marketplaces		281
	References		285
9	**Decentralized Finance (DeFi)**		**287**
	9.1 The Architecture of Decentralized Finance		287
		A Closer Look at Liquidity Pools	288
		A Closer Look at Automated Market Makers	290
	9.2 DeFi vs Traditional Finance		290
		The Ethereum Name Service, ENS	290
		A Hypothetical Venture Capital Protocol	293
	9.3 The Blockchain		295
		Traditional Versus Blockchain Networks	300
		Blockchain and Its "Nodes" in a DeFi Protocols	302
	9.4 The Value of the DeFi		303
	9.5 Key Characteristics of DeFi		305
	9.6 Benefits and Potential of DeFi		306
	9.7 A DeFi Project in Deep		307
		The Protocol	309
		The Players	310
		Pools	313
		The Process	314
		Process of Choice of Investment by Voting Pool	315
		Control Over the Target Company	316
		Smart Contracts	316
		Required Standards of the Projects	316
	9.8 Challenges and Risks of DeFi		317

		Systemic Risk	320
9.9		DeFi Valuation	320
		Market Approach	321
		Income Approach	326
		Further Elements to Be Analyzed in Any Valuation Approach of DeFi Projects	332
		Risk Assessment	337
	References		338
10	Cybersecurity		341
	10.1	Introduction	341
	10.2	SWOT Analysis	345
	10.3	Digital Tokens and Cybersecurity	346
	10.4	Valuation	350
	References		354
11	Digital Token Valuation: Looking for a New Gold Standard?		355
	11.1	The Digital Token Underlying as a Prerequisite for the Valuation	355
		Tokenomics	361
	11.2	Asset Class Valuation	364
	11.3	Digital Token Valuation	366
	11.4	Valuation of the Digital Tokens Linked to the DeFi Projects	370
	11.5	Income approach	374
		The perpetuity growth rate	375
		The Discount or Required Rate of Return	377
	11.6	Market Approach	378
	11.7	The Total Value Locked ratio	381
	11.8	The Market Cap to Total Value Locked Ratio	385
	11.9	The Price to Earnings Ratio (P/E)	387
	11.10	Valuation of Non-backed Cryptocurrencies Locked Up in Staking on a Proof-of-Stake Network	389
	11.11	Conclusion	391
	References		393
12	The Cryptocurrency Crash of 2022: Which Lessons for the Future?		395
	12.1	Annus horribilis	395

12.2	The Cryptocurrency Bubble	395
12.3	Which Lessons for the Future?	397
12.4	Volatility Does Not Give Guarantees	398
	The Role of the Exchanges in the Volatility of the Cryptocurrencies	400
	Ownership Concentration	401
	The Ghost of Charles Ponzi is Still Among Us	401
12.5	Due Diligence is Still in Fashion	402
12.6	Pump and dump	404
12.7	The Crypto Assets Are of This World	405
12.8	"Too Big to Fail" Doesn't Work in the Crypto World	407
12.9	Contagion is Real	408
12.10	Let's Get Physical	409
References		409

13 FinTech and Digital Payment Systems Valuation — 411

13.1	Introduction	411
13.2	The Digital Ecosystem	416
13.3	Financial Bottlenecks: Inefficiencies and Friction Points	418
13.4	The Accounting Background for Valuation	420
13.5	FinTech Business Models	420
13.6	Digital Payment Systems	425
13.7	Banks Versus FinTechs: Cross-Pollination and Scalability	436
	Cross-Pollination	436
	Scalability	437
13.8	Insights from Listed FinTechs	438
13.9	Valuation Methods	440
	The Financial Approach	443
	Empirical Approaches (Market Multipliers)	450
13.10	Market Stress Tests and Business Model Sensitivity	452
13.11	Challenges and Failures: Why FinTechs Burn Out	453
13.12	Concluding Remarks	456
References		456

14 Digitalization and ESG-Driven Valuation — 459

14.1	Introduction	459
14.2	Sustainable Business Planning	462

14.3	The Cost of Collecting Capital: A Comparison between Traditional and ESG-Firms	466
14.4	Sustainability Patterns	469
	Circular Economy	474
	Resilient Supply and Value Chains	478
	Sharing Economy and Collaborative Commons	480
	Scalability and Real Options	483
	Impact of ESG Parameters on the Valuation of Digital Tokens and Cryptocurrencies	486
References		494

Index 497

List of Figures

Fig. 2.1	From the enterprise to the equity value	30
Fig. 2.2	Functional analysis, business planning, and firm valuation	33
Fig. 2.3	From market trends to business models and firm valuation	34
Fig. 2.4	From the balance sheet to the asset classes	36
Fig. 2.5	The Financial-Economic Cycle	39
Fig. 2.6	Firm valuation approaches: a taxonomy	40
Fig. 2.7	Balance sheet-based approach	41
Fig. 2.8	Voting and investment rights	42
Fig. 2.9	Book, monetary, tangible, and intangible equity	46
Fig. 2.10	Revenue normalization	48
Fig. 2.11	Partitioning of the value-added pie	57
Fig. 2.12	Operating and net cash flows	59
Fig. 2.13	Value of the firm and cash flows	62
Fig. 2.14	WACC determinants	66
Fig. 2.15	From the EBITDA multiplier to the enterprise and equity value	75
Fig. 2.16	Terminal value applications	76
Fig. 2.17	Terminal value estimation process	77
Fig. 3.1	Intangible interaction	82
Fig. 3.2	Information value chain	82
Fig. 3.3	The integrated equity—economic—financial—empirical and market valuation	89
Fig. 3.4	Approaches of valuation of intangible assets	92
Fig. 3.5	Network valuation approaches	99
Fig. 4.1	Digitalization, scalability, and cryptocurrencies	114

Fig. 4.2	Volatility of Bitcoin vs Dow Jones Industrial	130
Fig. 4.3	Variations of prices of Bitcoin vs Dow Jones Industrial	131
Fig. 4.4	Variations of prices of ether vs Dow Jones Industrial	131
Fig. 4.5	Variations of Dow Jones Industrial vs Nasdaq Composite	132
Fig. 4.6	Cryptocurrencies, NFTs, and blockchains	135
Fig. 5.1	Interaction between digital art and intangible assets	150
Fig. 5.2	Digital art evaluation methodologies	158
Fig. 5.3	Primary and secondary market	163
Fig. 6.1	Blockchain as a sequential chain of data	170
Fig. 6.2	Blockchain formation	171
Fig. 6.3	Public, private, and consortium Blockchain	187
Fig. 7.1	From physical reality to the internet and metaverse	201
Fig. 7.2	Metaverse constituents	202
Fig. 7.3	Multilayer networks	215
Fig. 7.4	Multisided platforms bridging to the metaverse	219
Fig. 7.5	The metaverse building features	221
Fig. 7.6	The metaverse technological input factors	222
Fig. 7.7	The Avatar value chain	225
Fig. 7.8	From physical reality to the Internet and the Metaverse	228
Fig. 8.1	Platform taxonomy	246
Fig. 8.2	Internal and external stakeholders linked to the firm and the digital platform	256
Fig. 8.3	From traditional to networked digital value chains	263
Fig. 9.1	Traditional venture capital model	293
Fig. 9.2	A decentralized venture capital model	294
Fig. 9.3	Distributed network	298
Fig. 9.4	Types of blockchains	300
Fig. 9.5	Private blockchain	301
Fig. 9.6	Simplified representation of a DeFi venture capital on Ethereum blockchain	302
Fig. 9.7	TVL from 2020 to the first quarter of 2023	304
Fig. 9.8	TVL is related to the price of cryptocurrencies	305
Fig. 9.9	Business model of a DeFi venture capital protocol totally decentralized and disintermediated	310
Fig. 9.10	A DeFi protocol is a multilayer network	312
Fig. 9.11	TVL of 10 DeFi protocols on June 2, 2023 (*Source* DefiLlama.com)	322
Fig. 9.12	Processing of data extracted from DefiLlama.com and Coinmarketcap.com on June 2, 2023	323
Fig. 9.13	Processing of data published by DefiLlama.com and CoinMarketCap.com on June 2, 2023	324

Fig. 9.14	Process of calculation of the value of a DeFi protocol with the DCF approach	326
Fig. 9.15	Price variations of UNI and DOT, 2021–2022 (*Data source* Coinmarketcap.com)	330
Fig. 11.1	From the balance sheet to the asset classes	366
Fig. 12.1	Prices of BTC. 6 years	396
Fig. 12.2	Prices of LUNC token 2021–2022	399
Fig. 12.3	Prices of USTC 2021–2022	399
Fig. 12.4	Prices of FTT token 2021–2022	403
Fig. 12.5	Prices of PEPE token April 2023–May 2023	403
Fig. 12.6	Correlation between BTC and Fed's interest rates	405
Fig. 12.7	Correlation between DeFi TVL and Fed's interest rates	406
Fig. 13.1	Main FinTech activities	415
Fig. 13.2	Interaction of FinTech with BigTechs and traditional banks	419
Fig. 13.3	Evaluation methodology	424
Fig. 13.4	Business model and value drivers	425
Fig. 13.5	FinTech versus technological and banking stock market index	439
Fig. 13.6	Business model and valuation approach of FinTechs	442
Fig. 14.1	Cost of capital: comparison between traditional and ESG-firms	468
Fig. 14.2	Sustainability patterns	473
Fig. 14.3	Circular economy FlowChart	477
Fig. 14.4	The Impact of the Intangible Investments on the EBITDA	485

List of Tables

Table 2.1	Cash flow statement and link with the cost of capital	61
Table 2.2	Income statement of the target firm	78
Table 2.3	Valuation multiples	78
Table 2.4	Enterprise and equity value	78
Table 3.1	Economic and financial marginality	96
Table 3.2	Value co-creation and economic-financial impact	101
Table 4.1	Cryptocurrency features and valuation	115
Table 4.2	SWOT analysis	128
Table 5.1	Digital art—taxonomy	143
Table 7.1	Network scalability laws	209
Table 9.1	Characteristics of traditional intermediaries, blockchain, and DeFi	296
Table 9.2	Dex exchanges	323
Table 9.3	DEX statistics	324
Table 9.4	DCF of DeFi protocols	330
Table 11.1	Digital tokens and their underlying	368
Table 13.1	FinTech typologies and business models	422
Table 13.2	Comparison of the main evaluation approaches of traditional firms, technological startups, and banks	444
Table 13.3	FinTech valuation approaches	444
Table 13.4	Cash flow statement of a FinTech and link with the cost of capital	449
Table 14.1	Real options	486

CHAPTER 1

Introduction

Cryptocurrency valuation is highly speculative and can be influenced by a wide range of factors, including market sentiment, speculation, and investor psychology. As a result, cryptocurrency prices can be extremely volatile, and valuing them is inherently uncertain. Digital finance, strongly related to this topic, refers to the integration of technology into financial systems and processes, enabling the digitization of financial transactions, services, and products, and including digital tokens. It encompasses a wide range of activities, including online banking, digital payments, mobile banking, peer-to-peer lending, crowdfunding, and more. Some of the main features of digital finance include:

1. Online and Mobile Access: Digital finance provides individuals and businesses with convenient access to financial services through online platforms and mobile applications. Users can perform various transactions and manage their finances anytime and anywhere.
2. Speed and Efficiency: Digital finance significantly improves the speed and efficiency of financial transactions. With instant processing and real-time updates, funds can be transferred quickly, reducing the time and effort required for traditional financial processes.
3. Enhanced Security: Digital finance employs advanced security measures, such as encryption, two-factor authentication, and biometric verification, to protect financial transactions and user data.

© The Author(s), under exclusive license to Springer Nature Switzerland AG 2023
R. Moro-Visconti and A. Cesaretti, *Digital Token Valuation*, https://doi.org/10.1007/978-3-031-42971-2_1

This helps mitigate the risks associated with fraud and unauthorized access.
4. Financial Inclusion: Digital finance has the potential to increase financial inclusion by providing access to financial services to previously underserved populations. Individuals without traditional bank accounts can utilize digital wallets and mobile banking services to store, transfer, and receive funds.
5. Automation and Streamlining: Through digital finance, manual financial tasks can be automated, leading to increased efficiency and reduced errors. Processes such as account reconciliation, data entry, and regulatory compliance can be streamlined, saving time and resources.

Cryptocurrencies, such as Bitcoin and Ethereum, are, as anticipated, a subset of digital finance and are closely related to it. Cryptocurrencies are digital or virtual currencies that utilize cryptography for security and operate independently of a central authority, such as a government or financial institution. They leverage blockchain technology, a decentralized and distributed ledger system, to record and verify transactions.

Cryptocurrencies offer several unique features within the realm of digital finance:

1. Decentralization: Cryptocurrencies operate on decentralized networks, meaning there is no central authority controlling or governing them. This decentralized nature increases transparency, reduces the risk of censorship, and enables greater user control over funds.
2. Security and Privacy: Cryptocurrencies employ cryptographic techniques to ensure the security and privacy of transactions. Participants are identified through pseudonyms rather than personal information, and cryptographic protocols protect the integrity and confidentiality of the data.
3. Borderless Transactions: Cryptocurrencies facilitate global transactions without the need for intermediaries or traditional banking systems. Users can send and receive funds across borders quickly and at lower costs compared to traditional remittance methods.
4. Investment Opportunities: Cryptocurrencies provide investment opportunities for individuals seeking potential returns. The volatile

nature of cryptocurrencies can lead to significant price fluctuations, offering the potential for speculative gains.

While cryptocurrencies are a part of digital finance, they represent only one aspect of the broader digital transformation occurring in the financial industry.

As shown in Chapter 2, the asset class taxonomy refers to the categorization of different types of assets based on their characteristics and investment attributes. The classification of cryptocurrencies within the asset class taxonomy can have an impact on the valuation approaches used for cryptocurrencies as an asset class. Here are a few ways the asset class taxonomy can influence cryptocurrency valuation:

1. Traditional Valuation Methods: If cryptocurrencies are classified within the asset class taxonomy as a form of currency or digital cash, traditional valuation methods used for currencies and monetary assets may be applied. These methods include measures such as purchasing power parity, money supply analysis, and relative value assessments against other currencies.
2. Commodity-Like Valuation: If cryptocurrencies are classified as commodity-like assets, valuation approaches like those used for commodities may be utilized. These methods might involve supply and demand analysis, cost of production considerations, and comparisons with other commodities.
3. Equity-Like Valuation: cryptocurrencies exhibit characteristics like equities, representing ownership in a digital network or platform. In this case, valuation methods used for equities, such as discounted cash flow analysis, earnings multiples, and market capitalization, could be applied.
4. Network Valuation: Cryptocurrencies often derive value from the underlying network or blockchain technology they operate on. If cryptocurrencies are classified within the asset class taxonomy as network assets, valuation approaches might focus on evaluating the adoption, user base, transaction volume, and overall network effects of the underlying platform.
5. Hybrid Valuation Approaches: Cryptocurrencies possess unique characteristics that may require the development of hybrid valuation approaches that combine elements from various traditional valuation

methods. For example, a valuation model for a cryptocurrency could consider aspects of both currency valuation and network valuation.

The asset class taxonomy for cryptocurrencies is still a subject of debate and evolving regulatory frameworks. As the understanding and acceptance of cryptocurrencies continue to evolve, the approaches to valuing them as an asset class are also likely to evolve accordingly.

Chapter 3 is concerned with the Scalable Valuation of digital intangibles which refers to the process of assessing the value of intangible assets that are digital in nature and can potentially scale rapidly. Digital intangibles include a wide range of assets such as software, algorithms, patents, copyrights, brands, customer databases, and other intellectual property.

Valuing digital intangibles can be challenging due to their unique characteristics, including the ability to scale quickly and the potential for rapid innovation. Here are some considerations for the scalable valuation of digital intangibles:

1. Income-Based Approaches: Income-based valuation approaches, such as discounted cash flow (DCF) analysis, can be used to estimate the present value of expected future cash flows generated by digital intangibles. This approach requires making projections of revenue streams, considering factors such as market size, growth potential, and competitive landscape. The scalability of digital intangibles should be factored into the growth assumptions.
2. Market-Based Approaches: Market-based valuation approaches involve comparing the digital intangible to similar assets that have been recently sold or valued in the market. For digital intangibles, this can be challenging due to limited comparable transactions. However, if there are comparable digital intangibles or transactions involving similar technologies or business models, they can provide insights into the potential value of the asset.
3. Cost-Based Approaches: Cost-based valuation approaches focus on estimating the cost to recreate or replace the digital intangible. This approach considers factors such as development costs, research and development expenses, and intellectual property protection costs. However, it may not capture the full value of the intangible, especially if it has unique features or competitive advantages.

4. Network Effects and User Base: For certain digital intangibles, such as social media platforms or online marketplaces, the value may be driven by network effects and the size of the user base. Valuation methods that incorporate network effects and the potential for rapid user growth can be used to estimate the value of such assets.
5. Technology and Innovation: Digital intangibles often rely on underlying technology and innovation. Valuation approaches that consider the quality, uniqueness, and potential disruption of the technology can provide insights into the value of the intangible asset. Factors such as patents, trade secrets, and competitive advantages can also influence the valuation.

The scalable valuation of digital intangibles may require a combination of different approaches, and the specific valuation method used will depend on the nature of the intangible asset, the industry, and the available data. Additionally, the valuation of digital intangibles may require ongoing monitoring and adjustment due to the dynamic and evolving nature of digital markets.

Cryptocurrencies, examined in Chapter 4, have several main features that distinguish them from traditional forms of currency and financial assets. These features include:

1. Decentralization: Cryptocurrencies operate on decentralized networks, such as blockchain technology, where transactions are verified and recorded by a distributed network of participants. This decentralized nature eliminates the need for intermediaries like banks and allows for peer-to-peer transactions.
2. Security: Cryptocurrencies utilize cryptographic techniques to secure transactions and control the creation of new units. These techniques ensure the integrity and immutability of the transaction history, making it difficult to alter or tamper with the records.
3. Anonymity and Privacy: While not all cryptocurrencies offer complete anonymity, many provide users with a certain level of privacy. Participants in cryptocurrency transactions are identified by cryptographic addresses rather than personal information, offering some level of pseudonymity.
4. Digital Scarcity: Cryptocurrencies often have limited or predetermined supplies, meaning there is a finite number of units that can

be created. This feature creates scarcity and can impact the value of cryptocurrencies.
5. Global Accessibility: Cryptocurrencies enable cross-border transactions with relatively low fees compared to traditional banking systems. They are accessible to anyone with an internet connection, allowing for financial inclusion and access to the global economy.

Cryptocurrency valuation is a complex process that combines elements of traditional financial analysis, market dynamics, and unique factors specific to cryptocurrencies. Here are some common methods and factors used in cryptocurrency valuation:

1. Market Capitalization: Market capitalization is a straightforward valuation metric calculated by multiplying the current price of a cryptocurrency by its total circulating supply. It provides a measure of the overall size and value of a cryptocurrency relative to other assets in the market.
2. Supply and Demand Dynamics: The valuation of a cryptocurrency is influenced by the interaction between its supply and demand. Factors such as scarcity, utility, adoption, and market sentiment play a role in determining the demand for a cryptocurrency, which can impact its price.
3. Tokenomics and Utility: The utility and functionality of a cryptocurrency within its respective ecosystem can affect its valuation. Factors such as the token's use in powering decentralized applications (DApps), governance rights, staking, or payment functions can contribute to its perceived value.
4. Network Effects and Adoption: The value of a cryptocurrency can be influenced by the size and growth of its user base, as well as the level of adoption within the industry or community. Network effects, where the value of a cryptocurrency increases as more participants join the network, can play a significant role in its valuation.
5. Fundamental Analysis: Fundamental analysis involves assessing the underlying technology, team, partnerships, regulatory environment, and potential risks associated with a cryptocurrency. This analysis helps evaluate the long-term viability and prospects of a cryptocurrency.

6. Technical Analysis: Technical analysis involves studying historical price patterns, trading volumes, and market trends to make predictions about future price movements. Technical indicators and chart patterns are used to identify potential buying and selling opportunities.

Cryptocurrency valuation is highly speculative and subject to significant volatility. The valuation methods employed can vary depending on the specific cryptocurrency and the preferences of investors and analysts.

Chapter 4 also considers non-fungible tokens (NFTs), whose distinct features differentiate them from other types of tokens or cryptocurrencies:

1. Unique and Non-Fungible: Unlike cryptocurrencies like Bitcoin or Ethereum, which are fungible and interchangeable, each NFT is unique and cannot be replicated or exchanged on a one-to-one basis. NFTs represent ownership of a specific digital asset, such as artwork, collectibles, virtual real estate, or in-game items.
2. Ownership and Authenticity: NFTs utilize blockchain technology to establish proof of ownership and authenticate the digital assets they represent. The blockchain acts as a decentralized ledger that verifies and records the ownership history and transaction details of the NFT.
3. Indivisible and Divisibility: NFTs are indivisible by nature, meaning they cannot be divided into smaller units like cryptocurrencies. However, some NFT platforms or marketplaces allow for fractional ownership, where multiple individuals can collectively own a percentage of an NFT.
4. Programmability: NFTs can be programmed with smart contracts, which enable customizable features and functionalities. Smart contracts can include provisions such as royalty payments to creators, time-limited ownership, or unlock additional content or benefits tied to the NFT.
5. Diverse Applications: NFTs have found applications in various domains, including digital art, gaming, music, virtual real estate, and more. They enable new avenues for creators, artists, and collectors to monetize and engage with digital assets in unique ways.

When it comes to the valuation of NFTs, several parameters and factors are considered:

1. Rarity: Rarity is a significant factor in valuing NFTs. The scarcity or uniqueness of a digital asset can greatly impact its perceived value. Rare or one-of-a-kind NFTs tend to attract higher valuations as they are often considered more desirable by collectors.
2. Popularity and Demand: The demand for a particular NFT plays a crucial role in its valuation. High demand driven by factors such as the popularity of the artist or creator, media coverage, or community interest can drive up the value of an NFT.
3. Reputation and Pedigree: The reputation and track record of the artist or creator behind an NFT can influence its valuation. Established artists or creators with a strong following and recognized body of work may command higher prices for their NFTs.
4. Scarcity within a Collection: In cases where NFTs are part of a limited collection or series, the scarcity of a particular item within the collection can affect its value. Rare items within a limited edition set can be highly sought after by collectors.
5. Utility and Functionality: The utility and functionality associated with an NFT can contribute to its value. NFTs that provide additional benefits, such as access to exclusive content, experiences, or membership perks, may be valued higher compared to NFTs with limited utility.
6. Secondary Market Activity: The prices at which similar NFTs have been sold in the secondary market can provide insights into the valuation of an NFT. Marketplaces and auction platforms often serve as indicators of market sentiment and can impact the perceived value of an NFT.

NFT valuation is subjective and influenced by various factors, including individual preferences, market trends, and the evolving nature of the NFT ecosystem. Valuation methodologies for NFTs are still emerging, and there is ongoing exploration and innovation in this space.

As shown in Chapter 5, (NFTs) have distinct features that differentiate them from other types of tokens or cryptocurrencies. Here are the main features of NFTs (already introduced in Chapter 4):

1. Unique and Non-Fungible: Unlike cryptocurrencies like Bitcoin or Ethereum, which are fungible and interchangeable, each NFT is unique and cannot be replicated or exchanged on a one-to-one basis. NFTs represent ownership of a specific digital asset, such as artwork, collectibles, virtual real estate, or in-game items.
2. Ownership and Authenticity: NFTs utilize blockchain technology to establish proof of ownership and authenticate the digital assets they represent. The blockchain acts as a decentralized ledger that verifies and records the ownership history and transaction details of the NFT.
3. Indivisible and Divisibility: NFTs are indivisible by nature, meaning they cannot be divided into smaller units like cryptocurrencies. However, some NFT platforms or marketplaces allow for fractional ownership, where multiple individuals can collectively own a percentage of an NFT.
4. Programmability: NFTs can be programmed with smart contracts, which enable customizable features and functionalities. Smart contracts can include provisions such as royalty payments to creators, time-limited ownership, or unlocking additional content or benefits tied to the NFT.
5. Diverse Applications: NFTs have found applications in various domains, including digital art, gaming, music, virtual real estate, and more. They enable new avenues for creators, artists, and collectors to monetize and engage with digital assets in unique ways.

When it comes to the valuation of NFTs, several parameters and factors are considered:

1. Rarity: Rarity is a significant factor in valuing NFTs. The scarcity or uniqueness of a digital asset can greatly impact its perceived value. Rare or one-of-a-kind NFTs tend to attract higher valuations as they are often considered more desirable by collectors.
2. Popularity and Demand: The demand for a particular NFT plays a crucial role in its valuation. High demand driven by factors such as the popularity of the artist or creator, media coverage, or community interest can drive up the value of an NFT.

3. Reputation and Pedigree: The reputation and track record of the artist or creator behind an NFT can influence its valuation. Established artists or creators with a strong following and recognized body of work may command higher prices for their NFTs.
4. Scarcity within a Collection: In cases where NFTs are part of a limited collection or series, the scarcity of a particular item within the collection can affect its value. Rare items within a limited edition set can be highly sought after by collectors.
5. Utility and Functionality: The utility and functionality associated with an NFT can contribute to its value. NFTs that provide additional benefits, such as access to exclusive content, experiences, or membership perks, may be valued higher compared to NFTs with limited utility.
6. Secondary Market Activity: The prices at which similar NFTs have been sold in the secondary market can provide insights into the valuation of an NFT. Marketplaces and auction platforms often serve as indicators of market sentiment and can impact the perceived value of an NFT.

NFT valuation is subjective and influenced by various factors, including individual preferences, market trends, and the evolving nature of the NFT ecosystem. Valuation methodologies for NFTs are still emerging, and there is ongoing exploration and innovation in this space.

Chapter 6 shows that the interaction between blockchains, the Internet of Value, and smart transactions is intertwined and represents a new paradigm for decentralized, secure, and efficient value exchange. Here's a breakdown of how these concepts relate to each other:

1. Blockchains: Blockchains are distributed ledger systems that enable the recording, verification, and storage of transactions in a secure and transparent manner. They utilize cryptographic techniques to ensure the integrity and immutability of the data. Blockchains serve as the underlying technology for various applications, including cryptocurrencies, smart contracts, and decentralized applications (DApps).
2. Internet of Value: The Internet of Value is a concept that envisions a connected, digital ecosystem where value, in the form of assets, currencies, or other digital representations of value, can be

exchanged seamlessly and instantly. It refers to the ability to transfer and transact value with the same ease and speed as information is exchanged on the internet. Blockchains play a crucial role in enabling the Internet of Value by providing the infrastructure for secure and efficient value transfer without intermediaries.
3. Smart Transactions: Smart transactions, also known as smart contracts, are self-executing contracts with the terms and conditions directly written into the code of the contract. These contracts automatically execute and enforce the agreed-upon conditions when predetermined criteria are met. Smart transactions leverage blockchain technology, enabling trust, transparency, and automation in various scenarios such as financial transactions, supply chain management, and asset ownership transfer.

The interaction between these concepts can be described as follows:

- Blockchains provide the foundational technology for the Internet of Value. They enable the secure and transparent recording and transfer of value in the form of digital assets or currencies. Blockchains facilitate peer-to-peer transactions, eliminating the need for intermediaries and reducing transaction costs and settlement times.
- Smart transactions, powered by blockchain technology, enhance the efficiency and automation of value exchange. They eliminate the need for intermediaries by executing predefined conditions automatically. These smart contracts are self-verifying, tamper-resistant, and can facilitate complex transactions with multiple parties, ensuring trust and reducing the risk of fraud.
- The Internet of Value encompasses the broader vision of interconnected digital systems where value can flow seamlessly. Blockchains, with their decentralized and secure nature, enable the Internet of Value by providing the infrastructure for trustless value transfer. Smart transactions add a layer of programmability and automation to this ecosystem, enabling more sophisticated and efficient value exchange.

Together, blockchains, the Internet of Value, and smart transactions are transforming traditional financial systems and opening up new possibilities for secure, transparent, and efficient value exchange in various domains beyond finance.

Valuating blockchains can be a complex task as they are not traditional assets or entities that generate cash flows. However, there are a few patterns and approaches that can be considered when assessing the value or potential value of blockchains:

1. Network Adoption and Activity: The value of a blockchain can be influenced by the level of network adoption and activity. Factors such as the number of active users, developers, and nodes on the network, transaction volume, and growth in usage can indicate the potential value of the blockchain. Higher adoption and activity may suggest a valuable ecosystem with network effects.
2. Token Economics: Many blockchains have native tokens that play a vital role in their ecosystems. Token economics, including token supply and distribution, utility, and governance mechanisms, can impact the valuation of a blockchain. Factors like scarcity, demand for the token, and its use in powering the network, accessing services, or participating in governance can contribute to the perceived value.
3. Security and Consensus Mechanisms: The security and robustness of a blockchain's consensus mechanism can affect its value. Proof of Work (PoW), Proof of Stake (PoS), or other consensus algorithms determine the security, scalability, and efficiency of a blockchain. A secure and well-designed consensus mechanism can increase the trust and value associated with the blockchain.
4. Development and Ecosystem: The strength and activity of the developer community and the broader ecosystem surrounding a blockchain can impact its value. The presence of active developers, vibrant projects, partnerships with established organizations, and the development of decentralized applications (DApps) can contribute to the potential value and adoption of the blockchain.
5. Interoperability and Scalability: Interoperability, the ability of a blockchain to interact and exchange value with other blockchains

or traditional systems, can add value to a blockchain. Similarly, scalability solutions that address transaction throughput and latency challenges can impact the perceived value of a blockchain by enabling broader adoption and use cases.
6. Regulatory Environment and Adoption: The regulatory environment and acceptance of blockchain technology within various jurisdictions can influence the value of a blockchain. Favorable regulatory frameworks or partnerships with regulatory-compliant entities may contribute to the value and adoption of the blockchain.

The valuation of blockchains is subject to market dynamics, investor sentiment, and the evolving nature of the blockchain industry. As the technology and ecosystem continue to develop, new valuation approaches and metrics specific to blockchains may emerge.

Chapter 7 refers to the metaverse, a virtual universe or a collective virtual space where users can interact with each other and digital entities in real time, often through immersive technologies. While the metaverse is an evolving concept, it typically exhibits the following main features:

1. Virtual Environment: The metaverse provides a simulated environment that may encompass 2D or 3D spaces, virtual worlds, augmented reality (AR), or virtual reality (VR) experiences. Users can explore and interact with the virtual environment using avatars or digital representations of themselves.
2. Persistent and Shared Space: The metaverse is a persistent and shared space, meaning it exists and can be accessed by users at any time. Users can coexist and interact with each other simultaneously, fostering social connections and collaborative experiences.
3. User-Generated Content: The metaverse encourages user-generated content creation. Users can create, modify, and trade digital assets, virtual goods, and services within the metaverse. This aspect promotes creativity, entrepreneurship, and economic opportunities for users.
4. Interconnectivity: The metaverse is interconnected, allowing seamless movement and interaction across different virtual spaces, platforms, and applications. It enables continuity of experiences and the potential for cross-platform interactions.

5. Immersive and Interactive Experiences: The metaverse leverages immersive technologies like VR and AR to provide engaging and interactive experiences. Users can engage in various activities such as gaming, socializing, shopping, learning, and more, blurring the boundaries between the physical and virtual worlds.

The features of the metaverse can impact economic valuation patterns in several ways:

1. Digital Asset Valuation: The metaverse facilitates the creation, ownership, and trading of digital assets and virtual goods. The economic value of these assets can be influenced by factors such as scarcity, demand, utility, and cultural significance within the metaverse ecosystem.
2. Virtual Property and Real Estate: Within the metaverse, virtual property and real estate can have economic value. Similar to physical real estate, the location, desirability, and potential for revenue generation within the metaverse can impact the valuation of virtual properties.
3. Virtual Economy: The metaverse supports a virtual economy where users can engage in various economic activities, such as buying and selling virtual goods, offering services, and participating in virtual marketplaces. The valuation of the metaverse can be influenced by the size, activity, and economic growth of this virtual economy.
4. Interoperability and Standards: Interoperability between different metaverse platforms and applications can impact the valuation patterns. The development of standards for asset exchange, cross-platform interactions, and seamless movement between virtual environments can enhance the economic potential and valuation of the metaverse as a whole.
5. Market Dynamics and Adoption: Economic valuation patterns in the metaverse are also influenced by market dynamics, user adoption, and investor sentiment. Factors such as user engagement, user growth, the presence of established brands, and regulatory frameworks can affect the perceived value and potential for economic activity within the metaverse.

The concept of the metaverse is still evolving, and there are ongoing discussions, technological advancements, and market developments shaping its features and economic implications.

Networking digital platforms and Virtual Marketplaces are examined in Chapter 8.

They represent interconnected concepts that facilitate online interactions, transactions, and economic activities. Here's how they can be defined and the main valuation approaches associated with them:

Networking Digital Platforms: Networking digital platforms refer to online platforms that enable individuals or entities to connect, collaborate, and interact with each other. These platforms create a virtual space for users to share information, engage in social or professional relationships, and exchange resources. Examples of networking digital platforms include social media platforms (e.g., Facebook, LinkedIn), professional networking platforms (e.g., Upwork, LinkedIn), and community-based platforms (e.g., Reddit, Discord).

Valuation Approaches for Networking Digital Platforms:

1. User Base and Engagement: The size, growth rate, and engagement level of the user base are important valuation metrics. Platforms with a large and active user base tend to attract more attention from advertisers, investors, and potential acquirers.
2. Network Effects: Network effects occur when the value of a platform increases as more users join and interact with each other. The strength of network effects and the platform's ability to leverage them can influence its valuation. Metrics such as user acquisition, retention, and user activity patterns are considered in assessing the strength of network effects.
3. Revenue Generation: Revenue generation models, such as advertising, subscriptions, or transaction fees, impact the valuation of networking digital platforms. The scalability and sustainability of the revenue model are key factors, along with revenue growth and profitability.

Virtual Marketplaces: Virtual marketplaces are online platforms that facilitate the buying and selling of goods, services, or digital assets between multiple parties. These marketplaces provide a digital space for sellers and buyers to transact, often connecting them through a common platform. Examples of virtual marketplaces include e-commerce platforms (e.g., Amazon, Alibaba), peer-to-peer marketplaces (e.g., eBay, Etsy), and digital asset marketplaces (e.g., NFT marketplaces, cryptocurrency exchanges).

Valuation Approaches for Virtual Marketplaces:

1. Transaction Volume and GMV: Gross Merchandise Volume (GMV) is a metric that represents the total value of transactions processed on the marketplace. Higher transaction volume and GMV generally indicate a more active and valuable marketplace.
2. Network Effects: Like networking digital platforms, network effects play a role in the valuation of virtual marketplaces. The size of the user base, the number of active buyers and sellers, and the liquidity of the marketplace can impact its valuation.
3. Revenue and Commission Structure: The revenue generated through transaction fees or commissions is an important factor in the valuation of virtual marketplaces. The marketplace's ability to capture a portion of the value exchanged between buyers and sellers, along with revenue growth and profitability, influences its valuation.
4. Competitive Landscape and Market Position: The competitive landscape and the market position of the virtual marketplace are considered in its valuation. Factors such as market share, differentiation, barriers to entry, and potential disruption affect the perceived value of the marketplace.

The valuation of networking digital platforms and virtual marketplaces can be influenced by industry-specific dynamics, user behavior, technological advancements, and market trends. Valuation methodologies may vary based on the specific characteristics and growth prospects of the platform or marketplace being assessed.

Decentralized Finance (De.Fi.) examined in Chapter 9 refers to a set of financial applications and platforms built on blockchain networks, typically utilizing smart contracts. DeFi aims to provide decentralized, open, and permissionless alternatives to traditional financial intermediaries and services. Here are some main definitions and how they impact valuation approaches in DeFi:

1. Decentralization: DeFi emphasizes the use of decentralized networks, primarily public blockchains, to enable financial activities without relying on centralized intermediaries such as banks. The decentralized nature of DeFi platforms impacts valuation by promoting transparency, reducing counterparty risk, and potentially increasing user trust.
2. Smart Contracts: DeFi platforms utilize smart contracts, which are self-executing contracts with the terms and conditions directly written into code. Smart contracts automate financial processes, allowing for seamless and programmable execution of transactions. The use of smart contracts can impact valuation by enhancing operational efficiency, reducing costs, and enabling new types of financial services.
3. Openness and Interoperability: DeFi aims to foster openness and interoperability, allowing different protocols and applications to integrate and interact with each other. This interoperability enables composability, where various DeFi building blocks can be combined to create more complex financial products or services. Valuation approaches need to consider the network effects, adoption, and potential synergies resulting from the openness and interoperability of DeFi protocols.
4. Token Economics: DeFi often utilizes native tokens that have various functions within the ecosystem. These tokens may serve as governance rights, provide access to specific services, or act as collateral for borrowing and lending. The valuation of DeFi protocols can be influenced by token economics, including factors such as token supply, distribution, demand, and utility within the ecosystem.
5. User Activity and Adoption: The activity level and adoption of DeFi platforms are crucial factors in valuation. Metrics such as the number of active users, trading volume, liquidity, and assets locked in the protocols can provide insights into the usage and potential value of the platforms. Higher user activity and adoption often correlate with increased valuation potential.
6. Risk Management and Auditing: DeFi platforms present unique risks such as smart contract vulnerabilities, market volatility, and liquidity risks. Valuation approaches need to consider the risk management practices implemented by DeFi platforms, including security audits, insurance mechanisms, and governance processes. Strong risk

management practices can enhance the perceived value and reduce risk premiums associated with DeFi protocols.

The valuation of DeFi protocols and platforms can be challenging due to the dynamic nature of the space, the evolving regulatory environment, and the potential for rapid innovation. Valuation approaches need to consider both traditional financial analysis methods and specific factors related to DeFi, such as user adoption, composability, token economics, and risk management practices.

Cybersecurity, examined in Chapter 10, refers to the practice of protecting computer systems, networks, and data from unauthorized access, breaches, damage, or disruption. It encompasses a wide range of technologies, processes, and practices aimed at safeguarding digital assets and ensuring the confidentiality, integrity, and availability of information. Here are the main features of cybersecurity and how it can be evaluated:

1. Confidentiality: Confidentiality ensures that data and information are accessible only to authorized individuals or entities. Evaluation of confidentiality involves assessing the effectiveness of access controls, encryption techniques, data classification, and user authentication mechanisms in place to prevent unauthorized access.
2. Integrity: Integrity ensures that data and information are accurate, complete, and unaltered. Evaluation of integrity involves examining the measures in place to detect and prevent data tampering, unauthorized modifications, or data corruption. Techniques such as checksums, digital signatures, and version controls can be assessed for their effectiveness.
3. Availability: Availability ensures that systems, networks, and data are accessible and operational when needed. Evaluation of availability involves assessing the robustness of infrastructure, redundancy measures, backup and recovery processes, and resilience against disruptions such as cyberattacks or natural disasters.
4. Authentication and Authorization: Evaluation of authentication involves assessing the effectiveness of mechanisms to verify the identity of users and systems, such as passwords, multi-factor authentication, or biometric authentication. Authorization evaluation focuses on assessing the controls and policies in place to determine access privileges and permissions based on user roles and responsibilities.

5. Vulnerability Management: Evaluation of vulnerability management involves assessing the processes and tools in place to identify, track, and remediate vulnerabilities in systems and software. Vulnerability scanning, penetration testing, and patch management practices can be evaluated for their effectiveness in minimizing the risk of exploitation.
6. Incident Response and Recovery: Evaluation of incident response and recovery capabilities involves assessing the processes, procedures, and resources in place to detect, respond to, and recover from cybersecurity incidents. Incident response plans, backup strategies, and incident handling practices can be evaluated for their effectiveness in minimizing the impact of security incidents.
7. Security Awareness and Training: Evaluation of security awareness and training involves assessing the effectiveness of programs and initiatives aimed at educating users about cybersecurity threats, best practices, and the proper handling of sensitive information. The evaluation can include assessing the level of awareness, training effectiveness, and adherence to security policies and procedures.

Evaluation of cybersecurity can be performed through various methods, including:

- Security Audits and Assessments: Independent assessments of cybersecurity controls and practices can be conducted to identify vulnerabilities, gaps, and areas for improvement. These assessments can involve technical testing, interviews, and review of policies and procedures.
- Risk Assessments: Evaluating cybersecurity risks involves identifying potential threats, vulnerabilities, and impacts to determine the level of risk and prioritize mitigation efforts. Risk assessments help organizations understand their cybersecurity posture and make informed decisions about resource allocation.
- Compliance Assessments: Evaluation of compliance with regulatory requirements and industry standards helps ensure that cybersecurity practices meet legal and regulatory obligations. Compliance assessments involve reviewing controls, policies, and procedures against applicable requirements.

- Incident Response Exercises: Conducting simulated cybersecurity incidents helps evaluate the effectiveness of incident response plans, communication protocols, and coordination among stakeholders. These exercises test the organization's readiness to handle and recover from security incidents.

Cybersecurity is an ongoing process, and evaluation should be conducted regularly to adapt to evolving threats, technologies, and regulatory requirements.

Digital token valuation, examined in Chapter 11, refers to the process of assessing the value of digital tokens, which are typically assets or units of value that exist on a blockchain or distributed ledger technology. Digital tokens can represent various forms of value, such as cryptocurrencies, utility tokens, security tokens, or non-fungible tokens (NFTs). Valuation methods for digital tokens vary based on the type of token and its underlying characteristics:

1. Cryptocurrencies: Cryptocurrencies like Bitcoin or Ethereum are typically valued based on market dynamics, supply and demand, and investor sentiment. Market capitalization, which is calculated by multiplying the current price by the total circulating supply, is a commonly used valuation metric. Other factors include liquidity, trading volume, network effects, technological developments, and adoption metrics.
2. Utility Tokens: Utility tokens are designed to provide access to a specific product, service, or platform. The valuation of utility tokens can be influenced by factors such as the utility and demand for the underlying product or service, the projected usage or adoption, and the economic model tied to the token. Discounted cash flow analysis or comparing the value of the token to the potential value of the utility it provides can be used for valuation.
3. Security Tokens: Security tokens represent ownership in an underlying asset or entity, such as shares in a company or ownership of real estate. Valuing security tokens can involve traditional financial valuation methods, including discounted cash flow analysis, comparable company analysis, or market multiples. Additionally, compliance with securities regulations and the legal framework surrounding security tokens should be considered.

4. Non-Fungible Tokens (NFTs): NFTs represent unique digital assets, such as artwork, collectibles, or virtual real estate. Valuation of NFTs can be subjective and influenced by factors such as the artist's reputation, scarcity, historical sales, cultural significance, and market demand. Marketplaces and recent sales of similar NFTs can provide insights into their valuation.
5. Hybrid Approaches: Some digital tokens may have hybrid characteristics, combining elements of different token types. In such cases, a combination of valuation approaches might be employed, considering both market dynamics and specific factors related to the token's utility, underlying assets, or unique features.

The valuation of digital tokens can be highly speculative and subject to volatility. Market sentiment, regulatory changes, technological advancements, and the evolving nature of the token ecosystem can impact their perceived value. Valuation approaches should consider a combination of traditional financial analysis, market dynamics, and token-specific factors to make informed assessments.

Cryptocurrency crashes, examined in Chapter 12, refer to significant and rapid declines in the prices of cryptocurrencies, resulting in a substantial loss of value for investors and holders. Cryptocurrency markets, like any other financial market, can be subject to price volatility and periods of sharp declines. Several factors can contribute to cryptocurrency crashes, including:

1. Market Sentiment and Speculation: Cryptocurrency markets are influenced by market sentiment and speculative trading. Positive or negative news, regulatory announcements, market rumors, or investor sentiment can trigger large price swings, leading to crashes.
2. Regulatory Actions: Regulatory actions or announcements by governments or financial authorities can have a significant impact on cryptocurrency markets. Regulatory crackdowns, bans, or restrictions on cryptocurrency trading, initial coin offerings (ICOs), or cryptocurrency exchanges can cause market uncertainty and trigger sell-offs.
3. Security Breaches and Hacks: The occurrence of security breaches or hacks on cryptocurrency exchanges or wallets can erode investor confidence and lead to market downturns. High-profile incidents of

theft or loss of cryptocurrencies can contribute to market panic and sell-offs.
4. Market Manipulation: Cryptocurrency markets, like other financial markets, are susceptible to market manipulation. Large-scale trading activities or coordinated efforts to artificially inflate or deflate prices can create market instability and trigger crashes.
5. Technology and Network Issues: Technological vulnerabilities or network issues within specific cryptocurrencies or blockchain networks can lead to crashes. For example, software bugs, network congestion, scalability challenges, or consensus algorithm failures can cause disruptions and impact market confidence.
6. Economic Factors: Broader economic factors, such as global economic downturns, inflation concerns, or financial market turbulence, can also influence cryptocurrency markets. Cryptocurrencies may be considered risky assets, and during periods of economic uncertainty, investors may shift toward safer assets, leading to cryptocurrency sell-offs and crashes.

During cryptocurrency crashes, investors may experience significant losses, and market volatility can be amplified due to the speculative nature of the cryptocurrency market. It's important for investors to exercise caution, conduct thorough research, and diversify their investment portfolios to mitigate risks associated with cryptocurrency investments.

While cryptocurrency crashes can result in short-term losses, the market has also demonstrated the potential for recovery and long-term growth. Cryptocurrency markets have historically experienced cycles of volatility, including both periods of significant declines and subsequent periods of price appreciation.

Fintechs are examined in Chapter 13. Valuation of FinTech companies and digital payment systems involves assessing their financial performance, growth prospects, market position, and potential risks. Valuation methods used for traditional companies can be applied to FinTech firms, but certain factors specific to the FinTech and digital payment industry should be considered. Here are some key aspects and valuation approaches:

1. Revenue and Profitability: Evaluating the revenue streams and profitability of a FinTech company or digital payment system is essential. This includes assessing transaction fees, subscription fees, licensing

fees, or other revenue sources. Profitability metrics such as gross margins, net margins, and EBITDA (Earnings Before Interest, Taxes, Depreciation, and Amortization) are considered.
2. User Base and Adoption: The size and growth rate of the user base are important factors in valuing FinTech companies. Metrics such as active users, customer acquisition costs, retention rates, and user engagement levels provide insights into the potential market reach and growth prospects. Higher user adoption and engagement generally correlate with increased valuation potential.
3. Market Share and Competitive Landscape: The market share of a digital payment system or FinTech company is significant in determining its value. Assessing the competitive landscape, including the presence of established players, market barriers, and differentiation factors, helps evaluate the potential market position and long-term viability.
4. Technology and Innovation: The quality and uniqueness of the technology employed by a FinTech company or digital payment system impact its valuation. Evaluation includes assessing the scalability, security, and efficiency of the technology, as well as any intellectual property or patents held by the company.
5. Regulatory Compliance: The ability to navigate and comply with regulatory requirements is critical for FinTech companies and digital payment systems. Compliance with financial regulations, data protection laws, and anti-money laundering (AML) regulations is crucial. Valuation considerations include the company's ability to meet regulatory obligations, manage compliance costs, and adapt to evolving regulations.
6. Partnerships and Ecosystem: Evaluating partnerships with banks, financial institutions, merchants, or other key players in the ecosystem provides insights into the growth potential and strategic positioning of a FinTech company or digital payment system. The strength and quality of partnerships can impact valuation.
7. Market Size and Growth Potential: Understanding the size and growth potential of the digital payment and FinTech market is essential. Analyzing market trends, forecasts, and the addressable market size helps assess the growth opportunities and revenue potential for the company.

Valuation approaches for FinTech companies and digital payment systems may include discounted cash flow (DCF) analysis, comparable company analysis, market multiples, and revenue or user-based valuation models. Additionally, factors such as industry-specific growth rates, unique risks associated with the industry (e.g., cybersecurity, regulatory changes), and the potential for disruptive technologies should be considered in the valuation process.

ESG-driven valuations, examined in Chapter 14, refer to the consideration of Environmental, Social, and Governance factors in the assessment of a company's value. ESG factors have gained prominence in investment analysis and decision-making as they provide insights into a company's sustainability, social impact, and overall governance practices. ESG-driven valuations aim to evaluate the financial risks and opportunities associated with these factors:

1. Environmental Factors: Environmental factors assess a company's impact on the environment, including its carbon footprint, resource consumption, waste management, and adherence to environmental regulations. ESG-driven valuations consider the potential financial risks associated with climate change, environmental liabilities, and the company's ability to adapt to emerging environmental trends and regulations. Positive environmental performance and sustainability practices can enhance a company's long-term value and resilience.
2. Social Factors: Social factors evaluate a company's impact on society, including its treatment of employees, community relations, product safety, diversity and inclusion, and labor practices. ESG-driven valuations analyze the financial implications of social factors, such as employee satisfaction, brand reputation, customer loyalty, and social license to operate. Strong social performance can contribute to enhanced value creation and stakeholder trust.
3. Governance Factors: Governance factors assess the quality and effectiveness of a company's governance structure, board composition, executive compensation, risk management practices, and adherence to ethical standards. ESG-driven valuations consider the impact of governance practices on financial performance, risk management, and shareholder rights. Strong governance practices can enhance transparency, reduce operational risks, and attract long-term investors.

4. Integration of ESG Metrics: ESG-driven valuations involve incorporating ESG metrics into traditional financial analysis and valuation models. This integration can include assessing ESG risks and opportunities in cash flow projections, discount rate adjustments, cost of capital estimation, and scenario analysis. ESG metrics can also inform the selection of comparable companies and market multiples used in valuation analysis.
5. ESG Performance Indicators: ESG-driven valuations leverage ESG performance indicators and data to assess a company's sustainability performance and its alignment with industry peers. These indicators can be derived from third-party ESG ratings, company disclosures, industry benchmarks, or specific ESG frameworks and standards. The evaluation of a company's ESG performance against its peers can provide insights into its competitive position and potential risks or advantages.

ESG-driven valuations recognize that ESG factors can impact a company's financial performance, reputation, and long-term sustainability. By incorporating ESG considerations into the valuation process, investors and analysts can better understand the potential risks and opportunities associated with a company's ESG performance and make more informed investment decisions.

ESG-driven valuations are still evolving, and there is an ongoing development in standardization, measurement methodologies, and reporting practices related to ESG factors.

* * *

The book has been jointly conceived and written by the two co-authors. However, chapters 2, 3, 5, 6, 7, 8, 13 and 14 are mainly attributable to Roberto Moro-Visconti, while chapters 4, 9, 10, 11, 12 are mainly attributable to Andrea Cesaretti. Any digital comment may be sent to roberto.moro@unicatt.it (or by visiting www.morovisconti.com/en) or to andrea.cesaretti@gmail.com. This book is dedicated to the loving memory of Adele Borghi (1952–2023), who has dedicated Her whole professional life to needy cardiopathic children.

Milan, Italy, Università Cattolica del Sacro Cuore, October, 2023

CHAPTER 2

Asset Class Taxonomy and General Valuation Approaches

2.1 Purpose of the Firm Evaluation

The general principles of corporate valuation are synthetically recalled in this chapter. Even if digital tokens—the core issue of this book—are very different from traditional firms, some common principles need to be recalled and shortly investigated, to understand if and to which extent they can apply to tokens. Cryptocurrency valuation is still a relatively nascent field, and there is ongoing debate and research on the best valuation methods and models. Intermediating cryptocurrencies can be highly speculative, and investors should exercise caution and consider multiple factors when assessing their value. Additionally, the unique characteristics of each cryptocurrency may require tailored appraisal approaches.

The value of a company (for instance, a firm issuing cryptocurrencies) is primarily the result of a series of factors, including:

- Net assets, i.e., all the funds contributed by the partners to finance the business activity;
- Ability to generate income, i.e., the capacity to produce positive income flows;
- Financial capacity.

The attitude of the net assets to produce income depends on the quality of the means of production and the entrepreneurial capacity. This last

© The Author(s), under exclusive license to Springer Nature Switzerland AG 2023
R. Moro-Visconti and A. Cesaretti, *Digital Token Valuation*,
https://doi.org/10.1007/978-3-031-42971-2_2

circumstance allows an understanding of the presence of different profit margins between companies operating in the same sector. Under ideal conditions, the subjective internal "value" must tend to coincide with an objective external (market-driven) "price" at the negotiation stage.

Value is estimated from the application of one or more valuation criteria, chosen concerning the type of corporate transaction, the identity of the parties involved, and the activity of the firm. It is ideally independent of the contractual strength of the parties and other subjective factors, as it expresses a "fair market" value. The value should not be confused with a price: value is subjective, whereas market-driven price is objective. But (intrinsic) value influences prices and eases the detection of over- or under-valuated stocks, whose price is far from their intrinsic fundamental value.

The price is the meeting point of economic expectations and benefits formulated by the supply and demand involved in the negotiation of the company. A firm can be evaluated, among other things:

1. To trade (transaction purposes);
    - Purchases/sales of shareholdings (the underlying company is valued), companies, or business units;
    - Extraordinary financial transactions (relating to the company/ branch of business), M&A, demergers, contributions, disposals, transformations, securitization …;
2. For litigation (e.g., compute damage awards in an infringement lawsuit);
3. For arbitration or similar proceedings;
4. For bankruptcy (valuation is required by the Court to dispose of the assets properly, and pay back creditors);
5. Because of changes in equity:
    - Issue of shares (excluding pre-emptive rights; with share premium …);
    - Issue of convertible bonds;
    - Issue of warrants;
    - Linked to extraordinary operations (transfers, transformations, mergers, contributions, demergers, etc.);
6. With a view to the purchase of assets by the founding partners;
7. To provide guarantees;

8. For listing on the Stock Exchange (IPO);
9. For "internal" cognitive purposes (financial reporting, etc.);
10. For the evaluation of the withdrawal of the shareholder;
11. For tax purposes (transfer pricing issues, etc.).

The main approaches for estimating the market value of companies are different and can be divided into empirical and analytical approaches.

Empirical approaches are based on the practical observation of market prices of assets that are sufficiently similar and, as such, comparable.

Analytical approaches, on the other hand, have a more solid scientific basis and a more significant tradition in the professional sphere and are based on a revenue-financial approach, to estimate what an asset is worth today based on expected future returns or an estimate of the costs incurred for its reproduction/replacement. Analytical approaches are the cornerstone of fundamental analysis—a method of measuring a security's intrinsic value by examining related economic and financial factors.

The main approaches to evaluating companies commonly used in practice are:

1. The balance sheet-based approach (simple and adjusted);
2. The income approach;
3. The mixed capital-income approach (a combination of 1 + 2);
4. The financial approach; and
5. Market approaches and valuation through multiples.

Value creation and option-driven approaches are also used as complementary tools. A comprehensive picture is shown in Fig. 2.7.

The central element in determining the equity value of a firm is the estimate of its future ability to generate an income or financial flow capable of adequately rewarding its shareholders after debt service.

Among the approaches used by operators to identify the market value of the firm, the financial and income approaches are the most appropriate to represent the expected fair remuneration of shareholders.

Whereas the equity value residually relates to shareholders (equity holders), the wider enterprise value reflects the comprehensive market value of the firm including its debt structure, as shown in Fig. 2.1.

Implicit goodwill represents the extra value differential between the market and the book value of the assets, counterbalanced by a "Δ

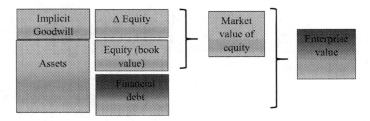

Fig. 2.1 From the enterprise to the equity value

Equity". The market value of equity/book value of equity is known as the price/book-value ratio.

In M&A transactions, reference to the enterprise value is frequent, if an investor willing to purchase a target firm considers not only its residual equity value but also the outstanding financial debt to be served. Operating debt (included in the Net Working Capital) is not considered within the enterprise value since it is "rolling" and paid out in the short term, showing "trading" features that prevail over the "financial" ones.

While the balance sheet-based approach values tangible and intangible resources summing up the values of individual assets, income, and financial approaches considers them as comprehensive elements able to participate in the context of the entire set of factors for the creation of value. The firm's market value is the result of the interaction of internal variables relating to its tangible and intangible assets and external variables relating to the market. The combined consideration of both makes it possible to estimate the firm's future results and assess its risk.

The target of any different approach is to estimate the market value, starting from different parameters. Ideally, the estimated market values obtained considering the different approaches should converge to a common value. In most cases, valuators use a principal and a secondary approach to estimate the firm's intrinsic value. Whenever the difference between the two approaches is too wide (i.e., beyond 25–30%), further investigation is needed to understand the causes and to fix them.

Recent valuation trends have led to the use of two main approaches:

1. the financial approach based on the estimate of discounted operating cash flows at the weighted average cost of capital (WACC);

the estimate of the equity value discounts net cash flows at the cost of equity; and
2. the market approach based on the EBITDA multipliers of comparable companies. In both cases, the enterprise value (value of the firm, including debt) is estimated, which is then added algebraically to the net financial position to arrive at the residual equity value.

Whereas the two approaches dominate among practitioners, the other ones are still used in peculiar cases. For instance, the balance sheet-based approach is often used in the evaluation of real estate firms (where the market value of property replaces, in the assets, its book value that expresses the net worth) or holding companies (replacing the book value of the participations with their estimated market value).

In the evaluation of the intangibles, considered in Chapter 3, "*distinctions are sometimes made between trade intangibles and marketing intangibles, between 'soft' intangibles and 'hard' intangibles, between routine and non-routine intangibles, and between other classes and categories of intangibles*" (OECD, 2022). The intangibles possibly represent the harder parameter to estimate but also the most important source of growth and differential value. It is not surprising that intangibles, together with derivatives, are the biggest puzzle for accountants.

2.2 Back-to-the Earth: Functional Analysis and Business Planning as a Prerequisite for Valuation

The choice of the correct approach and parameters depends on a bottom-up analysis of the business plan of the target firm. This helps in the estimate of trendy parameters (operating and net cash flows; economic margins, etc.) and in the functional analysis that eases the selection of comparable firms.

The functional analysis is traditionally used for transfer pricing purposes (OECD, 2022). It analyzes the functions performed (considering assets used and risks assumed) by associated firms in a transaction, providing an overview of value creation within the supply chain. Transfer pricing guidelines, with their analytical exposure, provide useful insights for the performing of functional analysis even beyond the specific transfer pricing case, so representing a valuable albeit unconventional best practice benchmark for evaluators.

The sequential steps from functional analysis to business planning and firm valuation are synthetized in Fig. 2.2.

Business models incorporate market trends and contain the input factors for firm valuation (consistently with Fig. 2.2), as shown in Fig. 2.3.

These general valuation methodologies need to be applied to digital tokens, whenever possible. Sensitive data are extracted from business models (that depend on functional analysis) and embedded in business plans. Valuation parameters are economic (revenues; EBITDA; EBIT; pre-tax profit; net profit), financial (EBITDA; operating cash flows; net cash flows), and asset-based (Equity Value, Net Financial Position, Enterprise Value). These forward-looking raw data are included in composite formulation (Discounted Cash Flows, etc.) that provide the best estimate of the firm's value.

The main thesis of this chapter is that digital tokens need to be compliant with these general rules, should we assess their potential value. If they are not, then they are worthless, since rational investors accept to buy and sell firms (or assets, tokens, etc.) only if they can expect to extract some future value (especially in terms of expected cash flows). A core issue in the evaluation of digital tokens is represented by the very fact that they represent a shell (box) that is potentially worthless unless we consider the embedded value of its underlying asset. The relationship between the "box" and its contents is, however, uneasy to analyze (as shown in the token definitions).

A further complication is represented by the fact that it is not always clear if and to which extent the "box/shell" token adds value to its underlying. This dilemma is like that concerning derivative or holding companies. The value of a derivative depends both on its underlying asset (stock, commodity, interest, currency rate, etc.) and on its very nature (speculative or defensive, if detained for hedging purposes).

Holding companies are represented by a legal "shell" that controls one or more underlying stocks. A holding discount typically occurs, since the holding company's market capitalization is often lower than the sum of investments it holds. This discount is due to inefficiencies or frictions like limited Free float of a holding company, tax inefficiencies associated with the Holding company, and the additional administrative costs any Holding company incurs. A rational investor may be tempted to buy at a discount the holding company, sell off at premium content, and lock in a profitable arbitrage that would soon decrease the discount,

2 ASSET CLASS TAXONOMY AND GENERAL VALUATION ...

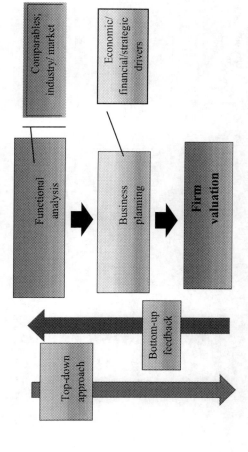

Fig. 2.2 Functional analysis, business planning, and firm valuation

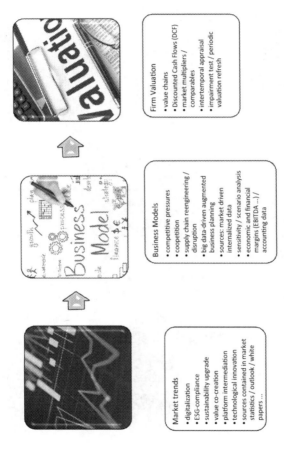

Fig. 2.3 From market trends to business models and firm valuation

reaching par value—but this does not normally happen, representing a conundrum in appraisal theories.

Something similar may happen with digital tokens, raising a Hamletic concern: do they add value to their underlying contents? (If not, they may be useless or, even more, damaging, as they destroy value).

Information asymmetries should be considered in this analysis since they increase the overall risk of the package ("shell" token + underlying asset). Empirical evidence shows that the returns of the tokens are not always in line with the trend of their underlying. The risk profile may be mitigated or exacerbated, influencing the comprehensive valuation. Should we ask investors what is behind the digital token they buy and sell, we may get embarrassing or confused answers: many of them simply do not know what the token represents, and they are happy with their ignorance, but only if prices go up and speculative bubbles seem far away.

2.3 Are Cryptocurrencies an Asset Class?

Investors choose an asset class which refers to a set of items with some features in common. Historically there have been five main types of asset classes:

1. Stocks (equities)
2. Bonds
3. Cash equivalents (money market vehicles)
4. Real estate
5. Commodities

Cryptocurrencies are considered a further asset class, even if the question is still debated (see: https://www.wealthmanagement.com/opinions/opinion-crypto-not-asset-class), as many investors do not consider it a currency and realize that it has no independent value or inherent utility.

Others, however, consider cryptocurrencies an asset class since they possess certain characteristics that align them with traditional asset classes. They can be bought, sold, and traded on various cryptocurrency exchanges, and their value can fluctuate based on market supply and demand dynamics. Cryptocurrencies also exhibit varying degrees of risk, potential returns, and correlations with other asset classes.

Others still consider them as a subset of alternative investments. The classification may vary depending on the context and the methodology used for categorization. Nonetheless, cryptocurrencies have attracted significant attention as investment vehicles and are often included in discussions of asset allocation and diversification strategies.

Asset classes can be comprehensively considered within a balance sheet that expresses the assets and liabilities of a firm, as shown in Fig. 2.4.

The comprehensive valuation of a firm typically considers either the Enterprise Value (equity + bonds = financial debt) or the residual Equity Value, ultimately belonging to the shareholders.

Should cryptocurrencies be considered an asset class, they would be allocated within the assets (invested capital).

Valuating cryptocurrencies can be challenging due to their unique characteristics and the dynamic nature of the crypto market. While there is no universally agreed-upon "best" valuation approach for cryptocurrencies, here are some commonly used methods:

1. Market-based Approach: This approach relies on comparing the cryptocurrency to similar digital assets that have been recently traded in the market. It involves examining factors such as trading volume, liquidity, market capitalization, and price movements. Market-based approaches often use metrics like market multiples (e.g., price-to-earnings ratio or price-to-sales ratio) or price comparisons against similar cryptocurrencies.

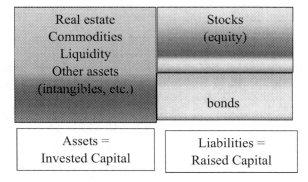

Fig. 2.4 From the balance sheet to the asset classes

2. Network-based Approach: Cryptocurrencies often derive their value from the network or ecosystem they operate within. This approach assesses factors such as the number of active users, transaction volume, developer activity, community engagement, and network effects. It considers the growth and adoption potential of the cryptocurrency's underlying platform or technology.
3. Cost of Production: This approach considers the cost of mining a cryptocurrency. It assumes that the cost of production is the minimum value of a cryptocurrency.
4. Fundamental Analysis: This approach involves analyzing the fundamental factors that can impact a cryptocurrency's value. This includes examining aspects such as the project's whitepaper, technology, team, partnerships, regulatory environment, and competitive landscape. Fundamental analysis attempts to assess the intrinsic value of the cryptocurrency based on its underlying fundamentals and potential future utility.
5. Tokenomics and Utility-based Approach: Many cryptocurrencies have specific use cases and utility within their respective platforms. This approach evaluates the tokenomics of the cryptocurrency, including its token supply, distribution mechanisms, governance structure, and utility within the ecosystem. It considers factors such as token demand, scarcity, and the role of cryptocurrency in facilitating transactions or accessing platform services.
6. Hybrid Approaches: Given the complexity of valuing cryptocurrencies, many analysts and investors combine multiple approaches to arrive at a more comprehensive valuation. They may use a combination of market-based, fundamental, and network-based analysis to gain a holistic understanding of the cryptocurrency's potential value.

2.4 General Valuation Approaches

Fernandez (2019b) and Damodaran (1996) describe the most widely used company valuation methods:

1. balance sheet-based methods;
2. income statement-based methods (including market comparables);
3. mixed methods; and
4. cash flow discounting-based methods.

The conceptually correct methods are those based on cash flow discounting (Singh, 2013).

The main valuation methods (see also Damodaran, 2018; Fazzini, 2018; Koller & Goedhart, 2015) are recalled in Fig. 2.6.

The valuation approaches, as shown in Fig. 2.5, are based on the business model that incorporates all the key parameters for valuation (e.g., EBITDA; operating and net cash flows; Net Financial Position, etc.). The assets represent the invested capital backed by the raised capital (represented by the liabilities = equity + financial debt). Within the assets, the core component is represented by the CAPEX (fixed assets, tangible and intangible). The CAPEX is the key input driver that presides over the output represented by the income statement (revenues and costs) and the cash flow statement.

Within the invested capital, the main input factor for productivity is represented by the CAPEX, as anticipated, because the Net Working Capital is just an ancillary component. The stock and the accounts receivable are ancillary to the sales (but are not the real "engine" behind that is represented by the CAPEX), and the accounts payable are linked to the OPEX (costs paid to the suppliers).

The Balance Sheet-Based Approach

Balance sheet-based methods try to assess the company's value by estimating the value of its assets. The balance sheet-based approach (seldom used in Anglo-Saxon countries but diffused in the Continental European UEC valuation school—see Viel et al., 1973) estimates value starting from the book value of equity (see Fig. 2.1). The basic idea behind this approach is that value can be inferred from the size of equity (book value, adjusted to express the market value).

A firm's book value, or net worth, is the accounting value of the shareholders' equity reported in the balance sheet (paid-in capital + reserves). The book value of equity is also the difference between total assets and liabilities the surplus of the firm's total tangible and intangible assets over its total debts. Whenever the book value of equity becomes negative, due to equity burnout (frequent in startups during the "Death valley" passage), the firms need to be recapitalized or liquidated.

The book value is then adjusted to consider, as a final output, the market value of equity, as shown in Fig. 2.7. The adjustments typically

2 ASSET CLASS TAXONOMY AND GENERAL VALUATION ...   39

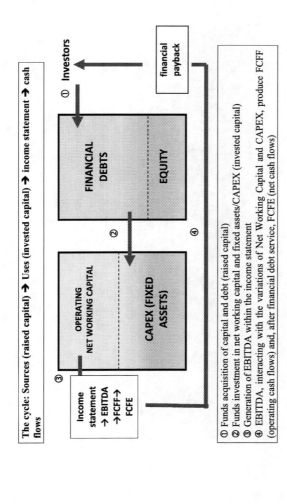

Fig. 2.5 The Financial-Economic Cycle

Fig. 2.6 Firm valuation approaches: a taxonomy

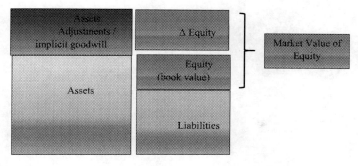

Fig. 2.7 Balance sheet-based approach

consist of revaluation of some assets (typically the intangibles and occasionally some fixed assets, always considering the CAPEX, since current assets are intrinsically unfit for consideration in any revaluation).

The equity is considered the value reserve belonging to the ultimate stakeholders, represented by the shareholders who underwrite risky capital and so are the last to be satisfied, following the absolute priority rule according to which the firm uses its liquidity to serve secured debt, then junior (subordinated) debt, followed by quasi-equity (e.g., financial debt underwritten by the shareholders; convertible bonds, etc.), preferred equity and eventually "standard" equity (represented by ordinary shares, with full voting rights). Share valuation follows the distinction between voting rights and investment rights, together with its legal consequences, as shown in Fig. 2.8.

Whereas ordinary shares typically embody both voting and investment rights, preferred shares have limited voting capacity (in specific meetings), compensated by prior or higher remuneration (dividends or liquidation payback). During takeovers, the value of ordinary shares typically sours, whereas non-voting shares are not considered interesting by market raiders who seek control of the (ordinary) shareholders' meeting. This reflects in the relative valuation of ordinary versus preferred shares. A peculiar case is represented by the merger between two firms with different categories of shares: the share swaps are two—ordinary versus ordinary and ordinary versus non-voting shares.

As equity represents, in broader terms, the net wealth belonging to the shareholders, it is intrinsically associated with the concept of private property (of the firm). According to Aristotle, property should be private

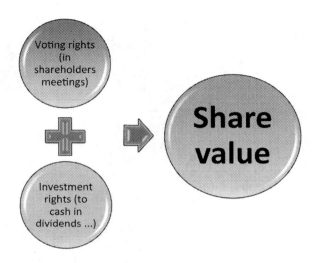

Fig. 2.8 Voting and investment rights

but the use of it is common, and the special business of the legislator is to create in men this benevolent disposition. So, property should be private because when the property is held in common it prevents people from acting benevolently people cannot be generous if they do not have anything to give away, so property provides little incentive for individuals to trade and invest if it is held in common and in this very case no one maintains it. The property right has been pointed out even by John Locke who talks about individual rights saying that as God gave us dominion over our bodies, we also have dominion over the things we make the German philosopher Emmanuel Kant later argued that private property is a legitimate expression of the self, however, Karl Marx insisted that private property is a mean of expropriation in a capitalistic way of the labor of the proletarian.

The valuation of the market value according to the balance-sheet approach (Fernandez, 2001, 2019a) is based on the current value of the equity contained in the last available balance sheet. Fernandez, possibly the most famous and "downloaded" expert on corporate valuations with Damodaran, shows a good synthesis between the Anglo-Saxon and the Continental European schools—sharply different in the past decades, not so now, thanks to the centripetal forces of globalization.

There are three approaches:

1. Simple balance sheet-based approach;
2. Adjusted balance sheet-based approach—Grade I; and
3. Adjusted balance sheet-based approach—Grade II.

As anticipated, this approach has been traditionally used in continental Europe and less so in Anglo-Saxon countries.

The starting point for the use of the balance sheet-based approach, both simple and adjusted, is represented by the shareholders' equity of the financial statements including the profit for the year net of the amounts approved for distribution (dividends).

Based on the values shown in the financial statements, a balance sheet analysis of assets and liabilities must be carried out, representing non-monetary assets (technical fixed assets, inventories of goods, securities, and, depending on the approach used, intangible fixed assets) in terms of current values, to highlight implicit capital gains or losses compared to the accounting data. For assets with a significant exchange market (e.g., real estate or traded securities), the calculation of present values is generally based on the prices recorded during the most recent negotiations. When there is no reference market, estimates based on reconstruction or training costs may be alternatively used—this being the typical circumstance with unconventional intangibles, as shown in Chapter 3.

The simple balance sheet-based approach is significant in the case of companies with high equity content (real estate companies, holding companies, etc.). In such companies, the overall profitability/risk profile may represent the synthesis of the patterns implicitly or explicitly considered in the valuation of the individual assets.

This methodology makes the value of the capital coincide with the difference between the current value of the assets and the value of the liabilities that contribute to determining the company's assets. The value can be inferred starting from the differential book value of equity and then adding up market adjustments. The asset value corresponds with the net investment that would be necessary to start a new company with the same asset structure as the one being valued (a sort of replacement cost). The simple asset value is, therefore, not the liquidation value of the assets, but the value of their reconstruction from a business operating perspective. Reconstruction (replacement) cost is one of the three standard methodologies to evaluate intangibles, as shown in Chapter 3.

Accounting of liabilities should never be underestimated and so their value should be consistent with their bookkeeping or lower—it is not so, the approved and then deposited balance sheet is false, with criminal consequences, especially for listed firms.

The formula, consistent with Fig. 2.1, is:

$$\text{Enterprise value} = \text{book equity} + \text{asset adjustments} - \text{liability adjustments} = \text{adjusted equity} = K_1 = W_1 \quad (2.1)$$

where asset and liability adjustments are defined as capital gains and losses net of the tax impact. These gains/losses express the difference between market and book (accounting) values.

The simple valuation considers, to estimate equity stocks, only tangible assets in addition to loans and liquidity.

The valuation provides for a detailed estimate of the assets at current replacement values, in particular:

- Assets at current repurchase value;
- Assets and liabilities, based on settlement values.

The "first-grade adjusted balance sheet-based approach" also considers intangible assets that are not accounted for but have a market value. In formulae:

$$K_1 + \text{intangible assets not accounted for but with market value} = K_2 = W_2 \quad (2.2)$$

(e.g., bank deposits, insurance premium portfolio, shop licenses, large-scale distribution, etc.)

Where K_1 is the value of assets determined according to the principles of the simple balance sheet-based approach.

Finally, the adjusted Tier II balance sheet-based approach also refers to intangible assets that are not accounted for and do not have a specific market value, bringing to the "second-grade adjusted balance sheet-based approach".

$$K_2 + \text{unrecognized intangible assets without market value} = K_3 = W_3 \quad (2.3)$$

(e.g., product portfolio, patents, industrial concessions, know-how, market shares and corporate image sales network, management, the value of human capital, etc.)

Where K_2 is the value of assets determined according to the adjusted-grade I balance sheet-based approach.

Intangible assets (beyond those described in Chapter 3) that are not accounted for and do not have a market value are:

- Strategy, concerning products and life cycle, customers, markets, market positioning, and market share achieved, orientation toward growth and partnership policies;
- Customers and market share;
- Processes and innovation;
- The organization, which includes all the elements related to corporate governance; and
- Human resources.

Monetary Equity

Whenever a firm valuation considers "equity" as a key parameter for appraisal, several complementary definitions emerge and compete. The "book" value of equity, consistent with the representation of Fig. 2.1, indicates the accounting difference between assets and liabilities, within the balance sheet, whereas the "market" value is the expression of the external fair value of the equity. The difference, if positive, is represented by an internally generated goodwill (badwill, if negative) that cannot be recorded but is to be considered in any market-oriented appraisal. Other equity definitions are, however, important for a comprehensive evaluation.

Figure 2.9 accordingly shows in graphical terms the various definitions of book, monetary, tangible, and intangible equity.

Monetary equity has a temporal dimension, and it may be subdivided in:

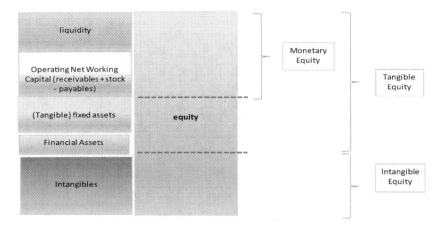

Fig. 2.9 Book, monetary, tangible, and intangible equity

- "immediate" monetary equity, considering in the assets only the liquidity; and
- short-term ("net working") monetary equity, also including the liquidity that is going to be generated (and absorbed) by the evolution of the operating net working capital (cashed-in receivables, paid-out payables, etc.).

The concept of monetary equity allows bypassing the controversial accounting treatment of intangibles that include capitalized costs (CAPEX, as opposed to OPEX, recorded in the income statement).

Work-for-equity is common in startups that wish to mix retention policies with monetary savings. The promised working effort from workers (especially for skilled co-operators) may be paid in kind with a capital increase.

Apart from the legal issues and the necessity to estimate this contribution to avoid any unjustified equity dilution, what matters here is the financial issue. Since work-for-equity is a cashless contribution, it does not have any immediate impact on monetary equity. Nevertheless, it can bring future monetary OPEX savings, if (monetary) staff cost is replaced by a dedicated equity increase.

The monetary equity represents a natural bridge between balance sheet approaches and financial methodologies rotating around Discounted Cash Flows.

2.5 The Income Approach

According to the income approach, the estimated value of the firm can be inferred considering its profits (revenues), referring to economic margins like the EBITDA (that is also a monetary margin, representing the difference between monetary operating revenues and costs), the EBIT, the pre-tax profit or, eventually, the net profit.

The "higher" the parameter in the consequential income statement (starting with sales, and then descending to EBITDA, EBIT, pre-tax, and net profit), the lower its significance but the better its reliability. In other words, sales are much less sensitive to creative accounting than net profits, being so more reliable, even if they do not incorporate any cost structure or economic marginality. A common compromise is represented by mid-way EBITDA, since it is an economic but also financial margin that reflects the managerial impact on the overall outcome of the firm, without considering financial leverage, taxation, or other factors that the management can hardly control. For this very reason, managerial compensation is often based on EBITDA.

Profit, representing the bottom line of the income statement, is a controversial concept, longly debated in philosophy, theology, and economics, on a moral and factual basis. According to the Summa Theologiae of Saint Thomas Aquinas, no man should sell a thing to another man for more than it's worth. So we introduce the concept of just price; of course, the market needs goods, and traders are going to supply them only if they have an appropriate reward but according to Saint Thomas there is also a moral dimension and prices do not have to be unjust. Profit should not be excessive because otherwise it would become a sin, and no deception can be involved in setting the value of the goods; also the buyer must freely accept the price.

Profitability valuation can be particularly appropriate when the company has a sufficiently defined profitability trend, or the approach is deemed reliable for company projections. Or even if the degree of capitalization (the discount rate of expected income streams) is not too high, due also to a significant intangible component. This is why the income

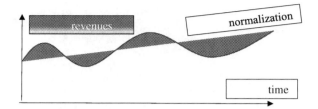

Fig. 2.10 Revenue normalization

approach is hardly applicable to startups and, more generally, to volatile firms whose future revenues are difficult to forecast.

The income approach makes it possible to estimate the market value based on expected profits, which the company is deemed to be able to produce in future years. Multi-year contractual agreements and customer loyalty, whenever available and meaningful, can help.

This methodology is also suitable for the evaluation of cyclical companies, which have volatile incomes, only if they show a tendency to compensate for overtime. In the presence of cyclical companies, normalization is a process that can identify a stable trend line, underlying the volatile trend of income flows that occur in the various periods of management. Figure 2.10 shows a possible trend normalization.

The fundamental elements in an evaluation of an income approach are:

a. The estimate of normalized income;
b. The choice of the capitalization rate; and
c. The choice of the capitalization formula, based on the valuation time horizon.

Estimated Normalized Income

As regards the determination of the income to be used as a basis for the valuation, reference is made to the average normalized value of income that the company is expected to produce permanently in future years, as graphically exemplified in Fig. 2.10.

Therefore, it is not considered as a series of future incomes, but rather as the expected normalized (average) value able to reflect the company's average long-term income capacity, in a time horizon consistent with the business model.

Normalized income can be derived from:

- Study of the income statement (historical and perspective);
- Analysis of the financial structure (leverage);
- Consistency between the normalized operating result and the equity evaluation process;
- Normalized income, i.e., average perspective income; and
- Alternatively, the evaluator may consider operating result / EBIT, pre-tax result, net income, operating or net cash flow (if referring to a complementary financial approach).

It is essential to transform the net profit (income) into a "normalized and integrated value" capable of expressing the company's ability to generate income, through three corrective processes:

1. Normalization: this is an articulated process aimed primarily at:
    - Redistribute "extraordinary" income and expenses over time;
    - Eliminate "non-operating" income and expenses; and
    - Neutralization of the effects caused by budgetary policies;
2. The integration of changes in the stock of intangible assets; and
3. Neutralization of the distorting impacts of inflation, to avoid fictitious losses or profits that could affect the valuation process.

The longer the extension of the evaluation scenario, the likelier the distortions.

The normalization process aims to subtract a series of income components from randomness, to bring them back to a relationship of adequate competence (accrual) with the reference period.

Extraordinary income and expenses are significant (and sometimes non-recurring) components of operating income. Extraordinary income may, for example, include the realization of substantial assets on the assets side, such as real estate.

Costs include the economic consequences of exceptional events, such as restructuring costs, costs arising from the effects of natural disasters (e.g., the Covid-19 pandemic), and plant removals.

These elements must be redistributed over time to express a measure of normalized income, not burdened by components that do not present the usual manifestation. The objective of the redistribution is to replace a random size with an average value to avoid that some businesses are particularly underweighted, and others are overestimated.

The elimination of income and costs unrelated to ordinary operations must be carried out by bringing the values in the income statement to size in line with the market or practice.

As regards the neutralization of budgetary policies, reference is made to the fundamental estimates (amortization and depreciation, inventories, provisions for risks in industrial and commercial firms, and fiscal policies).

The integration process is based on the observation that the dynamics of some values regarding intangible assets are or are not adequately recorded in the accounts.

The neutralization of the inflation distortive effects makes it possible to separate real outcomes from apparent and illusory results since they derive from the sum of values that are not uniform in monetary terms. The most commonly used corrections are as follows:

- The adjustment of the depreciation rates of fixed technical assets at reconstruction costs, i.e., to the updated values of recent estimates;
- Adoption of the LIFO procedure in the valuation of inventories of products, semi-finished products, and raw materials; and
- Determination of economic results.

Income subjective normalization can be completely avoided if the evaluator only considers "objective" revenues (invoiced sales) in her/his estimates. The obvious reply is that revenues completely dismiss the implications of the cost structure and, consequently, economic marginality, from EBITDA onward.

Turnover is, however, widely used as a "rule of thumb" parameter in many evaluations. The main rationale behind this irrational decision is not only to refer to "quick and dirty" shortcuts that tend to eliminate subjectivity but also (mainly) considering that, in many cases, firm evaluators (and the potential buyers behind them) are interested in the business activity, forgetting the "legal shell" that incorporates it in a firm.

In other words, buyers are often attracted by the clientele portfolio and its goodwill (expressed by the sales), considering that after the purchase they can merge the target firm inside their own; at that point, they can cut the costs of the prey company, exploiting economies of scale and experience and, eventually, forgetting the original cost structure of the acquired firm.

The M&A of chemist shops (pharmacies) is a well-known example of this practical methodology.

Choice of the Capitalization Rate

The capitalization rate of normalized income represents the opportunity cost of capital employed. The opportunity cost measures the value of choices that have been rejected.

This rate, used to discount the normalized stream of expected revenues, depends on the expected return on the risk-free securities and the risk premium that the market is expected to require for the type of investment being valued. The expected return on risk-free securities is generally identified with that on government bonds. The market return refers to all risky investments available on the market. This is consistent with the Capital Asset Pricing Model.

An alternative criterion for determining the capitalization rate may be to base it on the cost of invested capital from the perspective of the purchaser.

In this case, the value of the company is understood as a series of future incomes that must be discounted based on the average cost of money for the purchaser. Its value, therefore, no longer depends on the degree of risk of the company.

The first approach of determining the rate of capitalization presents a theoretical-practical structure of greater importance but presupposes efficient financial markets (where stock prices reflect all available information) since the entire evaluation is based on indicators that can be traced back to them.

Choice of the Capitalization Formula

The determination of the market value, through the discounting of future income flows, occurs in many cases using the perpetual annuity formula since the company is an institution destined to last over time.

The attribution, instead, of limited duration to the production of income (from 3–5 to 8–10 years) is an assumption not verified in the business reality and tends to be arbitrary, considering the determination of the time boundary. An unlimited time horizon (∞) also disregards the terminal value that is theoretically present anyway but whose discounted value tends to zero (terminal value $/\infty \approx 0$).

It is, therefore, possible to proceed with the calculation of the value of the firm, based on the average normalized value of the income flows, synthetically estimated, and generated in protracted-time horizons, consistent with the business plan.

Based on the chosen capitalization period, one of the two alternative formulas can be used:

- The limited capitalization (for a finite period):

$$W_2 = Ra_{n-i} \qquad (2.4)$$

- The unlimited capitalization:

$$W_1 = R/i \qquad (2.5)$$

- W is the market value of the firm;
- R is the integrated normalized income;
- i is the income capitalization rate (a discount rate, similar to the cost of capital, that incorporates both the time value of money and the risk that the real realized return differs from the expected one); and
- n is the period (years) of limited capitalization.

The capitalization rate is given by the sum of:

a. the riskless real rate of return;
b. expected inflation; and
c. risk.

According to the Fisher equation, $1 + 2$ = nominal rate of return. Risk-free returns can be estimated considering a proxy recently issued Government bonds (of the country of the target firm) with a maturity similar to the capitalization time. Inflation expectations are easily available from Internet sources (IMF, World Bank, Central banks, OECD, etc.) If the capitalization is unlimited, evaluators normally choose the Government bond with the longest maturity. The risk premium may consider not only the volatility of the forecast revenues but also country risk factors traditionally embedded in equity risk premia. As Fernandez (2019c) notes "The equity premium designates four different concepts: Historical Equity Premium (HEP); Expected Equity Premium (EEP); Required Equity Premium (REP); and Implied Equity Premium (IEP)."

Country and equity risk premia are easily available from free databases.

2.6 The Value Added

The value added is a key parameter in financial statement analysis since it concerns the economic value that a company internally creates, just considering its typical managerial activities, i.e., without considering extraordinary items, financial issues, or taxes (that are ancillary to the ordinary management).

A value-added Statement is an income statement that depicts wealth created by a corporation and its distribution among various stakeholders. The various stakeholders comprise the employees, shareholders, government, creditors, and the wealth that is retained in the business.

As per the concept of Enterprise Theory, profit is calculated for various stakeholders by a corporation. Value added is this profit generated by the collective efforts of management, employees, capital, and the utilization of its capacity that is distributed among its various stakeholders.

Consider a manufacturing firm. A typical firm would buy raw materials from the market. Process the raw materials and assemble them to produce the finished goods. The finished goods are then sold in the market. The additional work that the firm does to the raw materials for it to be sold in the market is the value added by that firm. Value added can also be defined as the difference between the value that the customers are willing to pay for the finished goods and the cost of materials.

Sales Revenue	3000
Less: Cost of bought in goods and services	600
Value added	**2400**
Application of Value added	
Employee Benefits	750
To capital providers (Creditors and Lenders)	300

(continued)

(continued)

Taxes	300
Value retained (depreciation and expansion of business)	1050
Value added	**2400**

From the above illustration, the difference between sales and cost of bought-in materials and services gives the value added by the corporation. The second part of the statement gives the distribution of the value added by the corporation. Of the €800 added by the firm, €250 is utilized for employee benefits. €100 is given as interest on loans and dividends to shareholders. Another €100 is contributed to the government in the form of taxes. Whereas €350 is retained for the expansion of the current business, and part of it is kept aside for depreciation amount. Thus, the value-added statement not only gives the value added by the corporation but also the distribution of it across various stakeholders.

These are the main advantages of a value-added statement:

- It is easy to calculate.
- It helps a company to apportion the value to various stakeholders. The company can use this to analyze what proportion of value added is allocated to which stakeholder.
- It is useful for doing a direct comparison with your competitors.
- It is useful for internal comparison purposes and for devising employee incentive schemes.

The Difference Between Value Added and Profit can be synthesized as follows:

- Profit subtracts all the costs incurred in the process of generating revenues. The value added, on the other hand only subtracts the cost of bought-in goods and services. Profits are meant for shareholders whereas value added is meant for stakeholders who include shareholders also. Therefore, value added is a wider term.

Use Value and Exchange Value

Use value or value in use is a concept in the classical political economy, dating back from Aristoteles and then developed by Adam Smith and Karl Marx. It refers to the tangible features of a commodity (a tradeable object) that can satisfy some human requirement, want, or need, or which serves a useful purpose. In Marx's critique of political economy, any product has a labor-value and a use-value, and if it is traded as a commodity in markets, it additionally has an exchange value, most often expressed as a money price. Marx acknowledges that commodities being traded also have a general utility, implied by the fact that people want them, but he argues that this by itself tells us nothing about the specific character of the economy in which they are produced and sold.

A commodity has:

- a value
- a use-value (or utility)
- an exchange value
- a price (it could be an actual selling price or an imputed ideal price)

The difference between use-value and exchange-value is a key component of the process of creating (added) value.

This concept is linked to the paradox of value (also known as the diamond–water paradox) is the apparent contradiction that, although water is, on the whole, more useful, in terms of survival than diamonds, diamonds command a higher price in the market. The philosopher Adam Smith is often considered to be the classic presenter of this paradox, although it had already appeared as early as Plato's Euthydemus. Nicolaus Copernicus, John Locke, John Law, and others had previously tried to explain the disparity.

Whenever the use-value is higher than the exchange value, the company has an economic incentive to purchase a good (or commodity or service). When the exchange value exceeds the use-value, then the company is motivated to sell out its goods, to earn an economic profit.

The value-added, in broader terms, is the value that the company creates (adds up) by combining different factors (labor, capital, etc.) in a synergistic mix.

VALUE-ADDED

Labor cost	→	Remuneration of labor
Depreciation	→	Remuneration of capital
Negative interest rates	→	Remuneration of debtholders
Taxes	→	Remuneration of the Government
Net result	→	Remuneration of shareholders

Practical Example—The Value-Added Cake

The value-added is value created by assembling different components (labor + capital, etc.).

It can be compared to a cake made of composite ingredients. The two key issues are:

a. the dimension of the cake (the bigger, the better); and
b. the criteria for cutting the slices.

does issue b) impact issue a)? Yes, if we can say that fair criteria represent an incentive for all the stakeholders that contribute to producing a bigger and tastier cake (with a higher added value).

A further question is represented by the link, if any, between the cake's added value and each slice.

The first slice is represented by labor cost. Is it proportional to the added value and so variable? Or is it fixed? Labor costs are mainly fixed and so independent of the value-added, even if they may partially be variables (incentives, extra salary, etc.).

After labor costs, a residual cake is left for the other stakeholders:

Is it big enough for the appetite of the remaining stakeholders? And is the slice cut for employees fair and stimulating?

A further "pie" is represented by capital remuneration of investments (fixed assets, intangibles, etc.).

In our example, mainly the oven and the kitchen furniture.

Is this slice proportional to the value-added?

Not really: the slice represents the economic depreciation of the investments, which is linked to the "cake" fixed assets. Are fixed assets related to value-added? Yes, at least partially: we need investments to produce a value-added. Productivity may minimize the investment needed for that output, but up to a certain point.

Negative interests represent a further slice. They are not directly linked to the value-added. They are related to outstanding debt, recorded in the liabilities of the balance sheet. Debt is needed to back investments. So negative interests are related to debt and then investments and then depreciation and finally value-added. A long value chain, with different possible interactions.

Taxes are fixed in their % rate, but they depend on a floating taxable income that is linked to the value-added.

Eventually, as shown in Fig. 2.11, the ultimate slice that is left over belongs to the shareholders. It is completely flexible: the bigger the cake that is left, the higher the remuneration of the equity holders. But if they are too greedy, the other stakeholders may lack the incentive to cooperate for bigger and tastier cakes.

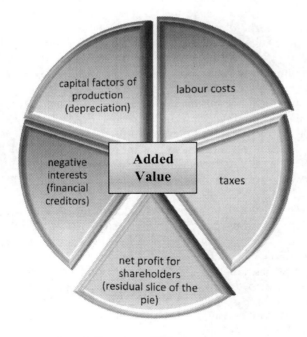

Fig. 2.11 Partitioning of the value-added pie

Cash is King: The Superiority of the Financial Approach

According to Peter Bernstein (Introduction to Rappaport & Mauboussin, 2021) "assets producing cash flows will ultimately return the owner's investment without depending on the whims of other investors. Even if those cash flows are some distance in the future, their prospects endow them with a present value. Financial markets are nothing more than arenas where investors who need cash today can obtain it by selling the present value of future cash flows to other investors willing to wait for the cash payoffs from their capital. The payment medium in this transaction is money. The crucial point: If you invest without expecting future cash flows, then you might as well collect art or play the slot machines".

The financial approach is based on the principle that the market value of the company is equal to the discounted value of the cash flows that the company can generate ("cash is king"). The determination of the cash flows is of primary importance in the application of the approach, as is the consistency of the discount rates adopted.

The doctrine (especially the Anglo-Saxon one) believes that the financial approach is the "ideal" solution for estimating the market value for limited periods. It is not possible to make reliable estimates of cash flows for longer periods. "The conceptually correct methods are those based on cash flow discounting" (Fernandez, 2019b); and "nowadays, the cash flow discounting method is generally used because it is the only conceptually correct valuation method".

This approach is of practical importance if the individual investor or company with high cash flows (leasing companies, retail trade, public, and motorway services, financial trading, project financing SPVs, etc.) is valued.

Financial evaluation can be particularly appropriate when the company's ability to generate cash flow for investors is significantly different from its ability to generate income and forecasts can be formulated with a sufficient degree of credibility and are demonstrable.

There are two criteria for determining cash flows, respectively bringing (if appropriately discounted) to the estimate of the equity or the enterprise value, as shown in Fig. 2.12. In the evaluation of CAPEX investments where the Net Present Value (NPV) is to be estimated, the two criteria can be assimilated, respectively, to the NPV_{equity} or $NPV_{project}$, where the former expresses the residual net return for the investing shareholders (as remuneration of the Equity Value), whereas the latter estimate the return for all the raised capital underwriters (shareholders + financial creditors). The Internal Rate of Return (IRR) is, mathematically, the break-even financial rate that makes the NPV = 0. In the income statement structure, operating cash flows can be compared to operating profit (= EBIT), and net cash flows to net profits.

I The Cash Flow Available to Shareholders (Free Cash Flow to Equity—FCFE)

It is a measure of cash flow that considers the financial structure of the company (levered cash flow). It is the ultimate cash flow that remains after the payment of interest and the repayment of equity shares and after the coverage of equity expenditures necessary to maintain existing assets and

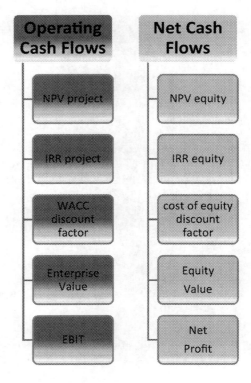

Fig. 2.12 Operating and net cash flows

to create the conditions for business growth. That is why it is also called "free" (=residually available) liquidity for the equity holders.

In M&A operations, the Free Cash Flow to the Firm (FCFF) (operating cash flow) is normally calculated, to estimate the Enterprise Value (comprehensive of financial debt). The residual Equity Value is then derived by subtracting the Net Financial Position.

The cash flow for the shareholders can be determined, starting from the net profit:

Net profit (loss)
+ amortization/depreciation and provisions
+ divestments (−investments) in technical equipment
+ divestments (−investments) in other assets
+ decrease (−increase) in net operating working capital
+ increases (−decreases) in loans
+ equity increases (−decreases)
= **Cash flows available to shareholders**
(Net cash flow or Free cash flow to equity − FCFE)

Alternatively to this bottom-up calculation, the net cash flow can be calculated with top-down steps, starting from the sales (monetary revenues) in the income statement, arriving at the operating cash flow—see II. below) and eventually the net cash flow (see Table 2.1).

The discounting of the free cash flow for the shareholders takes place at a rate equal to the cost of the shareholders' equity, consistent with the representation of Fig. 2.12. This flow identifies the theoretical measure of the company's ability to distribute dividends, even if it may not coincide with the dividend paid. The dividend policy of the firm influences the Dividend Discount Model, used as a proxy for calculating the cost of equity.

II The Cash Flow Available to the Company (Free Cash Flow to the Firm—FCFF)

The second configuration of flows is used in the practice of Enterprise Value estimate.

Table 2.1 Cash flow statement and link with the cost of capital

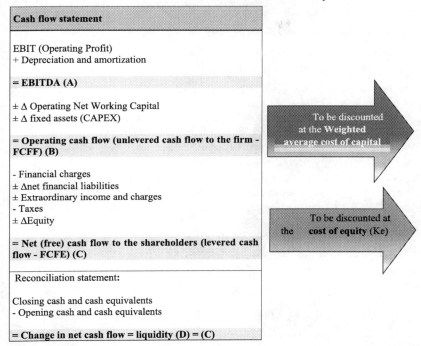

It is a measure of cash flows independent of the financial structure of the company (unlevered cash flows) that is particularly suitable to evaluate companies with high levels of indebtedness, or that do not have a debt plan (as happens in most debt-free startups). If the firm is debt-free, then FCFF≈FCFE, cost of debt ≈ cost of equity ≈ WACC, operating profit ≈ net profit, raised capital ≈ equity, ROE ≈ ROI, etc.

This methodology is based on the operating flows generated by the management of the company, based on the operating income available for the remuneration of own and third-party means net of the relative tax effect. Unlevered cash flows are typically determined with a bottom-up procedure starting from the income statement by using operating income before taxes and financial charges:

Net operating income(EBIT) − taxes on operating income

+ amortization/depreciation and provisions(non − monetary operating costs)
+ technical divestments(−investments)
+ divestments(−investments)in other assets
+ decrease(−increase)in operating net working capital
= **Cash flow available to shareholders and lenders**
   (operating cash flow or free cash flow to the firm − FCFF)

The cash flow available to the firm is, therefore, determined as the cash flow available to shareholders, plus financial charges after tax, plus loan repayments and equity repayments, minus new borrowings and flows arising from equity increases. An example is given in Fig. 2.13.

The difference between the two approaches is, therefore, given by the different meanings of cash flows associated with debt and equity repayments. Debt service comes first unless the firm is debt-free: in this case, as anticipated above, FCFF = FCFE.

Cash flows from operating activities are discounted to present value at the weighted average cost of capital (WACC), analyzed in the formula Eq. (2.12).

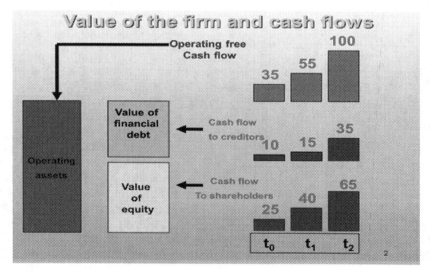

Fig. 2.13 Value of the firm and cash flows

This DCF metrics offers an evaluation of the whole company, independently from its financial structure (whose impact is considered later, both in the income and cash flow statement). The value of the debt must be subtracted from the value of the company to rejoin the market value of equity, obtained by discounting the residual cash flows available for the shareholders (FCFE).

The relationship between the two concepts of cash flow, consistent with Table 2.1, is as follows:

Cash flow available to the company(CFFF)
= cash flow available to shareholders(CFFE) + financial charges
(net of taxes) + loan repayments − new loans   (2.6)

An example of the Enterprise Value of the firm (value of financial debt + equity) and its partitioning between financial debtholders and eventually shareholders is illustrated in Fig. 2.13.

Cash flow estimates can be applied to any type of asset. The differential element is represented by its duration. Many assets have a defined time horizon, while others assume a perpetual time horizon such as shares. That is why firm valuation should theoretically always be unlimited, without any time constraint. In many cases, as it has been shown with the estimate of a limited capitalization of expected revenues (par. 2.5.), it is not, but only because unlimited forecasts may prove too subjective.

Cash flows (CF) can, therefore, be estimated using a normalized projection of cash flows that it uses, alternatively:

$$-\text{unlimited capitalization}: \quad W_1 = CF/i \qquad (2.7)$$

$$-\text{limited capitalization}: \quad W_2 = CFa_{n-i} \qquad (2.8)$$

where W_1 and W_2 represent the present value of future cash flows. Depending on the numerator of the formula, W_1 or W_2 measures either the Enterprise Value or the Equity Value.

This formulation is like that of expected revenues (see formulae Eqs. (2.4) and (2.5)), simply replacing expected revenues for forecast cash flows. Theoretical accountants claim that, in the long run, the projection of cash flows should converge to that of comparable revenue returns (and so, operating cash flow ≈ EBIT; net cash flow ≈ net profit). If so, income and financial methodologies should be converging to common estimates.

The discount rate to be applied to expected cash flows is determined as the sum of the cost of equity and the cost of debt, appropriately weighted according to the leverage of the company (the ratio between financial debt and equity). This produces the Weighted Average Cost of Capital (WACC):

$$WACC = k_i(1-t)\frac{D}{D+E} + k_e\frac{E}{D+E} \qquad (2.9)$$

where:

- k_i = cost of debt;
- t = corporate tax rate;
- D = market value of debt;
- E = market value of equity;
- D + E = raised capital;
- k_e = cost of equity.

The consistency between the numerator and the denominator in the discounted FCFF is evident since both parameters represent a mix of financial debt and equity.

The cost of debt capital is easy to determine, as it can be inferred from the financial statements of the company, representing the ratio between negative interests and financial debt. The cost of equity or share capital, which represents the minimum rate of return required by investors for equity investments, is instead more complex and may use the Capital Asset Pricing Model or the Dividend Discount Model (see paragraph 2.7.1.). Equity is traditionally riskier than financial debt (whose periodical remuneration and payback are contractually predetermined), and so the cost of equity > cost of debt, and also the cost of equity > WACC.

Once the present value of the cash flows has been determined, the calculation of the market value (W) of the company may correspond to:

a. the unlevered cash flow approach (to estimate the Enterprise Value):

$$W = \sum \frac{CF_0}{WACC} + TV - D \qquad (2.10)$$

b. the levered cash flow approach (to estimate the Equity Value):

$$W = \sum \frac{CF_n}{K_e} + TV \qquad (2.11)$$

where:

- $\sum CF_0/WACC$ = present value of operating cash flows (FCFF)
- $\sum CF_n/K_e$ = present value of net cash flows (FCFE)
- TV = terminal (residual) value
- D = initial net financial position (financial debt − liquidity)
- WACC = average after-tax cost of a company's various capital sources (cost of collecting external capital), including common stock, preferred stock, bonds, and any other long-term financial debt.

What matters in formulae Eqs. (2.10) and (2.11) is, once again, the consistency between the numerator and the denominator. Operating cash flows are unlevered since they are considered before debt service, and they so need to be discounted using an "operating" (unlevered) cost of capital that considers both the cost of debt and the residual cost of equity. Net cash flows are consistently discounted at the cost of equity since both the numerator and the denominator refer to the residual claims of the equity holders. Preferred equity is slightly safer than ordinary equity, as it commands a (small) premium and a priority in dividends—that is why a different cost of equity is used.

The WACC is the weighted average of the following cost of capital sources (Fig. 2.14):

The residual (terminal) value, more comprehensively described in paragraph 2.13., is the result of discounting the value at the time n (before which the cash flows are estimated analytically). It is often the greatest component of the global value W (above all in intangible-intensive companies) and tends to zero if the time horizon of the capitalization is infinite (VR $/ \infty = 0$).

The two variants (levered versus unlevered) give the same result if the overall DCF value of the firm, determined through the cash flows available to the lenders (FCFF), is deducted from the value of the net financial debts. In this case: equity value = enterprise value ± net financial position.

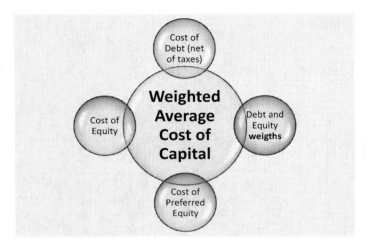

Fig. 2.14 WACC determinants

Operating cash flows (unlevered – FCFF) and net cash flows for shareholders (levered – FCFE) is determined by comparing the last two balance sheets (to consider changes in operating Net Working Capital, fixed assets/CAPEX, financial liabilities, and shareholders' equity) with the income statement of the last year, as shown in Table 2.1 that illustrates the accounting scheme of the cash flow statement.

This cash flow statement is different from the scheme proposed by the international accounting principles (see, for instance, IAS 7) since it considers both the EBITDA and the Operating Cash Flows, whose importance for firm valuation emerges from this chapter. Even if both statements—the one proposed here and the IAS 7-compliant scheme—arrive at the same net result (FCFE), they show some differences "on the road".

The net cash flow for the shareholders coincides with the free cash flow to equity (FCFE) and, therefore, with the dividends that can be paid out, once it has been verified that enough internal liquidity resources remain in the firm to back its going concern perspectives. This feature, associated with the ability to raise equity from third parties and shareholders, is such as to allow the company to find adequate financial coverage for the investments deemed necessary to maintain the company's business continuity and remain on the market in economic conditions (minimum objectives).

They should allow for the creation of incremental value in favor of the shareholders, who are the residual claimants (being, as subscribers of risky capital, the only beneficiaries of the variable net returns, which, as such, are residual and subordinate to the fixed remuneration of the other stakeholders).

The estimate of cash flows can be ideally applied to any activity.

A core differential element is service life. Many activities have a defined time horizon, while others assume a perpetual time horizon such as company shares, as anticipated.

The discounted cash flow (DCF) approach can be complemented with real options that incorporate intangible-driven flexibility in the forecasts. Real options improve the flexibility of capital budgeting estimates, fostering the NPV (higher resilience decreases the risk that is a major component of the discount factor in the denominator of DCF).

DCF is ubiquitous in financial valuation and constitutes the cornerstone of contemporary valuation theory (Singh, 2013). The robustness of the model, as well as its compatibility with the conventional two-dimensional risk-return structure of investment appraisal, makes it suited to a multitude of valuations. Accounting standards across the globe recognize the efficacy of this model and advocate its use, wherever practicable. FAS 141 and 142 of the United States and IAS 39 which relate to the accounting of intangible assets recommend the use of DCF methodology for attributing a value to such assets.

Some caveats should be considered. According to OECD (2022):

- *"Valuation techniques that estimate the discounted value of projected future cash flows derived from the exploitation of the transferred intangible or intangibles can be particularly useful when properly applied. There are many variations of these valuation techniques. In general terms, such techniques measure the value of an intangible by the estimated value of future cash flows it may generate over its expected remaining lifetime. The value can be calculated by discounting the expected future cash flows to present value. Under this approach valuation requires, among other things, defining realistic and reliable financial projections, growth rates, discount rates, the useful life of intangibles, and the tax effects of the transaction. Moreover, it entails consideration of terminal values when appropriate"* (par. 6.157).

- "When applying valuation techniques, including valuation techniques based on projected cash flows, it is important to recognize that the estimates of value based on such techniques can be volatile. Small changes in one or another of the assumptions underlying the valuation approach or in one or more of the valuation parameters can lead to large differences in the intangible value the approach produces. A small percentage change in the discount rate, a small percentage change in the growth rates assumed in producing financial projections, or a small change in the assumptions regarding the useful life of the intangible can each have a profound effect on the ultimate valuation. Moreover, this volatility is often compounded when changes are made simultaneously to two or more valuation assumptions or parameters" (par. 6.158).
- "The reliability of a valuation of a transferred intangible using discounted cash flow valuation techniques is dependent on the accuracy of the projections of future cash flows or income on which the valuation is based" (par. 6.163).
- "The discount rate or rates used in converting a stream of projected cash flows into a present value is a critical element of a valuation approach. The discount rate considers the time value of money and the risk or uncertainty of the anticipated cash flows. As small variations in selected discount rates can generate large variations in the calculated value of intangibles using these techniques" (par. 6.170).
- "It should be recognized in determining and evaluating discount rates that in some instances, particularly those associated with the valuation of intangibles still in development, intangibles may be among the riskiest components" (par. 6.172).

Empirical Approaches

The empirical approaches (that some authors, like Fernandez, 2019b, consider as a part of income methodologies since they use the EBITDA as the benchmarking parameter) represent a wide set of appraisal methodologies that are mostly based on market comparisons. The market value identifies:

a. The value attributable to a share of the equity, expressed at stock exchange prices;
b. The price of the controlling interest or the entire share equity;

c. The traded value for the controlling equity of comparable undertakings;
d. The value derived from the stock exchange quotations of comparable undertakings.

Market comparisons have long been used in appraisals (e.g., when evaluating a real estate property, considering recent transactions for similar apartments) and represent a precious benchmark to infer fair market value.

Evaluators sometimes use comparable trades of companies belonging to the same product sector with similar characteristics (in terms of cash flows, sales, costs, etc.).

The market approach has direct application in listed firms, whose value can be inferred by recorded daily transactions. The total capitalization is a proxy of the overall equity value of the listed firm. Unlisted companies can be compared to listed ones—and their valuation metrics (Enterprise Value/EBITDA, Price-Earnings, etc.), typically applying a discount factor that reflects the lack of marketability, the lower liquidity, etc.

Market prices incorporate the assumption that investors are rational. Adam Smith was the first philosopher and economist to talk about the rational economic man and to establish the principles of the business economy. The economic man is a cold and rational calculator as individuals we are self-interested, we aim to improve our well-being by consuming goods and services and achieving goals we make decisions by collecting information and calculating which actions will help us achieve our aims without being too costly.

In practice, an examination of the prices used in negotiations with companies in the same sector leads to quantifying average parameters:

- *Price/EBIT*
- *Price/cash flow*
- *Price/book value*
- *Price/earnings*
- *Price/dividend*

These ratios seek to estimate the average rate to be applied to the company being assessed. However, there may be distorting effects of prices based on special interest rates, on a historical context, on difficulties of comparison, etc.

In financial market practice, the multiples methodology is frequently applied. Based on multiples, the company's value is derived from the market price profit referring to comparable listed companies, such as net profit, before tax or operating profit, cash flow, equity, or turnover.

The attractiveness of the multiples approach stems from its ease of use: multiples can be used to obtain quick but dirty estimates of the company's value and are useful when there are many comparable companies listed on the financial markets and the market sets correct prices for them on average.

Because of the simplicity of the calculation, these indicators are easily manipulated and susceptible to misuse, especially if they refer to companies that are not entirely similar. Since there are no identical companies in terms of entrepreneurial risk and growth rate, the assumption of multiples for the processing of the valuation can be misleading, bringing "fake multipliers".

The use of multiples can be implemented through:

A Use of fundamentals;
B Use of comparable data:

    B.1. Comparable companies;
    B.2. Comparable transactions.

The first approach links multiples to the fundamentals of the company being assessed: profit growth and cash flow, dividend distribution ratio, and risk. It is equivalent to the use of cash flow discounting approaches.

Discount factors incorporate risk. According to the OECD (2022):

- *"When identifying risks in relation to an investment with specificity, it is important to distinguish between the financial risks that are linked to the funding provided for the investments and the operational risks that are linked to the operational activities for which the funding is used, such as for example the development risk when the funding is used for developing a new intangible"* (par. 6.61).
- *"Particular types of risk that may have importance in a functional analysis relating to transactions involving intangibles include:*
- *risks related to development of intangibles, including the risk that costly research and development or marketing activities will prove to be unsuccessful, and considering the timing of the investment (for*

example, whether the investment is made at an early stage, mid-way through the development process, or at a late stage will impact the level of the underlying investment risk);
- *the risk of product obsolescence, including the possibility that technological advances of competitors will adversely affect the value of the intangibles;*
- *infringement risk, including the risk that defense of intangible rights or defense against other persons' claims of infringement may prove to be time-consuming, costly and/or unavailing;*
- *product liability and similar risks related to products and services based on the intangibles;*
- *exploitation risks, uncertainties in relation to the returns to be generated by the intangible"* (par. 6.65).

In some industries, products protected by intangibles can become obsolete or uncompetitive in a relatively short period in the absence of continuing development and enhancement of the intangibles. As a result, having access to updates and enhancements can be the difference between deriving a short-term advantage from the intangibles and deriving a longer-term advantage.

The following types of risks, among others, should be considered:

- Risks related to the future development of the intangibles. This includes an evaluation of whether the intangibles relate to commercially viable products, whether the intangibles may support commercially viable products in the future, the expected cost of required future development and testing, the likelihood that such development and testing will prove successful, and similar considerations.
- Risks related to product obsolescence and depreciation in the value of the intangibles. This includes an evaluation of the likelihood that competitors will introduce products or services in the future that would materially erode the market for products dependent on the intangibles being analyzed.
- Risks related to the infringement of intangible rights.
- Product liability and similar risks related to the future use of the intangibles (par. 6.128).
- For the second approach, it is necessary to distinguish whether it is a valuation of comparable companies or comparable transactions.

- The comparability concerns different firms but is also related to their contents. Intangible assets are however often hard to compare.

According again to the OECD (2022):

- *"Unique and valuable"* intangibles are those intangibles (i) that are not comparable to intangibles used by or available to parties to potentially comparable transactions, and (ii) whose use in business operations (e.g., manufacturing, provision of services, marketing, sales or administration) is expected to yield greater future economic benefits than would be expected in the absence of the intangible" (par. 6.17) *"intangibles often have unique characteristics, and as a result have the potential for generating returns and creating future benefits that could differ widely. In conducting a comparability analysis with regard to a transfer of intangibles, it is, therefore, essential to consider the unique features of the intangibles"* (par. 6.116).
- *"In conducting a comparability analysis, it may be important to consider the stage of development of particular intangibles"* (par. 6.123).

In the case of comparable companies, the approach estimates multiples by observing similar companies. The problem is to determine what is meant by similar companies. In theory, the analyst should check all the variables that influence the multiple.

In practice, companies should estimate the most likely price for a non-listed company, taking as a reference some listed companies, operating in the same sector and considered homogeneous. Two companies can be defined as homogeneous when they present, the same risk, similar characteristics, and expectations.

The calculation is:

- A company whose price is known (P_1),
- A variable closely related to its value (X_1)

The ratio (P_1)/(X_1) is assumed to apply to the company to be valued, for which the size of the reference variable (X_2) is known.

Therefore:

$$(P1)/(X1) = (P2)/(X2) \qquad (2.12)$$

so that the desired value P_2 will be:

$$P2 = X2[(P1)/(X1)] \qquad (2.13)$$

According to widespread estimates, the main factors to establish whether a company is comparable are:

- Size;
- Belonging to the same sector (See for instance the Statistical Classification of Economic Activities in the European Community, commonly referred to as NACE Rev 2 (https://ec.europa.eu/eurostat/documents/3859598/5902521/KS-RA-07-015-EN.PDF);
- Financial risks (leverage);
- Historical trends and prospects for the development of results and markets;
- Geographical diversification;
- Degree of reputation and credibility;
- Management skills;
- Ability to pay dividends.

The basis of valuation is founded on comparable transactions and exploits information about actual negotiations (or mergers) of similar—i.e., comparable—companies.

Among the empirical criteria, the approach of the multiplier of the EBITDA (Earnings Before Interest, Taxes, Depreciation, and Amortization) is widely diffused. The EBIDTA multiplier brings to an estimate of the enterprise value—and not the equity value—because the EBITDA is an economic/financial margin calculated *before* debt service.

When the net financial position is algebraically added to the enterprise value, the equity value can be estimated:

$$\begin{aligned} W &= \text{average perspective EBITDA} * \text{Enterprise Value/industry EBITDA} \\ &= \text{Enterprise Value of the Company} \end{aligned} \qquad (2.14)$$

And then:

$$\text{Equity Value} = \text{Enterprise Value} \pm \text{Net Financial Position} \qquad (2.15)$$

The graphical representation of this process is illustrated in Fig. 2.15.

2.7 Terminal Value

Terminal value (TV) is the value of an asset, business, or project beyond the forecasted period when future cash flows can be estimated. Terminal value assumes a business will grow at a set growth rate forever after the forecast period. Terminal value often comprises a large percentage of the total assessed value.

In all the valuation processes that forecast (limited) future streams of revenues, cash flows, or similar items (e.g., dividends, as it happens in the Dividend Discount Model), the terminal value issue arises and as anticipated above, is often material. In some exceptional cases, the terminal value percentage, compared to the overall estimated value, can well exceed 100%, meaning that the remaining value-adding factors (cash flows, etc.) in the preceding years have a negative value.

Abuses in terminal value estimation are frequent, especially when mighty startups are evaluated—that is why any valuation that embeds substantial terminal value contribution should be carefully interpreted, undergoing periodical impairment testing.

Figure 2.16 shows the alternative applications of terminal value.

The two most common types of Terminal Values considered by evaluators are:

A. Perpetuity Method

Discounting is a necessary algebraic process to incorporate the time value of money (nominal rate of interest, following Fisher's equation, according to which nominal interest is given by real interests + expected inflation) in the stream of future flows (revenues, cash flows, dividends, etc.). Operating (or net) cash flows or dividends can be forecast for a discrete period, beyond which estimates become too uncertain. Moreover, it is difficult to determine the precise time when a firm may cease operations.

To overcome these well-known practical limitations, evaluators often consider that future streams will grow at a stable rate forever, starting at some point in the next years. This represents the terminal value.

Terminal value is calculated by dividing the last flow forecast by the difference between the discount rate and the terminal growth rate.

2 ASSET CLASS TAXONOMY AND GENERAL VALUATION ... 75

Fig. 2.15 From the EBITDA multiplier to the enterprise and equity value

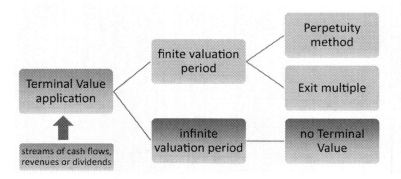

Fig. 2.16 Terminal value applications

The terminal value calculation estimates the value of the company after the forecast period. The formula shows similarities with the Dividend Discount Model:

$$\text{Terminal Value} = [CF \times (1 + g)]/(d - g) \qquad (2.16)$$

where:

- CF = cash flow for the last forecast period
- g = terminal growth rate
- d = discount rate (which is usually the weighted average cost of capital, consistently with operating cash flows—or the cost of equity, if the numerator is represented by a stream of forecast net cash flows)

The terminal growth rate is the constant rate at a company is expected to grow forever. This growth rate starts at the end of the last forecasted cash flow period in a discounted cash flow model and goes into perpetuity. A terminal growth rate is usually in line with the long-term rate of inflation, but not higher than the historical gross domestic product growth rate.

B. Exit Multiple Method

If the evaluators assume a finite set of operations, there is no need to use the perpetuity growth model. Instead, the terminal value must reflect the net realizable value of a company's assets at that time. This often implies that the equity will be acquired by a larger firm, and the value of acquisitions is often calculated with exit multiples.

Exit multiples estimate a fair price by multiplying financial statistics, such as sales, profits, or earnings before interest, taxes, depreciation, and amortization (EBITDA) by a factor that is common for similar firms that were recently acquired. The terminal value formula using the exit multiple methods is the most recent metric (i.e., sales, EBITDA, etc.) multiplied by the decided-upon multiple (usually an average of recent exit multiples for other transactions). Investment banks often employ this valuation method, but some detractors hesitate to use intrinsic and relative valuation techniques simultaneously.

An exit multiple assumes that the value of a business can be determined at the end of a projected period, based on the existing public market valuations of comparable companies. The most commonly used multiples are EV/EBITDA and EV/EBIT, where EV stands for Enterprise Value. Both ratios have intrinsic consistency between the numerator and the denominator, since the EV is the market value of equity and financial debt, whereas EBITDA or EBIT are economic margins calculated before financial debt service (Fig. 2.17).

An example of terminal value calculation is illustrated in the following tables (Table 2.2).

A firm has the following income statement:

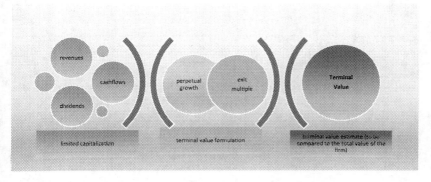

Fig. 2.17 Terminal value estimation process

Table 2.2 Income statement of the target firm

Income Statement	T2	T1	T0
Value of production (A)	€ 2,11,28,866	€ 2,14,18,006	€ 2,71,05,916
Costs of prodution (B)	-€ 2,05,54,608	-€ 2,09,10,069	-€ 2,63,41,730
EBIT (A−B)	€ 5,74,258	€ 5,07,937	€ 7,64,186
Depreciations, ammortisation and provisions		€ 39,703	€ 37,222
EBITDA	€ 5,74,258	€ 5,47,640	€ 8,01,408
Financial incomes and charges	-€ 2,27,229	-€ 2,67,327	-€ 2,51,253
Pre-tax Result	€ 3,42,544	€ 2,30,795	€ 5,06,108
Net result	**€ 2,19,789**	**€ 1,46,279**	**€ 3,36,537**

The multiples (extracted from the Orbis database) are recalled in Table 2.3.

A 40% discount is applied to market multipliers of listed firms, to consider the fact that the target company is unlisted, illiquid, and small. The terminal value with an EV/EBITDA exit multiple brings to the enterprise and equity value shown in Table 2.4.

Table 2.3 Valuation multiples

	Orbis
MULTIPLE (EV/EBITDA)	T0–T2
Average	10.98
Size discount	15%
Illiquidity discount	25%
Total discount	40%
Adjusted multiple	**6.59**

Table 2.4 Enterprise and equity value

Av. EBITDA T0–T2	€ 6,41,102
* Adj. multiple [EV/EBITDA]	6.59
= Enterprise value	€ 42,21,959
+ /− av. Net Financial Position T0–T2	-€ 37,12,560
= Equity value 100%	€ 5,09,399

References

Damodaran, A. (1996). *The stable growth DDM: Gordon growth model.* http://people.stern.nyu.edu/adamodar/pdfiles/ddm.pdf.
Damodaran, A. (2018). *The dark side of valuation.* Pearson FT Press PTG.
Fazzini, M. (2018). *Business valuation: Theory and practice.* Palgrave Macmillan.
Fernandez, P. (2001). *Valuation using multiples. How do analysts reach their conclusions?* IESE Business School. https://www.researchgate.net/publication/4803035_Valuation_Using_Multiples_How_Do_Analysts_Reach_their_Conclusions
Fernandez, P. (2019a). *CAPM: An absurd model.* https://ssrn.com/abstract=2505597
Fernandez, P. (2019b). *Valuation and common sense.* https://web.iese.edu/PabloFernandez/Book_VaCS/ContentsValuation.pdf
Fernandez, P. (2019c). *Equity premium: Historical, expected, required and implied.* https://ssrn.com/abstract=933070.
Koller, T., & Goedhart, M. (2015). *Valuation: Measuring and managing the value of companies.* McKinsey & Company.
OECD. (2022). *Transfer pricing guidelines for multinational enterprises and tax administrations.* https://www.oecd.org/tax/oecd-transfer-pricing-guidelines-for-multinational-enterprises-and-tax-administrations-20769717.htm
Rappaport, A., & Mauboussin, M. J. (2021). *Expectations investing.* Harvard Business School Press.
Singh, J. P. (2013). On the Intricacies of cash flow corporate valuation. *Advances in Management, 6*(3), 15–22.
Viel, J., Bredt, O., & Renard, M. (1973). *Valuation models and financial statements.* ETAS.

CHAPTER 3

The Scalable Valuation of Digital Intangibles

3.1 THE INTANGIBLE ROADMAP

Due to their immaterial nature and lack of "physicality", intangible assets are often characterized by undefined boundaries and plasticity that make them easily interchangeable, adaptable, and flexible. These properties are typically exalted if the intangible has a digital dimension, as it can be used, and exchanged in real-time within the web.

Intangibles often overlap, as shown in Fig. 3.1. An example is given by know-how that eventually may evolve to protected patenting, (implicit) goodwill that expresses the non-recorded potential of trademarks, or even the information value chain recalled in Fig. 3.2. Software is ubiquitous, as it interacts with most intangibles, and algorithms are at the base of artificial intelligence (machine learning) patterns. Cryptocurrency are not formally considered an "intangible asset", even if they share with innovative intangibles (e.g., software, blockchains, etc.) many common features.

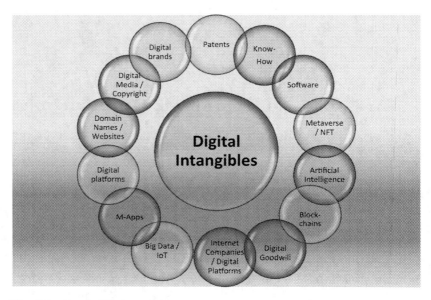

Fig. 3.1 Intangible interaction

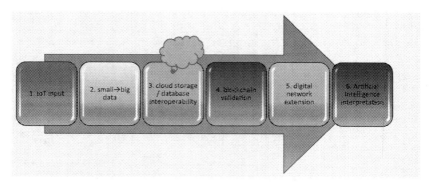

Fig. 3.2 Information value chain

3.2 Accounting for Intellectual Property as a Prerequisite for Valuation

Intangibles constitute an ongoing challenge for accountants, and their recording is a constant dispute, with problematic consequences even on market and performance valuation, exemplified by the increasing gap—softened during recessions—between market and book values, mostly attributable to relevant but not (adequately) accounted intangibles. International homogeneous accounting treatment for intangibles is still a daunting target.

Intangible value is hidden in the balance sheet by inadequate accounting, but not in the income or in the cash flow statement, where the intangible contribution to profit is detectable.

Issues relating to the valuation of intangibles are surfacing with unprecedented regularity and posit an intriguing challenge for the accounting fraternity that is entrenched in the traditional ascendancy of "reliability" over "relevance" (Singh, 2013).

As the intangibles are non-monetary assets with no physical form, it is difficult to find evidence for their existence. Intangible assets may be recorded as an asset in the balance sheet if future economic benefits can be expected.

An intangible asset is identifiable when it: is separable (capable of being separated and sold, transferred, licensed, rented, or exchanged, either individually or together with a related contract) or arises from contractual or other legal rights, regardless of whether those rights are transferable or separable from the entity or other rights and obligations (IAS 38.12).

The requirement for an intangible asset to be "identifiable" is included to distinguish the asset from the (internally generated) goodwill that cannot be recorded.

Many intangibles will not be recognized in the financial statements as they fail to meet the definition of an asset or the recognition criteria. Examples include staff training, brand-building through advertising, and the development of new business processes. As no asset is recognized because of expenditure on such activities, it will be reported as an expense, even though it is undertaken to enhance the financial returns in subsequent accounting periods (Lennard, 2018).

Financial statements can only deal with those intangibles that meet the definition of assets and satisfy the recognition criteria, as set out in the IASB's Conceptual Framework.

Intangibles can be acquired by:

a. Separate purchase;
b. Being part of a business combination;
c. Government grant;
d. Exchange of assets; and
e. Self-creation (internal generation).

IAS 38 permits intangible assets to be recognized at fair value, measured by reference to an active market. While acknowledging that such markets may exist for assets such as "freely transferable taxi licenses, fishing licenses or production quotas" it states that "it is uncommon for an active market to exist for an intangible asset".

The lack of an active market makes it difficult to estimate the fair market value of an intangible.

It should be noted that:

- Most of the strategic, value-creating resources of business firms, such as patents, IT, or brands, are currently expensed, and, therefore, not recognized as assets in financial reports, thereby understating the earnings and assets of intangibles-growing firms, and overstating the earnings and assets of intangibles-declining firms;
- The fundamental inconsistency between the accounting treatment of internally generated intangibles (expensed) and that of the functionally similar acquired intangibles (capitalized) precludes a meaningful performance comparison of peer companies with different innovation strategies (internal generation vs. acquisition); and
- The disclosure of intangible expenditures in financial reports is seriously deficient. Except for R&D, all other intangible expenditures are generally aggregated within large expense items, mainly the cost of sales and Selling General &Administrative expenses.

These inconsistencies severely impair the capacity to rely on accounting data to infer the market value of the intangibles.

The accounting treatment is nevertheless a prerequisite for valuation. The issue is very complex, given that intangible assets are often not directly accounted for in the balance sheet or, in some cases, only appear in the income statement, within the operating expenses (OPEX).

In the attribution of value to intangible assets, it is necessary to consider the income capacity they generate, without which it is difficult to assign a specific value to the "intangible".

The accounting treatment and the consequent under-representation in the balance sheet of the real value of the intangibles often imply the necessity to appraise the growth opportunities that are naturally embedded in the intangibles.

Another accounting issue concerns the net present value of growth opportunities (NPVGO) which calculates the net present value of all future cash flows involved with the growth opportunities of the firm. The NPVGO is not recorded in the balance sheet and is used to determine the intrinsic value of these opportunities to determine how much of the firm's current per-share value is determined by them. The estimation of NPVGO is consistent with the appraisal of the intrinsic value of the real options linked to the intangible assets.

According to Damodaran (2018), firms with intangible assets have the following characteristics:

a. Inconsistent accounting rules that prudentially prevent capitalization of most operating expenses (OPEX);
b. Conservative financing since intangibles lack any physical collateral;
c. Extensive use of stock options to remunerate the management; and
d. The compressed life cycle of tech firms grows faster and stays mature for shorter periods.

Intellectual property (IP) is an umbrella term for a set of intangible assets that provide a competitive advantage or economic value to a company. IP can include patents, trademarks, copyrights, trade secrets, proprietary software, algorithms, and data assets. Each type of IP should be carefully assessed for its uniqueness, market potential, and competitive advantage. Here are some considerations regarding the accounting treatment of intellectual property in the valuation process:

1. Intellectual Property Valuation Methods: Various valuation methods can be employed to determine the value of intellectual property. Common approaches include the cost approach (based on the cost to create or replace the IP), the market approach (comparing the

IP to similar transactions in the market), and the income approach (assessing the expected future cash flows generated by the IP).
2. Legal Protection and Ownership: Legal protection and ownership of intellectual property are crucial aspects to consider. Confirming that the company has proper documentation, such as patents, trademarks, or copyrights, in place is important for assessing the strength and enforceability of the IP.
3. Revenue Generation Potential: Intellectual property assets can contribute to a company's revenue generation potential. For instance, a patented technology or proprietary software may offer licensing or royalty opportunities. Estimating the revenue streams and growth prospects associated with the IP is important for determining its value.
4. Risk and Competitive Landscape: Assessing the risk factors related to intellectual property is essential. This includes evaluating the IP's longevity, potential infringement risks, and the competitive landscape in which the company operates. Understanding the IP's positioning and its ability to withstand competition will influence its valuation.
5. Financial Reporting: From an accounting perspective, intellectual property is typically recorded as an intangible asset on the balance sheet. The valuation of intellectual property assets may impact financial reporting, as it can affect asset values, depreciation or amortization expenses, and potential impairment considerations.

Intangible Assets and Capitalized Costs

Accounting practice tends to divide intangible assets into two categories:

a. Intangible assets in the strict sense; and
b. Intangible assets not represented by assets.

The first category includes patents, intellectual property rights (IPR), concession or rights, licenses, and trademarks; the second category includes capitalized costs, such as startup and expansion costs, bond issue discounts, study and research costs, design costs, advertising, and propaganda costs and representation costs (...).

Capitalized costs (intangible assets not represented by assets, like all elements not identifiable with certainty and not separable from the company) are not independently transferable and, therefore, do not represent straightforward intangible assets.

The valuation of intangible assets cannot fail to consider the subdivision into specific and generic (not represented by assets) intangibles: the former usually are subject to a separate estimate, which mainly uses the criterion of the cost of reproduction or the incremental income that the intangible asset guarantees.

Intangible assets are characterized by a lack of tangibility. They are made up of costs that do not exhaust their usefulness in a single period but show economic benefits for several years. Intangible (fixed) assets include:

- Deferred charges (startup and expansion costs; development costs);
- Intangible assets (industrial patents and intellectual property rights; concessions, licenses, trademarks, and similar rights);
- Goodwill;
- Intangible assets in progress; and
- Advances.

Future economic benefits arising from an intangible asset include revenues from the sale of products or services, cost savings, or other benefits arising from the use of the intangible asset by the company.

Valuation Drivers, Overcoming the Accounting Puzzle

The continued growth of intangible investments is the hallmark of developed economies, initiating significant changes in the business models, strategies, and performance of business firms. Accounting standard-setters, however, by and large, are oblivious to this worldwide development.

The two biggest challenges in accounting principles are probably represented by the valuation of intangible assets and derivatives. Concerning the former, the international accounting standards (IAS, IFRS) have long adopted a strict view, and the capitalization of intangibles is admitted in very limited cases (such as development costs if they show an expected useful life). This approach privileges prudence over representativeness and may underestimate the real value of the intangibles.

Capitalized intangibles are part of the Capital Expenditure (CAPEX), whereas intangible costs recorded in the income statement are part of the monetary OPEX. Amortization is a non-monetary operating cost that reduces the balance value of the intangible CAPEX.

The two most common valuation approaches for the estimate of the enterprise value are based on the operating cash flows discounted at the WACC or on the EBITDA times a multiple of comparable firms.

The following formulation recalls the two methodologies (for simplicity, DCF does not consider any terminal value):

Enterprise Value

$$= \sum_{i=1}^{n} \frac{sales - monetary\ OPEX \pm \Delta Net\ Working\ Capital \pm \Delta CAPEX}{(1 + WACC)^n}$$

$$= \frac{Operating\ Cash\ Flow}{(1 + WACC)^n}$$

$$\cong (basic\ EBITDA + intangible-driven\ EBITDA) * market\ multiplier$$

(3.1)

Intangibles impact sales (due to the scalability effect), monetary OPEX (cost of not-capitalized intangibles, net of the savings from synergies), and the CAPEX (capitalized intangibles less the yearly amortization).

The DCF formulation estimates the Enterprise Value of the firm discounting its Operating Cash Flow at the WACC. Since the Operating Cash flow includes both the monetary OPEX represented by the intangibles (intangible costs net of the synergies) and the intangible part of the CAPEX (incremental CAPEX due to the intangible capitalized investments net of the yearly amortization), the numerator of the DCF formula is not affected by the accounting policies of the firm.

The book value of the intangible assets is expressed by the information available from the balance sheet, income statement, and cash flow statement, following the format shown in Fig. 3.3, which comprehensively represents the different valuation approaches.

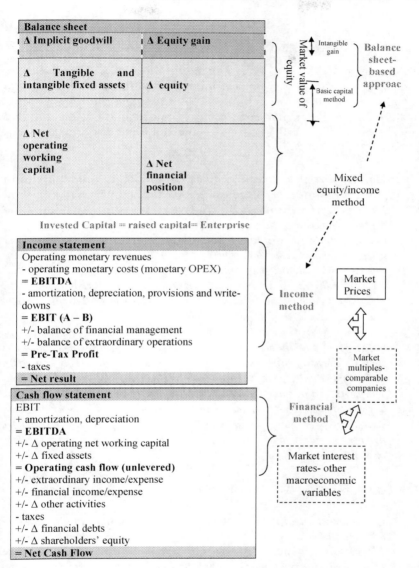

Fig. 3.3 The integrated equity—economic—financial—empirical and market valuation

3.3 Intangible Assets Valuation According to IVS 210

According to IVS 210 § 20.1. *"an intangible asset is a non-monetary asset that manifests itself by its economic properties. It does not have physical substance but grants rights and economic benefits to its owner"*.

§ 20.3. indicates that there are many intangible assets, but they are often considered to fall into one of the following five categories (or goodwill):

a. *Marketing-related: marketing-related intangible assets are used primarily in the marketing or promotion of products or services. Examples include trademarks, trade names, unique trade design and internet domain names,*
b. *Customer-related: customer-related intangible assets include customer lists, backlog, customer contracts, and contractual and non-contractual customer relationships,*
c. *Artistic-related: artistic-related intangible assets arising from the right to benefits such as royalties from artistic works such as plays, books, films and music, and from non-contractual copyright protection,*
d. *Contract-related: contract-related intangible assets represent the value of rights that arise from contractual agreements. Examples include licensing and royalty agreements, service or supply contracts, lease agreements, permits, broadcast rights, servicing contracts, non-competition agreements and natural resource rights, and*
e. *Technology-based: technology-related intangible assets arise from contractual or non-contractual rights to use patented technology, unpatented technology, databases, formulae, designs, software, processes or recipes.*

OECD (2022) distinguishes between:

a. *Commercial intangibles: patents, know-how, industrial designs and ornamental models used to produce a good or to provide a service;*
b. *Marketing intangibles, as a special category of commercial intangibles, including trademarks, trade names, customer lists, distribution channels, symbols or logos or unique names which have promotional value.*

Other, more precise classifications distinguish first between intangible goods linked to marketing and technology, to which should be added the world of the Internet (hence the subtitle of this book).

IVS 210 § 30.1. recalls that the three principal valuation approaches described in IVS 105 Valuation Approaches (income approach; market approach; cost approach) can all be applied to the valuation of intangible assets.

In terms of intangible resources, specific valuation issues arise, which derive from the nature of these assets. The reproducibility of such goods, the absence of rivalry in consumption (the use of a branded product by a consumer does not prejudice a simultaneous use by others) and scalability can be noticed.

The empirical approaches are based on the practical observation of the market prices of the intangible goods, identical in characteristics, from which formulas and parameters of evaluation can be derived. The use of practical criteria is dictated by the speed of updating the value of the fixed assets in similar and homogeneous companies.

Analytical approaches, on the contrary, are more reliable because they are accepted by theory and consolidated by practice, even if they are often less intuitive.

The three principal valuation approaches described in IVS 105 Valuation Approaches (consistent with IFRS 13—Fair Value Measurement) used individually or in a complementary way—by professional practice for the economic estimation of the value of intangible assets are (see Fig. 3.4):

1. The market approach;
2. The cost approach (reconstruction or replacement capital); and
3. The (incremental) income approach.

According to the valuation practice, the appraisal of an intangible asset can be made by reference to each of the three known valuation approaches. In selecting the most appropriate approach, the expert should consider the characteristics of the intangible asset and its reproducibility, the nature of the benefits it can generate for the owner (current or potential) and the user, and the existence or otherwise of a reference market.

Some intangibles, such as trademarks and patents, are particularly complex to evaluate, considering their intrinsic immaterial nature, and

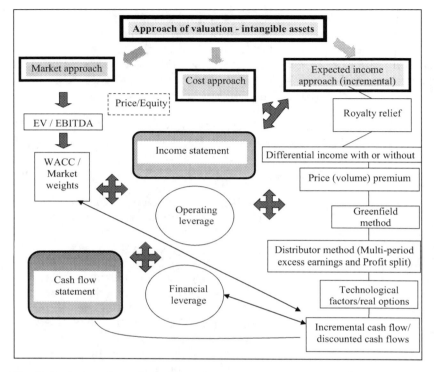

Fig. 3.4 Approaches of valuation of intangible assets

different (complementary) approaches of evaluation, quantitative and qualitative, are traditionally used by the evaluation practice.

Valuation issues are even more complex for other intangibles, such as know-how, industrial secrets, unpatented research and development costs, goodwill, etc., which are characterized by limited or absent negotiability, greater information asymmetries, and less defined legal boundaries, particularly in specific sectors.

The valuation of intangible assets not registered or specifically protected, such as know-how, is subject to high inter-temporal variability, being anchored to provisions aimed at drawing up the strategic, industrial, and financial plans applicable to joint-stock companies. Variability is incorporated in the risk, and the information contained in the report on operations can provide valuable insights.

The breadth of the valuation interval is demarcated by upper and lower limits, in the case of (full) going concern (full business continuity) or in break-up (liquidation) scenarios, in which intangible resources traditionally lose most of their value. This happens especially if they are not independently negotiable or can be synergistically linked to other assets. In the case of discontinuity, the "organized complex of assets" that keeps together the company is eliminated.

The choice of the approaches to be used depends on the type of intangible resource and the purpose and context of the evaluation, but also on the ease with which reliable information can be found.

Of the different approaches, the complementarity in identifying—from different angles—the multifaceted aspects of the intangible object of evaluation, suitable to allow an integrated assessment, must be grasped. For example, the relief from royalties is in the function of the incomes or incremental cash flows that derive from the exploitation of the intangible resource and that interact with the market surplus value or the multipliers of comparable companies. Incremental equity derives from an accumulation of differential income. The cost of reproduction estimates the future benefits and differential goodwill. The different approaches should theoretically lead to similar results, although the relief from royalties and reproduction cost approach sometimes tends to provide lower valuations than the differential income approach or the market comparisons.

3.4 Financial Evaluation

A comprehensive model for the evaluation of intangibles considers their economic (incremental) marginality as a starting point to assess their capacity to generate liquidity. Coherently with IAS 38 prescriptions, DCF is the key parameter for both accounting and appraisal estimates, representing the unifying common denominator of cost, income, or market-based approaches which regularly all need to find out their monetary value.

A synthesis of the market, cost, and income approach may be found in a financial appraisal methodology (consistent with a more general evaluation of a firm) where the estimate is based on the capacity to generate liquidity, remembering that "cash is king".

Market valuations may use as preferred approaches either DCF or directly an EBITDA multiplier, deriving from multiple comparisons of intangibles. DCF theoretically stands out as the optimal method, being inspired by the golden rule according to which cash is king.

DCF is ubiquitous in financial valuation and is the cornerstone of contemporary valuation theory (Singh, 2013). The reliability of the model, as well as its compatibility with the conventional two-dimensional risk-return structure of investment appraisal, adapts it to a multitude of asset/liability valuations. Accounting standards across the globe recognize the efficacy of this model and advocate its use wherever practicable. FAS 141 and 142 of the United States and IAS 39, related to the accounting of intangible assets, recommend the use of the DCF method to evaluate such assets.

Market valuations frequently use a standardized EBITDA multiplied over time (from 2/3 up to 15 or more times/years, in exceptional cases) and this (apparently) simple multiplication brings an Enterprise Value (EV), to be divided between debtholders and equity holders. This approach is consistent with the accounting nature of EBITDA, which is calculated before debt servicing.

EV/EBITDA multipliers can be connected to price/book value or Tobin q parameters which reflect the differential value of intangibles under a hypothetical cost reproduction hypothesis. They are a precious bridge between the otherwise disconnected market and cost appraisal approaches.

As a rough calculation, the EV multiple indicates how long it would take for the complete acquisition of the entire company (including its debt) to earn enough to pay off its costs (assuming no change in EBITDA and a constantly added value contribution from the intangible portfolio). Temporal mismatches between the numerator and the denominator may bias the ratio and should be minimized accordingly.

Equity and debt value may be jointly inferred from an EBITDA multiplier which estimates EV and, after deduction of the market value of debt, the residual market value of equity.

Debt and equity underwriters recognize that the stream of growing Operating Cash Flows (O_{CF}) (marginally attributable to the intangible strategic contribution to the overall value) incorporates growth factors, whereas the weighted average cost of capital (WACC) discounting denominator embodies market risk elements. Moreover, cash flows are a cornerstone of debt service. Qualitative issues such as consistency, durability, depth of coverage, etc., concerning the intangible assets, may strategically impact future EBITDA, cash flows, and consequent value. WACC may be affected by the asset substitution problem and inherent wealth transfer from debt- to equity holders (or vice-versa).

Should the valuation consider an intangible-driven marginal contribution to the overall company's value, what matters is just the differential/incremental O_{CF} or EBITDA made possible by the strategic contribution of the blockchain, although often uneasy to isolate. Additional value, not attributable to specific intangible components, is allocated as goodwill.

Since O_{CF} is derived from EBITDA, the link between market approaches and DCF is evident. This finding is significant, and it has an essential impact on valuation.

Calculation of expected benefits with Net Present Value (NPV) is given by the following formula, considering NPV accruing to equity holders:

$$NPV_{equity} = \sum_{t=1}^{n} \frac{CFN_t}{(1+K_e)^t} - CF_0 \qquad (3.2)$$

where:

- CFN = Net Cash Flow;
- t = time;
- K_e = Cost of equity; and
- CF_0 = initial investment.

A more detailed calculation of NPV should include even the other factors, incorporating in Net Cash Flows geographic limitations, restrictions, exclusivity, etc.

The synthesis between the two methodologies is represented by the calculation of Operating Cash Flows that reflect the impact of scalability. Liquidity is calculated by comparing changes in balance sheet figures/numbers with the current income statement. Blockchains are expected to improve the EBITDA through higher revenues and lower costs.

"With or Without" Incremental Valuation

The incremental evaluation can be useful to external users of the blockchain that incorporate its functions in their (traditional) business model or use its certified data.

The "with or without" methodology is currently used to evaluate intangibles and estimate the fair value of an asset by comparing the value of the business inclusive of the asset to the possible value of the same business excluding the asset.

The economic and financial (incremental) marginality is represented in Table 3.1.

Operating cash flows eventually bring to net cash flows.

Table 3.1 Economic and financial marginality

Economic/Financial marginality	Standard company	Blockchain extension
Revenues	These parameters depend on the traditional business model of the firm, without the impact of the blockchain applications	• New business models and opportunities real options for expansion and development
• Fixed monetary costs • Variable monetary costs		• Validation of data can decrease costs and speed up processes, with time savings
= EBITDA		• Economic and financial marginality grows because of higher revenues and lower costs
± Δ Operating Net Working Capital (NWC)		• Blockchains may shorten the supply chain, making payments more straightforward and quicker, reducing the accounts receivable and payable. Even the stock might be decreased
± Δ Net Investments ± Δ Capex)		• Blockchains may reduce some fixed investments, with a positive consequence on some fixed costs and depreciation
= Operating Cash Flow		• Liquidity may increase because of the higher EBITDA and lower NWC and Capex

EBITDA and Operating cash flow are the cornerstones of the two primary evaluation criteria.

The with-and-without methodology is traditionally used in the evaluation of intangibles. For instance, the International Valuation Standard (IVS) 210 considers this method within the income approach methods (§ 60.5), then shows its application criteria:

> **With-and-Without Method**
>
> 60.22. The with-and-without method indicates the value of an intangible asset by comparing two scenarios: one in which the business uses the subject intangible asset and one in which the business does not use the subject intangible asset (but all other factors are kept constant).
>
> 60.23. The comparison of the two scenarios can be done in two ways:
>
> a. calculating the value of the business under each scenario with the difference in the business values being the value of the subject intangible asset, and
> b. calculating, for each future period, the difference between the profits in the two scenarios. The present value of those amounts is then used to reach the value of the subject intangible asset.
>
> 60.24. In theory, either method should reach a similar value for the intangible asset provided the value considers not only the impact on the entity's profit, but additional factors such as differences between the two scenarios in working capital needs and capital expenditures.
>
> 60.25. The with-and-without method is frequently used in the valuation of non-competition agreements but may be appropriate in the valuation of other intangible assets in certain circumstances.
>
> 60.26. The key steps in applying the with-and-without method are to:
>
> a. prepare projections of revenue, expenses, capital expenditures, and working capital needs for the business assuming the use of

all of the assets of the business including the subject intangible asset. These are the cash flows in the "with" scenario,
b. use an appropriate discount rate to present value the future cash flows in the "with" scenario, and/or calculate the value of the business in the "with" scenario,
c. prepare projections of revenue, expenses, capital expenditures and working capital needs for the business assuming the use of all of the assets of the business except the subject intangible asset. These are the cash flows in the "without" scenario,
d. use an appropriate discount rate for the business, present value the future cash flows in the "with" scenario and/or calculate the value of the business in the "with" scenario,
e. deduct the present value of cash flows or the value of the business in the "without" scenario from the present value of cash flows or value of the business in the "with" scenario, and
f. if appropriate for the purpose of the valuation (see paras 110.1–110.4), calculate and add the TAB for the subject intangible asset.

60.27. As an additional step, the difference between the two scenarios may need to be probability-weighted. For example, when valuing a non-competition agreement, the individual or business subject to the agreement may choose not to compete, even if the agreement were not in place.

60.28. The differences in value between the two scenarios should be reflected solely in the cash flow projections rather than by using different discount rates in the two scenarios.

The incremental (marginal) value of an added network (Barabási, 2016), can be economically appraised by the with-and-without approach, and mathematically evaluated using (multilayer) network theory. The Network Effect Laws are complementary to these approaches, as shown in Fig. 3.5.

To the author's best knowledge, this joint approach has never been used in network valuation.

Every network can be expressed mathematically in the form of an adjacency matrix. In these matrices, the rows and columns are assigned to the

3 THE SCALABLE VALUATION OF DIGITAL INTANGIBLES   99

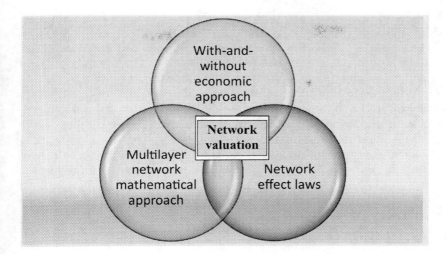

Fig. 3.5 Network valuation approaches

nodes in the network and the presence of an edge is symbolized by a numerical value.

The matrix representation is fully consistent with:

a. The with-and-without approach (each "with" is represented by the introduction of a new node and edging link; "without" represents node absence, deletion, or isolation);
b. Network effect laws that are enhanced by new nodes and edges;
c. Multilayer networks, where interconnections are mapped with adjacency matrices.

The with-and-without approach is also consistent with the differential analysis (confrontation) between networks without and then with interlinks (that depend on avatars or other linking nodes or edges). Digital links are intrinsically flexible and favor immediate linking through the web or the metaverse.

3.5 Value Co-creation and Economic Marginality

The valuation approaches indicated above are fully consistent with value co-creation patterns that exploit the network governance properties of digital platforms and, in perspective, their metaverse extension.

Value co-creation and economic marginality are two concepts that are relevant in the context of understanding business value and profitability.

Value co-creation refers to the collaborative process through which value is jointly created by companies and their customers or other stakeholders. It recognizes that value is not solely generated by the company, but rather emerges from interactions and engagements with customers. In a specific industry, value co-creation can occur through the development and delivery of innovative products, personalized services, and engaging customer experiences.

Companies can involve customers in the co-creation process by leveraging customer feedback, conducting user testing, and implementing iterative product development cycles. By actively engaging customers and addressing their needs and preferences, companies can enhance the value they deliver and build stronger customer relationships.

Value co-creation impacts economic marginality and its monetary outcomes, as ideally shown in Table 3.2.

Whereas the corporate players (metaverse enablers, platforms, etc.) have an economic, financial, and equity impact, users (represented by households and their avatars) typically enjoy the non-monetary value and some monetary savings (if they "monetize" their participation in the metaverse, the data, and feedback they share, etc.).

Economic marginality refers to the profitability or financial viability of a product, service, or business activity. It assesses the extent to which a particular offering contributes to the overall financial performance of a company. An activity or product is considered economically marginal when its contribution to revenue or profit is low or does not meet a specific threshold.

In an industry, economic marginality can be evaluated at various levels. It could involve assessing the profitability of individual product lines, business units, or specific customer segments companies may need to evaluate the economic marginality of their offerings to make informed decisions about resource allocation, product development, pricing strategies, and overall business sustainability.

Table 3.2 Value co-creation and economic-financial impact

Economic impact			
Revenues	Product/services sale	B2B2C intermediation fees	Revenues from data sharing
• Monetary OPEX	Running costs	Platform costs	Fees/purchasing costs, running expenses ...
= EBITDA			
• Non-monetary OPEX	Depreciation, amortization		Depreciation of technological investments
= EBIT			
EBITDA/revenues	Monetary Profitability ratio		
EBIT/revenues = Return on Sales	Operating Profitability ratio		
Financial impact			
EBITDA	Higher EBITDA improves monetary (financial) margins		Cash outflows (for metaverse fruition) net of co-creation gains/savings
Operating Cash Flows FCFF	Higher EBITDA improves FCFF		
Net Cash Flows FCFE	Higher FCFF improves FCFE		
Equity impact			
Book value of equity	Product/services sale, improving retained earnings and so book value of equity		Revenues from data sharing
Market value of equity	Higher book value of equity and goodwill improve the market value of equity		Fees/purchasing costs, running expenses ...
Investment capacity	Economic/financial marginality improves CAPEX		
Goodwill/brand equity	Depreciation, amortization		Depreciation of technological investments
Rating (debt service capacity)	Higher equity improves rating and bankability		

(continued)

Table 3.2 (continued)

Economic impact		
Non-monetary impact		
Reputation, visibility, standing ...	Corporate image improvement, with an impact on goodwill and revenues	Customer satisfaction, loyalty reinforcement, use value ...

Understanding the economic marginality of different activities or offerings helps companies prioritize their resources and focus on areas that generate significant value and contribute positively to the bottom line. It can also highlight areas that may require optimization or strategic adjustments to improve profitability.

Both value co-creation and economic marginality are important considerations for companies. Value co-creation emphasizes the importance of customer engagement and collaboration in creating meaningful and differentiated value propositions. Economic marginality, on the other hand, helps companies assess the financial viability and profitability of their activities, enabling them to make informed decisions and allocate resources effectively.

3.6 The Valuation of Scalable Digital Platforms

Valuing scalable digital platforms involves considering various factors that contribute to their growth potential, user base, revenue generation, and market position. Here are some key considerations when valuing scalable digital platforms:

1. User Base and Network Effects: The size and engagement of the platform's user base play a crucial role in its valuation. Platforms with a large and active user base are more attractive as they can leverage network effects, where the value of the platform increases as more users join and interact. Metrics such as user growth rate, user retention, and user activity levels are important indicators of a platform's potential and value.

2. Revenue Streams and Monetization: Assessing the platform's revenue streams and monetization strategies is essential. This could include advertising, subscription fees, transaction fees, data monetization, partnerships, or other revenue-generating mechanisms. Understanding the scalability and sustainability of these revenue streams is important in estimating the platform's future cash flows and potential profitability.
3. Market Opportunity and Competition: Evaluating the platform's market opportunity and the competitive landscape is crucial. Understanding the platform's target market, market size, growth potential, and competitive advantage helps in assessing its value. Platforms that operate in rapidly growing markets or have unique differentiators are generally more attractive to investors.
4. Technology and Scalability: Scalable digital platforms rely on robust and scalable technology infrastructure to handle increasing user demands. Evaluating the platform's technology stack, architecture, scalability potential, and ability to handle future growth is important for its valuation. Platforms that can efficiently scale their operations and accommodate a growing user base are typically more valuable.
5. Data and Analytics: Data is a valuable asset for scalable digital platforms. Assessing the platform's data assets, data collection capabilities, and data analytics capabilities is important. Platforms that can effectively collect, analyze, and leverage user data to enhance user experiences, personalize offerings, and drive insights have a competitive advantage and higher valuation potential.
6. Intellectual Property and Innovation: Evaluating the platform's intellectual property, such as patents, trademarks, copyrights, or proprietary algorithms, is essential. Intellectual property can provide a competitive advantage and enhance a platform's valuation. Additionally, considering the platform's innovation capabilities and its ability to stay ahead of market trends and customer demands is important in assessing its future growth potential.
7. Partnerships and Ecosystem: Assessing the platform's partnerships, ecosystem, and integration potential is relevant. Platforms that can form strategic partnerships, attract developers or third-party providers, and create a vibrant ecosystem around their platform have a higher valuation due to the increased potential for growth, innovation, and revenue diversification.

8. Financial Performance and Projections: Analyzing the platform's historical financial performance, revenue growth, profitability, and cash flow generation is crucial. Additionally, creating financial projections based on assumptions about user growth, revenue streams, and market dynamics is important in estimating the platform's future financial performance and potential returns.

Valuing scalable digital platforms requires a comprehensive understanding of their user base, revenue potential, technology infrastructure, competitive advantage, and market dynamics. Combining financial analysis with qualitative assessments of these factors helps in determining an appropriate valuation for such platforms.

3.7 Sliding Doors: Network-Bridging Multisided Platforms

Network-bridging multisided platforms are digital platforms that connect and facilitate interactions between two or more distinct user groups or networks. These platforms act as intermediaries, enabling transactions, collaborations, or exchanges between the different sides of the network. Here's an overview of network-bridging multisided platforms and their characteristics:

1. Multiple User Groups: Network-bridging platforms involve multiple user groups that have distinct needs and preferences. These user groups may include buyers and sellers, service providers and consumers, developers and users, or any other relevant combinations. The platform brings these groups together to create value through interactions and transactions.
2. Interactions and Transactions: The primary function of network-bridging multisided platforms is to facilitate interactions and transactions between the different user groups. The platform provides the infrastructure, tools, and services necessary for these interactions to occur, enabling users to connect, communicate, collaborate, or conduct transactions.
3. Network Effects: Network effects play a significant role in network-bridging multisided platforms. As more users join and participate on the platform, the value of the platform increases for all user groups.

Positive network effects occur when the presence of one user group attracts more participants from other groups, leading to a virtuous cycle of growth and value creation.
4. Value Creation and Exchange: Network-bridging platforms create value by facilitating exchanges or enabling collaborations between different user groups. The platform's success depends on its ability to provide value to all sides of the network. For example, an e-commerce platform connects buyers and sellers, allowing them to transact and exchange goods or services.
5. Trust and Reputation Systems: Building trust among the user groups is crucial for the success of network-bridging platforms. These platforms often implement trust and reputation systems to establish credibility, ensure quality, and mitigate risks. Trust and reputation mechanisms may include user ratings, reviews, verification processes, or escrow services to foster trust and enhance user experiences.
6. Platform Governance: Network-bridging multisided platforms typically establish rules, policies, and governance mechanisms to ensure fair and efficient interactions among user groups. Governance may include establishing guidelines for behavior, setting transaction rules, resolving disputes, or providing customer support. Effective governance helps maintain the platform's integrity and fosters a positive user experience.
7. Revenue Models: Network-bridging platforms generate revenue through various models. Common revenue sources include transaction fees, membership or subscription fees, advertising, data monetization, or commissions on transactions facilitated through the platform. The choice of revenue model depends on the platform's value proposition, user base, and the nature of interactions between the user groups.

Examples of network-bridging multisided platforms include e-commerce platforms like Amazon and Alibaba, ride-sharing platforms like Uber and Lyft, freelance marketplaces like Upwork, and app stores like Apple App Store or Google Play Store.

Understanding the dynamics, user interactions, and value exchange between multiple user groups is critical in evaluating and managing network-bridging multisided platforms. Leveraging network effects and creating a robust and trusted platform ecosystem is key to the success and long-term viability of these platforms.

REFERENCES

Barabási, A. (2016). *Network science*. Cambridge University Press. http://networksciencebook.com/

Damodaran, A. (2018). *The dark side of valuation*. Pearson FT Press PTG.

Lennard, A. (2018). *Intangibles: First thoughts*. Paper presented at IFASS meeting, Mumbai, 12–13 April 2018 Session 10.

OECD. (2022, January). *Transfer pricing guidelines for multinational enterprises and tax administrations*.

Singh, J. P. (2013). On the intricacies of cash flow corporate valuation. *Advances in Management, 6*(3), 15–22.

CHAPTER 4

Cryptocurrencies and Non-Fungible Tokens

4.1 Taxonomy and Features

Cryptocurrency is a digital or virtual currency that uses cryptography for security and operates independently of a central bank. A cryptocurrency is a digital currency, which is an alternative form of payment created using encryption algorithms. The use of encryption technologies means that cryptocurrencies function both as a currency and as a virtual accounting system. However, their function has evolved over time, and the various cryptocurrencies born over time have taken on different functions.

Probably, the most famous cryptocurrency is Bitcoin because it was born first. The history of its creation and its evolution can make the exact function of cryptocurrencies better understood. A look at the history also allows us to fully understand the concept of disintermediation applied to cryptocurrencies or how their creation and use are independent of monetary authorities and financial intermediaries.

It should first be made clear that cryptocurrencies use decentralized technology called blockchain, which is a distributed ledger enforced by a disparate network of computers that records all transactions securely and transparently. Cryptography and privacy-preserving were the original goals of the invention of blockchain in 1991 by Stuart Haber, a cryptographer and computer scientist, and Wakefield Scott Stornetta, a physicist and scientific researcher. Their paper "How to Time-Stamp a

---

© The Author(s), under exclusive license to Springer Nature Switzerland AG 2023
R. Moro-Visconti and A. Cesaretti, *Digital Token Valuation*,
https://doi.org/10.1007/978-3-031-42971-2_4

Digital Document" (1991) is considered to be one of the most important papers in the development of cryptocurrencies.

Another key concept to emphasize in understanding cryptocurrencies is the "Proof-of-Work". The cryptocurrencies are not generated by central monetary authorities but by a competitive and decentralized process called "mining", a process that involves individuals (the miners) who are rewarded by the Bitcoin network for their services. Miners compete to mine the new currency, each miner experiencing a success probability proportional to the computational effort expended. This process, in the case of Bitcoin, is called "Proof-of-Work".

The concept was invented by Moni Naor and Cynthia Dwork in 1993 but its application to cryptocurrencies is due to the computer scientist Hal Finney in 2004 who also was the recipient of the first Bitcoin transaction on 12 January 2009. Although he has always denied it, this last circumstance has led to suspect that Finney is the true inventor of the Bitcoin hidden behind the pseudonym of Satoshi Nakamoto. Nakamoto is the first to have published a paper on the operation and purposes of Bitcoin as well as describing an improved version of Proof-of-Work (2008).

The purpose of Bitcoin, in the intentions of Nakamoto, was to *"propose a solution to the double-spending problem using a peer-to-peer network"*. Double-spending is a potential flaw in a digital cash scheme in which the same single digital token can be spent more than once. Unlike physical cash, a digital token consists of a digital file that can be duplicated or falsified. As with counterfeit money, such double-spending leads to inflation by creating a new amount of copied currency that did not previously exist. This devalues the currency relative to other monetary units or goods and diminishes user trust as well as the circulation and retention of the currency. Prevention of double-spending is usually implemented using an online central trusted third party that can verify whether a token has been spent (Ryan, 2017).

Nakamoto, however, stressed that *"commerce on the Internet still suffers from the inherent weaknesses of the trust-based model. Completely non-reversible transactions are not possible, since financial institutions cannot avoid mediating disputes"* and that *"the cost of mediation increases transaction costs, limiting the minimum practical transaction size and cutting off the possibility for small casual transactions, and there is a broader cost in the loss of ability to make non-reversible payments for no reversible services. With the possibility of reversal, the need for trust spreads"* (Nakamoto, 2008).

The main features of cryptocurrencies are therefore:

- prevention of double-spending,
- use of encryption to ensure confidentiality and confidentiality of transactions,
- the management of the computer network (the blockchain) on which coins are issued and transactions is made by miners with the total absence of central authorities rendering the transactions theoretically immune to government interference or manipulation,
- the absence of centralized authorities determines the necessity for the members of the network of having to reach a diffused consent to proceed to a correct recording of the transactions and to render such definitive registrations in the ledger (the Proof-of-Work).

As anticipated, cryptocurrencies born in the wake of Bitcoin have taken on additional functions. Ether (ETH) is second for capitalization after Bitcoin. It is linked to the Ethereum network that allows the creation and peer-to-peer publication of smart contracts. To work, these smart contracts have to pay a price with ether currency, which therefore has the characteristics of cryptocurrency but also fuel for smart contracts.

Likewise, Binance Coin (BNB) is a cryptocurrency, but also a utility token that allows user applications that "run" in the Binance Smart Chain network.

So, while cryptocurrencies share general characteristics, there are numerous cryptocurrencies available, each with its unique features, purposes, and underlying technologies. Bitcoin (BTC) is the most well-known and widely adopted cryptocurrency, but there are also alternatives such as Ethereum (ETH), Ripple (XRP), Litecoin (LTC), Binance Coin (BNB), and many others, each with its own value proposition and use cases.

More in detail, here are the key features of cryptocurrencies:

1. Digital Nature: Cryptocurrencies exist purely in digital form and are not physical assets like traditional currencies. They are created, stored, and transferred electronically.
2. Decentralization: Cryptocurrencies are typically decentralized, meaning they operate on a peer-to-peer network without the need for a central authority like a government or financial institution. Transactions are verified and recorded by network participants, often referred to as "nodes" or "miners".

3. Cryptography: Cryptocurrencies use cryptographic techniques to secure transactions and control the creation of new units. Cryptography ensures the integrity, privacy, and security of the transactions and the underlying technology.
4. Blockchain Technology: Cryptocurrencies rely on blockchain technology, which is a distributed and transparent ledger that records all transactions across the network. The blockchain serves as a public record of every transaction and is maintained by the network participants.
5. Limited Supply: Many cryptocurrencies have a predetermined and limited supply. For example, Bitcoin has a maximum supply of 21 million coins, ensuring scarcity and potentially influencing value over time.
6. Transaction Transparency: while individual transactions are often pseudonymous, meaning they do not directly reveal the identity of the parties involved, the transaction history of most cryptocurrencies is transparent and publicly accessible on the blockchain. This transparency allows for verification and accountability.
7. Utility and Function: Cryptocurrencies can serve various functions, including facilitating peer-to-peer transactions, acting as a store of value, enabling smart contracts, or powering decentralized applications (DApps) on blockchain platforms.
8. Pseudonymity: Transactions on the cryptocurrency network are not tied to real-world identities, which provides a level of privacy and anonymity to users.
9. Volatility: Cryptocurrencies (other than stablecoins) can be highly volatile, experiencing significant price fluctuations due to factors such as market demand, investor sentiment, regulatory changes, or technological advancements. This volatility presents both risks and potential opportunities for investors and users.

What follows is a macro classification of digital tokens based on their purpose and function:

a. Cryptocurrencies. The cryptocurrency family includes:
  i. Non-backed Cryptocurrencies: these are digital tokens with an intrinsic value since their price is not anchored to assets with official values such as fiat coins, gold, or other exchange-traded

commodities. Bitcoin, Ether, Litecoin, etc. belong to this category.
   ii. Backed Stablecoins: these are tokens of the cryptocurrencies family where the price is pegged to fiat money or exchange-traded commodities (such as precious metals or industrial metals). Apart from the lower volatility, unlike other cryptocurrencies, stablecoins have one of the properties of the currency: the value reserve. Examples of Stablecoins are USD Tether, designed to maintain a value equal to the US dollar, and Paxos Gold backed by gold.
   iii. Crypto-Collateralized Stablecoins: these are digital tokens whose collateral is a cryptocurrency instead of a fiat or a commodity. An example of Crypto-Collateralized Stablecoins is DAI. DAI's price is pegged to the US dollar and is guaranteed by a mix of other cryptocurrencies that are deposited in smart contract safes every time a new DAI is minted.
   iv. Algorithmic Stablecoins: in this case, the collateralization is done on the blockchain. Instead of supporting the currency with some resources, an "algorithmic central bank" is created that manages supply and demand based on rules encoded in a smart contract. Examples of Algorithmic Stablecoins are Frax and Ampleforth.
b. Utility Tokens: these are digital tokens that give the holder the right to receive a specific service or good from the issuer or from a third party who has signed a commercial agreement or where the holder has the right to participate actively in a DeFi project for example by placing the token in a liquidity pool. One of the most important utility tokens is ETH, considering that it is used to power smart contract agreements. Another example is the BNB token, which fuels the Binance Smart Chain and offers discounts to traders on the main Binance exchange.
c. Security Tokens: these are tokens that incorporate the right to receive a specific payment or a future payment or tokens. Examples of security tokens are Sia Funds, Bcap (Blockchain Capital), and Science Blockchain.
d. Governance Tokens: these are digital tokens that give the holder the to vote by participating in a DAO. A decentralized autonomous organization (DAO) is an organization constructed by rules encoded as a computer program that is often transparent, controlled

by the organization's members, and not influenced by a central government. In general terms, DAOs are member-owned communities without centralized leadership. A DAO's transaction records and program rules are maintained on a blockchain. Examples of governance tokens are Curve DAO, Uniswap DAO, and Aave.

However, the above classification of digital tokens should not be considered rigid because, as anticipated, a digital token can belong to several categories simultaneously. For example. BNB token, as anticipated, is the fuel of the Binance Smart Chain and offers discounts to traders on the main Binance exchange. Therefore, it is classifiable as a utility token. However, it can be included in different online platforms allowing the holder to earn periodic percentage returns. In addition, an investor can buy a BNB token only in the expectation of its appreciation in the secondary market. In the latter two cases, the BNB token can be considered a security token since there is the co-existence of (i) capital use; (ii) a promise/expectation of a return of a financial nature; (iii) the assumption of a risk directly related to and related to capital use.

Like the BNB token, the ETH is classifiable in several categories. It is a Non-backed Cryptocurrency when required to buy thousands of ERC-20 tokens. It is a Utility Token when it is used to power smart contract agreements and it is a Security Token when the investor put it into staking or trades it in the secondary market. Finally, the ETH token can be classified as Backed Stablecoins. ETH is the fuel for the entire Ethereum ecosystem where most decentralized finance projects reside. Since it is only the decentralized finance that produces wealth within the Ethereum blockchain, we argue that decentralized finance is the underlying of the ETH. The further consideration is that, since ETH is the fuel of the Ethereum ecosystem, as the DeFi consolidates, the ETH will increasingly assume the function of utility token rather than cryptocurrency.

Consequently, the classification of most digital tokens does not depend on their nature, but on their use at the free choice of the holder.

Crypto assets can also be classified according to the following characteristics:

Blockchain Platform:

- Bitcoin-based: Cryptocurrencies that are built on the Bitcoin blockchain or follow a similar protocol. Examples include Bitcoin (BTC), Litecoin (LTC), and Bitcoin Cash (BCH).
- Ethereum-based: Cryptocurrencies built on the Ethereum blockchain or utilizing Ethereum's smart contract functionality. Examples include Ether (ETH), Chainlink (LINK), and UniSwap (UNI).
- Other Platforms: Cryptocurrencies built on alternative blockchain platforms. Examples include Ripple (XRP) on the RippleNet blockchain and Cardano (ADA) on the Cardano blockchain.

Consensus Mechanism:

- Proof-of-Work (PoW): Cryptocurrencies that rely on computational work to validate transactions and secure the network. Examples include Bitcoin (BTC) and Ethereum (ETH) (currently transitioning to Proof-of-Stake).
- Proof-of-Stake (PoS): Cryptocurrencies that use stake or ownership of coins to secure the network and validate transactions. Examples include Cardano (ADA) and Polkadot (DOT).
- Delegated Proof-of-Stake (DPoS): A variant of PoS where token holders delegate their voting power to elected block producers. Examples include EOS (EOS) and TRON (TRX).

Privacy-focused:

- Privacy Coins: Cryptocurrencies that prioritize privacy and anonymity in transactions. Examples include Monero (XMR), Zcash (ZEC), and Dash (DASH).

It is important to note that the digital token landscape is continuously evolving, and new tokens with unique characteristics emerge regularly. This taxonomy provides a general framework, but individual digital tokens may possess features that span multiple categories or introduce innovative elements not covered by this classification.

Cryptocurrency is a recent phenomenon that is receiving significant attention. On the one hand, it is based on fundamentally new technology, the potential of which is not fully understood. On the other hand, at least

Fig. 4.1 Digitalization, scalability, and cryptocurrencies

in its current form, it fulfills similar functions as other, more traditional assets.

Digital currency can either be centralized (with the central control point of the money supply, for instance, ruled by a Central Bank as it happens with fiat money) or decentralized, where supply control is regulated by the consensus and verified by a network of users, normally through Decentralised Finance (De.Fi.) ruled by blockchains. Despite the growing adoption of decentralized exchanges, not much is yet known about their market quality. To shed light on this issue, decentralized blockchain-based venues (DEX) are compared to centralized crypto exchanges (CEX) by assessing two key aspects of market quality: price efficiency and market liquidity.

Digitalization is a fundamental prerequisite behind scalability, and they both represent a basic feature of cryptocurrencies, as shown in Fig. 4.1.

Cryptocurrencies represent the monetary component of many digital networks (from basic blockchains to the metaverse) that otherwise would not be liquid. The absence of liquidity dries up a market, making it unattractive.

4.2 Taxonomy of the Main Cryptocurrencies, with Some Evaluation Hints

Table 4.1 contains a taxonomy of the main cryptocurrencies, with some evaluation hints. This classification is fully consistent with the aim of this study since it contributes to explaining the nature of the digital tokens that embed the cryptocurrencies.

Cryptocurrencies are valued using a variety of methods, including market capitalization, supply and demand, and investor sentiment. Market capitalization is a common method for determining the overall value of a particular cryptocurrency, which is calculated by multiplying the number

Table 4.1 Cryptocurrency features and valuation

Cryptocurrency typology	Value
Non-backed Cryptocurrencies	Their value is equally influenced by the level of demand, the level of the ownership concentration in the market, and the trading volume of the exchanges or exchange-like entities such as online wallets, OTC desks, and large institutional traders whether the subsequent use of the token is staking or pure portfolio investment Due to their extreme volatility, from an investor's point of view, the valuation methodology is that of very short-term technical analysis Some authors have proposed to evaluate Bitcoin based on the growth of the network on the assumption that, assuming user growth is a leading indicator, one can forecast how the price will react as the network adds more participants. Since the nodes of the network should be the addresses of the users, building a model based on user growth isn't as straightforward as it may seem. As pointed out by the same authors, the challenge is determining how many individuals use Bitcoin: an address could be for an exchange that represents countless users. Then, a single person can have multiple addresses, which would lead to overcounting Other authors speculated on the use of a modified Exchange Equation Model by John Stuart Mill. The original equation shows the relationship between the money supply, the velocity of money, the price level, and an index of expenditures. It assumes that the total amount of money in circulation is always equal to the total value of goods and services on the market. The modification of the model for cryptocurrencies consists in considering, instead of the GDP, (for example) the request to use Bitcoin for cross-border remittances or the request to use ether to pay gas fees for computing resources in the Ethereum network. The limit of this theory and its consequent inapplicability lies in the fact that the Exchange Equation Model is based on the assumption that money serves as a means of exchange while cryptocurrencies such as bitcoin and ether have lost over time the feature of the payment system and (especially the bitcoin) has become a speculative tool and, as for ether, the fuel of the Ethereum network ecosystem (Moro-Visconti et al., 2022)

(continued)

Table 4.1 (continued)

Cryptocurrency typology	Value
Backed Stablecoins	Their price is designed to be pegged to fiat money or exchange-traded commodities (such as precious metals or industrial metals). Consequently, the expectations of their price are the same as that of the fiat currencies or exchange-traded commodities to which they are anchored. When investors expect a hit in the crypto market, they put their money into stablecoins to protect their assets. The centralized entities operating this type of stablecoins must generate revenue and do so through the yield on their cash equivalents
Crypto-Collateralized Stablecoins	The value of these stablecoins is pegged 1:1 to a fiat currency (e.g., the US dollar). The stabilization mechanism for on-chain collateralized stablecoins relies on the option of the holder to redeem the stablecoins for the collateral assets on demand. The right to redeem at par value to the official currency of denomination is not always ensured, meaning redemptions are dependent on reserve valuation or must be made in kind. Due to the high volatility of the reserves which are cryptocurrencies, on-chain stablecoins are typically over-collateralized and their stabilization mechanisms rely on the continuous valuation of collateral
Algorithmic Stablecoins	The value of these stablecoins is pegged 1:1 to a fiat currency (e.g., the US dollar). While other stablecoins (USDC or Tether) are fiat-backed, these stablecoins are not backed by real assets. Instead, their value is backed by sisters' digital tokens created in the same blockchain of the stablecoins. To create these stablecoins, the sister digital token must be burned. If the value of this kind of stablecoin drops (for example, because investors liquidate positions), new sister cryptocurrencies must be minted for them to be burned so new stablecoins can be created. This creates a chain effect from the stable coin's price falling to the sister cryptocurrency price falling as well. This is what has happened to Luna Crypto since May 2022. The conclusion is that, despite what they claim, these stablecoins are not stable, but their value is variable like cryptocurrencies, and it is equally influenced by the level of demand, the level of ownership concentration in the market, and the trading volume

of coins in circulation by the current market price. The supply of a cryptocurrency can also impact its value, with limited supply typically leading to higher prices. Additionally, the level of demand for a particular cryptocurrency can impact its value, with increased demand typically leading to higher prices as well.

Several studies have been conducted on the correlation between bitcoin uncertainty, prices, and volatility in the cryptocurrency market. The result of these studies is a guide to forecasting the market for crypto assets. They show that:

- cryptocurrency markets experience an increase in volatility when investors' fears are increased (Akyildirim et al., 2020),
- the News-based Implied Volatility index (NVIX) affects long-term cryptocurrency volatility (Fang et al., 2020),
- the Trade Policy Uncertainty (TPU) in the USA negatively affects bitcoin returns (Gozgor et al., 2019),
- uncertainty hurts the Bitcoin market in the US and Japan whereas in China it has a positive effect (Shaikh, 2020),
- Chinese Economic Policy Uncertainty (EPU) index affects bitcoin returns positively (Chen et al., 2021),
- the twitter-based EPU positively affects the returns of cryptocurrencies (Wu et al., 2020),
- the uncertainty of cryptocurrency policy (UCRY Policy) negatively impacts Bitcoin (Lucey et al., 2021),
- the BC (Bitcoin in circulation) has a significant, positive relationship with the Bitcoin's price (BTC) in the long run; the EX (exchange rate) has a significant, negative relationship with the BTC, and the PO (popularity) has a significant, positive relationship with the BTC in the short run (Karaömer, 2022),
- there is a positive relation between the volatility of liquidity and expected returns. The volatility of liquidity is a currency-specific characteristic that measures the uncertainty associated with the level of liquidity of the currency at the time of the trade,
- since investors are exposed to not only the risk of the level of liquidity but also the variation in the level of liquidity, risk-averse investors require a risk premium for holding currencies with high variation in liquidity.

Finally, investor sentiment can also play a role in the valuation of cryptocurrencies, with positive sentiment leading to higher prices and negative sentiment leading to lower prices.

Valuing a cryptocurrency can be challenging due to its unique characteristics and market dynamics since the market for cryptocurrencies is subject to significant volatility and sentiment-driven price fluctuations. Valuing cryptocurrencies can be highly speculative, and the valuation approaches should be used as tools for estimation and are subject to various assumptions and limitations. In consequence, it is advisable to consider multiple valuation methods. The traditional financial valuation models used for stocks or other traditional assets may not directly apply. However, here are some common valuation approaches used for cryptocurrencies:

1. Fundamental Analysis: This approach involves analyzing the underlying factors that affect the value of a cryptocurrency, such as its technology, adoption rate, development team, the project's whitepaper, team expertise, technological innovation, market demand for the cryptocurrency's use case, regulatory environment, and overall market trends. Fundamental analysis aims to assess the long-term potential and viability of a cryptocurrency.
2. Comparable Analysis: Comparable analysis involves comparing a cryptocurrency to similar projects or assets within the crypto industry. This approach looks at factors such as the project's technology, team, market competition, partnerships, and adoption rate. By assessing the strengths and weaknesses of comparable projects, investors can make judgments about the relative value of a particular cryptocurrency.
3. Technical Analysis: This approach involves analyzing price charts and using various technical indicators to try and predict future price movements.
4. Market Capitalization: Market capitalization is a widely used method to value cryptocurrencies. It is calculated by multiplying the current price of a cryptocurrency by its total circulating supply. Market capitalization provides a relative measure of a cryptocurrency's value compared to other cryptocurrencies in the market.
5. Network Value-to-Transactions (NVT) Ratio: The NVT ratio compares the market capitalization of a cryptocurrency to its daily transaction volume. It measures the valuation relative to the utility

and transactional activity on the network. It considers factors such as the number of active users, transactions, and overall network activity. Network value attempts to assess the intrinsic value of a cryptocurrency based on its adoption and utility within its network. A lower NVT ratio may indicate that the cryptocurrency is undervalued relative to its usage, while a higher ratio may suggest it is overvalued.

6. Discounted Cash Flow (DCF) Analysis: DCF analysis estimates the present value of future cash flows generated by a cryptocurrency. It involves forecasting future cash flows based on factors such as adoption, transaction volume, fees, and network growth. These projected cash flows are then discounted back to the present using an appropriate discount rate.
7. Token Value Capture (TVC) Model: The TVC model considers the value capture potential of a cryptocurrency token within its ecosystem. It analyzes the token's utility, demand, scarcity, distribution model, inflation rate, staking rewards, governance features, any token burn mechanisms, and usage within decentralized applications (DApps) or platforms built on top of the cryptocurrency's blockchain. The model evaluates how the token's value is derived from its role in facilitating transactions or accessing platform services. Understanding tokenomics can provide insights into the potential value and sustainability of a cryptocurrency.
8. Metcalfe's Law and Network Effects: Metcalfe's Law states that the value of a network is proportional to the square of the number of participants or users. This concept is often applied to cryptocurrencies to estimate their value based on network effects and user adoption. It suggests that as more users join the network, the value of the cryptocurrency should increase.
9. Market Sentiment Analysis: This approach involves analyzing social media and other online sources to gauge market sentiment and predict future price movements.
10. Relative Valuation: Relative valuation compares a cryptocurrency to other similar cryptocurrencies or benchmark assets in terms of valuation metrics, such as price-to-earnings (P/E) ratio, price-to-sales (P/S) ratio, or price-to-book (P/B) ratio. This approach provides a relative measure of the cryptocurrency's value based on market comparables.

Backed Stablecoins—More on Value and Key Features

Backed stablecoins are a type of cryptocurrency that aims to maintain a stable value by being backed by assets or reserves. The main features of backed stablecoins are as follows:

1. Asset backing: Backed stablecoins are typically backed by real-world assets or reserves, such as fiat currencies (e.g., USD, EUR), commodities (e.g., gold, silver), or other cryptocurrencies. The backing provides stability by anchoring the value of the stablecoin to the value of the underlying assets.
2. Price stability: The primary objective of backed stablecoins is to maintain a stable value, often pegged to a specific asset or currency. For example, a stablecoin may be designed to maintain a 1:1 ratio with the value of the US dollar. This stability is achieved through mechanisms such as regular audits, collateralization, or reserve management.
3. Trust and transparency: Backed stablecoins aim to instill trust in the cryptocurrency market by providing transparency regarding their asset backing. They often undergo regular audits to verify that the reserves match the supply of stablecoins in circulation. This transparency helps users and investors have confidence in the stability and value preservation of the stablecoin.
4. Redemption and convertibility: Backed stablecoins typically offer a mechanism for users to redeem or convert their stablecoins back into the underlying assets or reserves. This feature allows users to maintain confidence in the stability of the stablecoin and provides an exit strategy should they choose to convert their holdings.
5. Centralized governance: Unlike some decentralized cryptocurrencies, backed stablecoins often have centralized governance structures. This means that a centralized entity or organization is responsible for managing the reserves, ensuring compliance, and maintaining the stability of the stablecoin. The centralized nature allows for more direct control over the stability mechanisms and asset management.
6. Regulatory compliance: Backed stablecoins often aim to comply with relevant regulations, particularly when they are backed by fiat currencies or other regulated assets. Compliance with regulatory

requirements helps to establish trust and confidence among users, financial institutions, and regulators.

It is important to note that while backed stablecoins offer stability, they are still subject to risks associated with the underlying assets, such as counterparty risk, regulatory changes, or liquidity challenges. Users should carefully assess the credibility and transparency of the stablecoin issuer and understand the mechanisms employed to maintain stability before utilizing or investing in backed stablecoins.

Crypto-Collateralized Stablecoins—More on Value and Key Features

Crypto-collateralized stablecoins are a type of stablecoin that maintain their value using cryptocurrency collateral. The main features of crypto-collateralized stablecoins are as follows:

1. Collateralization: Crypto-collateralized stablecoins are backed by a pool of cryptocurrencies held as collateral. The stablecoin issuer requires users to deposit a certain amount of cryptocurrency as collateral to mint or create stablecoins. The collateral provides a buffer to maintain the stability of the stablecoin's value.
2. Overcollateralization: To ensure stability and cover potential price fluctuations, crypto-collateralized stablecoins typically require overcollateralization. This means that the value of the collateral held exceeds the value of the stablecoins in circulation. Overcollateralization provides a cushion to absorb potential losses in the event of price volatility or defaults.
3. Price stability mechanism: Crypto-collateralized stablecoins employ price stabilization mechanisms to maintain their pegged value. These mechanisms may involve automated systems that monitor the collateralization ratio and trigger actions to maintain the stablecoin's value. For example, if the value of the collateral drops below a certain threshold, the stablecoin may be subject to liquidation or users may be required to add additional collateral.
4. Decentralized governance: Crypto-collateralized stablecoins often leverage decentralized governance models, where the decision-making process is distributed among token holders or participants. Decentralized governance allows for community participation in

determining the rules, parameters, and changes to the stablecoin protocol.
5. Liquidation and risk management: If the collateralization ratio falls below a specified threshold, crypto-collateralized stablecoins may trigger a liquidation process. This process involves selling a portion of the collateral to rebalance the system and maintain stability. Liquidation mechanisms are designed to manage the risk of default and maintain the stability of the stablecoin.
6. Transparency and audits: Crypto-collateralized stablecoins often emphasize transparency and regular audits to provide visibility into the collateralization and reserve holdings. Transparency helps to build trust among users and ensures that the stablecoin is backed by the appropriate amount of collateral.

It is important to note that while crypto-collateralized stablecoins aim to maintain stability, they still carry risks associated with the volatility and liquidity of the collateralized cryptocurrencies. Users should carefully consider the collateralization ratio, the mechanisms in place to maintain stability, and the transparency of the stablecoin protocol before using or investing in crypto-collateralized stablecoins.

Algorithmic Stablecoins—More on Value and Key Features

Algorithmic stablecoins are a type of stablecoin that utilize algorithms and smart contracts to maintain their value without relying on collateral or external assets. The main features of algorithmic stablecoins are as follows:

1. Algorithmic control: Algorithmic stablecoins are governed by algorithms and smart contracts, which dictate the supply and demand dynamics of the stablecoin. These algorithms aim to automatically adjust the supply and price of the stablecoin to maintain its pegged value.
2. Elastic supply: Algorithmic stablecoins typically employ an elastic supply mechanism, meaning that the supply of stablecoins can expand or contract based on market conditions. When the price of the stablecoin is above the pegged value, the algorithm may increase the supply to drive the price down. Conversely, when the price is

below the pegged value, the algorithm may reduce the supply to increase the price.
3. Seigniorage shares: Algorithmic stablecoins often introduce seigniorage shares, which are tokens that represent a claim on the future seigniorage, or profits generated by the stablecoin system. Seigniorage shares allow users to participate in the stability mechanism and potentially benefit from the expansion or contraction of the stablecoin supply.
4. Algorithmic stabilizing mechanisms: Algorithmic stablecoins employ various mechanisms to stabilize the price and supply. These mechanisms can include buying or selling stablecoins on the market, adjusting the interest rates, or introducing incentives for users to adjust their holdings. The algorithms aim to maintain the stability of the stablecoin's value through these dynamic mechanisms.
5. Decentralized governance: Algorithmic stablecoins often incorporate decentralized governance models, where decision-making power is distributed among token holders. The community can participate in proposing and voting on changes to the algorithm and other parameters of the stablecoin system, ensuring a decentralized and participatory approach to governance.
6. Market-driven stability: Unlike collateralized stablecoins, algorithmic stablecoins do not rely on external assets or collateral to maintain stability. Instead, their value is driven by market dynamics and the effectiveness of the algorithmic mechanisms. Market demand and user participation in the stability mechanisms play a crucial role in the stability and valuation of algorithmic stablecoins.

Algorithmic stablecoins are a relatively new and evolving concept, and their stability mechanisms may vary across different projects. Users should carefully evaluate the design, algorithmic mechanisms, and governance models of algorithmic stablecoins before using or investing in them, as they can still carry risks associated with market volatility and the effectiveness of the algorithm in maintaining stability.

4.3 Crypto Risk

The lack of intrinsic value or tangible assets backing cryptocurrencies can have consequences for their economic/financial valuation and investors. Here are some key points to consider:

1. Volatility: Cryptocurrencies can exhibit extreme price volatility due to their lack of underlying intrinsic value. Since their value primarily relies on market demand and investor sentiment, prices can fluctuate significantly in response to news, market trends, regulatory developments, or even social media activity. This volatility can make it challenging to determine the true underlying value of cryptocurrencies, leading to uncertainty for investors. Volatility can be influenced by factors such as market sentiment, regulatory announcements, technological advancements, or macroeconomic conditions. High volatility introduces uncertainty and can affect the valuation of cryptocurrencies, as it makes it challenging to determine their true underlying value.
2. Speculative nature: The absence of intrinsic value can make cryptocurrencies more susceptible to speculative trading. Investors may be attracted to cryptocurrencies solely based on the potential for price appreciation rather than any underlying fundamentals. Speculation can drive up prices in the short term but can also contribute to price bubbles and subsequent market crashes when the speculative demand subsides.
3. Lack of stability as a medium of exchange: Cryptocurrencies are often seen as a potential medium of exchange, but their value volatility can hinder their widespread adoption in everyday transactions. Merchants may be hesitant to accept a currency that can fluctuate significantly in value over a short period. Stability is an important characteristic for a currency to fulfill its role effectively.
4. Increased risk for investors: The lack of tangible assets backing cryptocurrencies poses higher risks for investors. Unlike traditional investments such as stocks or bonds, which are often backed by physical assets, cryptocurrencies rely on digital infrastructure and community adoption. If the technology or market sentiment surrounding a particular cryptocurrency weakens, the value can decline rapidly, potentially leading to significant financial losses for investors.

5. Regulatory uncertainties: The regulatory landscape for cryptocurrencies is still evolving in many jurisdictions. Uncertainty or unfavorable regulations can introduce additional risks for investors. Regulatory actions, such as bans or restrictions, can impact the liquidity and legality of cryptocurrencies, potentially affecting their valuation and investor confidence. Regulatory actions or changes can have a significant impact on the valuation of cryptocurrencies. Negative regulatory decisions, such as bans or restrictions, can decrease investor confidence and hinder adoption, leading to a decline in valuation. Conversely, positive regulatory developments that provide clarity and support can enhance valuation.
6. Security and Hacking Risks: The decentralized nature of many cryptocurrencies, along with the use of blockchain technology, introduces security risks. Hacks, security breaches, or vulnerabilities in the underlying technology can result in significant financial losses and damage the reputation of cryptocurrencies. Instances of security breaches can lead to decreased trust and confidence, which can negatively impact valuation.
7. Market Adoption and Utility: The valuation of cryptocurrencies is influenced by their adoption and utility in real-world applications. The more widely accepted and used a cryptocurrency is, the higher its potential valuation. Factors such as merchant acceptance, integration into financial systems, and user adoption play a role in determining the utility and valuation of cryptocurrencies.
8. Technology and Development Risks: Cryptocurrencies rely on complex technology, and their valuation can be affected by technological risks. Flaws or vulnerabilities in the underlying blockchain technology, scalability challenges, governance disputes, or delays in development and updates can impact the valuation of cryptocurrencies. Investors and users closely monitor the development progress and technological advancements of cryptocurrencies to assess their valuation potential.
9. Market Manipulation: The cryptocurrency market is susceptible to market manipulation, including practices such as pump-and-dump schemes, wash trading, and insider trading. These manipulative practices can artificially inflate or deflate the prices of cryptocurrencies, leading to distorted valuations. The presence of market manipulation can erode trust and hinder the accurate valuation of cryptocurrencies.

10. Competitive Landscape: Cryptocurrencies operate in a competitive environment with a multitude of projects and offerings. The presence of alternative cryptocurrencies or new technological advancements can impact the valuation of existing cryptocurrencies. The success or failure of competing projects, the emergence of new innovative solutions, or changing market dynamics can influence the valuation of cryptocurrencies.

The valuation of cryptocurrencies is also influenced by other traditional market factors such as supply and demand dynamics, investor sentiment, macroeconomic conditions, and overall market sentiment. Evaluating and managing these risk factors is crucial for investors and users to make informed decisions regarding the valuation and potential risks associated with cryptocurrencies. Understanding the underlying technology, assessing the credibility of the project, and evaluating the overall market conditions are essential steps in making informed investment decisions. Diversifying investment portfolios and being mindful of risk management strategies can also help mitigate the potential risks associated with cryptocurrencies.

The valuation patterns of cryptocurrencies are influenced by various factors, including market sentiment, investor behavior, technological advancements, regulatory developments, and macroeconomic conditions. While cryptocurrency markets can be highly volatile and subject to sudden price fluctuations, there are a few common patterns that can be observed. These patterns include:

1. Speculative Bubbles: Cryptocurrencies often experience periods of rapid price increases driven by hype, media attention, and speculative trading. These price surges are typically followed by sharp corrections or crash as market sentiment shifts or investors take profits.
2. Market Cycles: Cryptocurrency markets have historically exhibited cyclical patterns, characterized by periods of bullish (upward) and bearish (downward) trends. These cycles can last for months or even years and are influenced by factors such as market adoption, regulatory developments, and macroeconomic conditions.
3. Seasonal Effects: Some cryptocurrencies have shown seasonal patterns, where certain times of the year tend to have higher or

lower trading volumes and price movements. These effects can be influenced by factors like tax seasons, holidays, or specific events within the cryptocurrency ecosystem.
4. Correlation with Bitcoin: Bitcoin, as the largest and most well-known cryptocurrency, often sets the overall trend for the broader cryptocurrency market. Many cryptocurrencies exhibit a high degree of correlation with Bitcoin's price movements, meaning they tend to rise or fall in tandem with Bitcoin's performance.
5. News and Events: Significant news events, such as regulatory announcements, technological breakthroughs, security breaches, or major partnerships, can have a profound impact on cryptocurrency valuations. Positive news can lead to price increases, while negative news can trigger price declines.

The above valuation patterns can certainly affect the overall market valuation of cryptocurrencies. Sudden price movements, such as speculative bubbles or market crashes, can result in significant shifts in the total market capitalization of cryptocurrencies. Additionally, market cycles and correlations with Bitcoin can influence collective sentiment and investment behavior, thereby impacting the market valuation.

4.4 Impact of the SWOT Analysis on the Valuation of Cryptocurrencies

The risk and rewards of cryptocurrencies can be assessed even using SWOT analysis. SWOT analysis is a strategic framework used to evaluate the strengths, weaknesses, opportunities, and threats of a particular entity, in this case, cryptocurrencies. The impact of SWOT analysis on the economic, financial, and market valuation of cryptocurrencies can be substantial. By identifying strengths and opportunities, cryptocurrencies can leverage their unique features and potential to drive economic growth, attract investment, and increase market valuation. Conversely, weaknesses and threats can hinder adoption, and create risks for investors, and negatively (Table 2).

Table 4.2 SWOT analysis

Strengths	Weaknesses	Opportunities	Threats
a. **Decentralization:** Cryptocurrencies operate on decentralized blockchain technology, which eliminates the need for intermediaries and offers transparency, security, and immutability of transactions b. **Innovation and Technological Advancements:** Cryptocurrencies leverage innovative technologies like blockchain, smart contracts, and distributed ledger systems, enabling new applications and use cases c. **Global Accessibility:** Cryptocurrencies have the potential to provide financial services to the unbanked or underbanked populations globally, improving financial inclusion	a. **Volatility:** Cryptocurrencies are known for their high price volatility, which can make them risky for investors and hinder their mainstream adoption as stable stores of value b. **Scalability Challenges:** Some cryptocurrencies face scalability issues, resulting in slower transaction processing times and higher fees during periods of network congestion c. **Regulatory Uncertainty:** Cryptocurrencies operate in a regulatory grey area in many jurisdictions, which can create uncertainty and potentially lead to regulatory crackdowns or limitations d. **Energy Consumption:** Proof-of-Work (PoW) consensus mechanisms used by certain cryptocurrencies consume significant amounts of energy, raising concerns about their environmental impact	a. **Mainstream Adoption:** Cryptocurrencies have the potential to become widely accepted as a means of payment, investment vehicles, and store of value, leading to increased adoption and market liquidity b. **Financial Inclusion:** Cryptocurrencies can provide financial services to the unbanked and underbanked populations, particularly in developing countries where traditional banking infrastructure is lacking c. **Technological Innovation:** Ongoing advancements in blockchain technology can lead to the development of new features, scalability solutions, and improved user experiences, attracting more users and investors d. **Institutional Investment:**	a. **Regulatory and Legal Risks:** Increased regulatory scrutiny and potential bans or restrictions on cryptocurrencies could negatively impact their adoption and market valuation b. **Market Manipulation:** Cryptocurrency markets are susceptible to manipulation, including pump-and-dump schemes, price manipulation, and insider trading, which can erode investor trust c. **Security Breaches:**

Strengths	Weaknesses	Opportunities	Threats
d. Lower Transaction Costs: Cryptocurrencies can facilitate peer-to-peer transactions with lower fees compared to traditional financial systems, particularly for cross-border transactions **e. Privacy and Security:** Cryptocurrencies offer enhanced privacy features and cryptographic security protocols, protecting user identities and transactions	**e. Limited Merchant Acceptance:** While the acceptance of cryptocurrencies by merchants has been growing, it is still relatively limited compared to traditional payment methods	Growing interest from institutional investors, such as hedge funds and asset managers, can bring more capital and stability to the cryptocurrency market **e. DeFi and Smart Contracts:** Decentralized Finance (DeFi) applications and smart contracts built on blockchain platforms offer opportunities for innovative financial products, automated processes, and reduced intermediation	Hacking incidents, thefts, and vulnerabilities in cryptocurrency platforms can result in significant financial losses and undermine user confidence **d. Competition:** The cryptocurrency market is highly competitive, with numerous cryptocurrencies vying for market share, which could lead to consolidation or the emergence of dominant players **e. Technological Risks:** Flaws or vulnerabilities in blockchain technology, smart contracts, or consensus mechanisms could undermine the security and functionality of cryptocurrencies

4.5 THE IMPACT OF CRYPTOCURRENCY VOLATILITY ON MARKET VALUE

Cryptocurrency volatility can have both positive and negative impacts on its market value.

Volatility is defined in finance as the degree of variation of a trading price series over time as measured by the standard deviation of logarithmic returns.

The following figure shows the percentage changes in the price of bitcoin and the Dow Jones Industrial stock market index in each quarter over six years from 2017 to 2022 (Fig. 4.2).

The last figure shows that the changes almost always have the same direction, but the amplitude of those of Bitcoin is much greater than that of the stock index. The volatility of bitcoin is therefore higher than that of the stock market index. The standard deviation in the Bitcoin series is 0.75 versus Dow Jones's 0.09.

The following chart provides a clearer view of the different volatilities of the two financial instruments (Fig. 4.3).

The ETH (the cryptocurrency linked to the Ethereum network) is also extremely volatile. The standard deviation of its price changes in

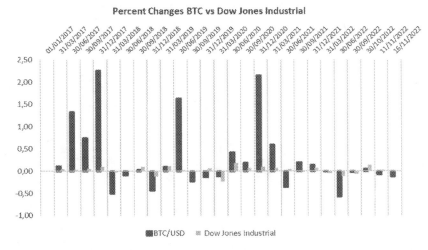

Fig. 4.2 Volatility of Bitcoin vs Dow Jones Industrial

4 CRYPTOCURRENCIES AND NON-FUNGIBLE TOKENS 131

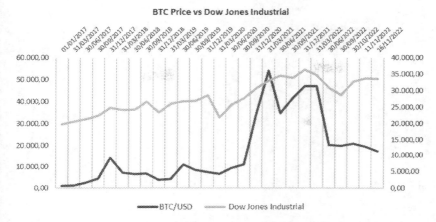

Fig. 4.3 Variations of prices of Bitcoin vs Dow Jones Industrial

percentage is even higher than bitcoin, 1.42 versus 0.75 in six years from 2017 to 2022 (Fig. 4.4):

Such strong volatility is not seen in traditional stock market indices (Fig. 4.5):

Some key points related to volatility to consider in the valuation of cryptocurrencies are the following:

Fig. 4.4 Variations of prices of ether vs Dow Jones Industrial

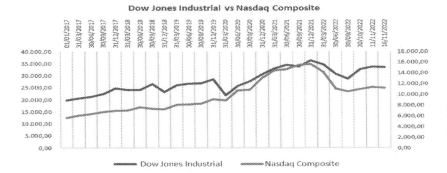

Fig. 4.5 Variations of Dow Jones Industrial vs Nasdaq Composite

1. Price Swings: Cryptocurrencies are known for their price volatility, with significant price swings occurring over short periods. Sharp price increases can attract investors and drive up the market value of a cryptocurrency, while rapid price declines can erode market value.
2. Investor Sentiment: Volatility can impact investor sentiment and behavior. When cryptocurrency prices are volatile, it can create a sense of uncertainty and risk among investors. This can lead to increased selling pressure during periods of high volatility, causing prices to drop further and impacting market value.
3. Speculation and Trading: Volatility often attracts traders and speculators looking to profit from price fluctuations. Increased trading activity can contribute to higher liquidity and trading volumes, potentially boosting market value. However, excessive speculation and short-term trading can also contribute to heightened volatility and instability.
4. Mainstream Adoption: High volatility can hinder the mainstream adoption of cryptocurrencies as a medium of exchange or store of value. Businesses and consumers may be hesitant to accept or hold a currency that experiences large price swings. Stability is often considered a crucial factor for widespread adoption and increasing market value.
5. Market Perception and Confidence: Volatility can influence the overall perception and confidence in cryptocurrencies. If volatility is perceived as a sign of instability or unpredictability, it may deter potential investors and limit market value growth. Conversely, if

volatility is seen as a characteristic of an emerging and potentially lucrative asset class, it can attract more investors and contribute to market value appreciation.
6. Institutional Investment: Institutional investors, such as hedge funds, asset managers, and pension funds, often have strict risk management policies and may be reluctant to invest in highly volatile assets. However, as the cryptocurrency market matures and volatility decreases, institutional investors may become more comfortable entering the market. Their participation can bring additional liquidity, stability, and increased market value.

The impact of volatility on market value can vary depending on the specific cryptocurrency, market conditions, and external factors. While some cryptocurrencies thrive on their volatility and attract traders, others may seek stability to gain wider acceptance and increase their market value.

4.6 Non-Fungible Tokens (NFT): Main Features

A non-fungible token (NFT) is a unique and indivisible digital asset that is stored on a blockchain that represents ownership or proof of authenticity of a unique item or piece of content, such as artwork, collectibles, virtual real estate, music, videos, or other digital creations. Unlike cryptocurrencies such as Bitcoin or Ethereum, which are fungible and can be exchanged on a one-to-one basis, NFTs are unique and cannot be exchanged on a like-for-like basis. This differs from fungible tokens like cryptocurrencies, which are identical to each other and, therefore, can serve as a medium for commercial transactions. NFTs are also considered in Chapter 5.

Here are some key characteristics of non-fungible tokens:

1. Unique and Indivisible: Each NFT is distinct and cannot be replicated or divided into smaller units. Each token represents a one-of-a-kind item or piece of content with its own set of attributes and properties.
2. Token Standard: NFTs are typically created and traded on blockchain platforms that support specific NFT standards, such as the ERC-721 standard on the Ethereum blockchain or the Binance

Smart Chain's BEP-721 standard. These standards define the technical specifications and functionality of NFTs, including ownership, transferability, and metadata storage.
3. Ownership and Authenticity: NFTs use blockchain technology to establish ownership and verify the authenticity of the associated digital asset. The ownership of an NFT is recorded and stored on a blockchain, providing a transparent and immutable record of ownership.
4. Smart Contracts: NFTs often utilize smart contracts, which are self-executing contracts with predefined rules and conditions. Smart contracts enable the automatic execution of transactions, royalties, or other programmed functionalities associated with the NFT, such as revenue sharing for creators.
5. Interoperability: NFTs can be bought, sold, and traded on various online marketplaces and platforms. Interoperability allows NFT owners to transfer their tokens across different platforms, enhancing liquidity and facilitating secondary market transactions.
6. Royalties and Secondary Sales: NFTs can be designed to include royalty mechanisms that allow creators or original rights holders to receive a percentage of subsequent sales or transactions involving their NFTs. This feature enables ongoing revenue for creators when their NFTs are resold in the secondary market.

As anticipated, an NFT is a digital asset that represents real-world objects like art, music, in-game items, and videos—new underlying physical assets are likely to be included in this list. It is more accurate to say that an NFT can be linked with a physical object rather than representing it because an NFT is an asset in its own right. It is a code—therefore an intangible good—and, as such, has a life of its own and, above all, has its independent quotation, almost always unrelated to the physical work of which it is a digital representation, although the latter may affect the value of the transaction.

Like all tokens, the NFT is linked to another code sequence, the smart contract that contains, in a nutshell, the rules of operation and the rights attributed to the holder such for example, the possibility or not of downloading the digital file representing the underlying work and/or its transferability, etc.

The presence of such a link to the work or the underlying asset that served to generate the NFT is not said to be always present: in most cases, it is functional to enhance the purchase because the buyer of an NFT is not satisfied with having purchased a string of numbers, and therefore has the need to have any physicality that can justify the economic transaction. This is the function of the link that allows the buyer to have the perception of the object of the transaction almost as if it were a detokenization of the NFT (even if it is not so). However, it is good to clarify it immediately: the link to the work is not the NFT: just think that a digital copy can be played countless times, Therefore, it is certainly not in the link to the work that concentrates the scarcity generated by the NFT but it is the sequence of numbers contained in the NFT to make it unique. Ultimately, the NFT is generated by a specific digital copy that becomes unflattering or, in another way: its code is unique.

The links among cryptocurrencies, NFTs, and blockchains, are depicted in Fig. 4.6, and can be reshaped forming different combinations, due to the intrinsic plasticity of digital intangibles. Even the difference between fungible cryptocurrencies and intrinsically non-fungible NFTs is softened by their osmotic connections.

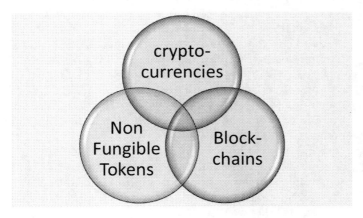

Fig. 4.6 Cryptocurrencies, NFTs, and blockchains

4.7 NFT Valuation

Valuing a non-fungible token (NFT) involves assessing its uniqueness, demand, scarcity, and overall market dynamics. Since NFTs represent unique digital assets, the valuation process can be subjective and influenced by factors such as the specific artwork, collectible, or digital content associated with the NFT. Here are some considerations for valuing an NFT:

1. Rarity and Scarcity: Evaluate the rarity and scarcity of the NFT. Consider factors such as the limited edition or unique nature of the digital asset represented by the NFT. High scarcity and limited supply can contribute to a higher value. Rarity and scarcity can have a significant impact on the economic evaluation of non-fungible tokens (NFTs). These factors influence the value of NFTs in several ways:

    a. Unique ownership: NFTs represent unique digital assets, often tied to digital art, collectibles, or virtual assets in games. Each NFT has a distinct identifier, making it one-of-a-kind and distinguishable from other tokens. Rarity adds value by creating a sense of exclusivity and uniqueness among collectors and enthusiasts.
    b. Limited supply: Scarcity refers to the limited availability of a particular NFT. Some NFTs are released in limited editions, meaning there are only a fixed number of tokens created. The scarcity of supply can increase the perceived value of an NFT, as collectors and investors seek to own something rare and potentially difficult to obtain.
    c. Demand from collectors: Rarity and scarcity contribute to the demand for NFTs among collectors and enthusiasts. Those who appreciate the unique characteristics of an NFT may be willing to pay a premium to acquire it, especially if they believe its rarity will increase its value over time.
    d. Perceived value and market dynamics: Rarity and scarcity create a perception of value in the NFT market. When a particular NFT is highly sought after due to its uniqueness and limited supply, it can attract more buyers and drive up its price. This dynamic is often fueled by the collector's mentality, where owning rare items holds intrinsic value beyond the underlying asset itself.

e. Secondary market dynamics: NFTs are often traded on secondary markets, such as NFT marketplaces. Rarity and scarcity can play a significant role in the pricing dynamics of these markets. Scarce NFTs that are in high demand may experience price appreciation as buyers compete to acquire them, while less rare or abundant NFTs may have lower valuations. The secondary market dynamics of non-fungible tokens (NFTs) refer to the buying and selling of NFTs after their initial release or minting. These dynamics play a crucial role in determining the economic valuation of NFTs. Here are some key aspects of secondary market dynamics and their impact on NFT valuation:
- Supply and demand: The interaction between supply and demand in the secondary market significantly influences the economic valuation of NFTs. If there is high demand for a particular NFT and limited supply, it can drive up the price as buyers compete to acquire it. Conversely, if supply exceeds demand, the price may decline as sellers lower their asking prices to attract buyers.
- Rarity and scarcity: As mentioned earlier, the rarity and scarcity of NFTs contribute to their economic valuation. When an NFT is rare, it tends to be more sought after by collectors, potentially leading to higher prices in the secondary market. The perception of exclusivity and uniqueness can drive up the value as collectors compete to own limited edition or one-of-a-kind NFTs.
- Market trends and popularity: The trends and overall popularity of NFTs can influence their economic valuation. Certain themes, artists, or collections may experience periods of high demand, which can result in increased prices. Market sentiment, social media buzz, and cultural relevance can all contribute to the popularity of NFTs and their subsequent valuation in the secondary market.
- Creator reputation: The reputation and recognition of the creator or artist behind an NFT can impact its economic valuation. Established artists with a strong following or a track record of successful works may command higher prices for their NFTs in the secondary market. Collectors and investors often consider the reputation and credibility of the creator when assessing the value of an NFT.

- Market liquidity and trading volume: The liquidity and trading volume of NFTs in the secondary market can also influence their economic valuation. Higher liquidity and trading activity provide more opportunities for buyers and sellers to engage in transactions, potentially leading to more accurate price discovery and competitive pricing.

It is important to note that the NFT market can be subject to fluctuations and speculative behavior, with valuations driven by market sentiment and investor behavior. Prices in the secondary market can be volatile, and buyers and sellers must exercise caution and conduct thorough research before engaging in NFT transactions. Assessing the underlying value of the NFT, considering market trends, and evaluating the overall demand and liquidity are all important factors in determining the economic valuation of NFTs in the secondary market.

Valuing NFTs can be highly subjective, and the value assigned to an NFT can vary significantly depending on individual preferences and market dynamics. Professional expertise, market research, and consultation with experts or appraisers specializing in digital art or collectibles can provide additional insights into NFT valuation.

References

Akyildirim, E., Corbet, S., Lucey, B., Sensoy, A., & Yarovaya, L. (2020). The relationship between implied volatility and cryptocurrency returns. *Finance Research Letters, 33*, 1–10.

Chen, T., Lau, C. K. M., Cheema, S., & Koo, C. K. (2021). Economic policy uncertainty in China and bitcoin returns: Evidence from the COVID-19 period. *Frontiers in Public Health, 9*(140), 1–7.

Dwork, C., & Naor, M. (1993). *Pricing via processing, or, combatting junk mail, advances in cryptology.* CRYPTO'92: Lecture Notes in Computer Science No. 740 (pp. 139–147). Springer.

Fang, T., Su, Z., & Yin, L. (2020). Economic fundamentals or investor perceptions? The role of uncertainty in predicting long-term cryptocurrency volatility. *International Review of Financial Analysis, 71*(101566), 1–12.

Gozgor, G., Tiwari, A. K., Demir, E., & Akron, S. (2019). The relationship between bitcoin returns and trade policy uncertainty. *Finance Research Letters, 29*, 75–82.

Haber, S., & Stornetta, W. S. (1991). How to time-stamp a digital document. *Journal of Cryptology, 3*, 99–111.

Karaömer, Y. (2022). *Is the cryptocurrency policy uncertainty a determinant of bitcoin's price?* (pp. 369–378). Pamukkale University Journal of Social Sciences Institute.

Lucey, B. M., Vigne, S. A., Yarovaya, L., & Wang, Y. (2021). The cryptocurrency uncertainty index. *Finance Research Letters, 102147*, 1–14.

Moro Visconti, R., Trevisi, C., & Cesaretti, A. (2022). *Non-fungible tokens, digital art and cultural heritage: A new form of financing and fruition*, Bancaria n. 2.

Nakamoto S. (2008). *Bitcoin: A peer-to-peer electronic cash system.* https://bitcoin.org/bitcoin.pdf.

Ryan, M. (2017). *Digital cash.* School of Computer Science, University of Birmingham.

Shaikh, I. (2020). Policy uncertainty and bitcoin returns. *Borsa Istanbul Review, 20*(3), 257–268.

Wu, W., Tiwari, A. K., Gozgor, G., & Leping, H. (2020). Does economic policy uncertainty affect cryptocurrency markets? Evidence from Twitter-based uncertainty measures. https://doi.org/10.2139/ssrn.3662748.

CHAPTER 5

Digital Art and Non-Fungible Tokens

5.1 Digital Art

Digital art refers to artworks that are created or presented using digital technology. It encompasses various forms of artistic expression, including visual art, multimedia installations, interactive experiences, animations, virtual reality (VR), and more. Digital art leverages digital tools, software, and platforms to create, manipulate, and display artistic content. Key characteristics of digital art include:

1. Digital Creation: Digital art is typically created using digital tools such as graphic design software, drawing tablets, 3D modeling software, or coding languages. Artists use these tools to create and manipulate digital images, animations, or interactive elements.
2. Technological Medium: Digital art relies on technology for its creation, display, and distribution. It takes advantage of advancements in digital media, computing power, and software capabilities to explore new artistic possibilities and techniques.
3. Interactivity and Immersion: Digital art often incorporates interactive elements, allowing viewers to engage with the artwork through touch, motion, or other interactive interfaces. It can also explore immersive experiences through virtual reality (VR), augmented reality (AR), or mixed reality (MR) technologies.

© The Author(s), under exclusive license to Springer Nature Switzerland AG 2023
R. Moro-Visconti and A. Cesaretti, *Digital Token Valuation*,
https://doi.org/10.1007/978-3-031-42971-2_5

4. Reproducibility and Distribution: Digital art can be easily reproduced and distributed in digital formats, making it accessible to a wider audience. Digital artworks can be shared and experienced online, through websites, social media platforms, or digital galleries.
5. Hybrid Forms: Digital art often blurs the boundaries between traditional art forms and digital media. It can incorporate elements of painting, sculpture, photography, video, sound, and performance, merging them with digital techniques and technologies.
6. Evolving and Dynamic: Digital art is responsive to advancements in technology and continually evolves as new tools, software, and platforms emerge. It embraces experimentation, pushing the boundaries of traditional artistic practices, and exploring new artistic expressions.

Digital art has gained recognition and acceptance within the art world, with dedicated exhibitions, galleries, and festivals. It has opened up new possibilities for artists, enabling them to explore innovative approaches, engage with a global audience, and challenge conventional notions of art and creativity.

Digital art (also called computer art) identifies a work or an artistic practice that uses digital technology as part of the creative process or exhibition presentation. Electronic art has a broader meaning than digital art, as it involves many interrelationships between art and technology.

Crypto art (cryptographic art) is a category of art related to blockchain technology and concerns digital artworks published directly on a blockchain in the form of non-fungible tokens (NFTs), which makes it possible to own, transfer, and sell artwork in a cryptographically secure and verifiable manner (see Anselmi & Petrella, 2023). NFTs have already been described in Chapter 4.

Neologisms such as video art, computer art, cybernetic art, virtual reality, multimedia art, digital art, and interactive art—nowadays preferably united in the broader and more ductile definition of electronic art—have been spreading for several decades in the language of artists, critics, and the public. Digital art traditionally identifies works of contemporary art, although there may be digitalization, even with creative reinterpretations, of works of classical art.

Digital art has many applications, among which the following are particularly relevant (Table 5.1):

Table 5.1 Digital art—taxonomy

Application/type description	Description
Digital photography	Procedure for the acquisition of static images, projected through an optical system, on a light-sensitive electronic device (sensor), with subsequent conversion into digital format and storage on a memory medium
Digital imaging	The creation of a visual representation of an object, through image acquisition, processing, compression, storage, printing, and representation
Digital publishing	The term digital publishing refers to the publishing phenomenon in which content, the entire publishing process, and access to content are implemented with the help of information technology. Digital publishing covers various fields of action, from the processing of printed content to the widespread distribution of digital content via the Internet
Electronic literature	Electronic literature, also known as digital literature, e-literature, or eLiterature, is a particular cross-sectoral phenomenon, ascribable to different fields, primarily literary, which through the use of innovative creative methodologies and the means offered by technological evolution, including computers, the web, and ICT (information and communication technologies), produces innovative literary works
Electronic poetry	Artistic experimentation that integrates poetic text and new media art (video art, digital art, net.art, installations, etc.). It can be distinguished into two major areas, often intertwined in research: video poetry, and computer poetry, which integrates the use of digital technologies
Internet art	Contemporary artistic discipline aimed at creating works of art with, for, and on the Internet
Electronic music	Music produced or modified through the use of electronic instrumentation
Pixel art	A type of computer graphics and a form of digital art. Pixel art is when the creator of an image can freely manipulate each pixel of the image
New media art	Artistic compositions are designed and reproduced with new media technologies (visual art; computer graphics; digital art; interactive art; sound art; cyborg art, etc.). See Catricalà (2015)
Digital Museums	Enable virtual tours of museums. Using the mouse and keyboard, clicking on the hotspots inserted in the environments, and navigating the interactive maps, the visit is deepened with contextual elements: photos, videos, and texts, and the route is freely chosen by the visitor
Collections/ digital databases	Databases uploaded and saved on digital media allow the online archiving and consultation of collections from digital museums or other archives

Digital art refers to artistic creations that are primarily produced or presented using digital technology. It encompasses a wide range of artistic forms and mediums, including but not limited to:

1. Digital painting and illustration: Artwork created using digital tools like graphics tablets, digital brushes, and software programs that mimic traditional painting techniques.
2. 3D modeling and sculpture: The creation of three-dimensional virtual objects, characters, or environments using specialized software.
3. Digital photography: Capturing and manipulating photographs using digital cameras and editing software.
4. Generative art: Artworks generated by algorithms or computer programs that produce unique visual or audiovisual compositions.
5. Digital installations and interactive art: Artworks that incorporate digital elements, multimedia, and interactive components to engage viewers in a participatory or immersive experience.
6. Video art and animation: The creation of moving images, animations, and videos using digital tools, often combining various techniques like digital drawing, compositing, and special effects.
7. Net art and web-based art: Artworks specifically created for or presented on the internet, exploring the possibilities of online platforms, interactivity, and networked environments.

Digital art often blurs the boundaries between traditional artistic practices and technology, offering artists new avenues for creative expression and experimentation. It can be displayed on various digital platforms, such as computer screens, projectors, and virtual reality (VR) headsets, or shared online through websites, social media, or digital galleries.

Digital art is based on digital platforms of interchange that connect the artist with the user of the work, with a typically B2C or C2C mechanism, through a virtual stage. Among the many differences between digital art and traditional art, the "viral usability" of the former is particularly noteworthy, compared to the "uniqueness" of the latter. Think, for example, of a digital painting, which can be reproduced and disseminated endlessly, with viral characteristics, compared to a "physical" painting, which represents a unique piece. The digital extension of traditional art represents its added value.

Digital art has intrinsic characteristics of immateriality and intangibility that are instead lacking in many more traditional artistic expressions (painting, sculpture, etc.), represented by physical goods. There are, however, artistic expressions, such as music, which overlap these two sets, originating from "physical" scores but assuming a diffusion over the air that, since the time of Napster, uses the Internet and immaterial modes of fruition (MP3 files or other).

The uniqueness of some "pieces", expression of traditional art is reflected intrinsically in the rarity and value; this is counterbalanced by the usability of digital art that, thanks to the support on which it is built, is intrinsically usable through the web. Even in traditional works of art, uniqueness is not, however, an exclusive element, since for many prints or serigraphic reproductions there is usually a print run, certified by the author, which increases the usability to tens or sometimes hundreds of copies (art multiples or numbered series). The higher the number of existing multiples, the lower the value becomes, following the property of supply and demand, intersected by an equilibrium price.

The immaterial goods have, as a rule, characteristics of non-rivalry, being able to be used even simultaneously by a large number of subjects. On the other hand, "physical" artistic goods have a more limited number of users, not only because they belong to a single owner, but also because of the constraints of usability in a physical presence, lacking the aforementioned characteristics of virality and scalability that are typical of the digital world (always, everywhere, potentially for everyone, especially in the absence of premium applications).

Among the many intersections between "physical" and "digital" art, there is no shortage of transpositions of traditional artistic assets onto digital format: thus, the reproduction of a painting or a sculpture, the performance of a musical score reproduced via the web, etc.

Another issue that has always been a concern for traditional artists is represented by plagiarism or theft of works of art. Digitization, on the one hand, increases this risk, making it much easier to acquire, manipulate, and disseminate the artistic creations of others, but on the other hand, it has IT tools, based primarily on the blockchain, which validate sources and information, protecting digital works from the start.

All these features, and more, affect the evaluation metrics. The increasing valorization of the contents published on the web, also based on the long-standing tug-of-war that pits the digital platforms of big tech against newspapers or the variegated world of authors, lies in the wake of these issues and grasps their evolutionary aspects, marking the difficult revenge of contents against communication platforms, with a view to a fairer sharing of advertising revenues and subscriptions for premium services.

The preservation of digital works of art is of particular importance, also for value durability.

5.2 Timestamps

A timestamp refers to a piece of information that denotes the date and time at which a particular event or data point occurred or was recorded. It serves as a reference point or chronological marker to indicate when something took place.

In computing and digital systems, timestamps are commonly used to track and record the timing of events, transactions, or data modifications. They are typically represented in a standardized format, such as the Coordinated Universal Time, which is based on the international time standard.

Timestamps are utilized in various contexts, including:

1. Data logging: Recording the time of data acquisition or data entry for reference and analysis purposes.
2. Transaction tracking: Verifying and documenting the time at which a transaction or event occurred, particularly in financial systems or distributed databases.
3. System monitoring and debugging: Logging the timing of system events, errors, or debugging information to troubleshoot and analyze software or hardware issues.
4. Content publishing and archiving: Indicating the publication time and date of articles, blog posts, social media updates, or other forms of digital content.
5. Legal and regulatory compliance: Establishing the sequence and timing of activities or events for legal or regulatory purposes, such as in electronic signatures or audit trails.

Timestamps provide a standardized and objective reference for organizing, analyzing, and understanding the temporal aspects of data and events within a given system or context.

The problem of literary or artistic plagiarism, or other forms of copyright infringement, has been known since ancient times.

In this context, the well-known claims on the subject of the prior art are also relevant.

The Temporal Mark is part of this application and consists of a service that allows associating date and time certain and legally valid to a computer document, thus allowing to associating of a temporal validation opposable to third parties.

The Temporal Marking service can also be used on files that are not digitally signed, guaranteeing a certain and legally valid temporal location.

SYSDATE	CURRENT_TIMESTAMP
7/29/2013 2:55:29 PM	7/29/2013 3:25:29.872577 PM +04:30

5.3 Evaluation Approaches

The evaluation of digital art can be approached in several ways, including:

1. Technical: Evaluating the artist's use of digital tools, software, and hardware to create their artwork.
2. Aesthetic: Assessing the artwork's beauty, emotional impact, and overall composition.
3. Conceptual: Evaluating the artist's message, meaning, and intent behind their artwork.
4. Interactive: Evaluating the user's experience when interacting with digital installations, video games, and virtual reality experiences.
5. Contextual: Evaluating the artwork's historical, cultural, and societal context, and how it relates to other works of art.

These approaches can be used individually or in combination to evaluate digital art. However, because digital art is a relatively new and constantly evolving field, there is still much debate and discussion about how best to evaluate and assess it.

The boundaries of digital art are particularly blurred and constantly evolving, under the propulsive thrust of technological innovation that opens the door to new forms of creation, experimentation, and dissemination of creativity. The legal protection of digital art and its classification as an intangible "asset" can be a valid aid to valuation, even if it suffers from the same uncertainties mentioned above.

In the writer's opinion, any attempt at valuation should follow a methodological approach in line with the sequence of reasoning and frameworks proposed here:

1. Classification of the artistic work being evaluated and its inclusion within a taxonomy, where existing (also for comparability with similar works);
2. Identification of legal issues regarding prior art, ownership, right of economic exploitation, etc.
3. Accounting of the work by the author;
4. Examination of royalty, sale, or other contracts relating to the work, if any;
5. Analogical reference to other types of intangible assets or rights being evaluated (copyright; software; blockchains; digital logos or trademarks; mobile apps; social networks; digital platforms, etc.);
6. Use of valuation approaches (cost, income, or market) traditionally used for the valuation of intangible assets.

The economic valuation of digital art is based on methodological approaches that differ, in part, from those used for traditional art, incorporating elements already illustrated such as (greater) usability, dematerialization, and reproducibility.

In more general terms, artistic works, like other activities based on the use and exploitation of culture, are difficult to evaluate, partly because the economic metrics derived from their exploitation and comparability with "similar" works are often inconvenient.

The framing of the artwork can be done through an "Expertise", used, in the technical language of art historians, to indicate an official document, which contains the technical characteristics of a work of art and certifies its authenticity, age, dating, and state of preservation. As a whole, it can be defined as the identity document of a work of art containing a description (as complete as possible) of the work's history, based also on any laboratory analysis, if deemed necessary. The expertise, therefore, consists of a detailed report for the evaluation of the originality and the historical-artistic framework of the work under examination, whatever the nature of the asset, i.e., a painting, a piece of furniture, or another figurative work. The expertise does not indicate the commercial value of the work.

The valuation techniques of works of art, even digital, follow the appraisal purposes (auction valuation, insurance, for hereditary purposes, to constitute a pledge or corollary on a loan, for inclusion in the budget, or judicial appraisals in case of civil or criminal litigation, etc.).

The valuation of a work of art must consider the author (emerging or already known), which suggests a range of indicative value, based on market comparisons for other works by the same author. The title of the work, date of creation, the technique of execution, dimensions of the work (not always easy to determine in the digital sphere), and certifications of authenticity, are relevant elements, as well as the origin (belonging to illustrious collections or families, though balanced by the short history of digital art), personal or collective exhibitions (mainly through the web channel, beyond the "physical" exhibition of traditional works of art). Also noteworthy is the presence of a catalog raisonné of the artist's works (facilitated by increasing digitization, which makes it possible to archive and search, mainly online, data and information). The traditional impact on the price and value of the state of preservation of work takes on different connotations in the digital sphere, given that digitization preserves the work from wear and tear and "physical" consumption while leaving it exposed to technological obsolescence and the emergence of new standards, which could hinder its preservation and use (think of analog works or digital formats that are no longer supported).

The distinction between the primary market (first sale) and the secondary market (subsequent resale, even through auction houses) is also relevant for digital art, even if it is balanced by the possibility of collective fruition that increases the diffusion but reduces the exclusivity of the buyer.

In particular cases, the so-called resale right can also be the object of evaluation.

The interaction between digital art and intangible assets (exemplified in Fig. 5.1) allows extending the traditional paradigms of evaluation of works of art, using innovative methodologies and tools of creation, dissemination, and use of the same. However, the problem of valuing works of art, including digital works, without a market remains unsolved.

The absence of a market would seem to suggest non-existence in terms of value, if not in terms of future potential.

The International Valuation Standards (IVS) 210 is entirely dedicated to intangible assets.

According to IVS 210, an intangible asset may be identifiable or unidentifiable (par. C3). An asset is identifiable if:

a. it is separable, i.e., it can be separated or spun off from the business and sold, transferred, licensed, leased, or exchanged, either individually or in connection with a contract or identifiable assets or liabilities, regardless of whether the business intends to do so; or
b. arises from contractual rights or other legal titles, regardless of whether such rights are transferable or separable from the business or other rights and obligations.

Goodwill is generally defined as any non-independently identifiable intangible asset associated with a business or group of businesses (par. C4).

Also according to IVS 210, the main classes of identifiable intangible assets are as follows (par. C5):

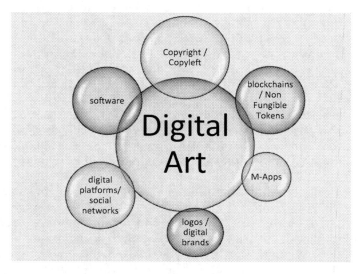

Fig. 5.1 Interaction between digital art and intangible assets

- intangible assets related to marketing;
- intangible assets linked to customers or suppliers;
- intangible assets linked to technology;
- intangible assets linked to art.

Marketing-related intangible assets (trademarks, trade names, logos, exclusive commercial design, digital branding, internet domain names, mastheads, and non-competition agreements) are primarily used in market research or the promotion of products or services (par. C7). Editorial titles may use content that is subject to copyright.

Intangible assets related to customers or suppliers (par. C8) arise from relationships with or knowledge of customers and suppliers (agreements for the provision of services or supplies, licensing or royalty agreements, customer portfolios, and employment contracts).

Intangible assets linked to technology and the Internet (par. C9) derive from contractual and non-contractual rights for the use of technology (patents, databases, formulas, designs, industrial drawings, ornamental models, software, know-how, procedures, or recipes). Databases (also related to the digital archiving of works of art) fall within the taxonomy provided for by Art. 2 of the l.d.a. (Italian law on copyright—l.d.a.—of April 22, 1941, n. 633).

Art-related intangible assets (par. C10) arise from the right to benefits such as royalties for works of art, including plays, books, films, and music, and non-contractual copyright protection.

The main methods (approaches) used—singly or in a complementary manner—by valuation standards for the economic estimation of the value of intangible assets are as follows:

1. market method;
2. cost method (of reconstruction or replacement);
3. expected income method (incremental).

According to the above-mentioned PIVs (par. III.5.5), the valuation of an intangible asset can be carried out by referring to each of the above three known valuation methods. To select the most appropriate method, the expert should consider the characteristics of the intangible asset, and in particular its reproducibility, the nature of the benefits it is capable of generating for the owner (current or potential, considering the resale right), and the user, and the existence or otherwise of a reference market.

The breadth of the possible valuation range is marked, in its extremes, by upper and lower limits, in hypotheses of (full) going concerned (full business continuity) or in break-up liquidation scenarios, in which intangible resources traditionally lose most of their value, especially if not independently negotiable or synergistically linked to other assets; in hypotheses of discontinuity, the "organized complex of assets" that frames the firm is completely lost. The different gradations of value also reflect the possibilities of growth and, with them, the possible scenarios with which to associate the estimates.

The choice of methods to be used, within the scope of those mentioned above or further variants, depends on the type of intangible resource and the purpose and context of the valuation, but also on the ease with which reliable and significant information can be found on the resource and the market in which it is strategically positioned.

5.4 Interactive Art (Participatory or Relational) and Value Co-Creation

Interactive art involves the viewer by giving him an active role in the contemplation of the work; it is a dynamic art form that responds to the audience and/or the environment. Unlike traditional art forms in which viewer interaction is mostly a mental event—of the order of reception—interactive art allows for different types of navigation, assembly, or participation in the artwork. Interactive art goes far beyond purely psychological activity. Interactive art installations are generally computerized and use sensors, which measure events such as temperature, movement, proximity, and weather phenomena that the author has programmed to elicit particular responses or reactions. In interactive works, the audience and the machine work or play together in a dialogue that produces a unique work of art in real time.

A declination of interactive art is a participatory art, which uses an approach to art-making that directly involves the audience in the creative process, empowering them to become co-authors, editors, and observers of the work itself. In some expressions, participatory art borders on tribal or traditional art.

Interactivity, inherent in the technological (digital) characteristics of artistic expression, encourages behaviors inspired by the co-creation of value between the inventor and the users, who participate in artistic creation with interactive strategies of value-based pricing based on consumer choices (pay-what-you-want; pay-as-you-wish).

5.5 Copyright Framework and Valuation

According to the Italian law on copyright—l.d.a.—of April 22, 1941, n. 633, copyright—right to copy—protects "the intellectual works of a creative nature that belong to literature, music, figurative arts, architecture, theater, and film, whatever the mode or form of expression" (art. 1). This taxonomy, with some adaptation, may be useful even outside Italy.

Article 2575 of the Italian Civil Code (which represents an example for other countries) states that: "intellectual works of a creative nature belonging to the sciences, literature, music, figurative arts, architecture, theater, and cinematography, whatever the mode or form of expression, form the subject matter of copyright".

At a general level (art. 1 l.d.a.) the creative works belonging to literature, music, figurative arts, architecture, theater and cinematography, computer programs, and databases are protected.

Copyright extends to a very varied and heterogeneous set of works or creations, creating problems with the taxonomy of typified works (from art. 2 of the l.d.a.) or, a fortiori, of non-typified creations; the following typified works are included in the protection:

1. literary, dramatic, scientific, educational, and religious works, whether in written or oral form;
2. Musical works and compositions, with or without words, dramatic-musical works, and musical variations constituting original works;
3. the choreographic and pantomime works, of which the trace is fixed in writing or otherwise;
4. works of sculpture, painting, drawing, engraving, and similar figurative arts, including set design;
5. the drawings and works of architecture;
6. works of cinematographic art, silent or sound, (…);
7. photographic works and those expressed by a process similar to that of photography (…);
8. computer programs [software, editor's note] (…);

9. databases (...), understood as collections of works, data, or other independent elements systematically or methodically arranged and individually accessible by electronic means or otherwise;
10. works of industrial design which in themselves have creative character and artistic value.

Then there are the non-typed creations:

1. critical editions and restoration;
2. sporting events;
3. advertising creations;
4. the fantasy character;
5. the television format;
6. museums;
7. multimedia works;
8. websites;
9. other cases (maps; floral arrangements; party symbols; collages; genetic engineering products; perfumes; sports commentaries; decoupage cards; public installations; SMS collections; embroidery; art historical itineraries, etc.).

Bently and Sherman (2014) propose a complementary taxonomy of copyright, in which they note:

1. literary works;
2. dramatic works;
3. musical works;
4. films;
5. the recording of sound;
6. broadcasts;
7. printed editions;
8. other related rights: of performers of a work; related to a database; technological protection measures in the digital environment; software; broadcasting; management of information rights; public lending right; resale right.

The varied perimeter of the works (simple; composite; collective; derivative) covered by copyright protection also entails economic problems, preparatory to the estimation of value. We refer, first of all, to the analysis of business models and the identification of the value creation levers connected to the exploitation of the work.

Copyright is an intangible asset, and its intangibility makes it easy to overlap with other assets (tangible or intangible) with which it can interact synergistically. Think, for example, of software fed by big data and the Internet of Things, with information flows that then flow into artificial intelligence applications, sometimes validated through blockchain, stored in the cloud, or interoperable databases.

Exploitation and Copyright Protection

There are two cases of copyright exploitation: the case in which the right is exploited by the author or the case in which it is transferred and therefore exploited by the third-party purchaser.

The transfer of copyright is regulated by the Italian l.d.a. (l. 633/1941, whose core principles, as anticipated, are often analogically applicable in other countries), which establishes that the author of the work has the exclusive right to use it economically; in particular, copyright can be divided into three parts:

1. right of publicity;
2. right of use;
3. right of paternity.

The l.d.a. lists a series of patrimonial rights:

- the right of reproduction in several copies of the work (art. 13);
- the right of transcription of the oral work (art. 14);
- the right of performance, representation, or recitation in public (articles 15 and 15 bis);
- the right of processing, translation, and publication of collected works (art. 18);
- the right of rental and lending (art. 18 bis).

Only the first and second rights mentioned above can be assigned, as in these cases they are patrimonial rights. The right of paternity, on the other hand, is a non-transferable personal right.

The rights granted to authors, in addition to those recognized by the Berne Convention, are:

- Distribution right (art. 6): the right to authorize the availability to the public of the original work or its copies through sale or other transfer of ownership;
- rental right (art. 7): the right to authorize the rental for the profit of the original work or its copies. It exclusively concerns three types of works: computer programs (except when the program is not the essential object of the rental), cinematographic works (unless the rental for profit has caused such a widespread reproduction of the work as to substantially compromise the exclusive right of reproduction), and works contained in phonograms;
- the right of communication to the public (Art. 8): the right to authorize any form of communication to the public, by wire or over the air, in such a way that "any person may freely access it from a place or at a time of his or her choosing," thus including on-demand services and interactive communication through the Internet.

Directive 2019/790, which was approved by the European Parliament on March 26, 2019, and by the Council of the European Union on April 15, 2019, aims to ensure adequate remuneration for content producers (and copyright holders) and to extend copyright rules to online content as well. The impact on copyright enhancement, also considering developments in digital applications, is potentially significant.

The patrimonial protection of copyright is a prerequisite for its economic use and subsequent valuation. The author is granted a patrimonial right, consequent to the moral right of unpublishing, which allows him to multiply the copies of the work, with copyright.

The patrimonial right guarantees the author the exclusivity of multiplying the copies of the work. According to Art. 12, paragraph 2, of the copyright law, the author "also has the exclusive right to use the work economically in any form and manner, original or derivative".

The right of reproduction includes all the ways of multiplying the original work into copies and that of representation, execution, and public performance. The work can be diffused at a distance, in the context of communication with the public. Note, even in this area, the potential of digital technologies.

In addition to exclusivity, the author has the right to compensation for certain uses of the work.

The right of economic use must be able to provide an economic benefit to the author, including any form of exploitation of the work, even without economic advantage.

The basis of copyright is the interest in remunerating creative work and investments, including entrepreneurial ones.

The protection of copyright and its consequent economic remuneration is based on various arguments of a juridical nature, which can be applied economically. In this regard, Bently and Sherman get inspired by the natural rights connected to the author's intellectual productions, to which it is considered fair to recognize a property right.

It follows, as a matter of fairness, that the author's effort should be protected through a reward represented by an exclusive right. The incentive for the author also has a public interest purpose, representing a stimulus to creativity and also a compensation for the costs incurred for the creation and production of a work which, in many cases, can be easily copied or manipulated, especially with modern digital technologies (think of serial duplication or photoshopping).

Among the interests protected based on the author's patrimonial rights, the interest in remunerating the creative work and the entrepreneurial investments necessary for the production and diffusion of works of culture and entertainment is of particular importance.

Among the patrimonial rights recognized by the l.d.a. there are:

- the right to publish the work (publication coincides with the first form of economic use);
- the right to reproduce copies in any way;
- the right to represent the work in public;
- the right to disseminate the work using a remote broadcasting medium, including satellite and cable;
- the right of distribution;
- the right to translate; the right to process;
- the right to hire and lend from libraries.

The rights of economic utilization are exclusive to the author, are all independent of each other (and therefore can lead to an incremental evaluation, in the presence of several rights economically endowed with autonomous or synergic valorization), and their economic exploitation is carried out according to agreements, contracts, and licenses.

The valuation of copyright can be carried out based on the three approaches outlined above. The cost approach has limited validity if not linked to the economic exploitation of copyright.

Royalties represent an important benchmark for the financial approach, even in hypothetical form (relief from royalties).

The useful life of copyright is typically extended; in general, rights last for the author's lifetime and 50/70 years after his death (depending on the law), or even longer in the case of anonymous or pseudonymous works.

The (long) duration of copyright, for valuation purposes, could therefore be considered almost perpetual (without application of the terminal value), even if in general the right of exploitation granted by the authors (in publishing contracts, etc..) often has a more limited duration than what is abstractly provided for by law.

For copyright valuation, the recent European Directive 2019/790 is also relevant, which provides (among other things) some innovations on the subject of remuneration of so-called content creators.

A summary of digital art valuation methodologies is reported in Fig. 5.2.

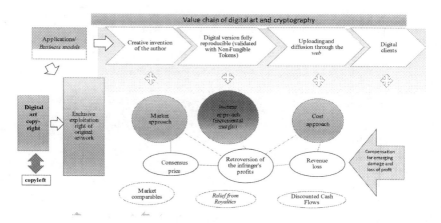

Fig. 5.2 Digital art evaluation methodologies

From Copyright to Copyleft and Creative Commons

Copyright, Copyleft, and Creative Commons are terms associated with intellectual property and licensing frameworks that aim to protect and regulate the rights of creators and users of creative works:

1. Copyright: Copyright is a legal framework that grants exclusive rights to creators or owners of original works, such as literary, artistic, musical, or audiovisual creations. It provides the creator with the authority to control the reproduction, distribution, adaptation, and public performance of their work. Copyright protection is automatically granted to a work upon its creation, and it generally lasts for a specified period, depending on the jurisdiction.
2. Copyleft: Copyleft is a concept that emerged as a response to copyright restrictions. It promotes the idea of granting broad permissions to users, allowing them to freely use, modify, and distribute creative works. Copyleft licenses, such as the GNU General Public License (GPL), use copyright law to enforce these permissions. Under copyleft, modified or derivative works based on the original must be made available under the same copyleft terms, ensuring that subsequent works maintain the same freedoms.
3. Creative Commons: Creative Commons (CC) is an organization that offers a set of standardized licenses that enable creators to specify the permissions and restrictions they want to apply to their works. CC licenses provide a more flexible alternative to traditional copyright by offering a range of permissions that allow creators to tailor the terms of use to their preferences. The licenses allow users to share, remix, and distribute the licensed works under specific conditions, such as attribution or non-commercial use. There are several types of CC licenses, each with its own set of permissions and restrictions.

Creative Commons licenses are widely used in various creative fields, including art, music, literature, and online content creation. They provide a way for creators to grant permissions to others while retaining some control over how their work is used and attributed. By using Creative Commons licenses, creators can encourage collaboration, sharing, and the building of a commons of freely available creative resources.

It's important to note that copyright, copyleft, and Creative Commons are legal frameworks that vary across jurisdictions, and the specific rights and obligations may differ based on local laws and the chosen license. It's advisable to consult the specific license terms and seek legal advice if necessary when using or licensing creative works.

In addition to copyright, there is a model of copyright management based on copyright permission, a system of licenses through which the author (as the original holder of rights on the work) indicates to the users of the work that it can be used, disseminated, and often modified freely while respecting some essential conditions. Copyleft (copyright permission) can be applied to a multitude of works, ranging from software to literary works, from videos to musical works, and databases to photographs.

The economic evaluation is sensitive to the passage from copyright to copyleft; in the second case, the author's monetization is less, even if the work can assume a much greater diffusion, generating non-economic benefits for the author (prestige; notoriety; visibility, even viral, etc.), which can then be subject to economic exploitation with new products or creations of authors who can become influencers.

Creative Commons licenses provide a simple and standardized way to communicate which copyright of the work is reserved and which others are renounced, to the benefit of users. Copyright is consequently relaxed and does not cover all rights but only some.

5.6 Reproducibility of Works, Real Options, and Digital Scalability

The digital platforms operating on the Web allow digitized art to implement a diffusion and a related immediate and global usability, with characteristics of "virality".

The issue of reproducibility of copyrighted works has a clear impact on their economic exploitation, on which the valuation, also in terms of the price of consent, depends.

Reproducibility is facilitated by a typical feature of intangible goods, represented by non-rivalry in consumption. The concept has traditionally been developed regarding public and private goods, exclusive or shareable. Rivalry in consumption is typical of private physical goods (e.g., a sandwich, which can be consumed by only one person, precluding enjoyment by others). Intangible goods—and typically those subject to copyright (e.g., a film, a song, etc.)—can instead be enjoyed simultaneously and shared by a potentially unlimited number of users, without being "consumed" by anyone. In the digital environment, reproducibility is further facilitated by the immediacy and ubiquity of the Internet.

In addition to this feature, there are others connected with the versatility of intangible assets (whose intangible nature makes them flexible and adaptable to multiple uses, regardless of "physical" problems that hinder their transportability and fungibility) or digital applications (think of a song or a film broadcast on the Internet). The synergic interaction of these characteristics affects the scalability of copyright-protected assets; this concept means the ability of a business model (also fed by intangible assets) to manage growing volumes (of sales, etc.) quickly and with reduced or even non-existent incremental costs. In the face of the greater revenues connected to scalability and the ontological invariance of fixed costs, a limited increase in variable costs emerges, with a consequent increase in economic and financial margins, which have a positive impact on valuation.

Think of accessing a website at the same time as watching a film: The circumstance that the number of connected users can grow exponentially in real time (if the film becomes viral) does not presuppose, as a rule, an appreciable increase in costs for the owner or host of the site, even by way of the web platform, aggregator site of news and other content or snippet. This is not the case, however, for the production of rival physical assets, which involves additional time and cost.

The transition from analog to digital involves a very significant potential increase in the usability of the work and its consequent economic exploitation. The effects on established business models can be disruptive, as occurred, for example, in the record industry with mass peer-to-peer systems such as Napster, at the end of the 90s of last century.

The driving force behind scalability is represented not only by the aforementioned characteristics of digitization of intangible assets but also by the presence of computer platforms on the Internet (linked to interoperable servers and databases with access through websites) where it is possible to share and simultaneously enjoy movies, songs, texts, images, etc., that is, works that, in a broad sense, are attributable to copyright protection.

A further catalyst is represented by social networks, which feed Internet traffic, promoting the virality of digital content. Artificial intelligence applications can also act as catalysts for the exploitation of copyrighted goods, with application scenarios yet to be discovered. Further support can be provided by the validation of information (for example on the authorship of a work of art) through blockchains.

From this area descend valuation issues that can conveniently exploit features of digital scalability to apply real options.

Real options, unlike the best-known financial options, allow to include in the model of estimation of prospective cash flows (traditionally used in the evaluation of companies) elements of flexibility and resilience, incorporating into it the reactions of the market, often difficult to predict. In this way, it is possible to have options (also linked to the right of resale of works of art) of deferment, temporary suspension, abandonment, contraction, or—in a more optimistic sense—expansion or development, which give elasticity and adaptability to patented inventions, increasing their potential value.

The ability to foresee and model future and uncertain events related to the actual economic and financial return deriving from the exploitation of the intangible asset (typically, a patent, but also a scalable asset protected by copyright) can be usefully codified in contractual earn-out clauses which, in sales, ensure the seller an additional price, if certain events occur, which are particularly aleatory and uncertain at the time of contract signing. This makes it possible to overcome delicate situations of deadlock, in which the seller is not willing to give up extra earnings (to the extent that the merits are attributable to him) and the buyer to recognize them without the presumable verifiability of the positive events associated with them being ascertained. Useful links can be established between earn-outs and real options, by contractually codifying the economic aspects of possible and uncertain events, also in the context of transactions in which the aim is to limit the uncertainty of the initial price, linking it to future increases subject to the achievement of pre-established milestones.

The Secondary Market

Secondary markets make primary markets more liquid and more valuable. The primary market refers to the market where securities or goods (art products, etc.) are created, while the secondary market is one in which they are traded among investors.

Without both primary and secondary markets, the overall capital markets would be much harder to deal with and much less profitable

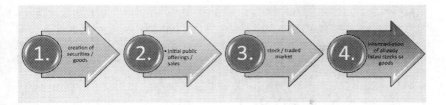

Fig. 5.3 Primary and secondary market

(Fig. 5.3). The primary and secondary market continuously interact with self-fulfilling links. The secondary market provides essential liquidity to primary issuing.

These standard features can be applied to this peculiar case, where cryptocurrencies are "minted" and then circulated. Something similar happens with NFTs or with digital art (that can be represented by NFTs or different forms).

Non-Fungible Tokens (NFT)

A non-fungible token (NFT) is a type of digital asset that represents ownership or proof of authenticity of a unique item or piece of content. Unlike cryptocurrencies such as Bitcoin or Ethereum, which are fungible and can be exchanged on a one-to-one basis, NFTs are distinct and cannot be exchanged on a like-for-like basis.

Here are some key characteristics and points to understand about NFTs:

1. Uniqueness: Each NFT has a distinct and verifiable digital identity, making it different from any other token. It can represent various types of digital or physical assets, such as artwork, music, videos, virtual real estate, virtual items in video games, collectibles, and more.
2. Blockchain-based: NFTs are typically built on blockchain technology, most commonly on platforms like Ethereum. The blockchain serves as a decentralized and transparent ledger that records ownership, transaction history, and metadata associated with each NFT, ensuring its authenticity and provenance.

3. Ownership and control: NFTs provide a means for individuals to claim ownership and control over digital assets in a way that was not easily possible before. The token serves as a digital certificate of ownership, allowing buyers to prove their exclusive ownership and control over the associated asset.
4. Indivisibility: NFTs cannot be divided or split into smaller units like cryptocurrencies. Each NFT represents a whole and unique asset. However, they can be bought, sold, or traded in part or as a whole, depending on the platform or marketplace where they are being transacted.
5. Smart contracts and royalties: NFTs can include smart contracts that define certain conditions or royalties for the original creator. For example, an artist can receive a percentage of future sales when their artwork is resold in the secondary market.
6. Marketplaces and value: NFTs can be bought, sold, and traded on various online marketplaces specifically designed for NFT transactions. The value of an NFT is determined by factors such as scarcity, demand, uniqueness, the reputation of the creator, and the perceived value attached to the associated asset.

NFTs have gained significant attention and popularity in the art world and beyond, as they provide new opportunities for creators, collectors, and investors to engage with and monetize digital assets. However, it's important to note that the NFT market is relatively new and highly speculative, with fluctuating trends and potential risks.

NFTs are assets that have been tokenized via a blockchain. They are assigned unique identification codes and metadata that distinguish them from other tokens. NFTs can be traded and exchanged for money, cryptocurrencies, or other NFTs—it all depends on the value the market and owners have placed on them. For instance, you could use an exchange to create a token for an image of a banana. Some people might pay millions for the NFT, while others might think it worthless. Cryptocurrencies are tokens as well; however, the key difference is that two cryptocurrencies from the same blockchain are interchangeable—they are fungible. Two NFTs from the same blockchain can look identical, but they are not interchangeable (https://www.investopedia.com/non-fungible-tokens-nft-5115211).

The NFT market is mushrooming in recent years. The concept of NFT originally comes from a token standard of Ethereum, aiming to distinguish each token with distinguishable signs. This type of token can be bound with virtual/digital properties as their unique identifications. With NFTs, all marked properties can be freely traded with customized values according to their ages, rarity, liquidity, etc. It has greatly stimulated the prosperity of the decentralized application market (Qin et al., 2021).

As shown in Trevisi, Moro Visconti, and Cesaretti (2022), an NFT is a unit of data stored on a digital ledger, called a blockchain, which can be sold and traded. The NFT can be associated with a particular digital or physical asset (such as a file or a physical object) and a license to use the asset for a specified purpose. An analysis of the business model and the legal aspects is propaedeutic to the market valuation. To the extent that NFTs can remove intermediaries, simplify and validate transactions, and create new markets, they can be used for several valuation purposes, according to the stakeholder involved (creator/artist; consumer, etc.).

The valuation of NFTs is a complex and dynamic process influenced by various factors. Some key factors that can affect the valuation of an NFT include:

1. Rarity: Rarity is a significant driver of value in the NFT market. The scarcer an NFT is, the higher its perceived value. If an NFT represents a unique or limited edition digital artwork or collectible, it may be more desirable and command a higher price.
2. Demand and Popularity: The level of demand for a particular NFT can greatly impact its valuation. Factors such as the popularity of the artist or creator, the perceived quality or uniqueness of the artwork, and current market trends can drive up demand and subsequently increase the value of an NFT.
3. Artist/Creator Reputation: The reputation and recognition of the artist or creator associated with an NFT can play a significant role in its valuation. Established and well-known artists may have a higher perceived value for their NFTs due to their track record, reputation, and existing fan base.
4. Scarcity and Supply: The scarcity of an NFT, in terms of limited edition releases or exclusivity, can drive up its value. If the supply of a particular NFT is limited, it can create a sense of urgency and exclusivity, potentially leading to higher valuations.

5. Utility and Functionality: Some NFTs have additional utility or functionality beyond being a mere collectible. For example, an NFT might grant access to exclusive content, virtual experiences, or special privileges. The added utility or functionality can contribute to the value of the NFT.
6. Secondary Market Activity: The prices at which similar NFTs have been bought and sold in the secondary market can influence the valuation of an NFT. Market trends and recent sales of comparable NFTs may be considered when determining the value of a specific NFT.

It's important to note that the valuation of NFTs can be highly subjective and influenced by market sentiment, trends, and individual preferences. The NFT market is still relatively new and evolving, and prices can be volatile. Buyers, sellers, and investors should conduct thorough research, consider multiple factors, and exercise caution when assessing the value of an NFT.

References

Anselmi, G., & Petrella, G. (2023). Non-fungible token artworks: More crypto than art?. *Finance Research Letters, 51.*

Bently, L., & Sherman, L. (2014). *Intellectual property law* (4th ed.). Oxford University Press.

Catricalà, V. (2015). *Media art. Towards a new definition of arts in the age of technology.* https://www.academia.edu/11185472/Media_Art_Towards_a_New_Definition_of_Arts_in_the_Age_of_Technology

Qin, W., Li, R., & Chen, S. (2021). Non-fungible token (NFT): Overview, evaluation, opportunities and challenges, tech report, Cornell University. https://arxiv.org/abs/2105.07447

Trevisi, C., Moro Visconti, R., & Cesaretti, A. (2022). Non-fungible tokens (NFT): Business models, legal aspects, and market valuation. *Media Laws, 1,* 1–26.

CHAPTER 6

Blockchains, Internet of Value, and Smart Transactions

6.1 BLOCKCHAINS: DEFINITION AND MAIN FEATURES

A blockchain is a consequential list (chain) of blocks (records) that are linked using cryptography. Each block contains a cryptographic hash of the previous block, a timestamp, and transaction data (generally represented as a Merkle tree root hash).

Blockchains are decentralized and distributed digital ledgers that record transactions across multiple computers or nodes in a transparent, secure, and immutable manner. They serve as a foundational technology for cryptocurrencies like Bitcoin and have applications beyond digital currencies, ranging from supply chain management to smart contracts. Here are the main features of blockchains:

1. Decentralization: Blockchains operate on a decentralized network, meaning there is no central authority or single point of control. Transactions are verified and recorded by multiple participants (nodes) in the network, ensuring transparency and preventing a single point of failure.
2. Distributed Ledger: The blockchain ledger is distributed across multiple nodes in the network. Each node has a copy of the entire transaction history, and new transactions are added to the ledger through consensus mechanisms, such as proof of work or proof of stake.

© The Author(s), under exclusive license to Springer Nature Switzerland AG 2023
R. Moro-Visconti and A. Cesaretti, *Digital Token Valuation*,
https://doi.org/10.1007/978-3-031-42971-2_6

3. Transparency and Immutability: Transactions recorded on a blockchain are transparent and can be viewed by anyone in the network. Once a transaction is recorded and verified, it is difficult to alter or delete due to cryptographic hashing and the distributed nature of the ledger. This immutability enhances trust and security in the system.
4. Security and Trust: Blockchains use advanced cryptographic algorithms to secure transactions and data. The distributed nature of the network makes it difficult for malicious actors to tamper with the ledger. Consensus mechanisms ensure agreement among nodes, further enhancing security and trust.
5. Smart Contracts: Smart contracts are self-executing contracts with predefined rules and conditions written into code on the blockchain. They automatically execute and enforce the terms of the contract once the conditions are met. Smart contracts enable the automation of various processes and eliminate the need for intermediaries.
6. Cryptocurrency and Tokenization: Blockchains are closely associated with cryptocurrencies like Bitcoin and Ethereum. These digital currencies utilize blockchain technology to facilitate secure and decentralized transactions. Additionally, blockchains enable the tokenization of assets, representing ownership or value of real-world assets on the blockchain.
7. Privacy and Permissioned Blockchains: While public blockchains offer open access and transparency, there are also permissioned or private blockchains that restrict access to authorized participants. Private blockchains are often used in enterprise settings where privacy and control over data are important.
8. Scalability and Performance: Blockchains face challenges related to scalability and performance. Public blockchains, in particular, may have limitations in terms of transaction throughput and speed. Various solutions and protocols, such as layer-two scaling solutions and consensus algorithm improvements, are being developed to address these challenges.
9. Interoperability and Standards: Interoperability refers to the ability of different blockchains to communicate and interact with each other seamlessly. As the blockchain ecosystem evolves, efforts are being made to establish interoperability standards and frameworks to facilitate the exchange of assets and information between different blockchains.

Blockchains offer a range of benefits, including decentralization, transparency, security, and automation through smart contracts. They have the potential to disrupt traditional industries (for example, healthcare, as shown by Lui, 2016) and enable new business models.

Blockchain could be regarded as a public ledger technology in which all committed transactions are stored in a chain of blocks. This chain continuously grows when new blocks are added to it. Blockchain technology has characteristics such as decentralization, persistence, anonymity, verifiability, and audibility. It can be then used to ensure the authenticity, reliability, and integrity of data and business activities. Blockchain can work in a decentralized environment thanks to the integration of technologies such as cryptographic hash, digital signature (based on asymmetric cryptography), and distributed consensus mechanisms. With blockchain technology, a transaction can take place in a decentralized manner. As a result, blockchain can reduce notable costs, producing efficiency gains (Fig. 6.1).

Blockchain formation is represented in Fig. 6.2. The main chain (black) consists of the most extended series of blocks from the first block (green) to the current block. Orphan blocks (blue) exist outside of the main chain.

A blockchain belongs to distributed ledger (database) technologies and represents a process where many subjects share IT data to make a virtual database available to a community of users. In most cases, this database is public, and the community is open, although there are examples of private implementations where each participant has a copy of the data.

A blockchain is mainly an open and distributed ledger that can memorize encrypted digital transactions (peer-to-peer) between two counterparts in a secure way that is verifiable and permanent. Electronic money transfers made from one person to another through an intermediary, are typically referred to as P2P payment applications. P2P payments can be directly sent and received via mobile device or any computer with access to the Internet, offering an alternative to traditional payment methods involving banks or other financial institutions.

Once recorded, the data within a block cannot be retroactively altered without modifying the subsequent blocks. Due to the nature of the protocol and the validation scheme, this would require the consensus of most of the network participants (Norman et al., 2018) and is practically unfeasible being the participants many, exponentially growing and hardly interrelated.

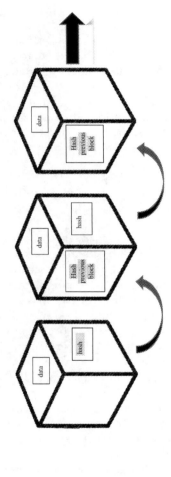

Fig. 6.1 Blockchain as a sequential chain of data

Fig. 6.2 Blockchain formation

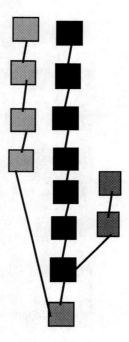

In summary, a blockchain has the following key characteristics:

1. Decentralization. In conventional centralized transaction systems, each transaction needs to be validated through the central trusted agency (e.g., the central bank) with a fixed cost and performance bottlenecks at the primary servers. A transaction in the blockchain network can instead be conducted between any two peers (P2P) without authentication by the central agency. In this manner, blockchain significantly reduces server costs (including development and operation costs) and mitigates the performance bottlenecks at the central server.
2. Persistency. Since each of the transactions spreading across the network needs to be confirmed and recorded in blocks distributed in the whole network, it is nearly impossible to tamper. Furthermore, each broadcasted block would need to be validated by other nodes

and transactions would be checked. In this way, any falsification could be detected easily.
3. Anonymity. Each user can interact with the blockchain network with a generated address. In addition to this, a user could create many addresses to avoid identity exposure. There is no longer a central party recording users' private information. This mechanism preserves the privacy of the transactions in the blockchain.
4. Auditability. Since each of the transactions on the blockchain is validated and recorded with a timestamp, users can easily verify and trace the previous records by accessing any node in the distributed network. In a Bitcoin blockchain, each transaction could be traced to previous transactions iteratively. This improves the traceability and transparency of the data stored in the blockchain.
5. Trust. Confidence is shifted away from human actors toward a cryptographic system, with incentives for participating actors.
6. Transparency: Blockchain transactions are transparent, meaning that they can be viewed by anyone on the network. This tion.
7. Immutability: Once a transaction is recorded on a blockchain, it cannot tant to tampering.
8. Consensus: Blockchains rely on a consensus mechanism to validate transactions and maintain the integrity of the network. Depending on the blockchain, this can anisms.
9. Smart Contracts: Many blockchains support smart contracts, which are s executing contracts that can automate complex processes and reduce the mediaries.

These are just a few of the key characteristics of blockchains.

6.2 Disrupting Traditional Business Models

Numerous industries are implementing blockchain as part of their business processes. Valuation patterns may thus be concerned not only with public or private blockchains (see Sect 6.4) but also with their impact on traditional businesses (see Goorha, 2018).

The employment of blockchain technologies and the possibility to apply them in different situations enables many industrial applications through increased efficiency and security, enhanced traceability and transparency, and reduced costs (Al-Jaroodi & Mohamed, 2019).

Blockchain technology has been initially used for controversial cryptocurrencies like bitcoins and FinTech applications and later in many other industries and supply chains (Blossey et al., 2019) such as:

- Energy (Fan et al., 2017; Sawa, 2019);
- IoT electric business model (Andoni et al., 2019; Veuger, 2018);
- Property transfer (intangibles, real estate property, registered movable property …);
- Industry/manufacturing;
- Logistics and transports (tracking of goods, etc.);
- Automotive (shipment of vehicles with frictionless information among connected systems; tracking of original spare parts; car-sharing; retention of the clients, etc.);
- Food supply chain (Mao et al., 2018);
- E-commerce;
- Stock markets (asset pricing; appraisal of shareholders, etc.). With blockchain technology, it is possible to automate and secure the entire process of selling, buying, and trading stocks;
- Healthcare (for track-record; clinical trials; personalized medicine; pharmaceutical supply chains; prescription drug management; health records management, etc.); see Singh (2013);
- Contemporary art (Lotti, 2016);
- Insurance (InsurTech);
- FinTech (validation of payments; P2P lending and crowdfunding, etc.);
- RegTech;
- Microfinance (assisting with smart contracts several microfinancing bodies without the need for mediators or central authorities);
- E-governance (transparency and accessibility of government information; information sharing, etc.);
- Crowdsourcing (decentralized and secured petition systems);
- Smart cities (Xie et al., 2019).

The list above is far from exhaustive and represents just an example of some applications of this versatile technology.

Since payments can be completed without any bank or intermediary, a blockchain can be used in various financial services such as digital assets, remittances, and online payments. Additionally, blockchain is becoming one of the most promising technologies for the next generation of Internet interaction systems such as smart contracts, public services, the Internet of Things (IoT), reputation systems, and security services.

Smart contracts are self-executing contracts with the terms of the agreement directly written into code on the blockchain. They automatically execute and enforce the predefined conditions of the contract without the need for intermediaries or manual intervention. Smart contracts facilitate trust and automation in transactions by eliminating the reliance on a centralized authority or third party.

Here are some key aspects of smart transactions or smart contracts:

1. Automation: Smart contracts enable the automation of transactions and business processes. Once the conditions specified in the contract's code are met, the contract executes automatically without requiring manual intervention.
2. Autonomy: Smart contracts operate autonomously, meaning they are self-executing and self-enforcing. Once deployed on the blockchain, they operate according to the predefined rules and conditions without the need for human intervention.
3. Transparency: Smart contracts are recorded on the blockchain, making them transparent and visible to all participants in the network. Anyone can view the code and terms of the contract, ensuring transparency and reducing the need for trust in a centralized authority.
4. Trust and Security: Smart contracts are secured by the cryptographic features of the underlying blockchain technology. The immutability and distributed nature of the blockchain ensure the integrity and security of the contract's execution and data.
5. Elimination of Intermediaries: Smart contracts eliminate the need for intermediaries, such as lawyers or brokers, as the contract terms are embedded in the code and automatically enforced. This reduces costs, speeds up transactions, and eliminates potential points of failure or disputes.
6. Use Cases: Smart contracts have various use cases, such as supply chain management, financial transactions, insurance claims processing, real estate transactions, and more. They can automate

and streamline complex processes, improve efficiency, and reduce the risk of fraud or error.

While smart contracts offer advantages in terms of automation and transparency, they are still subject to the accuracy and completeness of the code and the data provided to them. Careful development, auditing, and testing are necessary to ensure the reliability and security of smart contracts.

Smart transactions or smart contracts leverage the capabilities of blockchain technology to automate and enforce the terms of agreements, enabling secure and efficient transactions without the need for intermediaries.

Blockchains go well beyond the cryptocurrencies (like Bitcoins) that made them famous. Cryptocurrencies can fuel money laundering and other malpractices, given that their market is opaque, irrespective of any regulation, and subject to speculative bubbles. Cryptocurrencies should be regulated by Central Banks or, where not possible, prohibited. This, however, does not prejudice other useful applications of blockchain technology.

These many applications contribute to the valuation patterns, describing possible business models: the broader, the higher the potential value of a blockchain that can enable and forge new products, and processes.

For example, In the manufacturing industry blockchains are used to manage and control (audit) supply chains. Blockchains will also be used for Industry 4.0 (industrial automation) and IoT.

The Internet of Things (IoT) has been connecting an extraordinarily large number of devices to the Internet. Current solutions are mostly based on cloud computing infrastructures, which necessitate high-end servers and high-speed networks to provide services related to storage and computation. However, a cloud-enabled IoT framework manifests several significant disadvantages, such as high cloud server maintenance costs, weakness in supporting time-critical IoT applications, security and trust issues, etc., which impede its wide adoption. Therefore, it is essential for research communities to solve these problems associated with the cloud-enabled IoT frameworks and to develop new methods for IoT decentralization. Recently, blockchain is perceived as a promising technique to solve problems and design new decentralization frameworks for IoT.

There are innovative blockchain solutions for 3D printing where the widespread development of printed components (concerning, for instance, the rapid delivery of spare parts), creates a new challenge when differentiating between originals, copies, and counterfeits.

The current technological evolution will concern an extension of blockchain applications to many other sectors.

6.3 Internet of Value

The term "Internet of Value" refers to the vision of a digital ecosystem in which value, in the form of assets, currency, or data, can be seamlessly exchanged, transferred, and managed over the Internet. It encompasses the idea of using blockchain technology and decentralized systems to enable the frictionless transfer of value globally.

In the traditional financial system, value transfer often involves intermediaries such as banks or payment processors, which can introduce delays, fees, and complexities. The Internet of Value aims to overcome these limitations by leveraging blockchain technology, smart contracts, and cryptocurrencies to enable direct peer-to-peer value transfers with greater speed, security, and efficiency.

Here are key aspects of the Internet of Value:

1. Decentralization: The Internet of Value is based on decentralized networks, typically utilizing blockchain technology, which removes the need for central authorities or intermediaries. Value transfers occur directly between participants without the need for intermediaries, reducing costs and increasing efficiency.
2. Peer-to-Peer Transactions: The Internet of Value enables direct peer-to-peer transactions, allowing individuals and businesses to transact with each other directly without intermediaries. These transactions can involve various types of value, including cryptocurrencies, digital assets, or even traditional currencies represented on a blockchain.
3. Blockchain Technology: Blockchain technology provides the foundation for the Internet of Value. It ensures transparency, immutability, and security in value transfers by recording transactions on a distributed and decentralized ledger. Blockchains enable the verification and validation of transactions by multiple participants, ensuring trust and reliability.

4. Cryptocurrencies and Digital Assets: The Internet of Value is closely associated with cryptocurrencies and digital assets, which serve as the native units of value within the ecosystem. Cryptocurrencies, such as Bitcoin and Ethereum, provide a means of exchange and store of value, while digital assets represent ownership or rights to real-world assets like real estate, intellectual property, or financial instruments.
5. Smart Contracts: Smart contracts, powered by blockchain technology, play a vital role in the Internet of Value. They enable the automation and self-execution of predefined agreements and conditions, allowing for secure and transparent value transfers. Smart contracts eliminate the need for intermediaries and provide programmable logic for managing and enforcing agreements.
6. Cross-Border Transactions: The Internet of Value has the potential to simplify and accelerate cross-border transactions by bypassing the traditional financial system. It can facilitate fast and low-cost international transfers of value, eliminating intermediaries and reducing settlement times.
7. Financial Inclusion: The Internet of Value has the potential to improve financial inclusion by providing access to financial services to individuals and businesses that are currently underserved or excluded from traditional banking systems. With the Internet of Value, anyone with Internet access can participate in the global economy, transact, and store value securely.

The Internet of Value represents a paradigm shift in how value is exchanged and managed, leveraging decentralized technology to enable efficient, secure, and inclusive transactions. It has the potential to transform various industries, including finance, supply chain, remittances, and more, by providing a more transparent, efficient, and accessible ecosystem for value transfer.

The term "Internet of Value" refers to the vision of a connected network where value, in the form of digital assets or currencies, can be instantly and securely transferred and exchanged. It builds upon the concept of the Internet of Things (IoT) and extends it to include the exchange of economic value.

The Internet of Value represents a paradigm shift in the way value is created, transferred, and stored. It is facilitated by blockchain technology, which provides a decentralized and transparent framework for value transfer. Here are some key aspects of the Internet of Value:

1. Decentralization: The Internet of Value operates on decentralized networks, typically utilizing blockchain or distributed ledger technology. This eliminates the need for intermediaries, such as banks or payment processors, by allowing direct peer-to-peer value transfers. Decentralization enhances security, reduces costs, and promotes trust among participants.
2. Instant Transactions: The Internet of Value enables near-instantaneous transactions across geographical boundaries. Unlike traditional financial systems that involve delays and settlement periods, value transfers within the Internet of Value can occur in real-time or within seconds, promoting efficiency and enabling new business models.
3. Digital Assets and Cryptocurrencies: The Internet of Value relies on digital assets and cryptocurrencies as the units of value exchange. Cryptocurrencies, such as Bitcoin and Ethereum, serve as native digital currencies, while digital assets represent ownership or rights to tangible or intangible assets, such as real estate, intellectual property, or securities. These digital assets can be securely transferred and stored on the blockchain.
4. Smart Contracts: Smart contracts are self-executing contracts with the terms and conditions directly written into code on the blockchain. They automate and enforce agreements, eliminating the need for intermediaries and ensuring trust and transparency in value exchange. Smart contracts enable programmable and conditional transactions, opening up possibilities for innovative applications and business processes.
5. Interoperability: Interoperability is a crucial aspect of the Internet of Value, enabling different blockchain networks and systems to communicate and exchange value seamlessly. Standardization protocols and interoperability frameworks are being developed to facilitate the transfer of value across diverse blockchain platforms.
6. Global Accessibility: The Internet of Value promotes global accessibility, enabling anyone with internet connectivity to participate in the digital economy. It has the potential to empower individuals in underserved regions who lack access to traditional financial services, promoting financial inclusion and economic opportunities.
7. New Business Models: The Internet of Value fosters the emergence of new business models and ecosystems. It enables peer-to-peer

marketplaces, decentralized finance (DeFi) applications, tokenization of assets, crowdfunding platforms, and other innovative models that leverage the direct exchange of value between participants.

The Internet of Value represents the evolution of digital transactions and financial systems, harnessing the capabilities of blockchain technology to enable secure, efficient, and borderless value transfers. It has the potential to reshape industries, drive economic transformation, and unlock new opportunities for individuals and businesses worldwide.

Innovation is a critical element in a company's differentiation strategy that contributes to achieving Porter's competitive advantage and leads to monopolistic rents.

With the Internet of Value, a value transaction can happen instantly, at the same speed at which we share words, images, and videos online. The potential of the Internet of Value extends well beyond money. The Internet of Value will enable to exchange of any asset that is of value to someone, including stocks, votes, frequent flyer points, securities, intellectual property, music, scientific discoveries, and more.

Until now, selling, buying, or exchanging these assets always required an intermediary like a bank, a physical or digital marketplace a credit card company, or a third-party service. Blockchain technology allows assets to be transferred from one party to another without any intermediation. The transfer is immediately validated, completed, and will be recorded permanently.

Blockchain contributes to a new generation of web patterns (Internet of Value) consisting of a digital network built on open standards.

Corporate use of blockchains contributes to product and process innovation with a positive impact on the supply chain (Dujak & Sajter, 2019; Korpela et al., 2017; Saberi et al., 2018) thanks to the exploitation of big data.

Blockchain can generate a value increase in digital platforms (B2B, B2C …) through its secured transactions, facilitating e-commerce.

The sharing economy economic model is often defined as a peer-to-peer (P2P) based activity of the acquiring part, providing, or sharing access to goods and services that are facilitated by a community-based online platform. Information is exchanged through (virtual) communities that exchange data mainly through digital platforms linked to social networks.

Monopolies dominate the current sharing economy, and markets like this are vulnerable to disruption. The emergence of blockchain cuts out middlemen so savvy start-ups can create headaches for the likes of Uber and Airbnb.

As per the intangible capital, one area that seems particularly promising for blockchain is represented by value co-creation and open innovation.

There are meaningful correlations between blockchains and FinTech applications or artificial intelligence that influence the workings of blockchains and payment systems thanks to its machine learning patterns.

When evaluating the Internet of Value (IoV) or blockchain-based systems that facilitate the exchange and transfer of value, several key approaches can be considered. Here are some evaluation approaches for the Internet of Value:

1. Technical Feasibility: Assess the technical feasibility and capabilities of the underlying blockchain technology. Consider factors such as scalability, security, consensus mechanisms, interoperability, and the ability to handle transaction volume and throughput. Evaluate the blockchain's architecture, protocol, and development community to determine if it aligns with the requirements of the specific use case.
2. Use Case Alignment: Evaluate the alignment of the IoV solution with the intended use case. Assess whether the proposed application of blockchain technology brings significant advantages over existing systems or traditional approaches. Consider factors such as transparency, decentralization, automation, efficiency gains, and the potential for disintermediation.
3. Economic Viability: Evaluate the economic viability and sustainability of the IoV solution. Consider the potential cost savings, revenue generation models, and the potential for new business opportunities enabled by the technology. Assess the long-term viability and scalability of the IoV solution to determine if it can provide economic benefits for the participants involved.
4. Security and Privacy: Assess the security and privacy measures of the IoV solution. Evaluate the consensus mechanism, encryption techniques, and privacy protocols implemented in the blockchain. Consider the resilience against attacks, the level of data protection, and the ability to maintain confidentiality while ensuring transparency and audibility.

5. User Experience and Adoption: Evaluate the user experience and adoption potential of the IoV solution. Consider the ease of use, accessibility, and familiarity for users interacting with the system. Assess the potential barriers to adoption and the incentives for users to participate in the IoV ecosystem. User-centric design and intuitive interfaces can significantly impact the success and adoption of the solution.
6. Regulatory and Legal Compliance: Consider the regulatory and legal environment in which the IoV solution operates. Evaluate if the solution complies with existing regulations, such as data protection, anti-money laundering (AML), and know-your-customer (KYC) requirements. Assess the potential legal implications and the readiness of the IoV solution to adapt to evolving regulations.
7. Ecosystem and Governance: Evaluate the ecosystem and governance structure supporting the IoV solution. Assess the participation of key stakeholders, such as developers, users, and validators. Consider the governance model, decision-making processes, and mechanisms for resolving disputes or addressing upgrades and changes to the system.
8. Scalability and Interoperability: Assess the scalability and interoperability of the IoV solution. Consider the ability of the blockchain network to handle increasing transaction volumes without sacrificing performance. Evaluate the potential for interoperability with other blockchain networks or legacy systems to facilitate seamless value transfers and data exchange.

It is essential to conduct a comprehensive evaluation that takes into account the technical, economic, security, regulatory, user-centric, and ecosystem factors when considering the adoption and implementation of the Internet of Value. This evaluation process helps assess the suitability and potential benefits of the IoV solution in a particular context or use case.

There are several interdependent evaluation approaches for the Internet of Value. Some of them are:

1. Economic evaluation: This approach focuses on examining the economic impact of the Internet of Value by analyzing the costs and benefits associated with implementing blockchain technology and

decentralized systems. An economic evaluation of the Internet of Value involves analyzing the costs and benefits of implementing such a system. The benefits of the Internet of Value include increased efficiency, reduced transaction costs, and improved security and transparency. By enabling peer-to-peer transactions, the Internet of Value can eliminate the need for intermediaries, which can lead to lower fees and faster settlement times. Implementing the Internet of Value also involves significant costs, including the development and maintenance of the necessary infrastructure, as well as regulatory and legal compliance. Additionally, there may be upfront costs associated with transitioning from traditional financial systems to the Internet of Value., the economic evaluation of the Internet of Value suggests that while there are significant benefits to implementing such a system, careful consideration must be given to the costs and challenges involved. Nevertheless, the Internet of Value has the potential to revolutionize the financial industry and make financial services more accessible, efficient, and secure for all.

2. Technical evaluation: This approach evaluates the technical aspects of the Internet of Value, including the performance, scalability, security, and interoperability of blockchain networks. From a technical standpoint, the Internet of Value relies on the use of blockchain technology, which is a distributed ledger that is shared by all participating nodes. The ledger records all transactions and is updated in real-time, making it an ideal platform for enabling fast and secure transactions. One of the key advantages of the Internet of Value is that it operates on a decentralized network, which means that there is no central authority controlling it. This improves security as there is no single point of failure, making it more resilient against cyber attacks. In terms of scalability, the Internet of Value has the potential to handle millions of transactions per second. This is achieved through the use of various consensus algorithms that allow for fast and efficient processing of transactions., the Internet of Value has the potential to revolutionize the way we transfer value, enabling faster, cheaper, and more secure transactions than traditional financial systems.

3. Social evaluation: It examines the social impact of the Internet of Value by analyzing how it affects various stakeholders, such as businesses, governments, and individuals. From a social perspective, the Internet of Value has the potential to empower individuals and

communities by giving them more control over their assets and enabling them to participate in the global economy without relying on traditional financial institutions. This technology could also help to reduce inequality by providing access to financial services to people who are currently unbanked or underbanked. However, there are also potential risks and challenges associated with the Internet of Value. For example, the anonymity and decentralization of blockchain technology could make it easier for criminals to launder money or engage in other illegal activities. Additionally, there are concerns about the environmental impact of the energy-intensive mining process required to maintain the blockchain network., the Internet of Value has the potential to bring about significant benefits, but it will be important to address these challenges and ensure that the technology is used responsibly and ethically.
4. Legal evaluation: it focuses on evaluating the legal implications of the Internet of Value, including regulatory compliance, intellectual property issues, and privacy concerns. The legal implications of the Internet of Value will depend on the jurisdiction and the specific use case.
5. Environmental evaluation evaluates the environmental impact of the Internet of Value by analyzing the energy consumption and carbon footprint of blockchain networks. Firstly, the energy consumption of the blockchain network used in the Internet of Value can be quite significant. This is because blockchain relies on a distributed network of nodes to validate and process transactions, which requires a lot of computational power. As a result, the mining process can consume a significant amount of energy. However, there are efforts underway to improve the energy efficiency of blockchain, through the use of more efficient consensus algorithms and renewable energy sources. Secondly, the use of the Internet of Value can potentially reduce the environmental impact of traditional financial systems by enabling more efficient and transparent transactions. For example, it can reduce the need for intermediaries and associated paperwork, which can result in reduced resource consumption. Additionally, by enabling more efficient and secure transactions, the Internet of Value can potentially reduce fraud and associated environmental impacts., the environmental impact of the Internet of Value is complex and depends on a variety of factors. However, with efforts

to improve the efficiency of blockchain technology and the potential benefits of more efficient financial systems, there is potential for the Internet of Value to have a positive impact on the environment.

6.4 The Legal Nature of Public or Private Blockchains as a Prerequisite for Valuation

The legal nature of public or private blockchains can have implications for the valuation of blockchain-based assets or projects. The legal framework surrounding a blockchain network can impact factors such as regulatory compliance, the enforceability of smart contracts, intellectual property rights, and liability considerations. Here are some aspects to consider regarding the legal nature of public or private blockchains and their impact on valuation:

1. Regulatory Compliance: Public and private blockchains may be subject to different regulatory frameworks depending on their legal nature. Compliance with regulations, such as data protection, securities laws, anti-money laundering (AML), and know-your-customer (KYC) requirements, can impact the valuation of blockchain-based assets or projects. Failure to comply with relevant regulations can result in legal risks and potential penalties.
2. Legal Status of Smart Contracts: The legal recognition and enforceability of smart contracts can vary depending on the jurisdiction and the legal nature of the blockchain. The legal status of smart contracts affects their credibility, enforceability, and the level of trust associated with them. The valuation of blockchain projects that heavily rely on smart contracts may be influenced by the legal framework supporting their operation.
3. Intellectual Property Rights: The legal nature of the blockchain can impact intellectual property rights associated with blockchain-based assets, protocols, or innovations. Ownership, protection, and licensing of intellectual property assets can play a significant role in the valuation of blockchain projects. Clear legal frameworks and intellectual property rights protection can enhance the value of blockchain assets and incentivize innovation.

4. Liability Considerations: The legal nature of the blockchain may affect liability considerations for participants in the network. It can impact issues such as accountability for fraudulent or illicit activities, liability for data breaches or security incidents, and dispute resolution mechanisms. Clarity regarding liability and legal responsibilities can influence the perception of risk and, subsequently, the valuation of blockchain-based projects.
5. Contractual Agreements: The legal nature of public or private blockchains can influence contractual agreements between participants, stakeholders, or users. Agreements governing token sales, licensing, partnership agreements, or user agreements should align with the legal requirements and offer sufficient legal protection. Well-defined contractual relationships can enhance trust, reduce legal risks, and positively impact the valuation of blockchain projects.
6. Jurisdictional Considerations: The legal nature of public or private blockchains may depend on the jurisdiction in which they operate. Different jurisdictions have varying legal frameworks and regulatory approaches toward blockchain technology. Valuation considerations should account for the legal and regulatory environment in the relevant jurisdictions to ensure compliance and mitigate legal risks.

The legal nature of public or private blockchains is a complex and evolving area, with variations across jurisdictions.

The legal nature of the blockchain is essential for its valuation. There are three main kinds of blockchain:

1. Public;
2. Private;
3. Consortium.

There are different types of blockchains: some are open and public while others are private and only accessible to specific users.

A public blockchain is an open network. Anyone can download the protocol and read, write, or participate in the network. A public blockchain is distributed and decentralized.

Transactions are recorded as blocks and linked together to form a chain. Each new block must be timestamped and validated by all the computers connected to the network, known as nodes before it is written into the blockchain.

All transactions are public, and all nodes have the same importance (and value). Therefore, a public blockchain cannot be modified: once verified, data cannot be altered. The best-known public blockchains used for cryptocurrency are Bitcoin and Ethereum: open-source, smart contract blockchains.

A private blockchain is a controlled ledger governed by a single entity that can be accessed only by specific users. A new user requires permission to read, write, or audit the blockchain. There can be different levels of access restrictions and information can be encrypted to protect commercial confidentiality. Private blockchains allow organizations to employ distributed ledger technology without making the data public. However, this implies the lack of a defining feature of blockchains: decentralization. Some critics claim that private blockchains are not blockchains at all, but only centralized databases using distributed ledger technology. Private blockchains appear to be faster, more efficient, and more cost-effective than public blockchains, which require a lot of time and energy to validate transactions.

A blockchain does not represent a firm but a semi-public good (public or private) that is shared among different stakeholders that co-create value by constructing and implementing a sequential pattern of codes. As a result, the evaluation of a blockchain is very different from that of a firm or a physical asset (Fig. 6.3).

Public blockchains are open to everyone and anyone can participate in the network. They are decentralized and there is no central authority controlling the network. Private blockchains, on the other hand, are only accessible to a specific group of people or organizations, and they are typically centralized with controlling authority. Finally, consortium blockchains are a hybrid model that combines aspects of both public and private blockchains. In consortium blockchains, a group of organizations or entities come together to form a network that is controlled by a small number of trusted nodes.

Public blockchains are non-marketable, meaning that it is difficult to assess their potential value; they may have a symbolic value emerging from the public savings that they enable; the real value accrues to each user.

A firm may own a private blockchain, and valuation patterns may follow its innovative revenue model. Revenues deriving from new businesses are hard to assess since they lack historical performance records and do

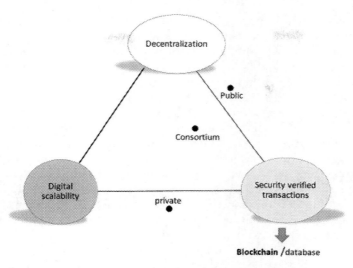

Fig. 6.3 Public, private, and consortium Blockchain

not follow traditional patterns. Profit streams can derive from subscriptions, pay-per-use income, performance-based fees (cashing in part of the savings of the blockchain users), or extraction of validated big data (sold outside for vertical advertising; e-commerce applications, etc.).

Public blockchains lack ultimate private ownership and may be harder to evaluate. They represent the only fully decentralized model.

Semi-public blockchains may somewhat resemble consortiums. A consortium is an association of two or more individuals, companies, organizations, or governments (or any combination of these entities) that participate in a shared activity or pool their resources to achieve a common goal. This may be consistent with blockchains, joint ventures, company networks, and value co-creation paradigms, representing an innovative business model. Different stakeholders may join in setting up co-opetition, by merging cooperation and competition. Co-opetition is used when companies that are, otherwise, competitors, collaborate in a consortium on areas non-strategic to their core businesses. They prefer to reduce their costs in these non-strategic areas and compete in other areas where they can differentiate better. The value of consortium membership is typically derived from the private rents that any participants can extract from it, being the consortium a non-profit alliance.

The business model of the blockchain influences its peculiar corporate governance issues (Yermack, 2017). Their peer-to-peer (P2P) interactions may link stakeholders and in general, do not coincide with the ordinary stakeholders of a firm (shareholders; debtholders; employees; managers; suppliers, clients, etc.). Whereas value co-creation is typical of digital businesses, sharing of co-created value tends to work differently. For example, social networks are based on shared information (personal data) that platforms can monetize unilaterally, through the tacit and unaware consent of the participants. Blockchains work differently, and their decentralization prevents the abuses of a pivoting platform since there are no dominant players able to distort competition, exploiting information asymmetries.

"Consortium blockchains differ from their public counterparts in that they require access permissions: the bare availability of an Internet connection is not enough to gain access to this sort of blockchain. Consortium blockchains can be semi-decentralized. Control over a consortium blockchain is not granted to a single entity, but rather to a group of approved individuals. With a consortium blockchain, the consensus process is likely to differ from that of a public blockchain. (…) Thus, consortium blockchains have the security features that are inherent to public blockchains while allowing for a greater degree of control over the network".

Each stakeholder has an interest in the decentralized blockchain and gets monetary or non-monetary remuneration from her or his participation. Stakeholders are like the participants of a consortium (so with no economic gain target) and may share the services and information that the blockchain offers or could be remunerated with crypto-assets (digital virtual units mainly represented by tokens or cryptocurrencies).

What matters is the capital gain or value-added that each participant could achieve in terms of incremental income from using the blockchain. It is in practice difficult to evaluate a blockchain per se, since, as stated above, it is neither a firm nor an asset but a good that is sharable among its participants.

Federated blockchains operate under multiple authorities instead of a single trusted node. Authority nodes are pre-selected from the adherents to the network.

6.5 Valuation Patterns

When evaluating blockchain technology for a specific use case or project, several key approaches can be considered. Here are some evaluation approaches for blockchain technology:

1. Problem–Solution Fit: Evaluate whether blockchain technology is the appropriate solution for the identified problem or challenge. Consider the characteristics of blockchain, such as decentralization, immutability, transparency, and trust, and assess if they align with the requirements and objectives of the use case.
2. Technical Feasibility: Assess the technical feasibility and capabilities of blockchain technology. Consider factors such as scalability, security, consensus mechanisms, interoperability, and the ability to handle transaction volume and throughput. Evaluate the maturity and robustness of the blockchain platform or protocol being considered.
3. Business Value and ROI: Determine the potential business value and return on investment (ROI) that blockchain technology can bring. Assess the expected cost savings, efficiency gains, revenue opportunities, and competitive advantages that can be achieved through blockchain implementation. Consider factors such as the elimination of intermediaries, process automation, enhanced data integrity, and improved customer experience.
4. Ecosystem and Network Effects: Evaluate the existing ecosystem and network effects surrounding blockchain technology. Assess the size, diversity, and engagement of the community, as well as the presence of supportive infrastructure, such as wallets, exchanges, and development tools. Consider the potential for collaboration, partnerships, and network effects that can amplify the value and adoption of the blockchain solution.
5. Regulatory and Legal Considerations: Assess the regulatory and legal landscape relevant to the use case and blockchain implementation. Determine if there are any legal barriers, compliance requirements, or potential risks associated with regulatory frameworks, data protection, intellectual property, or financial regulations. Ensure that the proposed use of blockchain aligns with applicable laws and regulations.

6. Security and Privacy: Evaluate the security and privacy measures provided by blockchain technology. Assess the consensus mechanism, encryption techniques, data storage mechanisms, and access controls implemented by the blockchain platform. Consider the potential risks and vulnerabilities associated with the technology and evaluate whether the chosen blockchain solution provides adequate security measures.
7. User Experience and Adoption: Assess the user experience and adoption potential of the blockchain solution. Consider factors such as ease of use, accessibility, and familiarity for end-users. Evaluate if the benefits of blockchain technology outweigh the potential challenges and complexities for users. User-centric design and seamless integration with existing systems can contribute to successful adoption and utilization.
8. Scalability and Interoperability: Evaluate the scalability and interoperability of the blockchain solution. Consider the ability of the blockchain network to handle increasing transaction volumes without sacrificing performance. Assess the potential for interoperability with other blockchain networks or legacy systems to facilitate seamless data exchange and integration.
9. Governance and Sustainability: Assess the governance and sustainability aspects of blockchain technology. Evaluate the decision-making processes, consensus mechanisms, and mechanisms for upgrades and changes to the blockchain protocol. Consider the governance structure and incentives that promote the long-term development, maintenance, and evolution of the blockchain ecosystem.
10. Total Cost of Ownership: Evaluate the total cost of ownership associated with the blockchain implementation. Consider the initial setup costs, ongoing maintenance expenses, and infrastructure requirements. Assess if the benefits of blockchain technology outweigh the costs over the long term.

A comprehensive evaluation should consider technical, business, regulatory, security, user-centric, and economic factors to determine the suitability and potential value of blockchain technology for a specific use case. Collaboration with domain experts, blockchain professionals, and stakeholders can provide valuable insights throughout the evaluation process.

There are several evaluation approaches for blockchain technology, including:

1. Security evaluation—ensuring that the blockchain is safe from malicious attacks and that user data is protected.
2. Performance evaluation—analyzing the blockchain's ability to handle large amounts of data and transactions without compromising its speed.
3. Scalability evaluation—assessing the blockchain's ability to grow and support an increasing number of users and transactions over time.
4. Interoperability evaluation—ensuring that the blockchain can interact with other blockchains and traditional systems.
5. Governance evaluation—assessing the governance mechanism of the blockchain network, including decision-making and dispute resolution processes.
6. Economic evaluation—analyzing the economic incentives of the blockchain and its impact on the broader ecosystem.

Concerning, in particular, the economic valuation approaches for blockchains, we should consider:

1. Token-based valuation: This approach values a blockchain network based on the price of its tokens or cryptocurrencies, as determined by market demand and supply. Token-based valuation for blockchains is a method of determining the value of a blockchain network based on the value of its native tokens. This method takes into account various factors such as the network's functionality, adoption rate, and ecosystem. One of the key aspects of token-based valuation is understanding the use cases of the token. For example, if a token is used to pay for transactions on the network, its value may be tied to the number of transactions taking place. Similarly, if a token is used for governance, its value may be linked to the level of participation and decision-making power within the network. Other factors that can impact token-based valuation include the token's scarcity, liquidity, and market demand. In general, the more useful and in-demand a token is within a blockchain ecosystem, the higher its valuation is likely to be.

2. Network-based valuation: This approach values a blockchain network based on its ability to attract and retain users, developers, and investors. The more users, developers, and investors a blockchain network has, the more valuable it is considered to be. Network-based valuation for blockchains refers to the measurement of the value of a blockchain network by analyzing the number and activity level of users on the network. This is typically done by examining metrics such as the number of transactions, the amount of computing power being used, and the level of network engagement. By analyzing these metrics, we can gain insights into the health and value of the network, which can be useful for investors, developers, and other stakeholders interested in the blockchain ecosystem.
3. Transaction-based valuation: This approach values a blockchain network based on the number and value of transactions that take place on the network. The more transactions that occur on a blockchain network, the more valuable it is considered to be. Transaction-based valuation for blockchains is a method of assessing the value of a particular blockchain network by analyzing the transactions that occur on that network. This approach looks at factors such as the number of transactions, transaction fees, and the value of the transactions processed on the blockchain. By examining these metrics, we can get a sense of the network's popularity, utility, and value. Of course, there are other factors to consider as well, such as the underlying technology, the development team, and the network's roadmap for future improvements. But analyzing transactions is certainly a useful tool for evaluating the potential value of a blockchain network.
4. Utility-based valuation: This approach values a blockchain network based on its ability to provide useful services and solutions to real-world problems. The more useful a blockchain network is, the more valuable it is considered to be. Utility-based valuation for blockchains is a method of assessing the potential value of blockchain technology or cryptocurrency based on its ability to solve real-world problems and provide useful solutions. This approach considers factors such as the functionality and ease of use of the technology, the size and growth potential of the user base, and the level of competition in the market. By considering these factors, a

utility-based valuation can provide a more accurate and comprehensive picture of the long-term potential of blockchain technology or cryptocurrency.

On a complementary side, there are several approaches to evaluating smart transactions, depending on the specific context and objectives. Some common evaluation methods include:

1. Technical evaluation: This involves assessing the technical capabilities of the smart contract, such as its security, scalability, and interoperability.
2. Performance evaluation: This involves measuring the efficiency and effectiveness of the smart contract in terms of its speed, accuracy, and responsiveness.
3. User-centered evaluation: This involves assessing the user experience and satisfaction with the smart contract, including its ease of use, accessibility, and value.
4. Economic evaluation: This involves analyzing the economic impact of the smart contract, including its cost-effectiveness and potential for generating value.
5. Social evaluation: This involves assessing the social impact of the smart contract, including its potential to promote social good, reduce inequality, and promote sustainable development.

The evaluation approach should be tailored to the specific needs of the smart contract and its stakeholders and should aim to provide a comprehensive understanding of its strengths, weaknesses, and potential for improvement.

6.6 Blockchains and Cryptocurrencies

There is a strong link between blockchains and cryptocurrencies. While blockchains are the underlying technology that enables cryptocurrencies, cryptocurrencies are digital assets that utilize blockchain technology for their creation, transfer, and storage. Here are some key aspects of the link between blockchains and cryptocurrencies:

1. Blockchain as the Foundation: Blockchains serve as the foundational technology for cryptocurrencies. A blockchain is a distributed ledger that records and verifies transactions across a network of computers or nodes. It ensures transparency, security, and immutability of transaction data. Cryptocurrencies are typically built on top of blockchains, utilizing them to facilitate secure and decentralized transactions.
2. Digital Asset Creation: Cryptocurrencies are digital assets that exist on blockchains. They are created through various mechanisms, such as mining (e.g., Bitcoin) or token issuance (e.g., Ethereum). Cryptocurrencies are designed to serve as mediums of exchange, stores of value, or units of account within their respective blockchain networks.
3. Transaction Validation and Consensus: Blockchains utilize consensus mechanisms, such as proof of work or proof of stake, to validate and confirm transactions. Cryptocurrencies rely on these consensus mechanisms to ensure the integrity and security of transactions. Miners or validators in the blockchain network validate transactions and add them to the blockchain's transaction history.
4. Decentralization and Trust: Blockchains provide a decentralized and trustless environment for cryptocurrencies. The decentralized nature of blockchains eliminates the need for intermediaries, such as banks or payment processors, by allowing direct peer-to-peer transactions. Cryptocurrencies leverage this decentralization to enable secure and transparent value transfers without relying on a central authority.
5. Wallets and Private Keys: Cryptocurrencies are stored and managed through digital wallets. Wallets contain private keys that allow users to access and control their cryptocurrency holdings. These private keys interact with the blockchain to authorize transactions and update ownership records. Wallets can be software-based, hardware-based, or even paper-based, depending on the level of security desired.
6. Tokenization and Smart Contracts: Blockchains enable the tokenization of assets and the creation of smart contracts. Tokens can represent various forms of value, such as ownership rights, voting rights, or access rights. Smart contracts are self-executing contracts with terms and conditions written into code on the blockchain. They enable programmable actions and automate the execution of

predefined conditions, adding functionality and utility to cryptocurrencies.
7. Market Dynamics: Cryptocurrencies operate within their respective markets, where they can be bought, sold, and exchanged for other cryptocurrencies or traditional fiat currencies. Cryptocurrency exchanges provide platforms for trading and liquidity, enabling users to buy, sell, and speculate on the value of cryptocurrencies. Market dynamics, such as supply and demand, investor sentiment, and regulatory factors, impact the value and volatility of cryptocurrencies.

While cryptocurrencies are a prominent application of blockchain technology, blockchains have broader applications beyond cryptocurrencies. They can be used for various purposes, including supply chain management, decentralized finance (DeFi), identity verification, and more. Nevertheless, cryptocurrencies remain one of the most significant and visible use cases of blockchain technology.

Blockchain technology plays a crucial role in the functioning and valuation of cryptocurrencies. Here are a few ways in which blockchain influences the value of cryptocurrencies:

1. Security: The distributed ledger technology of blockchain offers a high level of security, with its ability to be transparent and resistant to modification of the data. A blockchain that is considered secure and robust can increase the perceived value and trust in the associated cryptocurrency.
2. Scalability: The capability of the blockchain to handle a large number of transactions per second can influence the value of its associated cryptocurrency. Cryptocurrencies that can handle a high volume of transactions quickly and efficiently, like those based on more scalable blockchains, may be valued higher.
3. Decentralization: A key feature of blockchain technology is decentralization, which means that no single entity has control over the entire network. The degree of decentralization can influence a cryptocurrency's value, as it may be perceived as being more secure and less susceptible to manipulation.
4. Smart Contracts: Some blockchains, like Ethereum, allow for the execution of smart contracts. These are self-executing contracts with the terms directly written into code. Cryptocurrencies that support

smart contracts can potentially have additional utility, and this can affect their value.
5. Community and Developer Support: The development community around a blockchain can have a significant influence on the value of the associated cryptocurrency. Active development can lead to improvements, fixes, and new features, which can enhance the value of the cryptocurrency. Similarly, a large and active user community can increase demand for the cryptocurrency, driving up its value.
6. Adoption and Partnerships: Widespread adoption of a blockchain, as well as partnerships with businesses or other entities, can greatly influence the value of the associated cryptocurrency. The more widely a blockchain is used, the more valuable the associated cryptocurrency is likely to be.

The nature and quality of the underlying blockchain can significantly impact the valuation of a cryptocurrency. Factors such as security, scalability, decentralization, and the level of developer support all come into play when evaluating the potential value of a cryptocurrency.

REFERENCES

Al-Jaroodi, J., & Mohamed, N. (2019). *Blockchain in industries: A survey*. https://www.researchgate.net/publication/331600305_Blockchain_in_Industries_A_Survey

Andoni, M., et al. (2019, February). Blockchain technology in the energy sector: A systematic review of challenges and opportunities. *Renewable and Sustainable Energy Reviews, 100*, 143–174. https://www.sciencedirect.com/science/article/pii/S1364032118307184

Blossey, G., Eisenhardt, J., & Hahn, G. (2019). Blockchain technology in supply chain management: An application perspective. In *Proceedings of the 52nd Hawaii International Conference on System Sciences*. http://hdl.handle.net/10125/60124

Dujak, D., & Sajter, D. (2019). *Blockchain applications in supply chain*. Springer Verlag.

Fan, T., He, W., Nie, E., & Chen, S. (2017). *A study of pricing and trading model of blockchain & big data-based energy internet electricity*. Paper presented at IOP Conference Series, Earth, and Environmental Science.

Goorha, P. (2018, July). The return of 'The nature of the firm': The role of the blockchain. *Journal of the British Blockchain Association, 1*(1), 1–5.

Korpela, K., Hallikas, J., & Dahlber, T. (2017). *Digital supply chain transformation toward blockchain integration*. Paper presented at the 50th Hawaii International Conference on System Sciences, 4182.

Lotti, L. (2016). Contemporary art, capitalization and the blockchain: On the autonomy and automation of art's value. *Finance and Society, 2*(2), 96.

Lui, P. T. (2016). *Medical record systems using blockchain, big data, and tokenization*. Paper presented at the Information and Communications Security: 18th International Conference (pp. 254–261).

Mao, D., Wang, F., Hao, Z., & Li, H. (2018). Credit Evaluation system based on blockchain for multiple stakeholders in the food supply chain. *International Journal of Environmental Research and Public Health, 15*(8), 1627.

Norman, M. D., Karavas, Y. G., & Reed, H. (2018). *The emergence of trust and value in public blockchain networks*. https://www.researchgate.net/publication/325552991_The_Emergence_of_Trust_and_Value_in_Public_Blockchain_Networks

Saberi, S., Kouhizadeh, M., Sarkis, J., & Shen, L. (2018). Blockchain technology and its relationships to sustainable supply chain management. *International Journal of Production Researching*.

Sawa, T. (2019). Blockchain technology outline and its application to field of power and energy system. *IEEJ Transactions on Power and Energy, 138*(7), 537–540.

Singh, J. P. (2013). On the intricacies of cash flow corporate valuation. *Advances in Management, 6*(3), 15–22.

Veuger, J. (2018). Trust in a viable real estate economy with disruption and blockchain. *Facilities, 36*(1–2), 103–112.

Xie, J., et al. (2019). A survey of blockchain technology applied to smart cities: Research issues and challenges. *IEEE Communications Surveys & Tutorials, 21*(3), 2794–2830.

Yermack, D. (2017). Corporate governance and blockchains. *Review of Finance, 21*(1), 7–31.

CHAPTER 7

The Metaverse

7.1 THE METAVERSE: DEFINITION AND BUSINESS APPLICATIONS

The term "metaverse" refers to a virtual reality-based collective digital universe that encompasses multiple interconnected virtual worlds. It is an immersive and interactive digital space where people can explore, interact with other users, and engage in various activities, often blurring the boundaries between the physical and virtual worlds.

The metaverse can be thought of as a comprehensive and shared virtual/augmented reality digital ecosystem that enables users to create, customize, and inhabit digital avatars, interact with digital objects, and participate in virtual economies and social experiences. It is characterized by its persistent and evolving nature, where content and experiences are continuously created, shared, and interconnected.

The concept of the metaverse has been popularized in science fiction literature and movies, envisioning a future where individuals can seamlessly transition between the physical world and digital realms. It goes beyond traditional gaming environments, aiming to create a fully realized virtual universe that offers diverse experiences, ranging from entertainment and education to commerce and social interactions.

In the metaverse, users can engage in activities such as gaming, socializing, virtual events, education, commerce, art, and more. It often incorporates elements of augmented reality (AR) and virtual reality (VR)

© The Author(s), under exclusive license to Springer Nature Switzerland AG 2023
R. Moro-Visconti and A. Cesaretti, *Digital Token Valuation*, https://doi.org/10.1007/978-3-031-42971-2_7

technologies to provide immersive and interactive experiences. The metaverse is driven by advancements in technology, such as virtual reality headsets, haptic feedback devices, and spatial computing, that enhance the sense of presence and immersion within the digital space.

The concept of the metaverse is still evolving, and there is no universally accepted definition or specific implementation of the metaverse. Various companies, organizations, and developers are working on creating their interpretations and versions of the metaverse, each with their features, ecosystems, and user experiences.

A metaverse is a network of 3D virtual worlds focused on social connection; a set of virtual spaces where an individual can create and explore with other people who are not in the same physical space. It is a powered iteration of the web, designed to bring the digital and physical realms together. Several definitions are reported in https://metaverseroadmap.org/inputs4.html#glossary.

The term "metaverse" has its origins in the 1992 science fiction novel Snow Crash as a portmanteau of "meta" (in Greek $\mu\varepsilon\tau\alpha$ = beyond/transcending) + "universe".

The metaverse is a shared digital and online space that is inhabited by digital twins (avatars) of people, places, and things that interact in real-time, incorporating 3D graphics. Users are expected to be identified by their avatars who will interact in real-time with each other across multiple virtual locations. In addition, they will be able to purchase or build virtual items and environments, such as NFTs.

Regarded as the next iteration of the internet, the metaverse is where the physical and digital worlds come together. As an evolution of social technologies, the metaverse allows digital representations of people, and avatars, to interact with each other in a variety of settings. Whether it be at work, in an office, going to concerts or sports events, or even trying on clothes, the metaverse provides a space for endless, interconnected virtual communities using virtual reality (VR) headsets, augmented reality (AR) glasses, smartphone apps, or other devices (Johnson, 2022).

From a social perspective, the development of more immersive virtual experiences is helping people to build communities based on shared values and to express themselves in more authentic ways. Meanwhile, COVID-19 accelerated the digitization of our lives and normalized more persistent and multi-purpose online engagement and communication. It is this combination of technological, social, and economic drivers that is resulting in explosive interest in the metaverse (JP Morgan, 2022).

Metaverse seamlessly integrates the real world with the virtual world and allows avatars to carry out rich activities including creation, display, entertainment, social networking, and trading (Yang et al., 2022). Metaverses have existed for decades in the form of multiplayer online games. But we may soon enter an age of immersive experience hardly distinguishable from our real world—fostering new modes of interaction for gamers and non-gamers alike (https://www.ft.com/partnercontent/crypto-com/nfts-the-metaverse-economy.html).

The metaverse aims to create a shared virtual space that connects all virtual worlds via the Internet, where users, represented as digital avatars, can communicate, and collaborate as if they are in the physical world (Cheng et al., 2022).

According to Gartner's research (2022), the metaverse will require a host of technologies and combinatorial innovations to create a persistent and immersive digital environment. Product leaders across industries must invest selectively and not overspend in the short term, as a complete metaverse will take at least eight years to develop.

The three-step supply and value chain patterns from the physical world to the metaverse (synthesized in Fig. 7.1) pass through the Internet and follow a technological upgrade whose eventual outcome is still uncertain.

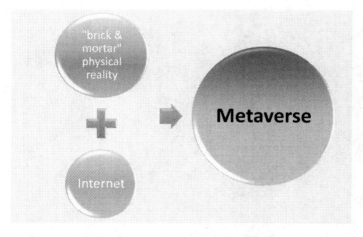

Fig. 7.1 From physical reality to the internet and metaverse

In the future, the metaverse is likely to fully incorporate the earlier-stage Internet dimension.

This study starts from the evidence that physical reality can be partially mapped with network theory, showing the edging links between connected nodes, and their spatial and intertemporal dynamic interaction. The Internet is a network of networks representing a global system of interconnected computer networks. The metaverse is a network of 3D virtual worlds focused on social connection. There is an evident Ariadne's thread between these ecosystems, interpreted with multilayer network theory that examines the connectivity and interdependency between nodes positioned in the physical world, the web, or the metaverse.

The metaverse is an Internet evolution that is oriented toward shared activities (mainly through social networking) with an exponential rise in creativeness, unleashed by a decentralized ecosystem, and integrated technologies, as shown in Fig. 7.2.

This pioneering study illustrates a new research avenue, analyzing the application of some of the most evident properties of network theory to the case, showing for instance how replica (corresponding) nodes can link through an avatar (an "augmented/virtual" replica node, acting as a

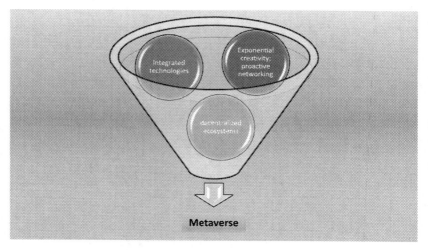

Fig. 7.2 Metaverse constituents

"digital twin") the physical world with the metaverse. Avatar is a concept within Hinduism that in Sanskrit literally means "descent". It signifies the material appearance or incarnation of a powerful deity, goddess, or spirit on Earth. Consistently with this framework, the main research question of this chapter is to investigate the potential market value of metaverse ecosystems, using a with-and-without differential approach, the scalable network approach, or multilayer network metrics.

7.2 Scale-Free Networks and the Metaverse Topology

Scale-free networks are a type of network topology characterized by the presence of a small number of highly connected nodes, often referred to as "hubs," and a large number of sparsely connected nodes. In a scale-free network, the distribution of connections or degrees follows a power law distribution, meaning that there are relatively few nodes with a high degree of connectivity and a large number of nodes with a low degree of connectivity.

The metaverse, as a concept, does not inherently have a prescribed or standardized topology. However, it is possible to explore how scale-free networks could potentially manifest within the metaverse context. Here are some considerations:

1. Hubs in the Metaverse: In the context of the metaverse, hubs could represent highly popular or influential virtual spaces, platforms, or experiences that attract a large number of users. These hubs could be the central gathering points or focal areas within the metaverse, offering a diverse range of activities and interactions.
2. Connectivity Distribution: The scale-free nature of the metaverse topology would imply that while there are a few highly connected hubs, the majority of nodes in the metaverse would have limited connections. This could be represented by users or virtual locations that have fewer connections but still contribute to the overall connectivity of the metaverse.
3. Information Flow and Influence: Scale-free networks can exhibit efficient information flow due to the presence of highly connected hubs that act as intermediaries or bridges between different parts of the network. In the metaverse, these hubs could play a significant

role in disseminating information, fostering social interactions, and influencing the overall dynamics of the virtual environment.
4. Resilience and Robustness: Scale-free networks are known to be resilient against random node failures but vulnerable to targeted attacks on highly connected hubs. This characteristic may have implications for the metaverse's stability and resilience. Protecting the integrity and availability of the metaverse's hubs could be crucial to maintaining a functional and robust virtual environment.

The metaverse is still a concept under development, and its exact topology and network characteristics may vary depending on the specific implementations and technological advancements. The interconnectivity and network structure within the metaverse will likely evolve based on user behavior, platform design, and the emergence of new technologies that support virtual interactions.

Network theory (see Barabási, 2016; Caldarelli & Catanzaro, 2011; Estrada & Knight, 2015; Jackson, 2008; Van Steen, 2010), is the study of graphs as a representation of either symmetric or asymmetric relations between discrete objects. Patients are a key albeit under-investigated stakeholder and smart technologies applied to public healthcare represent a trendy innovation that reshapes the value-driving proposition.

The World Wide Web is a network whose nodes are documents, and the links are the uniform resource locators (URLs) that allow one to "surf" with a click from one web document to the other (Barabási, 2016).

A scale-free network is a decentralized network whose degree distribution follows a power law and is characterized by the presence of large hubs. Decentralization is consistent with the web, blockchains, and the metaverse.

A scale-free network looks like an air-traffic network, whose nodes are airports and links are the direct flights between them. Most airports are tiny, with only a few flights. Yet, we have a few very large airports, like Chicago or Los Angeles, that act as major hubs, connecting many smaller airports.

Once hubs are present, they change the way we navigate the network. For example, if we travel from Boston to Los Angeles by car, we must drive through many cities. On the airplane network, however, we can reach most destinations via a single hub, like Chicago (Barabási, 2016).

Scale-free networks have a very heterogeneous distribution of degrees, and their dynamical behavior is dominated by the hub nodes having a degree order of magnitude larger than the average.

The topology of the metaverse influences its dynamics, workings, and wealth distribution. According to Radoff (2021), the metaverse, consistent with the Internet, is more like a scale-free network than a "hub and spoke" architecture, where every network node connects to a central authority that is responsible for controlling access and managing any of the exchanges.

In scale-free networks (e.g., the Internet, open-source software, smart contract blockchains, etc.), the central node acts more like a facilitator than an authority, and nodes are then free to connect.

The Barabási and Albert (2002) model is an algorithm for generating random scale-free networks using a preferential attachment mechanism. Several natural and human-made systems, including the Internet, the world wide web, citation networks, and some social networks are thought to be approximately scale-free and certainly contain few nodes (called hubs) with an unusually high degree as compared to the other nodes of the network. The Barabási and Albert model tries to explain the existence of such nodes in real networks.

7.3 Scalability and the Network Effect

Scalability and the network effect are two important concepts that are closely related in the context of platforms, technologies, and ecosystems. Scalability refers to the ability of a system, platform, or technology to handle increasing demand, user base, or workload without compromising performance, efficiency, or user experience. In other words, it's about the system's capacity to scale up or down to meet the needs of growing or fluctuating usage.

In the context of the metaverse or any digital platform, scalability is crucial. As the user base and activities within the metaverse grow, the platform must be able to handle the increasing number of users, transactions, interactions, and content without experiencing performance issues or degradation.

Scalability can be achieved through various means, including optimizing software architecture, utilizing distributed computing resources, implementing efficient data management techniques, and leveraging technologies like cloud computing or sharding. Scalability is essential for ensuring a seamless and enjoyable user experience within the metaverse.

The network effect refers to the phenomenon where the value or utility of a product, service, or platform increases as the number of users or participants grows. It suggests that the more people join and engage with a network, the more valuable it becomes for all users.

In the context of the metaverse, the network effect is significant. As more users join the metaverse and participate in virtual interactions, the value of the metaverse increases. This is because a larger user base leads to more content, social interactions, economic opportunities, and overall engagement within the virtual environment.

The network effect can create positive feedback loops, attracting more users and stakeholders, which further enhances the value and appeal of the metaverse. It fosters a sense of community, encourages collaboration, and drives the growth and sustainability of the metaverse ecosystem.

Scalability and the network effect are interconnected. The ability of a platform or technology to scale effectively is often critical for harnessing and sustaining the network effect. A scalable infrastructure ensures that as the network effect takes hold and the user base grows, the platform can accommodate the increased demand and continue to deliver value and quality experiences to users.

By addressing scalability challenges, platforms can support the increasing user base, capitalize on the network effect, and unlock the full potential of the metaverse as a thriving digital ecosystem.

Economic and financial margins that represent a primary parameter for valuation are boosted by cost savings and scalable increases in expected revenues. Digitalized intangibles synergistically interact through networked platforms that reshape traditional supply chains. Link (edge) overlaps and replica nodes foster these synergies.

The three main Laws of Network Effect are intrinsically consistent with the scalability properties:

(a) Sarnoff's Law: David Sarnoff led the Radio Corporation of America (which created NBC) from 1919 until 1970. It was one of the largest networks in the world during those years. Sarnoff observed that the value of his network seemed to increase in direct proportion to its size—proportional to N, where N is the total number of users on the network. Sarnoff's description of network value ended

up being an underestimate for SNS types of networks, although it was an accurate description of broadcast networks with a few central nodes broadcasting to many marginal nodes (a radio or television audience).
(b) Metcalfe's Law: Metcalfe's Law states that the value of a communications network grows in proportion to the square of the number of users on the network (N^2, where N is the total number of users on the network). The formulation of this concept is attributed to Robert Metcalfe, one of the inventors of the Ethernet standard. Metcalfe's Law seems to hold because the number of links between nodes on a network increases mathematically at a rate of N^2, where N is the number of nodes. Although originally formulated to describe communication networks like the ethernet, faxing, or phones, with the arrival of the Internet, it has evolved to describe SNSs as well.
(c) Reed's Law: it was published by Reed (2001). While Reed acknowledged that "many kinds of value grow proportionally to network size" and that some grow as a proportion to the square of network size, he suggested that "group-forming networks" that allow for the formation of clusters (as described above) scale value even faster than other networks. Group-forming networks, according to Reed, increase value at a rate of 2N, where N is the total number of nodes on the network. Reed suggested the formula of 2N instead of N^2 because the number of possible groups within a network that "supports easy group communication" is much higher than 1 so the total number of connections in the network (the network density) is not just a function of the total number of nodes (N). It is a function of the total number of nodes plus the total number of possible sub-groupings or clusters, which scales at a much faster rate with the addition of more users to the network. Since most online networks allow for the formation of clusters, they will likely behave at least somewhat as Reed's Law suggests and grow in value at a much faster rate than either Metcalfe's Law or Sarnoff's Law suggests.

Metcalfe's Law proposes that the value of a network increases geometrically with every device that's added. It explains why the telephone network and the Internet are so valuable and continue to increase in value.

Reed's Law posits that Metcalfe's Law underestimates the value of a network, especially those in which it is easy to form subgroups.

Table 7.1. (already analyzed in Chapter 3) synthesizes the main properties of some of the most known network laws. Many of these laws are empirical, with a weak scientific background and controversial evidence. Technological evolution is intrinsically difficult to forecast and so differs from its expected patterns. Most of the scalability laws recalled in the following table may so look outdated or imprecise. They are, however, useful since they recall some basic principles and retain an orientation predictive power, giving a rough idea of how scalability patterns may evolve. A common denominator is represented by statistical "power laws" (according to which one quantity varies as a power of another) that are intrinsically consistent with the scalability patterns.

Here are a few examples of Reed's Law in action:

- Social Media of all kinds (Facebook/Meta, TikTok, etc.) are so valuable because everyone is the center of their subgroups, and everyone can easily add content.
- Messaging applications like Discord allow you to easily form groups that serve as conversation hubs for games and projects.
- Open-Source software is incredibly powerful because projects can form and evolve rapidly, by opening participation from anyone who wants to contribute—building upon contributions from completely unrelated projects.
- Wikipedia became so important because content can be managed and evolved by the sphere of people who care most about certain topics. The collective value of Wikipedia increases as people maintain more content, which in turn expands the audience, resulting in people wanting to add more content to it.
- Online games with social features (multiplayer games, games featuring esports) are so sticky because each one acts as a type of social network where you join up with other people, participate in activities, and form friendships and rivalries.

Reed's Law is often mentioned when explaining the competitive dynamics of internet platforms. As the law states a network becomes more valuable when people can easily form subgroups to collaborate, while this value increases exponentially with the number of connections, a business

Table 7.1 Network scalability laws

Scalability law	Formula	Features/properties
Sarnoff's law	Network Value = n	The value of a network seemed to increase in direct proportion to the size of the network—proportional to N, where N is the total number of users on the network
Metcalfe's law	Network Value = n^2	Network value increases exponentially with an increasing number of devices on the network
Reed's law	Network Value = 2^n	Network value increases even more than Metcalfe's as subgroups (social networks; messaging apps, etc.) become easier to form. Reed's law is consistent with multilayer network extensions
Moore's law	$no = n02(yi - y0)/T2$, where n0n0 is the number of transistors in some reference year, y0y0, and T2 = 2T2 = 2 is the number of years taken to double this number	A doubling of real computing power has occurred every 2.3 years, on average since the birth of modern computing. Moore's Law is one of several enabling technological trends for Metaverse development. Rather than a law of physics, it is an empirical relationship linked to gains from experience in production
Henderson law		Henderson's Law also known as a variant of the "Power law" is a mathematical formula for calculating experience curves and their economic impact. It was first proposed by Bruce Henderson in 1968 while working for the Boston Consulting Group to generalize unit costs of production over time and by volume

(continued)

Table 7.1 (continued)

Scalability law	Formula	Features/properties
Wright's law	$C_n = C_1 n^{-a}$ where: C_1 is the cost of the first unit of production C_n is the cost of the n-th unit of production n is the cumulative volume of production a is the elasticity of cost regarding output	Wright found that every time total aircraft production doubled, the required labor time for a new aircraft fell by 20%. This has become known as "Wright's law". Studies in other industries have yielded different percentage values (ranging from only a couple of percent up to 30%), but in most cases, the value in each industry was a constant percentage and did not vary at different scales of operation. The learning curve model posits that for each doubling of the total quantity of items produced, costs decrease by a fixed proportion. Generally, the production of any good or service shows the learning curve or experience curve effect. Each time cumulative volume doubles, value-added costs (including administration, marketing, distribution, and manufacturing) fall by a constant percentage
Kryder's law		Storage capacity growth. Kryder's Law is the assumption that magnetic disk drive density, also known as areal density, will double every thirteen months. Kryder's Law implies that as areal density improves, storage will become cheaper
Butters' law		Butters' law says that the amount of data coming out of an optical fiber is doubling every nine months. Thus, the cost of transmitting a bit over an optical network decreases by half every nine months
Nielsen's law		Wired bandwidth growth
Gilder's law		The total bandwidth of communication systems triples every twelve months

(continued)

Table 7.1 (continued)

Scalability law	Formula	Features/properties
Cooper's law		Wireless bandwidth growth. The number of wireless signals that can simultaneously be transmitted without interfering with each other has been doubling approximately every 30 months since the early 1900s. This steady rise of wireless capabilities also has allowed access and distribution of news, entertainment, advertising, and other information to become truly mobile
Poor's law		Network address density growth
Beckström's law (2008)		The value of a network equals the net value added to each user's transactions conducted through that network, summed over all users. This model values the network by looking from the edge of the network at all of the transactions conducted and the value added to each. It states that one way to contemplate the value the network adds to each transaction is to imagine the network being shut off and what the additional transaction costs or loss would be
Radoff's law	[qualitative proposition]	The degree to which a network facilitates interconnections determines the extent of its emergent creativity, innovation, and wealth
Metaverse extension		3D dimension, increased networking, technological upgrade, etc. improve scalability and so value

platform that reaches enough members can generate network effects that dominate the overall economics of the system.

Other analysts of network value functions, including Odlyzko and Tilly (2005), have argued that both Reed's Law and Metcalfe's Law overstate network value because they fail to account for the restrictive impact of human cognitive limits on network formation.

7.4 Multilayer Networks

Multilayer networks refer to complex systems that consist of multiple interconnected layers, where each layer represents a distinct set of interactions or relationships. In the context of the metaverse, multilayer networks can be relevant to capture the diverse and interconnected nature of interactions within the virtual environment. Here's how multilayer networks relate to the metaverse:

1. Interactions Across Layers: The metaverse can involve multiple layers of interactions, each representing different aspects of the virtual environment. These layers could include social interactions, economic transactions, content creation, virtual object interactions, and more. Each layer represents a distinct network of connections and relationships. Multilayer networks provide a framework for understanding and analyzing these interconnected layers of interactions within the metaverse.
2. Layer Interdependencies: The layers within the metaverse are not isolated but often have interdependencies and interactions between them. For example, social interactions can influence economic transactions, and content creation can impact social dynamics. Multilayer network analysis helps identify and understand these interdependencies, providing insights into how changes in one layer may affect others within the metaverse ecosystem.
3. Network Dynamics: Multilayer networks can capture the dynamics and evolution of interactions within the metaverse over time. Changes in user behavior, the emergence of new content or services, or shifts in economic activities can all impact the structure and dynamics of the interconnected layers. Analyzing the multilayer network dynamics helps in understanding the evolving nature of the metaverse and its components.
4. Robustness and Resilience: Multilayer network analysis can provide insights into the robustness and resilience of the metaverse ecosystem. By examining the interdependencies and redundancies between layers, it becomes possible to assess how the metaverse can withstand disturbances or disruptions in one layer without cascading effects on other layers. This understanding helps in designing and building a more resilient and robust metaverse.

5. Optimization and Efficiency: Multilayer network analysis enables the identification of optimal strategies for resource allocation, content distribution, or user engagement across different layers of the metaverse. By considering the interconnectedness between layers, it becomes possible to optimize system-wide performance and efficiency. This can lead to improved user experiences, resource utilization, and overall effectiveness of the metaverse ecosystem.
6. Integration and Interoperability: Multilayer networks can help address the challenges of integration and interoperability between different platforms, technologies, or applications within the metaverse. As the metaverse evolves, it is likely to include diverse systems and technologies, each representing a different layer of interactions. Analyzing and understanding the interplay between these layers can facilitate seamless integration and interoperability, enhancing the overall metaverse experience.

By employing multilayer network analysis, stakeholders within the metaverse ecosystem can gain deeper insights into the complex dynamics, interdependencies, and optimization opportunities that arise from the diverse layers of interactions. This understanding can inform decision-making, system design, and policy development to create a more interconnected and vibrant metaverse environment.

Multilayer networks are networks with multiple kinds of relations with multiplex or multidimensional configurations (Bianconi, 2018; Lee et al., 2015). In a multiplex network, the same set of nodes is connected via more than one type of link, enhancing scalability.

The world is more complex than conventional economic models traditionally assume. Many real-world complex systems are accordingly best modeled by multiplex (multidimensional) networks of interacting layers (Lee et al., 2015). These interconnected systems are very sophisticated and may explain better the applications in the field of social network analysis, economics, operations management, finance, etc., being consistent with corporate governance concerns.

Multilayer networks are an extension of traditional networks and are fully consistent with the framing and research aim of this study. Multilayer networks are intrinsically fit for leveraging the scalability features already examined since they host bridging (replica) nodes, digital networks, or firms that are simultaneously present in several layers. These properties have deep, albeit non-investigated, governance consequences.

Complex multidimensional networks host multiple kinds of relations (multiplex, multilayer, multilevel, multi-relational, interconnected, interdependent, etc.), and may yield valuable insight into many interdisciplinary fields. These networks of networks may affect social networks that involve different types of connections, networks of airports connected by different air carriers, multiple infrastructures of a country that are mutually connected, etc.

Nodes that simultaneously belong to different layers (networks) can be represented mathematically by adjacency tensors with inter-layer edges that connect each network to the other. These links enhance the overall value of the network of networks, boosting Metcalfe's formulation.

Whereas the sophisticated mathematics that explains these relations (see Bianconi, 2018) goes far beyond this preliminary study, some economic implications may be worth considering.

In most real-world systems an individual network is one component within a much larger complex multilevel network (is part of a network of networks). Most real-world network systems continuously interact with other networks.

There is a wide range of systems in the real world where components cannot function independently so these components interact with others through different channels of connectivity and dependencies. Complex Networks theory is, in fact, the formal tool for describing and analyzing fields as disparate as sociology (social networks, acquaintances, or collaborations between individuals), biology (metabolic and protein networks, neural networks), or technology (phone call networks, computers in telecommunication networks).

The inter-layer edges (links) between the different nodes go beyond every single layer and connect two (or more) adjacent layers, resulting in a network of networks with multiple subsystems and connectivity properties. If the links between the nodes increase (both in the same layer and thanks to an inter-layer connection), there is a corresponding value growth of the systemic network of networks that might be estimated with Metcalfe's law. Figure 7.3 shows a simplified example of how multilayer networks interact.

Figure 7.3. shows at first sight that inter-network-bridging edges (that link node in country A with country B, product 1, and product 2) add value to the whole network ecosystem. This incremental value may be tentatively estimated (with a differential without/with approach) by

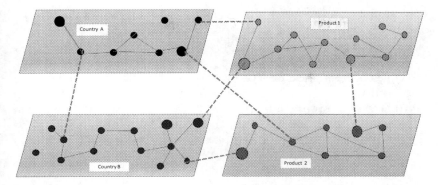

Fig. 7.3 Multilayer networks

comparing unrelated networks with linked ones. An economic interpretation of multiplex networks is—to the author's best knowledge—still underexplored and may be generalized (including further interacting layers in a dynamic ecosystem), giving an innovative explanation of the interactions between e-supply and e-value chains. As anticipated, digital platforms may once again act as the virtual linking edge among the networks.

A multilayer network—of which multiplex and interdependent networks are peculiar cases—is a network made up of multiple layers, each of which represents a given operation mode, social circle, or temporal instance.

In a multiplex network, each type of interaction between the nodes is described by a single-layer network and the different layers of networks describe the different modes of interaction.

Multilayer networks show connectivity links between the nodes of each layer that bring interdependency links.

A key feature of any network is represented by its dynamic properties: a network is hardly ever static, and this is never the case on the Internet–metaverse dimension. Many networks expand and grow by increasing their number of nodes and links over time, following dynamic rules. Examples include the Internet and social online networks this evidence is described by non-equilibrium dynamics important information can be gained by studying non-equilibrium models of growing networks that show scale-free properties that can emerge from simple dynamical rules of network growth.

Dynamical processes include:

(a) Percolation (the behavior of a network when nodes or links are added);
(b) Diffusion/propagation; (the ability to amplify association between nodes that lie in network proximity).
(c) Spreading processes on complex networks, show the transmission probability within and outside a network.

The interplay between the "random versus orderly" structure and the dynamics of multilayer networks contributes to explaining their essential features.

Relevant information from multilayer network data sets cannot be found by considering networks in isolation. Connectedness allows for the possibility of diffusing information and hyper-navigating the network. A further characteristic is represented by communicability—the number of paths that connect the node to the rest of the nodes within the network.

Precious informative sets are represented by big data that are gathered in cloud databases. The digital nature of data softens interoperability concerns, easing information dissemination and exploitation.

This contributes to explaining why interconnected (multilayer) networks are worth more than isolated networks. The implications for metaverse networks that are ontologically connected are evident, albeit hardly investigated.

A further feature is represented by navigability—the possibility of exploring large parts of the network by following its paths through connectedness. This concept can be associated with supply chains and shows which are the iterative patterns from the real world to the metaverse, passing through the Internet.

7.5 Sliding Doors: Network-Bridging Multisided Platforms

Network-bridging multisided platforms connect and facilitate interactions between multiple distinct user groups or networks. These platforms act as intermediaries, enabling transactions, information exchange, or collaboration between these different groups. Here's an overview of network-bridging multisided platforms and their characteristics:

1. Multiple User Groups: Network-bridging multisided platforms serve multiple user groups that have distinct needs, interests, or roles. These user groups can include buyers and sellers, service providers and consumers, content creators and consumers, or any other relevant combinations. The platform brings these groups together, creating value through their interactions.
2. Intermediary Role: The platform acts as an intermediary, providing the infrastructure, tools, and services necessary for users from different groups to connect and engage with each other. It facilitates the exchange of goods, services, information, or other resources, enabling transactions or collaborations that might not have occurred without the platform.
3. Value Creation and Capture: Network-bridging platforms create value by leveraging the interactions and transactions between the different user groups. They facilitate the exchange of goods, services, or information, which leads to value creation for the participating users. The platform captures value through various means, such as transaction fees, advertising revenue, subscription fees, or data monetization.
4. Network Effects: Network effects play a crucial role in the success of network-bridging multisided platforms. As more users join and engage with the platform, it becomes more attractive and valuable for other users, creating a positive feedback loop. The presence of multiple user groups amplifies the network effects, as the value of the platform increases with the growth and activity of each user group.
5. Trust and Reputation: Network-bridging platforms often establish mechanisms to build trust and reputation among user groups. They may implement user rating systems, reviews, verification processes, or escrow services to ensure trustworthiness and quality of interactions. Trust and reputation systems contribute to the smooth functioning of the platform and encourage participation from all user groups.
6. Platform Governance: Network-bridging platforms need to manage the interactions, rules, and policies governing the relationships between different user groups. They establish governance mechanisms that address conflicts of interest, resolve disputes, and make

decisions that impact the platform and its participants. Effective platform governance helps maintain fairness, transparency, and sustainability within the multisided ecosystem.
7. Ecosystem Expansion: Successful network-bridging platforms often aim to expand their ecosystem by attracting additional user groups or creating partnerships with complementary platforms. By expanding the ecosystem, the platform can offer more value, increase user engagement, and strengthen network effects. Ecosystem expansion requires strategic planning, collaboration, and integration with other platforms or services.

Examples of network-bridging multisided platforms include e-commerce marketplaces, sharing economy platforms, social media networks, and online advertising platforms. These platforms bring together different user groups and facilitate transactions, collaborations, or interactions between them, creating value and capturing a portion of it.

Network-bridging multisided platforms have the potential to unlock new business models, enhance market efficiency, and foster innovation by connecting and bridging previously disparate user groups or networks. Multilayer networks are consistent with multisided platforms—a service or product that connects two or more participant groups, playing a kind of intermediation role. Digital platforms, especially if multisided, are an access facilitator to both the web and the metaverse, thanks to their network effects and their virtual/digital nature. Platforms can be IoT-driven (Degrande et al., 2018), and they can incorporate big data or other digitized information.

The multisided platform is a bridging node between two counterparts that are put in contact through the intermediating platform to which each part is affiliated. The platform earns a commission from its mediation or, sometimes, a subscription. The platform may be extended to the metaverse, so representing a portal to this new ecosystem, as exemplified in Fig. 7.4.

The multisided platform business model is adopted by some of the most valuable start-ups in the world, such as PayPal, Uber, Alibaba, eBay, YouTube, and Facebook (Pereira, 2021).

To be useful for all the participant groups and, therefore, a profitable business, the multisided platforms must attract users. The more users,

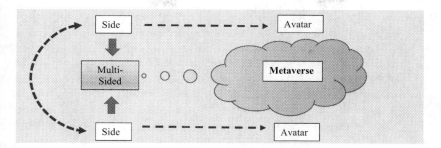

Fig. 7.4 Multisided platforms bridging to the metaverse

the more valuable the platform (https://businessmodelanalyst.com/multisided-platform-business-model/), due to a "snowball" effect ignited by scalability.

7.6 From the Internet to the Metaverse

The evolution from the Internet to the metaverse represents a shift in how we interact with digital content and virtual environments. Here's an overview of the journey from the Internet to the metaverse:

1. Internet: The Internet is a global network of interconnected computers and devices that enables the exchange of information and communication between users. It provides access to websites, online services, and digital content. The Internet revolutionized the way we access information, communicate, conduct business, and engage with digital media.
2. Web 2.0: Web 2.0 refers to the phase of the Internet characterized by user-generated content, social media, and interactive web applications. It marked a transition from static web pages to dynamic platforms that encouraged user participation, collaboration, and content creation. Web 2.0 introduced social networking, online communities, and user-generated content platforms like YouTube and Wikipedia. Content creators are increasingly protected by copyright legislation.

3. Virtual Worlds and Online Games: Virtual worlds and online games emerged as immersive digital environments where users could create avatars, explore virtual spaces, interact with other users, and engage in various activities. These platforms, such as Second Life, World of Warcraft, and Minecraft, showcased early elements of virtual socialization, virtual economies, and user-driven experiences.
4. Augmented Reality (AR) and Virtual Reality (VR): Augmented reality overlays digital content onto the physical world, enhancing real-world experiences, while virtual reality immerses users in entirely virtual environments. AR and VR technologies have advanced significantly, enabling more immersive and interactive digital experiences. They have been instrumental in bridging the gap between the physical and digital realms.
5. Metaverse Concept: The metaverse is an evolving concept that envisions a fully immersive and interconnected virtual reality-based digital universe. It represents a collective virtual space where people can interact, explore, create content, and engage in various activities using VR, AR, or other digital interfaces. The metaverse aims to blur the boundaries between the physical and digital worlds, offering a seamless and immersive user experience.
6. Interconnected Digital Ecosystem: The metaverse is expected to be a highly interconnected digital ecosystem, encompassing multiple virtual worlds, platforms, and experiences. It will integrate social interactions, gaming, virtual commerce, entertainment, education, and more. The metaverse emphasizes user agency, content creation, and collaborative experiences, allowing individuals and communities to shape the virtual environment.
7. Emerging Technologies: The realization of the metaverse relies on advancements in various technologies, including VR, AR, artificial intelligence, blockchain, cloud computing, and haptic feedback. These technologies contribute to immersive experiences, secure transactions, content distribution, and user interactions within the metaverse.

While the Internet has provided the foundation for digital connectivity and information exchange, the metaverse represents a vision of a more immersive and interactive digital realm. It expands upon the concepts of virtual worlds, social networks, and interactive media, aiming to create a fully realized virtual universe with extensive possibilities for exploration, socialization, creativity, and economic activities. The journey from the Internet to the metaverse reflects the ongoing evolution of digital experiences and our increasingly intertwined relationship with virtual environments.

The metaverse can be interpreted as a collection of different virtual worlds built on the blockchain by BigTechs. Segmentation matters and is profitable, at least in the short/medium term since it brings tailor-made ecosystems that reproduce exclusive environments. There is a diverse range of online networks, and dedicated environments allow for better experiences that produce greater engagement.

The metaverse building features are illustrated in Fig. 7.5.

There is no one technology underpinning the metaverse.

Broadly, the technologies that will make it up will include blockchain, cryptocurrencies, virtual and augmented reality, artificial intelligence (a

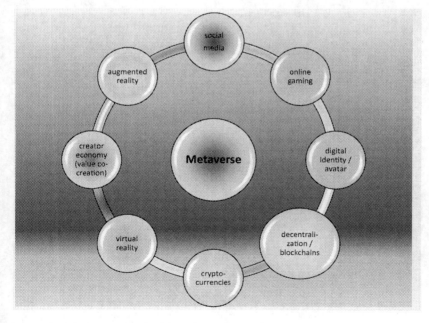

Fig. 7.5 The metaverse building features

key to unlock the metaverse), brain-computer interfaces, and the Internet of Things. Blockchain cryptocurrencies are consistent with Decentralized Finance (De.Fi.). De.Fi. disintermediates the payment system and is driven by FinTechs.

Blockchain technology provides a decentralized and transparent solution for digital proof of ownership, governance, accessibility, digital collectability, transfer of value, and interoperability among complementary databases. Cryptocurrencies enable users to transfer value while they work and socialize in the 3D digital world.

Complex and interdependent technologies are the core constituents of the metaverse ecosystems, as shown in Fig. 7.6.

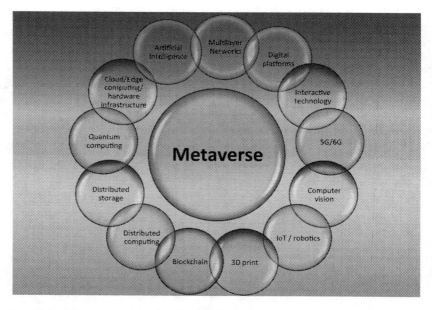

Fig. 7.6 The metaverse technological input factors

7.7 Synchronizing the Physical and Virtual: the Avatar Bridging Node

The concept of synchronizing the physical and virtual realms within the context of the metaverse involves bridging the gap between the real world and the digital environment. One approach to achieving this synchronization is through the use of an "avatar bridging node". Here's an overview of the avatar bridging node and its role in connecting the physical and virtual realms:

1. An avatar bridging node is a component or system that serves as an interface between a user's physical presence or actions and their representation in the virtual world. It enables users to control and interact with their digital avatars, allowing for real-time synchronization of movements, gestures, and actions.
2. Sensor Technologies: Avatar bridging nodes rely on sensor technologies to capture and translate physical movements and inputs into digital representations. These sensors can include motion capture devices, depth cameras, wearable sensors, or biometric sensors that track the user's body movements, facial expressions, or physiological responses.
3. Tracking and Mapping: The avatar bridging node tracks the user's physical movements and maps them onto the corresponding movements of the digital avatar in the virtual world. This mapping ensures that the avatar mimics the user's motions and gestures as accurately as possible, creating a sense of presence and embodiment within the virtual environment.
4. Real-Time Interaction: The avatar bridging node facilitates real-time interaction between the user and the virtual world. It enables users to manipulate virtual objects, engage in social interactions with other avatars, and participate in various activities within the metaverse. The avatar's movements and actions are synchronized with the user's physical inputs, allowing for seamless and immersive experiences.
5. Customization and Personalization: Avatar bridging nodes can also support customization and personalization options, allowing users to tailor their avatars to reflect their physical characteristics, preferences, or desired appearances. Users can choose their avatar's appearance, clothing, and accessories, or even customize its behavior and animations.

6. Multi-Modal Inputs: Avatar bridging nodes can integrate multiple modes of input to enhance the user's control over their avatar. This can include voice recognition, gesture recognition, haptic feedback, or even brain-computer interfaces. The use of multiple input modalities enables users to express themselves and interact with the virtual world in more natural and intuitive ways.
7. Social Presence and Collaboration: Avatar bridging nodes play a crucial role in enabling social presence and collaboration within the metaverse. By accurately reflecting users' physical expressions and actions, the avatars can convey non-verbal cues, emotions, and social interactions, enhancing the sense of shared presence and facilitating meaningful connections between users.

The avatar bridging node is an essential component in creating a seamless and immersive connection between the physical and virtual realms. By synchronizing the user's physical presence with their digital representation, it enhances the embodiment, agency, and interaction capabilities within the metaverse, creating more immersive and socially engaging experiences.

In computing, an avatar is a graphical representation of a user or the user's character or persona. It may take either a two-dimensional form as an icon in Internet forums and other online communities (where it is also known as a profile picture) or a three-dimensional form, as in games or virtual worlds. Another use of the avatar has emerged with the widespread use of social media platforms. There is a practice in social media sites: uploading avatars in place of the real profile image.

Avatars—a sort of virtual second life—can be considered the main bridging node connecting the real world to the metaverse (through the web), as shown in Fig. 7.7.

Even if avatars are traditionally linked to "light" applications (e.g., video games or social entertainment), they are increasingly used in more significant practices. For instance, digital twins are used in medicine.

A digital twin is a digital representation of real-world entities—an object, system, or process—that is synchronized with the real world. With sensors that relay information and two-way Internet of Things (IoT) object connections, this technology can synchronize the digital environment with the physical world and vice versa.

Fig. 7.7 The Avatar value chain

Any change in the material world is reflected in the digital representation (the twin) and feedback gets sent in the other direction. These intrinsic properties make digital twins one of the fundamental building blocks of the metaverse. In technical training programs, technicians can already use applications to operate 3D representations of complex systems (https://hellofuture.orange.com/en/journey-through-the-metaverse-digital-twins-are-synchronizing-the-physical-and-virtual).

Even if the original node in the real world (represented by a physical person) is different from Her digital avatar, they may tentatively be considered, as a necessary simplification in this study, substantially coincident.

Thanks to augmented (and virtual) reality, an avatar can be identified, copied, and measured, increasing Her value, if compared to the original.

According to Cozzo et al. (2016) "In Multiplex Networks a set of agents might interact in different ways, i.e., through different means. Since a subset of agents is present at the same time in different networks of interactions (layers), these layers become interconnected". These agents are represented, in our case, by bridging avatars and other players (digital platforms, etc.).

7.8 A Holistic Ecosystem: From Physical Reality to the Internet and the Metaverse

The evolution from physical reality to the Internet and eventually the metaverse represents the progression toward a holistic ecosystem of interconnected digital and physical realms. Let's explore this journey and the connections between these different domains:

1. Physical Reality: Physical reality refers to the tangible world we live in, consisting of physical objects, environments, and human interactions. It encompasses our physical presence, sensory experiences, and the traditional offline activities we engage in.
2. Internet: The Internet is a global network of interconnected computers and devices that enables the exchange of information and facilitates communication between users. It has transformed how we access information, communicate, conduct business, and interact with digital content. The Internet connects individuals across geographical boundaries and provides access to a vast array of online services, platforms, and resources.
3. Digital Transformation: The advent of the Internet sparked a digital transformation, reshaping various aspects of our lives. It brought about innovations such as e-commerce, social media, cloud computing, and online collaboration tools. Digital technologies have facilitated the creation, sharing, and consumption of digital content, opening up new opportunities for communication, commerce, and entertainment.
4. Interconnectivity: The Internet has fostered interconnectivity on a global scale. It has connected people, businesses, organizations, and devices, enabling seamless communication, data exchange, and collaboration. This interconnectivity has led to the emergence of virtual communities, online marketplaces, and shared digital experiences.
5. Virtual Reality and Augmented Reality: Virtual reality (VR) and augmented reality (AR) technologies have bridged the gap between physical reality and digital experiences. VR immerses users in entirely virtual environments, while AR overlays digital content onto the physical world. These technologies enhance our perception and interaction with the digital realm, enabling more immersive and interactive experiences.
6. Metaverse: The metaverse represents the concept of a fully immersive and interconnected virtual reality-based digital universe. It encompasses a collective virtual space where people can interact, explore, create content, and engage in various activities using VR, AR, or other digital interfaces. The metaverse aims to blur the boundaries between the physical and digital worlds, creating a seamless and immersive user experience.

7. Holistic Ecosystem: The vision of a holistic ecosystem involves the integration and harmonization of physical reality, the internet, and the metaverse. It envisions a seamless continuum of experiences, where individuals can seamlessly transition between physical and virtual realms. This ecosystem fosters interconnectedness, interoperability, and symbiotic relationships between different domains, enabling fluid interactions and value creation.

In this holistic ecosystem, physical reality continues to play a vital role as the foundation of our everyday lives, while the Internet and the metaverse provide additional layers of digital experiences and opportunities. The integration of these domains enables new forms of communication, collaboration, commerce, entertainment, and self-expression.

As technology advances and our understanding of the metaverse evolves, the vision of a holistic ecosystem will continue to shape the way we engage with digital content, connect with others, and explore new frontiers of virtual experiences.

The metaverse and the physical world interact in both directions, generating value-enhancing synergies.

According to Wang and Zhou (2017), "MetaEnterprises and MetaCities can be regarded as the mapping of real enterprises and cities in the virtual cyberspace. They are virtual enterprises and cities running parallel to real enterprises and cities, which can realize the description of real enterprises and cities. Corresponding to the human, material, organizations, scenarios, and other elements in real enterprises and cities, there are various virtual elements such as virtual humans, virtual objects, virtual organizations, and virtual scenarios in MetaEnterprises and MetaCities. These virtual elements in MetaEnterprises and MetaCities can be used to analyze and evaluate the decision-making scenarios with a computational experiments approach to realize the prediction of real enterprises and cities. Through the interaction and feedback between MetaEnterprises/MetaCities and real enterprises/cities, we can realize the prescription of decision-making in real enterprises and cities, to effectively improve the efficiency and effect of various decisions in real enterprises and cities".

The three-step pattern from the physical reality to the metaverse can be illustrated in Fig. 7.8 which represents an upgrade of Fig. 7.1.

Any consideration about the potential market value of the metaverse would be considered science fiction since the underlying concept is uneasy to define and impossible to measure.

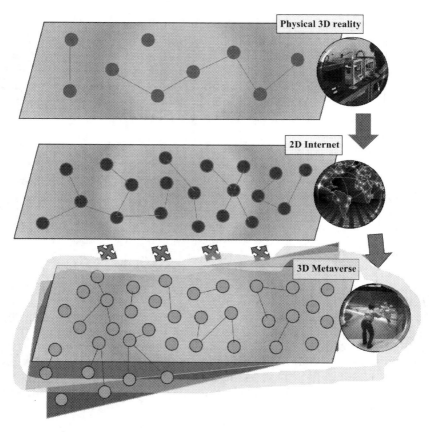

Fig. 7.8 From physical reality to the Internet and the Metaverse

An estimate of the value of the metaverse is, however, important because investors need market traction to drive their efforts, envisaging potential returns out of their expenditures.

The metaverses are spaces where you can not only admire places, monuments, and works of art but also conclude business. The metaverses represent worlds in which commercial exchanges are becoming increasingly important together with the market value of the companies that produce supporting technology. According to a Bloomberg Intelligence report, the market value of companies operating in metaverses is expected to reach $ 800 billion by the middle of this decade and $ 2.5 trillion by 2030.

Inside the metaverse, on the other hand, commercial exchanges take place on two floors. On the one hand, there is the presence of shops that act as a showcase and traditional e-commerce, while allowing a more immersive experience in which the customer chooses a product that exists in the real world and pays for it with fiat currency. At the same time, in the metaverse, there are properties, goods, and other values that are represented by NFTs or, more precisely, they are NFTs whose exchanges take place through digital currencies.

NFTs—records of digital ownership stored in the blockchain—will be the linchpin of the metaverse economy, by enabling authentication of possessions, property, and even identity. Since each NFT is secured by a cryptographic key that cannot be deleted, copied, or destroyed, it enables the robust, decentralized verification—of one's virtual identity and digital possessions—necessary for metaverse society to succeed and interact with other metaverse societies (https://www.ft.com/partnercontent/crypto-com/nfts-the-metaverse-economy.html).

The metaverse, through the interactions between avatars, makes possible strategies of value co-creation in which the single virtual nodes actively participate in this creation, receiving remuneration in tokens/cryptocurrencies that are usually lacking in many traditional business models. Even the feedback on the Internet (such as, for example, the reviews on TripAdvisor) does not involve any direct remuneration for the user, who for her part provides valuable big data that feeds increasingly advanced profiled marketing strategies. With the metaverse, there is a customer-centric qualitative leap, which places the user at the center of value co-creation and sharing of new value.

The currency of the metaverse is currently represented by controversial cryptocurrencies, linked to blockchain technologies potentially harbingers of tax evasion and money laundering. The boundaries and exchanges between fiat money and cryptocurrencies are still confused, although full convertibility could, in perspective, represent an important milestone in the convergence of ecosystems.

The value of the metaverse can be direct, if it concerns this integrated ecosystem (declined, as it has been shown, in many interrelated dimensions), or transferred to the real world and the Internet, which expands the range of goods and services exchanged, also in terms of usability, generating a differential / incremental surplus value.

The new paradigms of value co-creation rely, in many cases, on social networks and behavioral models inspired by the sharing economy, facilitated by the plasticity and resilience of the digital and virtual world.

The growing sensitivity toward development paths inspired by sustainability and ESG metrics must be confronted, first, with the energy-intensive trends of blockchains.

The pioneering investments in the metaverse are based on prospects of economic returns in the medium-long term, which in turn depend on the revenue model incorporated in the business models and disruptive strategies, with a highly innovative and discontinuous scope. These investments are made above all by Big Tech, intent on creating new lifestyles and entertainment, in the hope that they will become market standards, guaranteeing promoters the role of first movers and standard settlers, from which oligopolistic rents can derive (where barriers to entry are created for new competitors).

In the logic of the metaverse (a reality that is still predominantly conceptual, with no well-defined contents), the experiential experience and the contents shared between the virtual players will assume preponderant content in the co-creation of shared value. In perspective, the content will be able to count more than the technological infrastructure, destined to become a commodity (this trend is already visible in the world of digital media).

7.9 From Business Modeling to Economic Valuation

Business modeling for the metaverse involves defining the structure, revenue streams, and value proposition of businesses operating within the virtual environment. Here are some key considerations for business modeling in the metaverse:

1. Value Creation: Determine how your business will create value within the metaverse. This could involve providing virtual goods, services, experiences, or infrastructure. Consider the unique aspects of the metaverse, such as social interactions, virtual economies, and immersive experiences, and how your business can leverage those elements.

2. Revenue Streams: Identify the revenue streams that can sustain your business in the metaverse. This could include selling virtual goods, offering virtual services, hosting events or experiences, providing advertising opportunities, or monetizing user data. Explore different monetization models that align with the metaverse ecosystem and user expectations.
3. User Acquisition and Engagement: Develop strategies for attracting and engaging users within the metaverse. Consider how you can build a community, foster social interactions, and provide compelling experiences that keep users coming back. User acquisition and retention will be crucial for the success of your business in the competitive metaverse landscape.
4. Partnerships and Collaboration: Explore partnerships and collaborations with other businesses, creators, or platforms within the metaverse. Collaborations can enhance your offerings, expand your reach, and create synergies within the ecosystem. Look for opportunities to integrate your services or products with complementary offerings to provide more value to users.
5. Intellectual Property and Rights Management: Consider how you will protect and manage intellectual property within the metaverse. This could involve copyrights, trademarks, licensing agreements, or other mechanisms to safeguard your creations or assets. Understand the implications of virtual property rights and how they align with your business model.

Economic Valuation of the Metaverse: Economic valuation of the metaverse is a complex task due to its evolving nature and the diverse range of businesses, assets, and interactions within the virtual environment. Here are some factors to consider when attempting to evaluate the economic value of the metaverse:

1. User Base and Engagement: Assess the size, growth, and engagement of the user base within the metaverse. The number of active users, their demographics, and their level of engagement can indicate the market potential and attractiveness of the metaverse for businesses.
2. Virtual Asset Market: Examine the market for virtual assets within the metaverse, such as virtual real estate, digital collectibles, or

in-game items. Evaluate the trading volume, prices, and demand for these assets to gauge the economic activity and potential value creation within the metaverse.
3. Revenue Generation: Consider the revenue generated by businesses operating in the metaverse. This can include direct revenue from virtual goods sales, service fees, advertising revenue, or subscription models. Additionally, factor in the potential for indirect economic benefits, such as job creation, ecosystem growth, and multiplier effects.
4. Network Effects: Assess the strength of network effects within the metaverse ecosystem. The presence of network effects can amplify the value and potential growth of the metaverse as more users and businesses participate, leading to a virtuous cycle of increased value and engagement.
5. Market Sentiment and Adoption: Evaluate the market sentiment and adoption trends surrounding the metaverse. Monitor public perception, investor interest, regulatory developments, and industry trends to understand the market dynamics and potential risks or opportunities that may impact the economic valuation.
6. Technological Advancements: Consider the pace of technological advancements that can enhance the metaverse ecosystem. Innovations in virtual reality, augmented reality, blockchain, artificial intelligence, and other technologies can drive new possibilities, user experiences, and economic growth within the metaverse.

Due to the nascent stage of the metaverse, the economic valuation may be speculative and subject to uncertainties.

The metaverse presents several new business models that are not possible in the physical world. Some of these include:

1. Virtual events: Companies can hold virtual conferences, concerts, and other events in the metaverse, which can reach a much wider audience than physical events.
2. Virtual experiences: Companies can create immersive, interactive experiences in the metaverse that allow users to explore, learn, and engage with their brand in new ways.

3. Virtual services: Companies can offer virtual services in the metaverse, such as virtual consulting, virtual coaching, and virtual support.
4. Virtual economies: The metaverse can have its economies, with its currencies, supply chains, and marketplaces. This presents new opportunities for companies to participate in and benefit from these economies.
5. Virtual real estate development: Companies can invest in virtual real estate development in the metaverse, building and selling virtual properties to users.
6. Virtual advertising: Companies can advertise their products and services in the metaverse, using virtual billboards, virtual product placements, and other innovative methods.

These new business models provide opportunities for companies to generate revenue and engage with customers in new and exciting ways in the metaverse.

The economic evaluation of the metaverse is still in its early stages, as the concept of the metaverse is still evolving and developing. However, many experts believe that the metaverse has the potential to become a multi-billion dollar industry, as it represents a new frontier for digital commerce, gaming, entertainment, and social interaction. As more companies and developers invest in the metaverse, we can expect to see new business models, revenue streams, and economic opportunities emerge.

There are several potential revenue streams in the metaverse, including:

1. Virtual real estate: Similar to real-world real estate, the virtual property can be bought and sold in the metaverse, with prices varying depending on factors such as location, size, and popularity.
2. Virtual goods: From clothing and accessories to virtual weapons and vehicles, the metaverse offers a wide variety of digital products that can be sold to users.
3. Advertising: Just like in the real world, the metaverse offers opportunities for companies to advertise their products and services to a large audience.

4. Subscriptions and memberships: Many metaverse platforms offer premium memberships and subscriptions that provide users with additional features and benefits.
5. Fees for transactions: Like many digital marketplaces, the metaverse can charge small fees for transactions between users.
6. Gaming: Gaming is a key component of the metaverse, and revenues from in-game purchases, upgrades, and subscriptions can be significant.

As the metaverse continues to evolve, we can expect to see new revenue streams emerge as well.

The metaverse offers several unique advertising opportunities that are not possible in the physical world. Here are some of the advertising opportunities in the metaverse:

1. Immersive Ads: The metaverse allows for immersive ads that allow users to interact with the ad in a virtual environment. Advertisers can create unique experiences that engage users with their brand and products.
2. Product Placement: In the metaverse, advertisers can place their products and services in virtual environments, such as storefronts or billboards. This allows for a more natural promotion of products and services.
3. Personalized Advertising: With user data, advertisers can personalize ads for users based on their interests, preferences, and behaviors. This can lead to more effective advertising and higher engagement rates.
4. Sponsorships: Advertisers can sponsor events or virtual experiences in the metaverse, such as concerts or virtual conferences. This allows for high visibility and brand awareness.
5. Virtual Influencer Marketing: The metaverse presents opportunities for virtual influencers or avatars to promote brands and products to their followers.
6. Virtual Reality Advertising: Virtual Reality (VR) is becoming more popular in the metaverse, and advertisers can create VR experiences to promote products and services. This can be a highly engaging and immersive way to advertise.

Overall, the metaverse offers advertisers unique and innovative ways to reach audiences and promote their products and services. With its growing popularity and potential for growth, the metaverse may become a significant advertising platform in the future.

The economic evaluation of the metaverse is still in its early stages, as the concept of the metaverse is still evolving and developing. However, many experts believe that the metaverse has the potential to become a multi-billion dollar industry, as it represents a new frontier for digital commerce, gaming, entertainment, and social interaction. As more companies and developers invest in the metaverse, we can expect to see new business models, revenue streams, and economic opportunities emerge.

The expected cash flows from the metaverse are difficult to predict as the metaverse is still in its early stages of development. However, several potential sources of cash flows could emerge as the metaverse grows and matures.

7.10 Crypto-Backed Metaverse

A crypto-backed metaverse refers to a virtual world or digital environment that is built on blockchain technology and utilizes cryptocurrencies or blockchain-based assets as a fundamental component of its ecosystem. In a crypto-backed metaverse, digital assets, transactions, and interactions are facilitated by blockchain technology and cryptographic tokens. Cryptocurrencies are the predominant method of payment within the metaverse, with few if any alternatives.

Here are some key aspects of a crypto-backed metaverse:

1. Virtual Environment: A crypto-backed metaverse is a virtual environment that allows users to explore, interact, and engage with digital content, objects, and experiences. It can be accessed through virtual reality (VR), augmented reality (AR), or traditional web-based interfaces.
2. Blockchain Infrastructure: The metaverse is built on a blockchain infrastructure that provides the underlying framework for asset ownership, digital scarcity, provenance, and security. Blockchain technology ensures transparency, immutability, and decentralized control of assets and transactions within the metaverse.

3. Digital Assets and Tokens: In a crypto-backed metaverse, digital assets and tokens play a central role. These assets can represent virtual land, buildings, avatars, in-game items, virtual currencies, or other unique and tradable digital goods. They are typically represented as non-fungible tokens (NFTs) or fungible tokens (such as cryptocurrencies) on the blockchain.
4. Ownership and Value Exchange: The blockchain-based nature of the metaverse enables verifiable ownership and secure peer-to-peer value exchange of digital assets. Users can buy, sell, trade, and transfer assets within the metaverse using cryptocurrencies or other blockchain-based tokens. Ownership rights and transactions are recorded on the blockchain, ensuring transparency and authenticity.
5. Interoperability and Cross-Platform Integration: A crypto-backed metaverse may aim for interoperability with other blockchain-based platforms and systems, allowing users to move assets and value across different metaverses or applications. Cross-platform integration can enhance user experiences, facilitate asset portability, and create interconnected virtual economies.
6. User Engagement and Economy: The metaverse fosters user engagement and participation through various activities, including gaming, social interactions, virtual commerce, content creation, and more. Users can earn, spend, and monetize cryptocurrencies or digital assets within the metaverse, creating an economy where real-world value is intertwined with virtual experiences.
7. Community Governance: The governance of a crypto-backed metaverse is often driven by its community of users and stakeholders. Governance mechanisms can involve voting, consensus-building, or decentralized autonomous organization (DAO) structures. Token holders may have voting rights and influence over decisions related to the metaverse's development, policies, and evolution.
8. Potential Real-World Applications: A crypto-backed metaverse can extend beyond gaming and entertainment, with potential applications in areas such as virtual real estate, virtual events, education, art, virtual workplaces, and more. The ability to create unique and scarce digital assets, secure ownership, and enable peer-to-peer interactions presents opportunities for innovative and immersive experiences.

The concept of a crypto-backed metaverse is still evolving, and various projects are exploring different approaches to create decentralized virtual worlds with blockchain integration. The realization of a fully functional and widely adopted crypto-backed metaverse involves technological, social, and economic challenges that will continue to shape the development and potential of this concept.

7.11 Metaverse and Decentralized Finance

The metaverse and decentralized finance (DeFi) are two distinct concepts that are increasingly intersecting and influencing each other. Metaverse payments, incentrated on blockchains and cryptocurrencies, are intrinsically decentralized and this represents a strong link with DeFi.

The intersection between the metaverse and DeFi is driven by the desire to create a virtual economy within the metaverse, where users can engage in financial activities using blockchain-based assets and decentralized financial services. Here are some ways the Metaverse and DeFi are coming together:

(a) Virtual Currencies: Within the metaverse, cryptocurrencies or blockchain-based tokens can serve as the native currency for transactions, purchases, and value exchange. These virtual currencies can be integrated with DeFi protocols to enable decentralized lending, borrowing, and liquidity provision within the metaverse.

(b) Tokenized Assets: The metaverse can facilitate the tokenization of virtual assets, such as virtual real estate, virtual items, or virtual artwork. These tokenized assets can be traded, rented, or collateralized within the DeFi ecosystem, enabling new forms of value creation and financial activities.

(c) Decentralized Exchanges: Decentralized exchanges (DEXs) built on blockchain technology can provide liquidity and enable the exchange of virtual assets within the metaverse. These DEXs can leverage DeFi protocols to facilitate decentralized trading, ensuring transparent and secure transactions.

(d) Decentralized Lending and Borrowing: DeFi lending and borrowing protocols can enable users in the metaverse to access liquidity by leveraging their virtual assets as collateral. Users can borrow virtual currencies or other tokens for various purposes, such as purchasing virtual property or funding virtual businesses.

(e) Governance and DAOs: Decentralized Autonomous Organizations (DAOs) can play a role in governing aspects of the metaverse, such as decision-making, rules, and policies. DAOs can utilize DeFi governance mechanisms, enabling participants to have a say in the development and management of the metaverse's financial ecosystem.

The convergence of the metaverse and DeFi presents both challenges and opportunities. Challenges include scalability, user experience, interoperability, and regulatory considerations. However, the combination of the metaverse and DeFi offers opportunities for new economic models, decentralized marketplaces, virtual asset ownership, and innovative financial interactions within virtual worlds.

The development of the metaverse and its integration with DeFi is still in its early stages. Various projects and initiatives are exploring the potential of this intersection, and it will require ongoing technological advancements, user adoption, and regulatory clarity to fully realize the potential of a decentralized financial ecosystem within the metaverse.

7.12 Metaverse, Blockchains, and Cryptocurrencies

The metaverse could be powered by blockchain technology. Blockchain can ensure the ownership and scarcity of digital assets in the metaverse, helping to create a realistic and a fully functioning digital economy. Assets can be tracked and owned securely, and transactions can be verified independently and transparently.

Cryptocurrencies can be used as a medium of exchange in the metaverse. They can be used to buy and sell goods and services, similar to how they are used in the real world. Blockchain-based digital assets, sometimes known as Non-Fungible Tokens (NFTs), could also play a big part in the metaverse. NFTs can represent ownership of a unique item or piece of content in the digital world.

Smart contracts, which are self-executing contracts with the terms of the agreement directly written into code, can automate and secure transactions in the metaverse. This can enable trustless and efficient commerce, making the digital economy more accessible and efficient.

The metaverse, blockchains, and cryptocurrencies are all pieces of a bigger puzzle in the digital economy. Together, they can form a secure, efficient, and decentralized digital world where assets can be owned, exchanged, and interacted with in novel ways.

REFERENCES

Barabási, A. (2016). *Network science*. Cambridge University Press.
Barabási, A., & Albert, R. (2002). Statistical mechanics of complex networks. *Reviews of Modern Physics, 74*(1), 47–97.
Beckström, R. (2008). *The economics of networks and cybersecurity*. https://www.slideshare.net/RodBeckstrom/economics-of-networks-beckstrom-national-cybersecurity-center-department-of-homeland-security
Bianconi, G. (2018). *Multilayer networks*. Oxford University Press.
Caldarelli, G., & Catanzaro, M. (2011). *Networks: A very short introduction*. Oxford University Press.
Cheng, R., Wu, N., Chen, S., & Han, B. (2022). *Will metaverse be NextG internet? Vision, hype, and reality*. https://arxiv.org/abs/2201.12894
Cozzo, E., Ferraz de Arruda, G., Rodrigues F. A., & Moreno, Y. (2016). *Multilayer networks: Metrics and spectral properties*. https://cosnet.bifi.es/wp-content/uploads/2016/03/CFRM01.pdf
Degrande, T., Vannieuwenborg, F., Verbrugge, S., & Colle, D. (2018). Multisided Platforms for the Internet of Things. In B. Shishkov (Eds.), Business Modeling and Software Design. BMSD 205. *Lecture Notes in Business Information Processing* (Vol. 319). Springer.
Estrada, E., & Knight, P. A. (2015). *A first course in network theory*. Oxford University Press.
Gartner Research. (2022). *Emerging technologies: Critical insights on metaverse*. https://www.gartner.com/en/documents/4010017
Jackson, M. O. (2008). *Social and economic networks*. Princeton University Press.
Johnson, J. (2022, February). Metaverse—statistics & facts. *Statista*.
JP Morgan Onyx. (2022). *Opportunities in the metaverse: How businesses can explore the metaverse and navigate the hype vs. reality*. https://www.jpmorgan.com/content/dam/jpm/treasury-services/documents/opportunities-in-the-metaverse.pdf
Lee, K. M., Min, B., & Goh, K-I. (2015). Towards real-world complexity: An introduction to multiplex networks. *European Physical Journal B, 88*(2), 1–20.
Odlyzko, A., & Tilly, B. (2005). *A refutation of Metcalfe's law and a better estimate for the value of networks and network interconnections*. University of Minnesota.
Pereira, D. (2021). *Multisided platform business model*. https://businessmodelanalyst.com/multisided-platform-business-model/

Radoff, J. (2021). *Network effects in the metaverse.* https://medium.com/building-the-metaverse/network-effects-in-the-metaverse-5c39f9b94f5a

Reed, D. P. (2001, February). The law of the pack. *Harvard Business Review.*

Van Steen, M. (2010). *Graph theory and complex networks: An introduction.* Maarten Van Steen.

Wang, D., & Zhou, X. (2017). Control energy and controllability of multilayer networks. *Advances in Complex Systems, 20*(04n05), 1750008.

Yang, Q., Zhao, Y., Huang, H., & Zheng, Z. (2022). *Fusing blockchain and AI with metaverse: A survey.* https://arxiv.org/abs/2201.03201

CHAPTER 8

Networking Digital Platforms and Virtual Marketplaces

8.1 Definition and Features

Networking digital platforms and virtual marketplaces are interconnected concepts that have transformed the way businesses and individuals interact, trade, and collaborate.

Networking digital platforms are online platforms that facilitate connections, interactions, and collaborations between individuals or businesses. These platforms leverage technology to create virtual spaces where users can share information, exchange resources, and engage in various activities. Key features of networking digital platforms include:

1. User Profiles: Users create profiles that showcase their identity, skills, expertise, and interests. Profiles help establish connections and enable users to discover like-minded individuals or potential business partners.
2. Communication Tools: Networking platforms provide communication tools such as messaging systems, forums, or chat functionalities to facilitate direct interactions and collaboration between users.
3. Connection Building: Users can connect with others on the platform, forming networks of contacts and building professional relationships. Networking platforms often recommend potential connections based on shared interests, mutual connections, or algorithms that suggest relevant matches.

© The Author(s), under exclusive license to Springer Nature Switzerland AG 2023
R. Moro-Visconti and A. Cesaretti, *Digital Token Valuation*,
https://doi.org/10.1007/978-3-031-42971-2_8

4. Content Sharing: Users can share content such as articles, blog posts, presentations, or multimedia files to showcase their knowledge and expertise. Content sharing facilitates knowledge exchange and helps users establish credibility within the network.
5. Groups and Communities: Networking platforms often have groups or communities focused on specific topics, industries, or interests. These groups allow users to join discussions, share insights, and connect with individuals who share similar professional or personal interests.
6. Professional Development: Networking platforms offer opportunities for professional development through webinars, online courses, mentorship programs, or job boards. These features help users enhance their skills, gain industry knowledge, and find career opportunities.

Virtual marketplaces are online platforms that connect buyers and sellers, enabling the exchange of goods, services, or digital assets. These marketplaces create a digital ecosystem where individuals or businesses can make commercial transactions. Key features of virtual marketplaces include:

1. Product Listings: Sellers can create listings to showcase their products or services, including descriptions, images, pricing, and other relevant details. Buyers can browse these listings to find items of interest.
2. Search and Discovery: Virtual marketplaces provide search functionality and filters to help buyers discover products or services that meet their specific requirements. Algorithms or personalized recommendations assist in matching buyers with relevant offerings.
3. Transaction Facilitation: Virtual marketplaces facilitate transactions between buyers and sellers, often providing secure payment processing systems, escrow services, or dispute resolution mechanisms to ensure trust and mitigate risks.
4. Rating and Reviews: Users can provide ratings and reviews for sellers or their products/services based on their experiences. These ratings help establish trust and provide valuable feedback to buyers and sellers.

5. Global Reach: Virtual marketplaces enable businesses and individuals to reach a global audience, transcending geographical boundaries. Sellers can expand their customer base, and buyers have access to a wider range of offerings from various locations.
6. Niche Marketplaces: Virtual marketplaces exist for specific industries, niches, or product categories. These niche marketplaces cater to specialized needs and create targeted environments for specific types of transactions.

Networking digital platforms and virtual marketplaces are closely intertwined as they both facilitate connections and interactions in the digital realm. Networking platforms can serve as a foundation for building relationships and discovering potential business opportunities, while virtual marketplaces provide a platform for buying and selling goods or services within those networks. Together, they form a dynamic ecosystem that fosters collaboration, commerce, and community-building in the online world.

The interaction between networking digital platforms and virtual marketplaces is significant and mutually beneficial. Networking digital platforms, such as social media networks, professional networking sites, and online communities, provide a space for individuals and businesses to connect, collaborate, and share information. On the other hand, virtual marketplaces are online platforms that facilitate buying and selling of goods and services.

Here are a few key aspects of their interaction:

1. Enhanced Visibility: Networking digital platforms allow businesses to establish their presence, build brand awareness, and connect with potential customers. By leveraging these platforms, businesses can promote their products or services and redirect interested users to their virtual marketplace listings or storefronts. This interaction helps increase visibility and reach a wider audience.
2. Trust and Reputation: Networking platforms often include features like recommendations, endorsements, and reviews. These social validation elements contribute to building trust and credibility for businesses within the virtual marketplace. Positive interactions, recommendations, and endorsements on networking platforms can

translate into increased trust among potential customers on virtual marketplaces, leading to higher sales and conversions.
3. Targeted Marketing and Audience Insights: Networking platforms provide valuable demographic and behavioral insights about their users. Businesses can utilize this data to identify and target specific customer segments that align with their products or services. By integrating these insights into virtual marketplaces, businesses can optimize their marketing efforts, personalize product recommendations, and tailor their offerings to meet customer needs more effectively.
4. Seamless Integration: Many virtual marketplaces offer integration options with networking platforms to streamline the user experience. For example, businesses can sync their virtual marketplace listings with their social media profiles, allowing customers to view and purchase products directly from the social media platform. This integration reduces friction in the buying process and improves convenience for customers.
5. Collaborative Opportunities: Networking digital platforms foster collaboration between businesses, entrepreneurs, and industry professionals. Virtual marketplaces can benefit from these collaborations by enabling joint ventures, cross-promotions, or partnerships. Such collaborations can expand the range of products or services available on the marketplace and attract a broader customer base.

The interaction between networking digital platforms and virtual marketplaces creates a symbiotic relationship. Networking platforms enhance visibility, build trust, and provide valuable audience insights, while virtual marketplaces offer a platform for businesses to showcase their offerings, facilitate transactions, and drive sales. This integration allows businesses to leverage the power of networking and tap into the vast customer base of virtual marketplaces.

Digitalization is the process of transforming information or physical products into digital form, allowing businesses to "go paperless". Digitalization can be also interpreted as the process of converting data (not necessarily information) into a computer-readable format.

Thanks to digital solutions new forms of innovation and creativity are conceived while traditional business models are revised. Old-fashioned firms interact with digital startups, with a cross-pollination process that drives the analogic-to-digital transition. Digital links enable the real-time exchange of information or e-transactions (B2B2C), reducing information asymmetries and other frictions. Real-time interaction between stakeholders helps to minimize risk and enhance returns by win–win value co-creation paradigms.

Digital platforms are emerging as a virtual stakeholder that bridges nodes among players inside and outside the firm. The platform, as well as firm interactions, may conveniently be interpreted with network theory, showing which are the links among the stakeholders and how they concretely work.

Digital platforms are "software-based external platforms consisting of the extensible codebase of a software-based system that provides core functionality shared by the modules that interoperate with it and the interfaces through which they interoperate" (Tiwana et al., 2010). Software platforms are a technological meeting ground where application developers and end-users converge (Evans et al., 2006).

Platforms are facilitators of exchange (of goods, services, and information) between different types of stakeholders that could not otherwise interact with each other. Transactions are mediated through complementary players that share a network ecosystem (Armstrong, 2006; Rochet & Tirole, 2003). Due to their digital features, they have a global outreach that gives them the potential to scale. Platforms reshape traditional supply chains. Smoother interactions about each "ring" (passage) of the chain bear important consequences on cost savings, increasing the overall economic and financial marginality. Improved economic/financial marginality, incorporated in the EBITDA (difference between sales and monetary Operating Expenses) boosts economic value, bankability, and other value drivers.

A taxonomy of the platform typologies is recalled in Fig. 8.1.

A digital matchmaker is an online platform or service that connects individuals or entities based on specific criteria or preferences. It acts as a facilitator, helping people find suitable matches for various purposes, such as dating, professional networking, mentorship, or business partnerships. Here are some key aspects of digital matchmakers:

1. Matching Algorithm: Digital matchmakers utilize sophisticated algorithms to analyze user data, preferences, and characteristics. These algorithms aim to identify potential matches based on compatibility factors, shared interests, or specific criteria set by users.

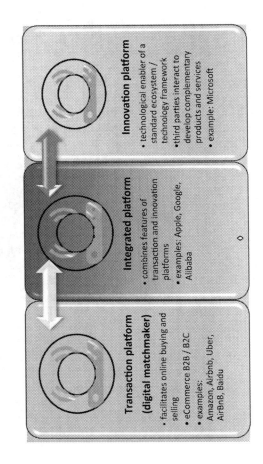

Fig. 8.1 Platform taxonomy

2. Profile Creation: Users typically create profiles on digital matchmaker platforms, providing information about themselves, their interests, and their preferences. These profiles help the algorithm understand user preferences and make suitable recommendations.
3. Personalized Recommendations: Based on the information provided by users and the matching algorithm, digital matchmakers generate personalized recommendations. These recommendations suggest potential matches that align with the user's preferences and criteria.
4. Communication and Interaction: Once a match is made, digital matchmakers often provide communication tools or messaging systems to facilitate interaction between matched individuals. These tools enable users to engage in conversations, exchange information, and explore potential connections.
5. Privacy and Security: Digital matchmakers prioritize user privacy and implement security measures to protect user data. They typically provide options for controlling the visibility of personal information and employ encryption and other security protocols to safeguard user communications.
6. Niche Matchmakers: Some digital matchmakers cater to specific niches or industries. For example, there are matchmakers focused on connecting professionals within a particular field, connecting mentors with mentees, or matching individuals based on specific interests or hobbies.
7. Continuous Learning and Improvement: Digital matchmakers continuously refine their algorithms and recommendations based on user feedback and interactions. This iterative process aims to enhance the accuracy and effectiveness of the matching process over time.

Digital matchmakers provide a convenient and efficient way to connect individuals, fostering relationships and collaborations. They leverage technology and data analysis to streamline the matchmaking process, helping users find suitable matches based on their preferences and objectives. Whether it's finding a romantic partner, a business collaborator, or a mentor, digital matchmakers offer a platform to discover and connect with like-minded individuals.

Digital platforms are the basis of technology-enabled business models that facilitate exchanges between multiple groups—such as end-users and producers—who do not necessarily know each other. The generated value is proportional to the size of the community, with scalable network effects thanks to the Internet. Interaction within digital platforms follows innovative paradigms where stakeholders co-create and share value. Supply and value chains flatten and incorporate learning curves (economies of experience) that are fueled by real-time big data.

The digital platform consists of an IT infrastructure (hardware typically associated with one or more software) that provides technological services and tools, programs, and applications, for the distribution, management, and creation of free or paid digital content and services, including through the integration of multiple media (integrated digital platform) (Spagnoletti et al., 2015). The platform can be open source or commercial and can be structured, respectively, for public access or a limited target, after registration. It may include information, interactive, file sharing, downloading and uploading, streaming services, as well as communication and sharing of multimedia material.

The use of online digital platforms is of primary importance for intermediation services and increasingly widespread applications such as e-commerce and payment services, Internet search engines, sharing economy, gig economy, e-learning, pay-TV and Video on Demand services, etc.

Digital businesses include transactions that are digitally mediated (often via m-apps) or that involve products or services that are used digitally by complementary users sharing a network (Kenney & Zisman, 2016).

Digital platforms consist of a complex set of software, hardware, information exchange operations (big data), or transactions and networks. Within digital platforms, the software, which oversees and manages its functions, is of particular importance. Software platforms are the technological place where application developers and end-users converge.

Digital platforms are the basis of innovative business models of highly profitable companies (such as Google or Facebook), thanks to the (presumed) gratuitousness of the services offered, typically offset by advertising revenues. Evaluation metrics take on relevance not only for the target companies but also to be able to enhance digital ecosystems that are increasingly pervasive and sophisticated in which users-consumers take on primary importance.

The monetary value of digital assets depends on parameters and value drivers that make it possible to overcome traditional free access, with the hypothesis of indirect or mixed remuneration (freemium).

The sharing economy is the basis of an innovative economic system, based on the sharing of goods and services by a community of users, who operate through ad hoc digital platforms.

An innovative interpretation of digital platforms can be provided by network theory, in which digital platforms represent a virtual node that connects with other nodes manned by stakeholders, allowing the circulation of information, the execution of transactions, etc.

A further extension concerns the application of the paradigms of the sharing economy whose stakeholders interact through digital platforms.

Consistently to Fig. 8.1, the main types of digital platforms are the following:

- e-commerce platforms (e.g., Amazon, Airbnb, eBay …), which facilitate online B2B/B2C/C2C exchanges, etc.;
- integrated platforms (e.g., Google, Apple, Alibaba …), which combine aspects of e-commerce platforms with innovative ones;
- innovative platforms (e.g., Microsoft), which allow third parties to develop complementary products and services, integrating proprietary business models with open-source extensions.

Digital platforms refer to a variety of complementary concepts that still need comprehensive systematization in the literature. A synthetic outlook of this recent research strand is important to make some critical remarks, consistent with the research question of this study.

A literature review on digital platforms is contained in Asadullah et al. (2018) and Sutherland and Jarrahi (2018) which analyze sharing economy platforms. Spagnoletti et al. (2015, p. 364) define a digital platform as "a building block that provides an essential function to a technological system and serves as a foundation upon which complementary products, technologies, or services can be developed". Cryptocurrencies are not conceivable without the background support of digital platforms.

Digital businesses are those that carry out transactions that are digitally mediated or involve products or services that are experienced digitally. Platforms are facilitators of exchange (of goods, services, and information). Transactions are mediated through complementary players that share a network ecosystem (Armstrong, 2006; Rochet & Tirole, 2003). This interpretation is consistent with the transaction cost theory that can be applied as a constructive stakeholder theory (Ketokivi & Mahoney, 2015).

Digital platforms are multisided digital frameworks that shape the terms on which participants interact. Digital platforms are also complex mixtures of software, hardware, operations, and networks (Gawer, 2014; Gawer & Cusumano, 2014). They provide a set of shared techniques, technologies, and interfaces to a broad set of users; social and economic interactions are mediated online, often by apps (Kenney & Zysman, 2016). Digital platforms are complementarily defined as "software-based external platforms consisting of the extensible codebase of a software-based system that provides core functionality shared by the modules that interoperate with it and the interfaces through which they interoperate" (Tiwana et al., 2010). Software platforms are a technological space where application developers and end-users converge (Evans et al., 2006).

Digital platforms have become a major mode for organizing a wide range of human activities, including economic, social, and political interactions (e.g., Kane et al., 2014; Tan et al., 2015). Platforms leverage networked technologies to facilitate economic exchange, transfer information, and connect people (Fenwick et al., 2019). Studies sharing this view focus on the technical developments and functions upon which complementary products and services can be developed, i.e., building on the top of the technical core that a platform owner offers and facilitates (Ceccagnoli et al., 2012; Ghazawneh & Henfridsson, 2015; Tiwana et al., 2010).

Other studies have conceptualized digital platforms based on a non-technical view that presents platforms as a commercial network or market that enables transactions in the form of business-to-business (B2B), business-to-customer (B2C), or even customer-to-customer (C2C) exchanges (Koh & Fichman, 2014; Pagani, 2013; Tan et al., 2015). Digital platforms may include crowdfunding and P2P stakeholders (Majchrzak & Malhotra, 2013) which are innovative ways of raising equity. Crowdfunding issues are a new frontier of corporate governance (Cumming et al., 2019).

An online marketplace (or online e-commerce marketplace) is a type of e-commerce website where product or service information is provided by multiple third parties. Online marketplaces are the primary type of e-Commerce and can be a way to streamline the production process.

8.2 Legal Aspects

Legal aspects of digital services and platforms encompass a wide range of topics and considerations. Here are some key aspects to consider:

1. Intellectual Property: Digital services and platforms often involve the creation, distribution, and consumption of intellectual property (IP). This includes copyright protection for content, trademarks for brand identities, and patents for inventions or unique technologies. Legal considerations involve understanding and respecting IP rights, obtaining necessary permissions or licenses, and addressing issues such as infringement, piracy, or unauthorized use.
2. Data Privacy and Protection: Digital services and platforms typically collect and process personal data from users. It is essential to comply with relevant data protection laws and regulations, such as the General Data Protection Regulation (GDPR) in the European Union or the California Consumer Privacy Act (CCPA) in the United States. Compliance involves obtaining user consent, implementing adequate security measures, and providing transparency regarding data collection, storage, and usage.
3. Terms of Service and User Agreements: Digital services and platforms often require users to agree to terms of service or user agreements. These agreements outline the rights and responsibilities of both the platform provider and the user. They cover aspects such as usage guidelines, intellectual property rights, liability limitations, dispute resolution mechanisms, and more. It is important to ensure these agreements are drafted, fairly, and in compliance with applicable laws.
4. E-Commerce and Consumer Protection: Digital platforms that facilitate e-commerce transactions must comply with laws and regulations related to consumer protection. This includes providing accurate product or service information, clear pricing and refund policies, secure payment processing, and handling customer complaints or disputes effectively. Compliance with local, national, and international consumer protection laws is crucial to maintain trust and avoid legal issues.
5. Liability and Content Moderation: Digital platforms may face legal challenges related to user-generated content, including issues of defamation, hate speech, copyright infringement, or illegal activities.

Platforms must establish content moderation policies and mechanisms to address these concerns. The legal framework, such as the Digital Millennium Copyright Act in the United States, provides safe harbor provisions for platforms that take reasonable steps to remove infringing content upon notification.
6. Competition and Antitrust: Digital platforms that dominate certain markets may be subject to scrutiny under competition and antitrust laws. Authorities assess whether these platforms engage in anti-competitive practices, such as unfair pricing, exclusionary behavior, or abuse of market power. Compliance with competition laws and regulations is crucial to avoid legal consequences and maintain a level playing field.
7. Jurisdictional Considerations: Digital services and platforms often operate globally, which raises jurisdictional challenges. Understanding which laws apply and complying with regulations in different jurisdictions can be complex. It is important to assess and address legal obligations based on the countries or regions where services are offered or accessed.

Digital services, as typically free, are sometimes assimilated into public goods. Typically these are so-called assets not rivals, as their use by a consumer does not prevent the consumption of others, even at the same time. For example, while a sandwich is a typical rival good (it can only be consumed by one person), the enjoyment of a streaming film is open to a potentially unlimited number of consumers.

The fact that the (free) use of a digital service usually presupposes a user registration and profiling (generating data which is then subject to commercial exploitation, even surreptitiously, by the provider) places digital services between public goods and private.

Digital platforms can easily give rise to monopolistic rents that lead to antitrust problems. The large players, typically belonging to big tech have an infrastructure based on a capillary and scalable IT network, which can be adapted with relative simplicity to different geographical contexts, offering global services and content. This can lead to numerous behaviors potentially harmful to free competition.

Among the main assets subject to use that is not always transparent, there are big data, collected through systematic and capillary profiling of user information. Big data can feed baggage of information surreptitiously characterized by anti-competitive effects, creating barriers to entry into a market dominated by incumbents who can strengthen their dominant positions. In this context, the protection of transparency in the use of data must be combined with consumer protection.

Problems in the field of labor law can also be relevant. Digital platforms such as Google, Facebook, or Amazon, but also Foodora or Deliveroo are now an integral part of the daily life of billions of individuals. The gig economy is based on the organization of digital platforms, associated with dedicated Mobile Apps, which orchestrate the precarious interaction of freelancers with clients, as seen during the lockdown. Poor regulation facilitates the flexibility of a model which, moreover, lends itself to abuses that proliferate also thanks to the regulatory vacuum.

The recent phenomena linked to the Covid-19 pandemic constantly draw attention to the role of the major players of digital platforms, equipped with business models that are much more organized than others to implement agile working tools quickly and on a large scale (smart working).

8.3 Networked Governance Around Digital Platforms

Networked governance refers to a collaborative and decentralized approach to decision-making and governance that involves multiple stakeholders within the context of digital platforms. In the realm of digital platforms, networked governance models have emerged to address the need for inclusive, transparent, and participatory decision-making processes. Here are some key aspects of networked governance around digital platforms:

1. Stakeholder Inclusion: Networked governance aims to include a wide range of stakeholders in decision-making processes. These stakeholders may include platform users, developers, service providers, regulators, policymakers, and other relevant actors. The goal is to ensure diverse perspectives are considered, promoting inclusivity and avoiding undue concentration of power.
2. Decentralization of Decision-making: Networked governance distributes decision-making authority across multiple stakeholders rather than relying solely on a central authority or platform owner. It may involve mechanisms such as voting, consensus building,

or participatory processes to ensure decisions reflect the collective interests and values of the network participants.
3. Transparent and Open Processes: Networked governance promotes transparency by making information about decision-making processes, rules, and policies accessible to all stakeholders. Open discussions, public forums, and documentation of decision-making proceedings can foster transparency and accountability.
4. Collaborative Problem Solving: Networked governance encourages collaboration and collective problem-solving. It involves engaging stakeholders in discussions, soliciting feedback, and leveraging their expertise to address challenges, make policy decisions, and shape the future direction of the platform.
5. Self-Regulation and Standards: Networked governance models often seek to establish self-regulatory mechanisms and industry standards. These mechanisms can define rules, best practices, and codes of conduct that govern the behavior of platform participants. Self-regulation can help address emerging issues, ensure compliance with ethical norms, and promote trust within the network.
6. Distributed Infrastructure and Interoperability: Networked governance may also extend to the technical infrastructure of digital platforms. Interoperability standards and protocols allow different platforms to communicate and interact with each other, fostering a networked ecosystem rather than isolated silos. This interoperability enables collaboration, innovation, and seamless user experiences across multiple platforms.
7. Hybrid Models and Partnerships: Networked governance can involve a mix of decentralized decision-making and collaboration with central authorities or industry organizations. Hybrid models may be adopted, where central entities provide coordination, support, and enforce certain rules while involving stakeholders in decision-making processes.
8. Evolving and Adaptive Structures: Networked governance recognizes the dynamic nature of digital platforms and adapts to changing circumstances and needs. It allows for iterative decision-making, continuous feedback loops, and mechanisms for updating policies and rules to keep pace with technological advancements and evolving user requirements.

Networked governance around digital platforms aims to foster a more democratic, inclusive, and responsive approach to decision-making. By involving diverse stakeholders, promoting transparency, and embracing collaboration, networked governance models seek to create fairer and more sustainable digital ecosystems. Cryptocurrencies may represent the "monetary glue" that links the stateholders and presides over their remuneration ("no money, no party").

The previous sections have proven how the firm, thanks to digitalization, can be considered a network of contracts. Some corporate governance implications have already been anticipated, consistent with the research question that is focused on the impact of digital platforms on networking stakeholders. This section investigates in further detail how internal and external stakeholders interact around two bridging nodes: the networked firm and the digital platform.

Digital networks use a common platform as a pivoting (bridging) node which centralizes information sharing and transactions. Innovation is continuously proposing new paradigms for value creation, reshaping governance interactions.

As described by de Reuven et al. (2018), digital technologies imply homogenization of data, editability, re-programmability, distributedness, and self-referentiality.

Internal stakeholders (mainly shareholders, managers, and employees) are the core part of the networked firm whereas external stakeholders are customers, suppliers, financial institutions (banks), and other players (P2P investors; competitors; partners, etc.). The firm may also be considered an "internal" platform (Gawer, 2014).

The digital platform is the bridging node between the firm and the external stakeholders (that may also have a direct link with the firm, bypassing the intermediating function of the platform) and it can be linked to a digital supply chain where suppliers interact with B2B transactions and e-Procurement.

Figure 8.2 shows a case where players (stakeholders) are interacting with nodes.

The two bridgings (hub) nodes shown in Fig. 8.2 are the networked firm and the digital platform. Internal stakeholders (shareholders, managers, employees, etc.) are a cohesive ecosystem within the firm that is linked to other external stakeholders (customers, suppliers, banks, interacting firms, etc.). These traditional internal and external stakeholders are complemented by the digital platform which is an innovative bridging

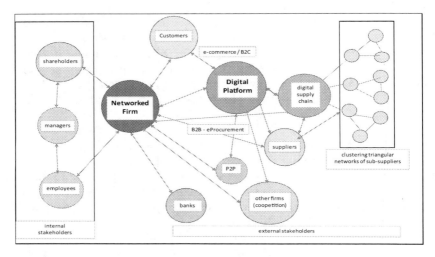

Fig. 8.2 Internal and external stakeholders linked to the firm and the digital platform

node, linked also to P2P lenders, and digitized supply chains, following B2B or B2C transactional patterns.

The digital supply chain is a further bridging node between the digital platform, and the traditional suppliers, and a further sub-network of e-suppliers that exchange information and trade in real-time (24 hours/ 7 days a week). B2B2C stakeholders that make transactions through the platform exchange data and so fuel big data stored in the cloud. This information then feeds interoperable databases, with consequent artificial intelligence interpretation (and possible blockchain validation). The digital platform acts as an intermediating hub, increasing the number of nodes (vertices) as well as the quantity and quality of the links. For instance, any interaction between two agents that are mediated through the platform is digitally recorded.

Internal stakeholders are individuals or groups within the firm or organization who have a direct interest in the digital platform and its success. They may include:

1. Management and Executives: These are the individuals responsible for overall strategic decisions and overseeing the digital platform's

operations. They provide guidance, allocate resources, and set goals to ensure the platform aligns with the firm's objectives.
2. Employees: Employees within various departments, such as marketing, technology, customer support, and operations, play a role in the development, maintenance, and promotion of the digital platform. Their expertise and efforts contribute to its success.
3. IT and Technical Staff: These professionals are responsible for the technical aspects of the digital platform, including development, maintenance, security, and infrastructure. They ensure the platform functions smoothly and remains secure.
4. Sales and Marketing Teams: These teams are responsible for promoting the digital platform, attracting users or customers, and driving adoption and engagement. They leverage marketing strategies, customer acquisition techniques, and customer relationship management to maximize the platform's potential.
5. Customer Support: The customer support team assists users or customers with inquiries, technical issues, and other platform-related concerns. They play a vital role in ensuring user satisfaction, resolving problems, and maintaining a positive user experience.

External stakeholders are individuals or entities outside the firm who have an interest in or are affected by the digital platform. They may include:

1. Customers or Users: The primary external stakeholders are the individuals or businesses who use the digital platform to access its services, products, or features. Their satisfaction, feedback, and engagement are critical for the success and growth of the platform.
2. Business Partners and Suppliers: These are the entities that collaborate with the firm to provide services, technologies, or content that enhance the digital platform's capabilities. Examples include payment processors, content providers, logistics partners, and integration partners.
3. Investors and Shareholders: Individuals or organizations that have invested in the firm and have a financial interest in its success are important stakeholders. They expect a return on their investment and monitor the platform's performance and growth.

4. Regulatory Authorities: Depending on the nature of the digital platform and its operations, regulatory authorities may be external stakeholders. They ensure compliance with relevant laws and regulations, such as data privacy, consumer protection, and competition laws.
5. Industry Associations and Communities: Associations and communities related to the firm's industry or the digital platform's niche can be external stakeholders. They may provide support, resources, networking opportunities, or industry-specific guidance.

Engaging and managing relationships with both internal and external stakeholders is crucial for the success of a digital platform. Their needs, expectations, and feedback should be considered in the platform's development, marketing, and ongoing improvements. Effective communication, collaboration, and addressing stakeholders' concerns are essential for building trust and long-term partnerships.

A digital platform that mediates different groups of users (such as buyers and sellers) may be denoted as multisided. In two-sided markets, two distinct groups have a relationship where the value for one group increases as the number of participants from the other group increases. As platforms bring together multiple user groups, they create the so-called network effects or network externalities. This is consistent with Metcalfe's property of networks and with the interpretation of platforms in networking terms. The added value of the eco-systemic network arises mainly from two synergistic features:

a) The "architectural" value of the network itself (depending on the outlay of the nodes and links) is measurable in numbers;
b) The functional value of the network (including the platform as a bridging node) depends on the intensity of the interactions among the different links (exchange of information; transactions, etc.). Architectural links are important to the extent that they incentive "traffic" among nodes (stakeholders).

Smart products in combination with innovative data-driven supply chain services help rethink supply chain management, leading to more self-organizing and self-optimizing systems. Digitization will play a growing role in global supply chains due to reasons such as the shift in values from the physical artifact to the data created by smart products, the emerging importance of services, the displacement of industry borders, the radical change of competitive structures, the transformation of business models and more in general, the symptomatic creative destruction of established structures and behavior patterns (Pflaum et al., 2017).

8.4 Digital (Smart) Supply Chains

A digital supply chain refers to the integration of digital technologies and systems into the traditional supply chain processes to enhance efficiency, visibility, and collaboration. It leverages digital tools, data analytics, automation, and connectivity to streamline operations, optimize decision-making, and improve overall supply chain performance. Here are the key aspects of a digital supply chain:

1. Connectivity and Integration: A digital supply chain relies on seamless connectivity and integration between various stakeholders, systems, and processes involved in the supply chain. It involves the integration of suppliers, manufacturers, distributors, logistics providers, and customers through digital platforms and data-sharing mechanisms.
2. Real-Time Data and Analytics: Digital technologies enable the collection, analysis, and utilization of real-time data throughout the supply chain. This includes data on inventory levels, demand patterns, production processes, transportation, and customer behavior. Advanced analytics, including machine learning and AI, can provide valuable insights for forecasting, inventory management, demand planning, and decision-making.
3. Automation and Robotics: Automation plays a vital role in a digital supply chain. Robotic process automation (RPA) automates repetitive tasks, such as order processing, inventory management, and data entry, improving speed and accuracy. Robotics and autonomous systems are used for tasks like warehouse automation, picking and packing, and transportation.
4. Internet of Things (IoT): The IoT enables the connection of physical objects, devices, and sensors to the internet, allowing real-time monitoring and control. In a digital supply chain, IoT

devices can provide data on product location, condition, temperature, and other variables, enhancing visibility and enabling proactive decision-making.
5. Blockchain Technology: Blockchain technology offers decentralized and transparent record-keeping capabilities, enabling secure and traceable transactions in the supply chain. It enhances trust, transparency, and efficiency by providing immutable and auditable records of transactions, product provenance, and compliance.
6. Supply Chain Visibility: Digital supply chains provide improved visibility across the entire supply chain. Through digital platforms and tools, stakeholders can track and monitor inventory levels, shipment status, production progress, and demand fluctuations. Real-time visibility enhances responsiveness, reduces lead times, and facilitates effective decision-making.
7. Collaboration and Communication: Digital supply chains enable enhanced collaboration and communication among supply chain partners. Cloud-based platforms, collaborative software, and digital communication tools facilitate real-time information sharing, collaborative planning, and coordination among stakeholders.
8. Agile and Responsive Operations: Digital supply chains enable agility and responsiveness by leveraging real-time data and analytics. They can quickly adapt to changes in demand, supply disruptions, or market dynamics. By leveraging predictive analytics and scenario modeling, supply chains can proactively identify risks and optimize operations.

Implementing a digital supply chain requires investment in technology infrastructure, data governance, talent, and change management. However, the benefits include improved operational efficiency, reduced costs, better customer service, enhanced sustainability, and increased supply chain resilience.

Digital supply (and value) chains are a further extension of the above considerations, consistent with the framework and aim of this study. Within a networked governance ecosystem, the information patterns and risk-return sharing of connected stakeholders are deeply affected by digitalization. This has an important impact on corporate governance.

A supply chain is a (physical) network between a company and its suppliers to produce and distribute a specific product to the final buyer. These links among the stakeholders shape their governance interactions and are reengineered by digitalization. Network theory and its digital extension are consistent with the architectural framework of the supply chain. To the extent that the single steps ("rings") of the chain are affected by digitalization (e.g., thanks to a disintermediation process that shortens the chain), it can be inferred that the digitalization process produces savings—in the form of lower transactional costs—that improve the risk-return profile of the stakeholders that also benefit from the softening of information asymmetries.

What makes supply chains resilient is:

- A mix of complementary intangibles (e.g., big data and IoT that fuel patented processes and in-cloud artificial intelligence applications);
- A scalable network of expanding nodes and linking edges (consistent with network theory and its digital applications), incorporating growth real options, and B2B2C relationships;
- Digital platform services (cloud computing platforms where customers can develop, run, and manage applications without the requirement of building and maintaining the infrastructure typically needed when developing and launching an app) (Butler, 2013).

Network theory is mainly related to digital platforms, which are in turn catalyzers of scalable intangibles. The most powerful active platforms nowadays are Amazon, Alibaba, Apple, Google, and Facebook. Their common features are technologies not based on physical assets. They benefit from innovative ecosystems with core interactions between platform participants as consumers, producers, and third parties (Jacobides et al., 2018).

Korpela et al. (2017) show that digital supply chain integration is becoming increasingly dynamic. Access to customer demand needs to be shared effectively, and product and service deliveries must be tracked to provide visibility in the supply chain. Business process integration is based on standards and reference architectures that should offer end-to-end integration of product data. Companies operating in supply chains integrate processes and data through intermediating companies, which establish interoperability by mapping and integrating company-specific data for various organizations and systems. This practice has high integration costs, and adoption is still low. Business-to-business (B2B) integration within the supply chain refers to the exchange of electronic data over the Internet between business partners and value-added service providers.

The principal value drivers of digital supply chains are:

- Fast (just-in-time) end-to-end integration through digital enablers;
- Traceability and visibility of deliveries through smart logistics partners;
- Cost-effective cloud solutions provided by ICT partners;
- Sharing of real-time information in the cloud;
- Standardized transactions and collaboration through digital platforms accessed by supply chain members;
- Networking with geo-localized e-commerce customers.

Digital (smart) supply and value chain technologies combine information, computing, communication, and connectivity innovation in applications or devices like Augmented reality; Big data; Cloud computing; Social media; Mobile, (cognitive) analytics, or embedded devices; Cognitive technologies (machine learning, neural networks, robotic process automation, NPL, AI, etc.); IoT, wearables and Sensor technology; Nanotechnology; Omni-channel (to improve customer experience); Robotics; Self-Driving Vehicles and Unmanned Aerial Vehicles; 3D printing.

The interactions among the networked firm, the digital platform, and the other external stakeholders can be examined with a value chain analysis that outlines its networked and digital features. The value chain is digitized by the devices/technologies reported above. An example is shown in Fig. 8.3.

Digital value chains tend to be flatter (more horizontal and less hierarchical) than traditional value chains and the bridging platform acts as a coordinating hub, as shown in Fig. 8.3. The digital network is intrinsically more valuable due to its highly interconnected architecture (higher number of links); value also depends on the increasing traffic of data or transactions among the linked nodes. This incremental value can be estimated using a with-or-without approach (consistent with the International Valuation Standard 210), according to which the value chain is estimated with and without its networked digital features, using the difference as a proxy for value.

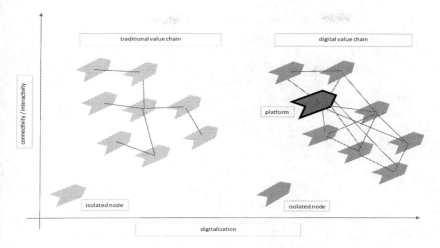

Fig. 8.3 From traditional to networked digital value chains

Digital supply and value chains may be represented by two separated network ecosystems that eventually interact, within a multilayer network (Bianconi, 2018). This interpretation is consistent with the cloud manufacturing paradigm, an advanced form of networked manufacturing. This process is based on a combination of existing manufacturing systems and emerging technologies, such as cloud computing, virtual manufacturing, agile manufacturing, manufacturing grid, IoT, and service-oriented technologies (Akbaripour et al., 2015). Global supply chains (and related value chains) are becoming increasingly connected due to the increased globalization in terms of network size, strength, and connectivity, showing significant intertemporal changes, and higher clustering (Tsekeris, 2017).

8.5 The Assumptions of Evaluation, Between Digital Scalability and Network Theory

The non-rivalry of digital platforms entails, in economic terms, the scalability of the business model. The business is scalable when an increase in revenues is significantly translated into the operating result, thanks to a mix of operating costs in which fixed costs are predominant, compared to variable costs. Since fixed costs by definition do not vary with changes in revenues, a rigid cost structure guarantees a more intense translation of increasing revenues on the operating margin (with a boomerang effect if revenues contract, in this case contributing to increasing losses or to achieve an economic balance between revenues and costs with greater difficulty).

Economies of scale and experience (the latter also referring to mechanisms of interaction with customers, who with their feedback participate in the creation of value) represent a fundamental strategic lever for interpreting innovative value drivers.

Scalability can be greatly increased in the presence of digital platforms that mediate between stakeholders in real-time (24/7) and everywhere, guaranteeing dissemination and comparability of information.

The proactive role of digital platforms can be better understood by considering their interactive properties in terms of network theory.

A network represents, in its most basic formulation, a set of points (vertices or nodes) connected by lines (sides or edges). Social networks take on particular importance, which rely on digital platforms (such as Facebook or LinkedIn) as a point of interchange (so-called "bridge node"—"bridge ring") between different individuals. The network theory assumes economic and legal importance also in the interpretation of corporate governance issues, where the stakeholders are considered to be interconnected nodes, also thanks to the intermediation of "bridge nodes" such as digital platforms that represent a new stakeholder intangible.

8.6 A Theoretical Background for the Economic Valuation

The economic evaluation of digital platforms involves assessing their financial performance, value creation, and overall economic impact. It aims to understand the economic viability, efficiency, and potential return on investment of digital platforms. Here are some key considerations for the economic evaluation of digital platforms:

1. Revenue Generation: Evaluate the revenue streams of the digital platform. This may include revenue from transaction fees, subscriptions, advertising, data monetization, or other platform-specific

sources. Analyze the growth and stability of revenue over time and assess the platform's ability to generate sustainable income.
2. Cost Structure: Understand the cost structure of the digital platform. Identify the key cost components, such as technology infrastructure, development and maintenance, marketing, customer acquisition, and operational expenses. Assess the efficiency and scalability of the cost structure to determine the platform's profitability and cost-effectiveness.
3. Value Proposition: Assess the value created by the digital platform. Determine the benefits it offers to users, such as convenience, cost savings, improved access to goods or services, or enhanced efficiency. Evaluate the platform's ability to attract and retain users, generate network effects, and create positive externalities in the broader economy.
4. User Adoption and Engagement: Analyze the user adoption and engagement metrics of the digital platform. Assess the growth rate of the user base, user retention, active user participation, and other relevant metrics. Higher user adoption and engagement can indicate the platform's attractiveness and potential for long-term success.
5. Network Effects: Consider the presence and strength of network effects within the digital platform. Network effects occur when the value of the platform increases as more users join or participate. Evaluate how network effects contribute to the platform's competitive advantage, user stickiness, and barriers to entry for potential competitors.
6. Market Size and Competition: Assess the market size and competition within the industry or sector in which the digital platform operates. Understand the competitive landscape, including the presence of other digital platforms, incumbents, and potential disruptors. Analyze the platform's market share and growth potential within the broader market context.
7. Scalability and Growth Potential: Evaluate the scalability and growth potential of the digital platform. Consider factors such as geographic expansion opportunities, diversification into new verticals or industries, and potential for innovation and product/service extensions. Assess the platform's ability to capture new markets, attract investment, and sustain growth over time.

8. Economic Impact: Consider the broader economic impact of the digital platform. Assess its contribution to employment generation, innovation, productivity, and economic growth. Evaluate the platform's ability to create value not only for its users but also for other stakeholders in the ecosystem.

In conducting an economic evaluation of digital platforms, it's important to consider both financial metrics and broader economic factors. This evaluation helps stakeholders understand the platform's economic viability, potential risks, and opportunities for value creation and growth.

The economic evaluation profiles depend above all on the type of platform being estimated (e.g., open-source or commercial). A further prerequisite is represented by the subject who relates to the platform to be evaluated: the owner, the consumer-user, and the intermediary (who provides hosting services or available M-App, etc.).

While the evaluation of the proprietary platform involves a relatively small number of subjects, the extension to consumers concerns a much wider audience of potentially interested parties. In this context, it is not the value of the platform itself, but rather the added value that it generates on the user's activity (net of intermediation costs for the use of the third-party platform).

If the economic evaluation refers to an asset (or business unit) that can be independently identified and susceptible to economic exploitation and consequent estimate in terms of value, no particular methodological findings emerge.

On the other hand, the estimate of the value for non-owners (such as consumers–users) is more complex. Profiles of co-creation of value emerge that enrich the traditional valuation landscape, inserting new stakeholders such as consumers, who, although not co-owners of the good or service being valued, participate (sometimes even with surreptitious strategies to which they are unwittingly subjected), with the release of personal information (habits and customs then profiled for vertical marketing strategies; feedback that feeds big data, etc.) that create a still strongly underestimated value.

The same characteristic of the "good" being valued—the digital platform—and its nature above all from the point of view of legal ownership (public, private, or consortium good?) Contributes to fueling a debate of an "ontological" nature on the rationale and objectives of the estimate. Analogously, a reference to blockchains can be hypothesized, which can also be of public, private, or consortium nature and which present significant intersections, especially in perspective, with digital platforms, being able to preside over a certification/authentication of digitized information that pass through the platform.

The interrelationships between digital platforms and other intangible assets can also be relevant, such as patents or know-how (with platforms that incorporate inventions), already mentioned intangibles such as software (which represents the essential IT infrastructure of digital platforms), blockchains, big data (which feed the platforms, leaving them enriched, with a surplus to be evaluated also economically), (social) networks, mobile apps (which represent an "IT shortcut" to access platforms). They also detect additional intangibles that process information intermediated by platforms, using algorithms orchestrated by artificial intelligence, which processes information data stored in the cloud in interoperable databases. Furthermore, brands should not be forgotten, even in their digital branding extensions, for platforms with high visibility, are often referable to as big tech.

From an evaluation point of view, the examination of the business model of the platform is aimed at identifying and estimating the value drivers that emanate from it. In this context, the following levers of value creation, first of all, stand out:

- Internet traffic conveyed by the platform, instrumental to the economic use of data and information, atomistically considered as "small data" but then aggregated at a "big data" level;
- The volumes of transactions conveyed by e-commerce platforms, with B2B / B2C profiling depend on the counterpart of the business operator, which can be another company or a consumer.

The digital platform and its virtual showcase function allow, thanks to the use of the web, to overcome space–time barriers, operating in a space–time context so-called "24/7" and allowing to pursue digital scalability strategies, also through a co-creation of value between providers and users.

8.7 Open Source Platforms

Open-source platforms refer to software or digital platforms that are developed and made available with an open-source license. Open source software allows users to access, use, modify, and distribute the source code freely, fostering collaboration, transparency, and community-driven development. Here are some key characteristics and benefits of open-source platforms:

1. Transparency: Open source platforms provide transparency as the source code is accessible to users. This transparency allows for peer review, identification of security vulnerabilities, and verification of the platform's functionality. Users can understand how the platform works and have visibility into any changes or updates.
2. Collaboration and Community: Open source platforms encourage collaboration and community participation. Developers and users can contribute to the platform's development, suggest improvements, and report bugs. The collective knowledge and efforts of the community can lead to rapid innovation, bug fixes, and feature enhancements.
3. Customization and Flexibility: Open source platforms offer customization and flexibility as users have the freedom to modify the source code to suit their specific needs. This enables businesses and individuals to tailor the platform to their unique requirements, leading to more adaptable and personalized solutions.
4. Cost-Effectiveness: Open source platforms often provide cost advantages as they are typically free to use and distribute. Organizations can avoid licensing fees associated with proprietary software, which can result in significant cost savings. Additionally, open-source platforms benefit from a large user community that provides support and resources.
5. Security and Reliability: Open source platforms benefit from community scrutiny, which can enhance security and reliability. With the code being open to review and contributions from the community, vulnerabilities and bugs can be quickly identified and addressed. The collaborative nature of open-source development often results in stable and robust platforms.

6. Innovation and Rapid Development: Open source platforms foster innovation and rapid development. The collective efforts of a diverse community of developers can lead to the introduction of new features, functionalities, and improvements at a faster pace. This agility can give open-source platforms a competitive edge in evolving markets.
7. Vendor Neutrality: Open source platforms provide vendor neutrality, reducing dependency on a single vendor for support, upgrades, or maintenance. Users have the freedom to choose service providers or internal resources to maintain and support the platform. This flexibility reduces the risk of vendor lock-in and offers greater control over the platform's future.
8. Longevity and Continuity: Open-source platforms tend to have a longer lifespan and continuity. Even if the original developer or organization discontinues support, the open nature of the code allows the community to continue development and support. This helps ensure the availability and sustainability of the platform over the long term.

Open source platforms have gained significant popularity and have been adopted in various domains, including operating systems (e.g., Linux), web servers (e.g., Apache), content management systems (e.g., WordPress), and enterprise software (e.g., OpenStack). Their collaborative nature and flexibility make open-source platforms attractive for organizations seeking cost-effective, customizable, and community-driven solutions.

The evaluation of open-source digital platforms has clear similarities with open-source software, in which the source codes are freely available by developers who contribute, equally free of charge, to improve their characteristics and performance.

In this context, the co-creation of value strategies is implemented, susceptible to an autonomous enhancement by the individual subjects participating in the initiative.

The estimate can be oriented, singularly, first of all by the analysis of cost savings and efficiency recoveries that the user can personally derive from the use of free software.

The evaluation of the usefulness of the use of open-source platforms can be estimated, consistently with the premises mentioned above, for example through a "with or without" approach, which estimates the value of the good or service or company, respectively before and after the appeal to the platform.

The "with or without" approach is traditionally used in the estimation of intangible assets and is explicitly recalled also by the International Valuation Standard 210, in the context of income approaches (because it considers, at a differential level, the increase in income made possible by 'use of the intangible asset being valued), comparing the valuation that incorporates the use of the platform ("with") with that without ("without") the platform.

8.8 Proprietary (Commercial) Platforms

Proprietary (commercial) platforms refer to digital platforms that are privately owned and operated by a specific company or organization for commercial purposes. These platforms are typically developed and maintained by the owning entity, which retains control over the platform's features, functionality, and access. Proprietary platforms often rely on Software as a Service (SaaS) products made available upon demand. Here are some key characteristics and features of proprietary platforms:

1. Ownership and Control: Proprietary platforms are owned and controlled by a specific company or organization. They have full decision-making authority over the platform's development, operation, and evolution. The owning entity can shape the platform's direction, features, and business model according to its strategic objectives.
2. Closed Ecosystem: Proprietary platforms often operate within a closed ecosystem, meaning that access to the platform and its services is controlled by the owning entity. Users typically need to abide by specific terms and conditions, and the platform provider can set rules and limitations on usage, content, and integration with third-party services.
3. Intellectual Property Protection: Proprietary platforms may involve the use of intellectual property, including proprietary software, algorithms, designs, or trademarks. The owning entity protects its intellectual property through various means, such as copyrights, patents, or trade secrets, to maintain a competitive advantage and prevent unauthorized use or replication.

4. Monetization and Revenue Generation: Commercial platforms are designed to generate revenue for the owning entity. They employ various monetization strategies, such as charging fees for access, selling products or services, displaying advertisements, or offering premium features or subscriptions. The primary goal is to create a profitable business model around the platform.
5. Customizability and Differentiation: Proprietary platforms allow the owning entity to tailor the platform's features, design, and user experience to suit their specific goals and target audience. This customization and differentiation enable the platform provider to create a unique value proposition and stand out from competitors in the market.
6. Support and Maintenance: The owning entity is responsible for providing support, maintenance, and updates for the proprietary platform. This ensures that the platform remains functional, secure, and up-to-date, addressing any issues or bugs that arise and implementing new features or improvements.
7. Branding and User Experience: Proprietary platforms often emphasize brand identity and provide a consistent user experience aligned with the owning entity's brand values. The platform's design, interface, and interactions reflect the branding and image of the company or organization, creating a cohesive experience for users.
8. Competitive Advantage: Proprietary platforms aim to establish a competitive advantage in the market by offering unique features, innovative solutions, or superior user experiences. This advantage can help attract and retain users, differentiate the platform from competitors, and secure a sustainable market position.

It's important to note that while proprietary platforms offer control and customization, they may also have limitations in terms of openness, interoperability, and potential vendor lock-in. Users must consider these factors when choosing to engage with proprietary platforms, as they may affect factors such as data portability, integration with other systems, and the ability to switch providers.

The proprietary platforms can implement e-commerce or data collection services (typically, big data, also powered by sensors—IoT). The services provided by the platform can also be used by non-owners, who "rent" them by paying fees (subject to economic evaluation and similar to royalties).

There can be models of Platform-as-a-Service (PaaS), an economic activity (connected to SaaS) that consists of the service of making available processing platforms (Computing platforms). The elements of PaaS allow you to develop, test, implement, and manage business applications without the costs and complexity associated with purchasing, configuring, optimizing, and managing basic hardware and software. Elements of PaaS can be used for application development and application services such as team collaboration, Web integration, database integration, security, and health management. These services can be used as an integrated solution on the web.

Platform-as-a-Service (PaaS) is a cloud computing service model that provides a platform for developing, deploying, and managing applications over the internet. PaaS abstracts the underlying infrastructure and provides developers with a ready-to-use platform, including operating systems, programming languages, development tools, and other resources necessary for application development. Here are some key characteristics and features of Platform-as-a-Service:

1. Infrastructure Abstraction: PaaS abstracts the complexities of infrastructure management, including hardware, networking, and server configurations. Users do not need to worry about the underlying infrastructure, as the service provider handles these aspects.
2. Development Tools and Frameworks: PaaS offers a range of development tools, frameworks, and runtime environments to support application development. These tools can include programming languages (such as Java, Python, or.NET), development frameworks (like Node.js, Django, or Ruby on Rails), and integrated development environments (IDEs) tailored for specific languages.
3. Scalability and Elasticity: PaaS platforms typically provide automatic scaling capabilities, allowing applications to handle increased traffic or workloads efficiently. Users can scale their applications up or down based on demand, without the need for manual infrastructure provisioning.
4. Multi-Tenancy and Resource Sharing: PaaS platforms often employ multi-tenancy, where multiple users or organizations share the same underlying resources securely. This resource sharing optimizes resource utilization and reduces costs for users.

5. Deployment and Management: PaaS facilitates the deployment and management of applications throughout their lifecycle. It offers features for application version control, testing, staging, and production deployment. PaaS platforms may also provide tools for monitoring, logging, and troubleshooting applications.
6. Integration and Middleware Services: PaaS often includes middleware services that facilitate integration with other systems or services. This can include databases, message queues, caching mechanisms, identity management, and more. These services streamline the development and deployment process by providing pre-built components.
7. Collaboration and Teamwork: PaaS platforms may offer collaboration features, allowing development teams to work together on projects. This can include features like code repositories, version control systems, project management tools, and communication channels.
8. Pay-as-You-Go Model: PaaS services typically follow a pay-as-you-go pricing model, where users pay for the resources and services they utilize. This allows for cost optimization, as users can scale resources based on actual needs and only pay for what they use.
9. Rapid Application Development: PaaS platforms aim to accelerate the application development process by providing pre-configured environments, ready-to-use components, and streamlined deployment options. This enables developers to focus on coding and innovation rather than infrastructure setup and maintenance.
10. Vendor Management and Support: PaaS service providers handle infrastructure maintenance, security updates, and overall platform management. They also provide customer support and may offer additional services such as training, consulting, or troubleshooting assistance.

PaaS provides a convenient and efficient platform for developers to build, deploy, and manage applications without the complexities of infrastructure management. It promotes faster time-to-market, scalability, and cost optimization, allowing developers to focus on application development and innovation.

Complementary, there are as-a-Service services in the fields of software, the Internet, or other applications.

The proprietary platforms are used by operators who carry out online transactions mainly compared to the use of outsourced digital shops.

8.9 Adaptation of the General Valuation Approaches

For the specific evaluation of digital platforms, it should, first of all, be noted that they are not—in their essence—easily identifiable by the rest of the companies that contain them (unless they constitute the corporate purpose). From this, it follows that, for their estimate, in most cases, it is necessary to refer to the evaluation of the entire company, the owner of the digital platform.

For evaluation purposes, first of all, the placement between the subjects intended for the estimate is noted: the owner of the platform or the user (belonging to a much more heterogeneous category) or any intermediaries, the value chain (supply/value chain).

Taking up the approaches described for the valuation of intangible assets, a brief critical examination of their applicability to the present case is possible.

The cost approach can only be used on a residual basis, as:

- the costs incurred for the development of the platform are not always clearly and autonomously identifiable and others can be separated;
- the historicity of costs is weakly correlated with the prospective value of the platform, which depends on scenarios and expectations based on expected market dynamics, rather than on costs incurred.

The income-financial approach is based, first of all, on the estimate of expected cash flows, to be discounted to represent the current value. Determining the size of these flows is of primary importance in applying the method and so is the consistency of the discount rates adopted.

Where the digital platform represents a business branch, its value can be estimated, incrementally, with the aforementioned differential income with or without an approach. The differential (incremental) income also represents a useful investigation tool for estimating the surplus value induced by the platform for the consumer.

The use of a differential method can also be useful for estimating the so-called profit of the infringer, often used in disputes relating to trademarks or patents, also considering the benefits achieved by the perpetrator of the violation.

The incremental value for the user can be estimated first of all by considering the scalability of revenues. Scalability is typical of non-rival intangible assets (that is, they can be used simultaneously by several subjects) and allows to increase in operating revenues exponentially and quickly, minimizing variable extra costs, thus giving the business model plasticity that enhances the key value drivers. Scalability is typical of digital applications and can also affect traditional sectors, even within its application limits (think of an e-commerce platform that allows the sale of local wine on a global scale).

The time horizon for discounting income or financial flows must consider the expected useful life of the platform, which depends on the persistence of its intrinsically ephemeral competitive advantage. The estimate of this horizon is one of the most critical parameters, considering the volatility of the reference markets and the related business models, in a highly competitive context, in which constant innovation implies elements of discontinuity that cannot be easily estimated.

Another methodology—also traditionally used in the estimation of intangible assets—is that of presumed royalties, based on the hypothetical fee that the company would pay if it were to obtain the license to use a platform owned by a third party.

The market approach is based on the assumption of being able to identify comparable transactions (of digital platforms or similar companies), from which to derive reliable benchmarks for evaluation.

The estimate of the market value is based on the screening of comparable transactions involving intangible assets, by way of sale or license, using the international databases now available on the web can provide useful clues about their value (also in terms of price comparison).

Still, in the context of the empirical approach, a further method of enhancement of so-called "Quick and dirty" digital platforms could concern, in partial analogy with the estimate of the value of internet sites, their diffusion (number of users), or the number of transactions and the volumes of traffic generated by them. This is information that feeds big data and, as such, can be subject to further enhancement (think of the profiling of customers' tastes and habits).

The taxonomy of the aforementioned approaches (cost, income, and market) intersects with the most frequently used methodologies for estimating companies tout court, based on discounted cash flows (which represent a subset of the income-financial approach) or on the stock market multipliers (Enterprise Value/EBITDA, etc.) of comparable companies, attributable to the market approach.

Both the accounting cash flows and the income parameter to which the multiplier is applied are, respectively, derived from or represented by the EBITDA (an economic/financial margin that incorporates the internally generated liquidity). A fortiori, the importance of EBITDA derives from it, which also derives from its fungibility, being the only parameter that simultaneously has the characteristics of an economic and financial margin, suitable for expressing the liquidity generated (or absorbed, if the algebraic sign is negative) in the context of typical or characteristic economic management (operational management, before debt service, taxes, and extraordinary operations). EBITDA is calculated by subtracting monetary operating costs (purchases, salaries, etc.) from operating monetary revenues (essentially sales). The application of the differential income to the EBITDA makes it possible to estimate the incremental impact, also for the consumer (which is the EBITDA increased thanks to the use of the digital platform?).

Big data, typically stored in the cloud, are included in the evaluation as assets with increasing value. They feed the interoperable databases with information input data from which information can be extracted to be interpreted with the aid of artificial intelligence. Artificial intelligence amplifies the potential of the digital world and helps make it more autonomous and self-referential, distancing it and abstracting it from its empirical substrate.

In evaluating digital platforms, the apps generally related to them and the internet sites themselves must also be considered.

Transactions of packages comprising multiple assets or multiple intangibles make the valuation of stand-alone intangibles more complicated based on an empirical method. These difficulties are even more evident taking into account that, from an accounting point of view, according to IAS 38, there is no active market for intangibles, which tend to be unaccounted for, and their fair value appears difficult to estimate.

The themes of overall evaluation are accompanied by those, no less insidious, of sharing the value among the stakeholders, who face traditional problems of negotiation asymmetry, such as monopoly rents (typical of the dominant platforms operated by big techs).

In more general terms, the broad theme of the enhancement of digital platforms cannot fail to intersect, at least at the level of interdisciplinary connection, with aspects of a sociological and psychological nature. This is because consumers' perceptions, attitudes, and expectations influence increasingly globalized choices and lifestyles, with evident economic impacts, which are also relevant in the context of evaluation metrics.

A still largely unexplored aspect concerns the link between the "physicality" of empirical reality and the parallel virtual world, which develops into ever more abstract digital platforms. The ancient link between immanent reality and the transcendent dimension intersects with a technological innovation destined to have profound socio-economic implications. The legal aspects and evaluation metrics are based on the analysis of an underlying reality whose boundaries, largely unexplored, must be the subject of constant interdisciplinary examination.

Technological evolution is bringing great progress in many fields of human life but also has a dangerous impact on his behavior. The smartphones on which we spend most of our time are today real prostheses of body and mind and are leading to a division between two brains: ours and the one we "carry in our pockets".

The "virtual splitting" of the user-consumer, which inspires innovative business models but at the same time surreptitiously suffers the consequences, re-proposes ancient themes. In this context, the hermeneutics of Plato's cave myth helps. The virtual shadows projected from the outside and viewed by the prisoners can well exemplify the ever-closer link between the real world and virtual reality, whose dangerous relationships manifest a hierarchical order that is not always defined.

8.10 Specific Valuation Approaches

The valuation of digital platforms typically involves several factors, including user engagement, revenue streams, market share, and growth potential. Some common methods for valuing digital platforms include discounted cash flow analysis, comparable company analysis, and precedent transaction analysis.

There are several specific evaluation approaches for digital platforms. Some of the most important include:

1. User Experience Evaluation: This approach focuses on how users interact with the platform, including usability, ease of navigation, and overall user satisfaction. Several user experience evaluation approaches can be used for digital platforms. One common approach is usability testing, which involves observing users as they interact with the platform and soliciting feedback on their experience. Another approach is user surveys, which can provide insights into user satisfaction, needs, and pain points. Additionally, heuristic evaluations can be used to identify usability issues and opportunities for improvement based on established design principles and guidelines. A/B testing is another approach that involves testing variations of the platform to determine which design or content changes are most effective in achieving user goals. These approaches can be used individually or in combination to provide a comprehensive understanding of the user experience and inform design decisions.
2. Performance Evaluation: This approach looks at the technical performance of the platform, including page load times, server response times, and other metrics related to speed and reliability. Some of the most common methods include analyzing user engagement and retention rates, tracking key performance indicators (KPIs) such as website traffic and conversion rates, and using machine learning algorithms to identify patterns and make predictions about user behavior. Other factors that may be considered in performance evaluation include user reviews and feedback, social media mentions and sentiment, and industry benchmarks and best practices. Ultimately, the most effective approach will depend on the specific goals and needs of the platform and its users.
3. Business Model Evaluation: This approach assesses the platform's ability to generate revenue and achieve profitability, including factors such as pricing structures, advertising revenue, and other revenue streams. The business model evaluation approach for digital platforms typically involves analyzing various components of the platform's business model, such as its value proposition, revenue streams, cost structure, customer segments, and key activities. This analysis helps to assess the overall viability and potential profitability of the platform's business model, as well as identify any potential

areas for improvement or optimization. Additionally, factors such as network effects, platform governance, and ecosystem dynamics may also be considered as part of the evaluation process.
4. Security Evaluation: it focuses on the platform's ability to protect user data and prevent security breaches, including measures such as encryption, firewalls, and other security protocols. A security risk assessment identifies potential vulnerabilities in the platform. This involves identifying potential threats and risks, assessing the likelihood and impact of those risks, and developing strategies to mitigate or prevent them.

Another approach is to conduct regular security audits, which involve a comprehensive review of the platform's security controls and policies to identify gaps and weaknesses. This can help organizations stay up-to-date with emerging threats and ensure that their security measures are adequate to protect against them. In addition, organizations may also implement security testing and penetration testing to simulate attacks and identify vulnerabilities before they can be exploited by malicious actors. This can help organizations identify and address potential security gaps before they can be exploited by attackers. A comprehensive security evaluation approach for digital platforms should involve a combination of risk assessment, security audits, and testing to ensure that the platform is adequately protected against a wide range of threats and vulnerabilities.

Valuing digital platforms involves assessing their financial performance, growth potential, market position, and overall value. Here are some commonly used methods and considerations for the valuation of digital platforms:

1. Market-Based Approach: This approach compares the digital platform to similar companies or platforms that have been recently sold or publicly traded. It involves analyzing market multiples such as the price-to-earnings (P/E) ratio, price-to-sales (P/S) ratio, or enterprise value-to-revenue (EV/Rev) ratio. This approach provides a relative valuation based on market comparables.
2. Income Approach: The income approach focuses on estimating the present value of future cash flows generated by the digital platform. The most common method under this approach is the discounted cash flow (DCF) analysis, which considers projected cash

flows, growth rates, and a discount rate to determine the platform's intrinsic value. This approach requires making assumptions about revenue growth, profitability, and capital expenditure.
3. Cost Approach: The cost approach evaluates the value of a digital platform based on the cost to recreate or reproduce it. It considers the expenses incurred in building and developing the platform, including research and development costs, infrastructure investments, and intellectual property. This approach may be less applicable to digital platforms that rely heavily on intangible assets and network effects.
4. User Metrics: User metrics play a significant role in valuing digital platforms. Key metrics to consider include the number of active users, user growth rate, user engagement, and user acquisition cost. User metrics can provide insights into the platform's market potential, customer retention, and overall attractiveness to potential investors or acquirers.
5. Technology and Intellectual Property: Assess the value of the platform's technology and intellectual property (IP). This includes analyzing the uniqueness, innovation, and defensibility of the platform's technology, algorithms, patents, copyrights, or trade secrets. Intellectual property and proprietary technology can enhance the platform's value and competitive advantage.
6. Growth Potential and Market Opportunity: Evaluate the platform's growth potential and addressable market opportunity. Consider factors such as market size, industry trends, competitive landscape, and the platform's ability to capture market share. Assess the scalability and expansion opportunities, including geographic reach and potential diversification into new product lines or services.
7. Strategic Partnerships and Ecosystem: Analyze the strategic partnerships, collaborations, and ecosystem surrounding the digital platform. Evaluate the value and contribution of these partnerships to the platform's growth, market access, and competitive advantage. Strong partnerships and ecosystem integration can enhance the platform's valuation.
8. Risk Assessment: Conduct a risk assessment of the digital platform, considering factors such as competition, regulatory risks, cybersecurity risks, operational risks, and market volatility. Evaluate the impact of these risks on the platform's financial performance, growth prospects, and long-term sustainability.

Valuing digital platforms can be complex, and different methods may be appropriate depending on the specific circumstances and characteristics of the platform. Additionally, market conditions, industry dynamics, and technological advancements should be considered when conducting a valuation. Engaging professional experts, such as financial analysts or valuation specialists, can provide further guidance and accuracy in the valuation process.

8.11 The Valuation of Virtual Marketplaces

Virtual marketplaces are online platforms where multiple sellers can list and sell their products or services to potential customers. These marketplaces have become increasingly popular in recent years, as they provide a convenient and efficient way for buyers to shop for a wide range of products and services from different sellers, all in one place. Examples of popular virtual marketplaces include Amazon, eBay, Etsy, and Airbnb.

To evaluate a virtual marketplace, you may want to consider the following factors:

1. User experience: The virtual marketplace should be easy to use and navigate, with clear and concise menus that allow users to find what they need quickly and easily. Evaluating user experience in a virtual marketplace involves analyzing many different factors such as website design, navigation, product descriptions, customer reviews, payment options, and checkout process. Various methods and tools can be used to gather feedback from users such as surveys, interviews, A/B testing, and heat maps.
2. Trust and security: Users should feel safe when using the platform, with secure payment options and data protection measures in place. To evaluate the trust and security of a virtual marketplace, there are several key factors to consider. These include the reputation of the platform, the quality of its security protocols, and the level of customer support they provide. One way to evaluate the reputation of a virtual marketplace is to read reviews from other users. This can give you a good sense of the experiences other people have had with the platform. Additionally, you can look for certifications or awards that the platform has earned, which can be a sign of its commitment to security and quality. Security protocols concern features like two-factor authentication, encryption, and regular security audits.

These can help protect your data and prevent unauthorized access to your account. Customer support is also important when evaluating a virtual marketplace. You'll want to look for a platform that offers responsive and helpful customer service so that you can get assistance if you ever run into an issue.
3. Product selection: The marketplace should offer a wide range of products or services to choose from, with high-quality images and detailed descriptions.
4. Pricing: The prices should be competitive and transparent, with no hidden fees or charges.
5. Customer service: The virtual marketplace should have a responsive and helpful customer service team that can quickly resolve any issues that arise.

By evaluating these factors, it is possible to determine if a virtual marketplace is a good fit for the user's needs and if it will provide a positive experience.

Valuing virtual marketplaces involves assessing their financial performance, market position, growth potential, and overall value. The valuation process typically considers several factors and methodologies. Here are key considerations for valuing virtual marketplaces:

1. Revenue and Business Model: Evaluate the revenue generation capabilities and business model of the virtual marketplace. This may include analyzing transaction fees, subscription fees, advertising revenue, data monetization, or any other sources of income. Assess the scalability and sustainability of the revenue model.
2. User Base and Engagement: Analyze the size and growth rate of the user base, including buyers and sellers, on the virtual marketplace. Consider metrics such as active users, retention rates, transaction volume, and user engagement levels. A large and engaged user base can indicate the platform's value and growth potential.
3. Market Size and Competition: Assess the size and growth potential of the market in which the virtual marketplace operates. Consider the market share of the platform and its ability to differentiate itself from competitors. Evaluate the competitive landscape, including other virtual marketplaces and potential disruptors.

4. Network Effects: Consider the presence and strength of network effects within the virtual marketplace. Network effects occur when the value of the platform increases as more users join or participate. Assess how network effects contribute to user acquisition, retention, and platform stickiness.
5. Technology and Infrastructure: Evaluate the technology infrastructure, features, and functionalities of the virtual marketplace. Consider the platform's user interface, ease of use, search capabilities, mobile compatibility, and security measures. Assess the scalability, reliability, and adaptability of the technology stack.
6. Financial Performance: Review financial metrics, such as revenue growth, profitability, and cash flow generation. Assess the platform's ability to monetize its user base and achieve sustainable financial performance. Consider historical financial data and projections for future growth.
7. Comparative Analysis: Compare the virtual marketplace to similar platforms in terms of market position, revenue multiples, or other relevant valuation metrics. This analysis helps understand the platform's relative valuation within the industry.
8. Ecosystem and Partnerships: Evaluate the ecosystem and partnerships surrounding the virtual marketplace. Consider strategic alliances, integrations with other platforms or services, and collaborations with key industry players. Assess how these partnerships contribute to the platform's value proposition and growth potential.

Valuing virtual marketplaces often involves using a combination of financial valuation methods, including discounted cash flow (DCF) analysis, comparable company analysis, or market-based multiples. These methods help estimate the present value of future cash flows or determine the platform's relative value compared to similar companies. It's important to consider both quantitative and qualitative factors, including market dynamics, competitive advantages, and the overall potential of the virtual marketplace.

Additionally, external factors such as the regulatory environment, market trends, and technological advancements can influence the valuation of virtual marketplaces. It's crucial to regularly reassess the valuation as the market landscape evolves and the platform's performance changes over time.

The valuation of virtual marketplaces can be influenced by cryptocurrencies, but the relationship is complex and multifaceted. Here are several ways in which cryptocurrencies can affect the value of virtual marketplaces:

1. Transaction Medium: Cryptocurrencies like Bitcoin and Ethereum are often used as a medium of exchange in virtual marketplaces, especially for purchasing digital goods and services. If a significant portion of a virtual marketplace's transactions are conducted in a particular cryptocurrency, the value of that marketplace could be influenced by the price volatility of the cryptocurrency.
2. Investor Interest: The popularity and acceptance of cryptocurrencies can drive interest and investment in related sectors, including virtual marketplaces. Increased investment can lead to increased valuation.
3. Digital Assets: The advent of non-fungible tokens (NFTs), which are unique digital assets stored on a blockchain, has introduced a new way of owning and trading digital goods in virtual marketplaces. NFTs have created significant value in these marketplaces, especially in sectors like digital art, virtual real estate, and digital collectibles.
4. Decentralization and Trust: Blockchain, the underlying technology of cryptocurrencies, can increase trust and transparency in virtual marketplaces by providing a decentralized and immutable ledger of transactions. This can increase the perceived value and reliability of the marketplace, potentially increasing its overall valuation.
5. Regulation and Legal Factors: Cryptocurrencies are subject to varying degrees of regulation around the world, and changes in these regulations can influence the valuation of virtual marketplaces. For example, if a country bans cryptocurrencies or introduces strict regulations, it could limit the growth of virtual marketplaces that rely heavily on cryptocurrency transactions.

While cryptocurrencies can influence the valuation of virtual marketplaces, they are just one of many factors. Other important factors include the user base, the volume of transactions, the variety and quality of goods and services offered, the technology and user experience of the platform, and competition from other marketplaces.

References

Akbaripour, H., Houshmand, M., & Valilai, O. F. (2015). Cloud-based global supply chain: A conceptual model and multilayer architecture. *Journal of Manufacturing Science Engineering, 137*(4), 040913.

Armstrong, M. (2006). Competition in two-sided markets. *Rand Journal of Economics, 37*(3), 668–691.

Asadullah, A., Faik, I., & Kankanhalli, A. (2018). Digital platforms: A review and future directions. Twenty-Second Pacific Asia Conference on Information Systems, Japan.

Bianconi, G. (2018). *Multilayer networks*. Oxford University Press.

Butler, B. (2013, February 11). PaaS Primer: What is platform as a service and why does it matter? *Network World*.

Ceccagnoli, M., Forman, C., Huang, P., & Wu, D. J. (2012). Co-creation of value in a platform ecosystem: The case of enterprise software. *MIS Quarterly, 36*(1), 263–290.

Cumming, D. J., Vanacker, T., & Zahra, S. A. (2019, January). Equity crowdfunding and governance: Toward an integrative model and research agenda. *Academy of Management Perspectives*.

de Reuven, M., Sørensen, C., & Basole, R. C. (2018). The digital platform: A research agenda. *Journal of Information Technology, 33*, 124–135.

Evans, D. S., Hagiu, A., & Schmalensee, R. (2006). *Invisible engines. How software platforms drive innovation and transform industries*. MIT University Press.

Fenwick, M., McCahery, J. A., & Vermeulen, E. P. M. (2019). The end of 'corporate' governance: Hello 'platform' governance. *European Business Organization Law Review, 20*(1), 171–199.

Gawer, A. (2014). Bridging differing perspectives on technological platforms: Toward an integrative framework. *Research Policy, 43*(7), 1239–1249.

Gawer, A., & Cusumano, M. A. (2014). Industry platforms and ecosystem innovation. *The Journal of Product Innovation Management, 31*(3), 417–433.

Ghazawneh, A., & Henfridsson, O. (2015). A paradigmatic analysis of digital application marketplaces. *Journal of Information Technology, 30*(3), 198–208.

Jacobides, M. G., Cernamo, C., & Gawer, A. (2018). Towards a theory of ecosystems. *Strategic Management Journal, 39*(8), 2255–2276.

Kane, G. C., Alavi, M., Labianca, G., & Borgatti, S. P. (2014). What's different about social media networks? A framework and research agenda. *MIS Quarterly, 38*(1), 275–304.

Kenney, M., & Zysman, J. (2016). The rise of the platform economy. *Issues in Science and Technology, 32*(3), 61.

Ketokivi, M., & Mahoney, J. T. (2015). Transaction cost economics as a constructive stakeholder theory. *Academy of Management Learning & Education, 15*(1), 123–138.

Koh, T. K., & Fichman, M. (2014). Multi-homing users' preferences for two-sided exchange networks. *Management Information Systems Quarterly, 38*(4), 977–996.

Korpela, K., Hallikas, J., & Dahlberg, T. (2017). Digital supply chain transformation toward blockchain integration. In *Proceedings of the 50th Hawaii International Conference on System Sciences*. https://scholarspace.manoa.hawaii.edu/handle/10125/41666

Majchrzak, A., & Malhotra, A. (2013). Towards an information systems perspective and research agenda on crowdsourcing for innovation. *Journal of Strategic Information Systems, 22*(4), 257–268.

Pagani, M. (2013). Digital business strategy and value creation: Framing the dynamic cycle of control points. *MIS Quarterly, 37*(2), 617–632.

Pflaum, A., Bodendorf, F., Prockl, G., & Chen, H. (2017). The digital supply chain of the future: Technologies, applications and business models minitrack. Hawaii International Conference on System Sciences. https://scholarspace.manoa.hawaii.edu/handle/10125/42513

Rochet, J. C., & Tirole, J. (2003). Platform competition in two-sided markets. *Journal of the European Economic Association, 1*(4), 990–1029.

Spagnoletti, P., Resca, A., & Lee, G. (2015). A design theory for digital platforms supporting online communities: A multiple case study. *Journal of Information Technology, 30*(4), 364–380.

Sutherland, W., & Jarrahi, M. H. (2018). The sharing economy and digital platforms: A review and research agenda. *International Journal of Information Management, 43*, 328–341.

Tan, B., Pan, S. L., Lu, X., & Huang, L. (2015). The role of IS capabilities in the development of multi-sided platforms: The digital ecosystem strategy of Alibaba.com. *Journal of the Association for Information Systems, 16*(4), 248–280.

Tiwana, A., Konsynsky, B., & Bush, A. A. (2010). Platform evolution: Coevolution of platform architecture, governance, and environmental dynamics. *Information Systems Research, 21*(4), 675–687.

Tsekeris, T. (2017). Global value chains: Building blocks and network dynamics. *Physica A: Statistical Mechanics and Its Applications, 488*, 187–204.

CHAPTER 9

Decentralized Finance (DeFi)

9.1 THE ARCHITECTURE OF DECENTRALIZED FINANCE

Decentralized finance, often referred to as DeFi, is a blockchain-based financial system that aims to provide open and permissionless access to financial services and products without the need for intermediaries, such as banks or traditional financial institutions. DeFi leverages the decentralized nature of blockchain technology to create transparent, secure, and programmable financial applications that operate on public or permissionless networks. The networking architecture does not have a barycenter, due to its decentralization.

Decentralized Finance was born with the Ethereum blockchain network in 2015.

One of the elements that have contributed most to the development of Ethereum and, therefore, the DeFi has been the possibility of creating and using the smart contracts on this network that, in turn, allows the creation of a wide range of decentralized applications, including the DeFi applications.

It is however in 2017 that DeFi begins its success when the first decentralized crypto exchanges are launched. The revolution consisted of the introduction of automated market makers that, with their liquidity pools, allow trading with any ERC-20 token. The other element that contributed to the success of DeFi in the same year was the ability to use it for initial public token offerings (ICO) that introduced the possibility of financing projects and startups by raising funds through the network.

In the following years, the phenomenon of ICOs has been progressively reduced also due to fraudulent practices unfortunately allowed by pseudo-anonymity and the lack of regulation and controls. This has not prevented the further development of the DeFi which, since then, has concentrated its activities on pooled funds. According to this philosophy, users do not interact directly with each other, but with smart contracts that regulate the operation of liquidity pools. One of the most successful DeFi protocols is Uniswap, a fully decentralized exchange launched in 2018, which allows users to exchange any token using automated market makers and liquidity pools. Users who feed the liquidity pools get rewards.

A Closer Look at Liquidity Pools

In DeFi, liquidity tokens play a crucial role in providing liquidity to decentralized exchanges (DEXs) and other liquidity protocols. These tokens represent users' shares in liquidity pools and enable the trading and swapping of assets within the DeFi ecosystem (Heimbach et al., 2021).

Here's a closer look at decentralized finance and liquidity tokens:

1. Liquidity Provision: Liquidity is essential for the efficient functioning of decentralized exchanges and other DeFi protocols. Liquidity providers (LPs) contribute their assets to liquidity pools, allowing users to trade or swap assets on DEXs. LPs are incentivized through earning fees or receiving rewards in the form of liquidity tokens.
2. Liquidity Pools: Liquidity pools are pools of assets held by LPs on decentralized platforms. These pools provide the liquidity required for users to make trades or execute other financial transactions. The pools typically consist of two or more assets, and LPs contribute proportional amounts of each asset to the pool.
3. Liquidity Tokens: Liquidity tokens are issued to LPs in exchange for their deposited assets in liquidity pools. These tokens represent LPs' share of the overall liquidity pool. Liquidity tokens act as proof of ownership and enable LPs to withdraw their proportionate share of the assets from the pool at any time. Liquidity tokens can be

freely traded, transferred, or used for other purposes within the DeFi ecosystem.
4. Impermanent Loss: LPs face the risk of impermanent loss when providing liquidity. Impermanent loss occurs when the value of the LP's deposited assets in the liquidity pool fluctuates relative to holding those assets outside the pool. It is a temporary loss that arises due to the dynamic nature of asset prices in the pool. However, LPs still earn fees or rewards, which can offset or compensate for impermanent loss.
5. Fee Distribution: When users trade or swap assets on DEXs, they pay transaction fees. These fees are distributed among the LPs in proportion to their share of the liquidity pool. Liquidity token holders, therefore, receive a portion of the fees generated by the platform, providing them with a passive income stream.
6. Incentives and Rewards: Some DeFi platforms incentivize liquidity provision by offering additional rewards or incentives to LPs. These incentives can come in the form of additional tokens, governance rights, or platform-specific rewards. These mechanisms encourage LPs to contribute assets to liquidity pools, enhancing the overall liquidity and functionality of the platform.
7. Liquidity Mining: Liquidity mining is a mechanism used by DeFi projects to incentivize liquidity provision. LPs are rewarded with additional tokens in proportion to their contribution to the liquidity pools. This practice helps bootstrap liquidity for new projects or protocols and encourages user participation.
8. Trading and Utility: Liquidity tokens can be traded on decentralized exchanges or used within the DeFi ecosystem for various purposes. They can be swapped for other assets, used for yield farming, or utilized in other DeFi protocols to earn additional rewards or benefits.

Liquidity tokens play a vital role in enabling efficient trading and liquidity provision in the decentralized finance space. They incentivize LPs to contribute assets to liquidity pools and participate in the growth and development of the DeFi ecosystem. However, it's important for LPs to carefully consider the risks and rewards associated with liquidity provision, including impermanent loss and market volatility.

A Closer Look at Automated Market Makers

Another element that forces the success of the DeFi is the presence of automatic market makers.

The automated market makers determine the price of the asset one wants to buy regardless of whether or not a counterparty wants to sell. Instead, they use an algorithm programmed to regulate the relationships between assets (typically two but could be more) present in a market (see Bartoletti et al., 2021).

The most popular of such systems is Uniswap which is based on the simple concept of the liquidity pool, a smart contract that holds two assets.

The algorithm keeps the product of the two assets constant and increases the price of the asset that becomes scarcer and on the contrary, decreases that of the asset that becomes more abundant.

9.2 DeFi vs Traditional Finance

To understand the difference between decentralized and traditional finance, it may be useful to use a couple of examples.

The Ethereum Name Service, ENS

The Ethereum Name Service, ENS is a decentralized domain name system built on the Ethereum blockchain. Similar to the traditional Internet's Domain Name System (DNS) that translates domain names into IP addresses, ENS translates human-readable domain names into Ethereum addresses and other decentralized content identifiers. ENS provides a decentralized and user-friendly approach to domain names in the Ethereum ecosystem. It simplifies the process of interacting with blockchain-based services and enables the creation of decentralized websites and content. Its integration with Wallets and DApps makes ENS fully a DeFi project (Brandinu, 2023).

Features of ENS domains are:

1. Decentralization. The traditional Internet's Domain Name Service (DNS) domain names are managed by central registrars and controlled by domain owners who have the authority to modify DNS records. This centralized control can lead to censorship

and single points of failure. In contrast, ENS domain names are decentralized, owned by individuals, and controlled by associated Ethereum addresses. Ownership and control of ENS domains are determined by the ownership of the corresponding private keys, providing a higher level of user autonomy and preventing censorship. ENS allows individuals to claim ownership of domain names by associating them with their Ethereum addresses. This ownership is secured by the Ethereum blockchain's consensus mechanism and cannot be altered by any central authority.
2. Ethereum Integration. ENS leverages the Ethereum blockchain to resolve and manage domain name ownership. Each ENS domain is associated with a unique Ethereum address, which can be used as a payment destination or for various decentralized applications (DApps) and services.
3. Customizable Records. ENS domains support various record types beyond simple address resolution. Owners can attach additional information to their domains, such as IPFS hashes, Swarm hashes, TXT records, and more. This flexibility enables ENS domains to be used for hosting decentralized websites, accessing decentralized content, and enabling various services.
4. Interoperability. ENS is designed to be interoperable with other systems and standards. It supports the Ethereum Name Service Public Resolver (EIP-137) standard, making it compatible with other Ethereum standards and DApps. Additionally, it can interact with DNS through the DNSSEC Integration specification (EIP-2222).
5. Registration and Auctions. ENS domains can be registered through a process of bidding and auctions, ensuring fair distribution and preventing domain squatting. The registration process involves placing a bid and committing to pay a certain amount of Ether (ETH) for the domain.
6. Integration with Wallets and DApps. ENS is widely supported by popular Ethereum wallets and decentralized applications. Users can easily associate their Ethereum addresses with ENS domains within these applications, making it more user-friendly to send and receive transactions.
7. Resolving Addresses. ENS provides a decentralized lookup system to resolve human-readable domain names to Ethereum addresses. This

makes it easier for users to interact with blockchain-based applications by replacing complex addresses with user-friendly names.

8. ENS solves Zooko's triangle problem. Zooko's triangle, also known as the Zooko's Triangle of Desiderata, is a conceptual framework that highlights three desirable properties in naming systems. It was proposed by Zooko Wilcox-O'Hearn, a computer scientist and cryptography expert. The triangle suggests that any global naming system can achieve at most two out of three properties: decentralization, security, and human-meaningful names (Wilcox, 2001). Here's a closer look at each property:

(a) Decentralization: Decentralization refers to the absence of a central authority controlling the naming system. In a decentralized system, no single entity has complete control over the assignment and management of names. Instead, the system is distributed among multiple participants or nodes, ensuring censorship resistance and resilience against single points of failure.

(b) Security: Security implies that the names within the system are unique, unforgeable, and tamper-resistant. It ensures that no two entities can claim the same name and that the integrity of the naming system is maintained. Security also encompasses the prevention of impersonation or spoofing, protecting users from fraudulent or malicious activities.

(c) Human-Meaningful Names: Human-meaningful names are names that are easy for people to remember, understand, and communicate. They are typically composed of words or phrases that have semantic value or are relevant to the entities they represent. Human-meaningful names enhance usability and user experience by making it easier for individuals to interact with the system and remember the names associated with specific entities.

(d) The triangle suggests that it is difficult to achieve all three properties simultaneously. Systems that prioritize decentralization and security may result in complex and cryptographically derived names that are not intuitive or human-friendly. Conversely, systems that prioritize human-meaningful names may sacrifice decentralization or security by relying on a central authority or introducing vulnerabilities.

(e) The traditional domain name systems (DNS) prioritize human-meaningful names and security but rely on centralized authorities, such as domain registrars, which limit decentralization.

Zooko's triangle serves as a useful framework for understanding the trade-offs involved in designing global naming systems. It highlights the challenges of achieving a balance between decentralization, security, and human-meaningful names, and encourages critical thinking in the development of naming systems.

A Hypothetical Venture Capital Protocol

The difference between a traditional financial structure and a DeFi infrastructure can be represented as follows. The next figures represent, for example, the business model of a venture capital infrastructure in both scenarios.

The next figure shows a traditional venture capital model where there are intermediaries and regulatory authorities between the capital market and the investee company.

For the moment, we provide a general description of the model only to clarify the differences between decentralized and traditional finance. The components of the decentralized business model will then be examined in detail in the next paragraphs (Fig. 9.1).

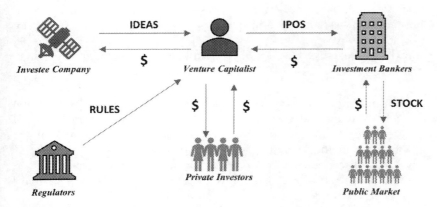

Fig. 9.1 Traditional venture capital model

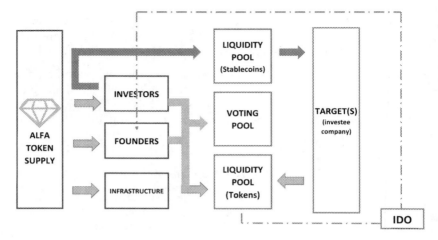

Fig. 9.2 A decentralized venture capital model

Figure 9.2 shows a decentralized venture capital model.

As can be seen, the traditional infrastructure is characterized by the presence of financial intermediaries that exercise control over transactions while in the DeFi infrastructure, such figures are completely absent especially when only cryptocurrencies and tokens are used. However, a DeFi protocol could provide for the presence of real subjects in certain processes for example when it includes transactions in fiat currency. In those cases, they are "hybrid DeFi protocols" (Anoop & Goldston, 2022).

A decentralized venture capital system has the following main characteristics:

- no intermediary. The first characteristic is the absence of a person who centralizes all transactions as is the case with traditional financial companies. All operations take place within the framework of the blockchain and, therefore, in a decentralized manner.
- the protocol takes resolutions only through parametric models,
- the execution of the operations based on "*if this ... then do that*" functions are delegated to smart contracts,
- the financing of the Liquidity Pool is open to any person wishing to contribute through the purchase of tokens;

- as a further effect of the decentralization and transparency inherent in the blockchain, all data collected within the protocol, including smart contract codes, are available to the public. The data of the subjects participating in the ecosystem naturally enjoy the pseudo-anonymity guaranteed by the blockchain;
- a DeFi protocol solves the problem of information asymmetry. In a traditional financial infrastructure, the relationships between the elements of the organization work only in one direction. The information is not fully shared between the parties involved in the economic process. Some subjects have more information than the rest of the participants. Due to information asymmetry, some individuals may benefit from the availability of information. Lack of information is also one of how systemic risk can spread between institutions, such as where the complexity of some financial instruments makes it difficult to identify the true underlying and the real counterparty of a contract. On the contrary, as a further effect of the decentralization and transparency inherent in the blockchain, all data collected within the DeFi protocols, including smart contract codes, are available to the public. The data of the subjects participating in the ecosystem naturally enjoy the pseudo-anonymity guaranteed by the blockchain;
- since the Blockchain can maintain a complete history of past transactions within the network, it can solve the problem of Byzantine Generals which is a "mathematical metaphor dealing with the questioning of the reliability of the transmissions and the integrity of the interlocutors" (Leloup, 2017).

Table 9.1 presents in more detail the characteristics of traditional intermediaries, blockchain, and DeFi.

9.3 The Blockchain

There would be no DeFi without the decentralized blockchain.

Blockchain technologies are part of the wider family of Distributed Ledger technologies (DLT). Distributed Ledger technologies are systems based on a distributed registry that is systems in which all nodes of a network have the same copy of a database that can be read and modified independently from the single nodes. Blockchain is therefore a distributed network (Fig. 9.3).

Table 9.1 Characteristics of traditional intermediaries, blockchain, and DeFi

Traditional financial intermediation networks	Blockchains	DeFi
Hierarchical structure The organizational structure follows the scheme of a pyramid. Each element, except for the upper element, is subordinate to someone else's element within the structure	**Decentralization** Every member of the blockchain structure can access the entire distributed database. Unlike in a centralized system, a consensus algorithm is responsible for network management	**Disintermediation** Absence of a person (institution) who centralizes all transactions as is the case with traditional financial companies. (Almost) All operations take place within the framework of the blockchain and, therefore, in a decentralized manner **No centralized decision-making** The protocol takes resolutions only through parametric models and/or by voting pools The execution of the operations based on "*if this … then do that*" functions is delegated to smart contracts **Equal access rights** The investment and the financing of the Liquidity Pools are open to any person wishing to contribute through the purchase of tokens

Traditional financial intermediation networks	Blockchains	DeFi
Asymmetries in relationships and information The relationships between the elements of the organization work only in one direction The information is not fully shared between the parties involved in the economic process Some subjects have more information than the rest of the participants Due to information asymmetry, some individuals may benefit from the availability of information Lack of information is also one of how systemic risk (see below) can spread between institutions, such as where the complexity of some financial instruments makes it difficult to identify the true underlying and the real counterparty of a contract	**Distribution** The information in blockchain is distributed across a network of connected computer systems, making it more secure and less prone to unauthorized data tampering. Blockchain maintains a complete history of past transactions within the network, which means that the user can track the data with full transparency. Blockchain relies on consensus protocols across a network of nodes to verify transactions executed on the network **Cryptography** Blockchain transactions are verified and trustworthy because of complex computations and cryptographic proof between the parties **Immutability** Records in a blockchain can't be modified or deleted **Provenance** It's possible to trace the origin of each transaction in the blockchain ledger **Anonymity** Every member of the blockchain network has a generated address, not a user ID (pseudo-anonymity). This preserves the anonymity of users, especially in a public blockchain **Transparency** The blockchain system is unlikely to be damaged as it takes enormous computing power to completely rewrite the blockchain network	**Full availability of information** As a further effect of the decentralization and transparency inherent in the blockchain, all data collected within the DeFi protocols, including smart contract codes, are available to the public. The data of the subjects participating in the ecosystem naturally enjoy the pseudo-anonymity guaranteed by the blockchain **The solution to the problem of Byzantine Generals** Since the Blockchain can maintain a complete history of past transactions within the network, it can solve the problem of Byzantine Generals which is a *"mathematical metaphor dealing with the questioning of the reliability of the transmissions and the integrity of the interlocutors"* (Leloup, 2017)

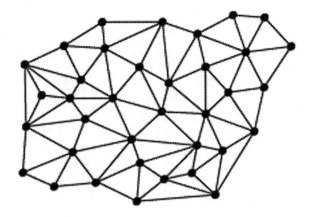

Fig. 9.3 Distributed network

A distributed network, also known as a decentralized network, refers to a network infrastructure in which data, resources, and decision-making are distributed across multiple nodes or computers. In a distributed network, no single central authority or entity has complete control over the network. Instead, control and decision-making authority are shared among the participating nodes.

Here are some key characteristics of distributed networks:

1. Peer-to-Peer Architecture: Distributed networks typically operate on a peer-to-peer (P2P) architecture, where each node in the network has equal capabilities and can act as both a client and a server. Nodes can directly communicate and interact with each other without relying on a central server.
2. Redundancy and Fault Tolerance: Distributed networks often exhibit redundancy, meaning that multiple copies of data or resources are distributed across different nodes. This redundancy helps ensure fault tolerance, meaning that if one node fails or goes offline, the network can continue to function and serve users without interruption.
3. Decentralized Decision-Making: In a distributed network, decision-making is decentralized, with each node having a degree of autonomy. Consensus mechanisms, such as majority voting or

consensus algorithms, may be employed to reach an agreement among nodes on network updates, data consistency, or transaction validation.
4. Data Distribution and Replication: Data in a distributed network is typically distributed and replicated across multiple nodes. This distribution helps improve data availability, accessibility, and resilience to failures or attacks. It also allows for parallel processing and efficient data retrieval.
5. A DeFi protocol solves the problem of information asymmetry. In a traditional financial infrastructure, the relationships between the elements of the organization work only in one direction. The information is not fully shared between the parties involved in the economic process. Some subjects have more information than the rest of the participants. Due to information asymmetry, some individuals may benefit from the availability of information. Lack of information is also one of how systemic risk can spread between institutions, such as where the complexity of some financial instruments makes it difficult to identify the true underlying and the real counterparty of a contract. On the contrary, as a further effect of the decentralization and transparency inherent in the blockchain, all data collected within the DeFi protocols, including smart contract codes, are available to the public. The data of the subjects participating in the ecosystem naturally enjoy the pseudo-anonymity guaranteed by the blockchain;
6. Scalability and Performance: Distributed networks can offer scalability advantages as the workload is distributed among multiple nodes. By adding more nodes to the network, the capacity and performance of the system can be increased to accommodate growing demand.
7. Security and Resilience: Distributed networks can enhance security and resilience. As data and control are distributed across multiple nodes, it becomes more challenging for malicious actors to compromise the entire network. In addition, distributed networks can withstand network failures or attacks on individual nodes, as the network can continue to operate using other available nodes.
8. Examples of Distributed Networks: Distributed networks are employed in various domains and technologies. Some examples include blockchain networks (used in cryptocurrencies and decentralized applications), peer-to-peer file-sharing networks (like

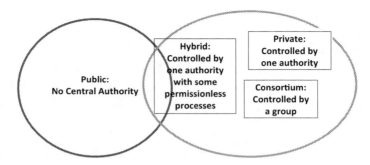

Fig. 9.4 Types of blockchains

BitTorrent), and content delivery networks (CDNs) that distribute content across geographically dispersed servers.

As anticipated, in distributed ledger systems, changes to the registry are regulated by consent algorithms. These algorithms allow consensus to be reached between the various versions of the registry, although they are updated independently by the network participants.

In addition to consent algorithms, to maintain the security and immutability of the registry, Distributed Ledger and Blockchain also make extensive use of encryption.

A blockchain is undoubtedly a distributed network since all its nodes have the same copy of a database but it may be centralized or decentralized depending on the rights of participants on the ledger. Based on this criterion, blockchains can be Public, Private, or Consortium (Figs. 9.4, 9.5).

Traditional Versus Blockchain Networks

Traditional networks and blockchains are fundamentally different in the way they operate.

Traditional Networks have the following main features:

1. Centralized Control: Traditional networks are typically controlled by a central authority or organization. This central entity manages

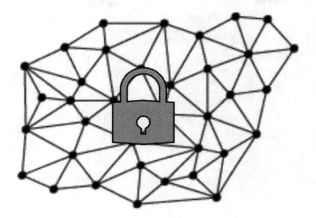

Fig. 9.5 Private blockchain

and controls the network, including decision-making, data storage, and access permissions.
2. Intermediaries: Traditional networks often rely on intermediaries, such as banks, payment processors, or central servers, to facilitate and verify transactions or data exchange. These intermediaries play a vital role in ensuring trust and security but can introduce inefficiencies and single points of failure.
3. Data Storage: Data in traditional networks is usually stored in centralized databases or servers controlled by the central authority or intermediaries. Users must rely on these centralized entities to manage and secure their data.
4. Trust: Trust in traditional networks is based on the reputation and credibility of the central authority or intermediaries. Users trust that these entities will act in their best interests and ensure the integrity of transactions and data.
5. Lack of Transparency: Traditional networks often lack transparency, as users have limited visibility into the inner workings of the network and the actions of the central authority or intermediaries.

Blockchain and Its "Nodes" in a DeFi Protocols

The next figure shows the use of blockchain by the decentralized venture capital model that we've taken as an example. In this example, we refer to the Ethereum blockchain since this network dominates, with almost 60% of the entire TVL (Fig. 9.6).

As has been seen, the blockchain consists of "nodes".

In a decentralized network like the blockchain, there is no central authority or single point of control. Instead, participants in the network collectively contribute to the operation, security, and decision-making processes. In this decentralized architecture, decision-making, control, and data are distributed across multiple nodes or participants.

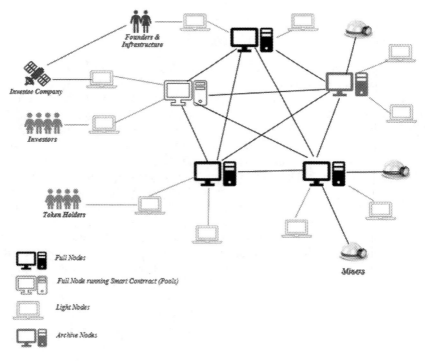

Fig. 9.6 Simplified representation of a DeFi venture capital on Ethereum blockchain

A "node" is a computer that performs a certain function on the Ethereum network and runs client software to do so. Depending on what the specific needs of the protocol are, whether it be a decentralized application (DApp) or a wallet, three different types of nodes can be run by any client: full nodes, light nodes, and archive nodes. Each node will interpret data differently and offer different methods for synchronization.

Full nodes store and distribute all the blockchain data from the Ethereum network. A full node will additionally participate in block validation (i.e., verify all blocks and states on the network). A full node can directly interact with any smart contract on the public blockchain. Full nodes can also directly deploy smart contracts into the public blockchain.

Light nodes are like the full node but handle less information. The light node stores header chain information (basic information stored in a block such as a timestamp and the hash of the previous block) but will only receive additional information upon request. They can verify the validity of data but do not fully participate in block validation.

Archive nodes are nodes that store all the information that a full node does and builds an archive of historical blockchain states. Archive nodes will retain historical data even after a client has finished synchronization. Full and light nodes, on the other hand, will "prune" the historical blockchain data, meaning they can rebuild, but do not retain this information.

9.4 The Value of the DeFi

The volume of funds invested in the DeFi is represented by Total Value Locked (TVL) which may refer to individual projects and the whole DeFi. Figure 9.7 shows the overall TVL performance from 2020 to the first quarter of 2023.

The factors influencing TVL can be identified by examining its value over time as shown in the chart below.

The growth of the TVL in 2021 was largely driven by three factors:

1. the growth in the value of cryptocurrencies since the TVL for the industry is heavily dependent on the underlying asset's price since the TVL for the industry is heavily dependent on the underlying asset's price;

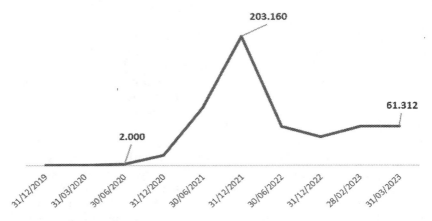

Fig. 9.7 TVL from 2020 to the first quarter of 2023

2. the development of applications for lending and borrowing digital assets, derivatives, insurance, and even the management of crypto assets;
3. the massive use of stablecoins used mainly by liquidity pools to make trading more convenient and intuitive. Additionally, DeFi applications rely on stablecoins to mitigate volatility in crypto markets, attracting investors in the long term.

The TVL explosion in 2021 was followed by a collapse due to:

1. the collapse in cryptocurrency prices. ETH lost 70.4% in the first six months of 2022;
2. the collapse of the Terra/Luna ecosystem in May 2022 that burned $40 billion and pushed cryptocurrency prices even lower;
3. the bankruptcy of FTX in November. To give an idea of the extent of this disaster, FTX reached a $3 trillion market capitalization at its maximum;
4. the domino effect that these defaults had on other financial players of the DeFi.

9 DECENTRALIZED FINANCE (DEFI)   305

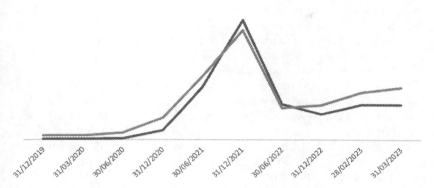

Fig. 9.8 TVL is related to the price of cryptocurrencies

Figure 9.8 shows how the TVL is strictly correlated to the price of the cryptocurrencies since the DeFi is heavily dependent on them.

9.5 Key Characteristics of DeFi

1. Openness and Accessibility: DeFi projects are built on public blockchains, allowing anyone with an internet connection to access and use financial services. DeFi aims to provide financial inclusion by removing barriers such as geographical restrictions, minimum account requirements, and identity verification processes.
2. Interoperability: DeFi protocols are designed to be interoperable, meaning they can interact and integrate with other protocols, applications, or services. This interoperability fosters composability, enabling developers to combine different DeFi building blocks to create new and innovative financial products and services.
3. Smart Contracts: DeFi applications rely on smart contracts, which are self-executing agreements with predefined rules and conditions. Smart contracts enable automation, transparency, and trust in financial transactions, removing the need for intermediaries. They execute transactions and enforce rules based on the code's logic and predefined conditions.

4. Decentralized Exchanges (DEXs): DeFi introduced decentralized exchanges, which allow users to trade cryptocurrencies directly with one another without relying on intermediaries or centralized entities. DEXs operate on blockchain networks, providing users with control over their funds and reducing counterparty risk.
5. Lending and Borrowing: DeFi platforms enable peer-to-peer lending and borrowing, allowing individuals to lend their cryptocurrencies and earn interest or borrow assets by providing collateral. These lending and borrowing protocols automate interest rate calculations, loan repayments, and collateral management through smart contracts.
6. Stablecoins: Stablecoins are cryptocurrencies designed to maintain a stable value, often pegged to a fiat currency like the US dollar. Stablecoins enable price stability within the volatile cryptocurrency market and facilitate seamless transactions and liquidity within DeFi applications.
7. Governance and Decentralized Autonomous Organizations (DAOs): DeFi projects often incorporate governance mechanisms that allow token holders to participate in decision-making processes. Decentralized Autonomous Organizations (DAOs) enable community governance, allowing stakeholders to vote on proposals, protocol upgrades, and the allocation of project resources.

9.6 Benefits and Potential of DeFi

Decentralized finance (DeFi) is a financial infrastructure based on distributed ledgers similar to those used by cryptocurrencies. It consists of open and interoperable protocols that operate based on smart contracts and decentralized applications (DApps) deposited in (permissionless) public blockchains that are open networks available to all. Contractual agreements are executed by the code and transactions are made in a safe and verifiable manner. Its main purpose is to remove the hierarchical control of financial intermediaries over money, products, and financial services.

Therefore, the DeFi architecture can create an immutable, interoperable, and transparent financial system with equal access rights and no need for custodians, central clearing houses, or escrow services as most of these roles can be assumed by smart contracts.

Here are the main key benefits of DeFi:

1. Financial Inclusion: DeFi aims to provide financial services to the unbanked or underbanked populations, offering access to loans, savings, and investments without traditional barriers;
2. Transparency: DeFi transactions are recorded on public blockchains, providing transparent and auditable records of financial activities;
3. Security: DeFi applications leverage blockchain's security features, such as cryptographic encryption and decentralized consensus, to protect user assets and data;
4. Programmability: Smart contracts enable the automation of financial processes, removing the need for intermediaries and reducing human error;
5. Innovation and Experimentation: DeFi fosters an environment for developers to experiment with new financial products and services, leading to innovative solutions and novel use cases.

9.7 A DeFi Project in Deep

To fully understand the components and operation of a DeFi project, the example of the decentralized venture capital business model is analyzed in detail.

DeFi Venture Capital refers to venture capital investments specifically focused on decentralized finance (DeFi) projects.

Here are some key features and considerations of DeFi Venture Capital:

1. Focus on DeFi: DeFi Venture Capital funds concentrate their investments on projects that operate within the decentralized finance ecosystem. These projects leverage blockchain technology, smart contracts, and other decentralized principles to offer financial services such as lending, borrowing, trading, asset management, and more.
2. Investment in Early-Stage Projects: DeFi VC funds often target early-stage or seed-stage projects in the DeFi space. They seek to identify promising projects with high growth potential and invest capital in exchange for equity or tokens.
3. Portfolio Diversification: DeFi VC funds typically maintain a diversified portfolio of investments across various DeFi projects. This

diversification strategy helps mitigate risks associated with individual projects and maximizes the potential for high returns by investing in different segments of the DeFi ecosystem.
4. Expertise and Support: DeFi VC funds provide not only a financial investment but also strategic guidance and support to the projects they invest in. They leverage their expertise, industry connections, and experience to assist portfolio projects in areas such as business development, technology, marketing, governance, and regulatory compliance.
5. Long-Term Investment Horizon: DeFi VC funds often have a long-term investment horizon, as the development and maturation of DeFi projects can take time. They aim to support the growth and success of their portfolio projects over the long term, allowing for value creation and capturing potential market opportunities.
6. Network and Ecosystem Building: DeFi VC funds actively contribute to building the DeFi ecosystem by fostering collaboration and partnerships among portfolio projects and other stakeholders. They facilitate connections and synergies within the DeFi space, which can enhance the growth and adoption of their portfolio projects.
7. Risk Assessment and Due Diligence: DeFi VC funds conduct thorough risk assessments and due diligence on potential investments. They evaluate the technological feasibility, market potential, team capabilities, token economics, regulatory compliance, and other factors to assess the viability and potential risks associated with a project.
8. Exit Strategies: DeFi VC funds consider exit strategies for their investments, aiming to realize returns on their investments at the appropriate time. Exit strategies may include options such as secondary market sales, initial public offerings (IPOs), token listings, or strategic partnerships.
9. No intermediary. The first characteristic is the absence of a person (institution) who centralizes all transactions as is the case with traditional financial companies. All operations take place within the framework of the blockchain and, therefore, in a decentralized manner (no centrality, no hubs).
10. the protocol takes resolutions only through parametric models,
11. the execution of the operations based on "if this ... then do that" functions is delegated to smart contracts,

12. the financing of the Liquidity Pool (stablecoins) is open to any person wishing to contribute through the purchase of tokens;
13. as a further effect of the decentralization and transparency inherent in the blockchain, all data collected within the protocol, including smart contract codes, are available to the public. The data of the subjects participating in the ecosystem naturally enjoy the pseudo-anonymity guaranteed by the blockchain.

DeFi Venture Capital plays a vital role in supporting the growth and development of the decentralized finance ecosystem. By providing capital, expertise, and guidance to early-stage DeFi projects, DeFi VC funds contribute to the innovation and expansion of the DeFi space while aiming to generate attractive returns for their investors.

The Protocol

In the DeFi world, there are no companies, but protocols. In this case, the Protocol is a combination of Players, Pools, Processes, Standards, Blockchain, Tokens, Smart Contracts, Oracles, and Licences.

To be precise, even in the DeFi ecosystem there are legal entities generally owned by the founders, but their function is to develop and update the system, hold licenses and legal authorizations, and coordinate the operational team.

The blockchain protocol is a coordination game, with multiple equilibria (Biais et al., 2018).

In this example, the protocol will use a token that we call ALFA (Fig. 9.9).

Keys:

- Transactions marked with a number in a circle and a red harrow are driven by user activity. They include the issuance of ALFA tokens by the founders, the purchase of ALFA tokens by the investors, and the deposit of ALFA tokens in stake by those who want to participate in the voting pool. All those transactions require a client interface between humans and the blockchain, for example, Metamask which is available as a browser extension. Metamask uses the information provided by users and signs them with their private key and then

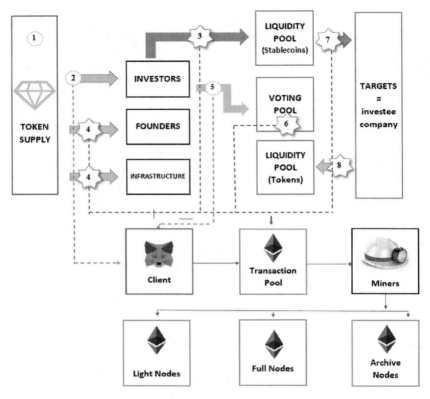

Fig. 9.9 Business model of a DeFi venture capital protocol totally decentralized and disintermediated

writes them on one of the Ethereum nodes. Services like Infura provide APIs that allow writing data to nodes.
- Transactions marked with a star and blue harrow are automatically executed via smart contract.

The Players

The community of subjects participating in the Protocol shall be composed of:

- Investors
- Founders
- Infrastructure
- Participants in the Voting Pools
- Participants in the Liquidity Pools
- Investee Companies

All these subjects make up the community that actively participates in the functioning of the system. All these subjects are linked by common denominators that can be emotional such as the desire for innovation or practical such as the hope of financial returns. However, a certain denominator of the entire community is the availability and use of the necessary tokens to participate, in various ways, in the project.

All of these subjects are elements of additional networks. Investors form a community of people looking for bargains. Developers are elements of a community of technicians linked by knowledge of specific computer languages. Voting pool participants constitute juries that influence choices within the protocol and so on.

Each subject can participate (and will participate) in more than one of these networks. Therefore, the ecosystem DeFi, in terms of networking, assumes the following configuration.

Figure 9.10 shows some of these networks, but they can be multiplied by each function within the protocol.

(a) Investors

Investors purchase the ALFA token during private and public offerings. The price must be paid in stablecoins.

The reasons for purchase are:

1. the ALFA token is freely negotiable. Therefore, the first reason is the forecast of an increase in its value,
2. participation in the Voting Pool, and subsequent remuneration,
3. participation in the Liquidity Pool (token) and consequent remuneration for staking and forecasting capital gain from investments in targets.

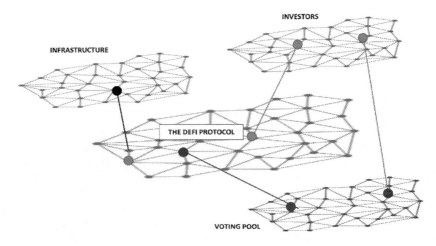

Fig. 9.10 A DeFi protocol is a multilayer network

In the DeFi model described in this chapter, the nature of tokens is fungible and hybrid.

The investors in the ALFA token are divided into two categories. The ones in the first category take an active role because they use the protocol taking on the role of venture capitalists and/or voting participants. Investors in this category are entitled to rewards from staking and capital gains. The investors in the second category take a passive role by investing in the token only in the expectation of its appreciation without having a real interest in the project. In consequence, they do not have property and/or administrative rights because they are not entitled to rewards from staking and capital gains.

What is interesting is that the property rights (right to rewards and capital gain) do not depend on the category of tokens, but on their use (in stake or not) at the free choice of the holder. These tokens are utility tokens because they contribute to the operations, but they assume the character of governance and/or security tokens when they are put in pools.

The question of whether tokens are security or not is sensitive because, if the ALFA tokens are considered security, then, in many countries, their offer to the public requires specific permissions. The debate is open. For example, on September 7, 2022, SEC President Gary Gensler gave an interview in which he stated that he believed that many cryptocurrencies are secure (Meshulam, 2022). For the sake of completeness, however, it should be remembered that some authors argue that the tokens of decentralized finance do not pass the Howey Test (and, therefore, are not secure) because their value isn't generated by the efforts of others (Kim, 2022). Moreover, in this protocol, the ALFA token also gives the holder (who deposits tokens in the voting pool) administrative rights (the right to vote on certain decisions). In this case, the token also assumes the function of a governance token.

(b) Founders

Founders receive ALFA tokens when created. One % must be locked for a certain time and one % can be used for staking in pools.

(c) The team

- Development team
- Legal team
- P.R. and marketing

All the components of the team receive ALFA tokens when created. One % must be locked for a certain time and one % can be used for staking in pools.

(d) Targets—Investee Companies

They issue their tokens. The Protocol purchases them to finance their projects in exchange for the fiat coins in the Liquidity Pool (stablecoins). After the purchase, the target's tokens are locked in the Liquidity Pool (token).

Pools

(a) The Liquidity Pool (stablecoins)

The Liquidity Pool (stablecoins) is fed by:

- stablecoins obtained from the sale of the ALFA token,

- stablecoins from offerings of Target's tokens.

It is decremented by the number of stablecoins sold to the targets in exchange for their tokens that, at the same time, are deposited in the Liquidity Pool (token).

To participate in the pool and participate in the capital gain at the time of placement, token holders must put a certain amount at stake.

(b) The Voting Pool

The Voting Pool shall decide:

- on which projects to invest,
- on the financing of the progress of the selected projects,
- on unlocking stablecoins for each work progress of the target,
- on the time of public offerings.

To participate in the Voting Pool, ALFA token holders must put a certain amount at stake. To ensure a high degree of independence from the founders and targets, for each decision, a certain number of voting participants shall be chosen randomly through a smart contract.

(c) The Liquidity Pool (token)

The Liquidity Pool (token) is fed by tokens received by the targets in exchange for fiat currency at the time of the investments. It decreases when tokens are placed through public or private offers.

The Process

The operating flow:

1. Creation of the ALFA token,
2. Distribution of ALFA tokens to founders and infrastructure components,
3. Sale of a % of the ALFA token via private, pre-sale, and public offerings,

4. Custody of stablecoins obtained from offerings in the (wallet) Liquidity Pool (stablecoins),
5. Receiving investment proposals from targets,
6. Even if the financing of the targets takes place according to the progress of the works of the Target, the Liquidity Pool (stablecoins) must have liquidity for the total investment. Therefore, further offering of ALFA tokens shall take place when the Liquidity Pool does not have sufficient liquidity for the overall investment (however, an inflationary risk should be avoided),
7. Random selection of the components of the Voting Pool via smart contract,
8. Investment decisions by the Voting Pool,
9. Purchase of tokens from Target in exchange for fiat money in the Liquidity Pool (stablecoins) for the first work progress,
10. Lock a % of the stablecoins to protect the community for a certain time,
11. For each subsequent work progress of the Target:

    - Random selection of the components of the Voting Pool via smart contract,
    - Investment decisions by the Voting Pool,
    - Purchase of tokens from the Target in exchange for stablecoins in the Liquidity Pool (stablecoins) for each work progress.

12. Public or private offering of Target's tokens,
13. Distribution of proceeds to ALFA token holders placed in staking in the Liquidity Pool (token).

Process of Choice of Investment by Voting Pool

When a potential target submits a project, it shall be communicated to the participants in the Voting Pool. For the process to take place exclusively through a smart contract, it must be parameterized. Therefore, the participants in the Voting Pool attribute a score to the set standards. If the overall result of the survey exceeds a certain score, the smart contract buys the tokens of the target in exchange for the stablecoins contained in the Liquidity Pool (stablecoins).

The same procedure applies to the release of funds at each stage of work progress.

Control Over the Target Company

As said, control over the target company is the most delicate activity within the protocol. In addition, it is to be expected that the target company will require program changes such as longer development times and/or increased financial resources. Since it is difficult to imagine an automatic system to evaluate and accept these requests, it is considered that human intervention is necessary. A solution could be the assignment to a leading law firm and a firm of auditors (at the expense of the target that will have to take this into account in the business plan) to certify the development of the company and the opportunity of its request. These subjects could insert the results of their analysis into a system that, in turn, transmits them to the smart contract through oracles.

Smart Contracts

Being a DAO protocol, the execution of the following operations is delegated to smart contracts:

- In and out transfers of stablecoins in and from the (wallet) Liquidity Pool (stablecoins),
- In and out transfers of Target's tokens in and from the (wallet) Liquidity Pool (token),
- Random selection of the components of the Voting Pool,
- Enforcement of decisions of the Voting Pool,
- Distribution of proceeds from the sale of Target's tokens to ALFA token holders.

Required Standards of the Projects

The selection of projects of the target companies should be based on predefined standards that must be carefully studied and established. The following are just examples:

- The specific economic sector of targets;

- Founders must have already collected seed capital;
- Expected multiples limit between the seed and the public rounds (to avoid unreasonable valuations);
- The total amount of tokens issued by the target company must cover its expenses for a further number of months compared to the expected time for the early stage in the business plan and increase a % of total estimated expenses;
- The maximum amount of investment by the Protocol;
- A % of the investment (in stablecoins) must be locked by Target in a wallet of the Protocol to protect the community;
- All tokens (equal to the total investment) must be delivered to the Protocol and no other tokens must be issued by the Target;
- Parameters of the reputation of the team which must include a legal team and financial auditors;
- Parameters of auditing of the smart contracts.

9.8 Challenges and Risks of DeFi

Risk management models in traditional finance are based on factors such as volatility and beta, and on the assumption that regulators, central banks, and other intermediaries make up a stable infrastructure and play a risk-reducing role. In DeFi, the replacement of intermediaries with programmable smart contracts does not allow the application of traditional theories of risk management and it is necessary to use a different approach.

(a) Operational Risk

Operational risk is one of the key challenges facing DeFi, as it is a relatively new and untested area.

There are a few different types of operational risks that DeFi projects face. One is the risk of smart contract bugs or vulnerabilities that could be exploited by attackers. Another is the risk of governance failure, where the decision-making processes of a project break down or become corrupted.

To mitigate these risks, many DeFi projects are implementing rigorous security audits and testing protocols, as well as establishing strong governance frameworks and community-driven decision-making processes. Additionally, many DeFi projects are exploring ways to decentralize their operations and reduce dependence on any one central authority or point of failure.

DeFi is an area with enormous potential, but projects need to take operational risk seriously and implement robust risk management strategies to ensure their long-term success.

Smart contracts are sequences of code, they are software and, as such, they can contain programming errors or, worse, malicious codes that allow intentional malfunctions or currency theft.

Oracles are also subject to the same risks. In addition, there is a risk of disservice to external providers about data transmitted to the blockchain utilizing oracles.

The codes used in the DeFi are open source. Since anyone can examine the code, the upside is that anyone can fix bugs. The downside is that even hackers can analyze the code and identify its weaknesses.

DeFi protocols depend on the infrastructure of the blockchain that presents vulnerabilities such as, for example, the compromise of consent mechanisms. In Proof-of-Stake networks, for example, cryptocurrency owners offer cryptocurrencies as collateral in exchange for the ability to validate transactions and earn rewards. In such a scenario, several subjects may form a "cartel" to influence the distribution of rewards and thereby compromise the functionality of the DeFi protocols.

Liquidity Risks: DeFi platforms heavily depend on sufficient liquidity to operate effectively. Insufficient liquidity can result in slippage, price manipulation, or challenges in executing transactions. In extreme cases, illiquidity can lead to systemic risks and contribute to market volatility. In the project described in this chapter, if target companies require additional finance, additional ALFA tokens must be issued and sold to the market. The increase in the mass of issued ALFA tokens can lead to an inflationary effect with a reduction in the market value of those in circulation. This may lead to a lower interest in the token for new investors and the disposal of tokens from the portfolios of those who already hold them and, in turn, a further decrease in their value. The additional perverse effect is that projects of target companies could be stopped even if they are already underway.

Smart contracts, in principle, reduce litigation because the conditions for the execution of specific contractual clauses depend on predefined objective factors. However, the likelihood of disputes cannot be ruled out. Many DeFi protocols provide for the devolution of disputes to arbitrators registered in blockchain whose probability of being chosen depends on the number of tokens placed in stakes. Not all disputes, however, can be submitted to arbitration and this circumstance can create difficulties or even the impossibility to resort to the judicial authority if the company holder of the protocol is domiciled in particular jurisdictions.

DeFi applications often rely on external data sources, known as oracles, to feed real-world information into smart contracts. Incorrect or manipulated data from oracles can compromise the integrity of DeFi protocols, leading to inaccurate pricing, faulty automated transactions, or financial losses.

An additional risk lies in the mechanisms of pool deposits. Platforms through which tokens can be pooled can suspend the right to put them in staking (and to withdraw them) reducing the possibility of underwriting policies at times when the market is unstable or hostile as well as for malfunctions or hacker attacks.

Governance Risks: Many DeFi projects incorporate governance mechanisms that allow token holders to participate in decision-making. However, decentralized governance can introduce risks, such as coordination challenges, governance attacks, or conflicts of interest among participants. Poor governance practices can lead to inefficient decision-making or contentious protocol upgrades (Xuan, 2023).

All smart contracts and DApps shall be best practices developed and audited. However, it would be unwise to consider that a system based on computer networks is completely immune to anomalies and hacker attacks. The Protocol therefore shall provide for insurance against the blocking of computer systems due to anomalies or hacker attacks.

Regulatory Uncertainty: The regulatory landscape for DeFi is still evolving, and regulatory actions can impact the operations and growth of DeFi projects. Compliance with financial regulations, such as anti-money laundering (AML) and know-your-customer (KYC) requirements, presents operational challenges. Failure to comply with regulatory obligations can lead to legal and reputational risks for DeFi projects and their users.

Market Volatility: DeFi projects and their associated tokens are subject to market volatility, which can impact the value of investments.

Scalability and User Experience: DeFi faces challenges in scaling to accommodate a larger user base, as well as improving user experience and onboarding for mainstream adoption.

Systemic Risk

The systemic "*risk in a network of interconnected agents, where distress caused to one or more agents is transmissible to several other agents in the network, generating widespread crisis*".

In a traditional financial network, it is "*the probability that cumulative losses will accrue from an event that sets in motion a series of successive losses along a chain of institutions or markets comprising a system [...] That is, systemic risk is the risk of a chain reaction of falling interconnected dominos*" (Kaufman & Scott, 2003).

The traditional financial system is composed of entities of different natures that are closely interconnected at the global level. The effects of the subprime mortgage crisis in the US on the financial markets and real economies of much of the globe have, unfortunately, demonstrated the correctness of this claim.

Of course, banks have very close relationships with each other in the interbank market. Moreover, the banks lend money to businesses and families and, in times of crisis, reduce credit, demand the repayment of loans, renegotiate interest rates, and enforce guarantees. Banks have relationships with insurance companies because banks increasingly sell insurance services and insurance companies build and sell financial products. The network of interconnected financial intermediaries also includes hedge funds and prime brokers. Many investors turn to hedge funds. Prime brokers streamline hedge funds by performing certain functions. They also contribute to investment choices and can lend securities to hedge funds.

In such a tightly interlinked network, a participant's default can easily and quickly spread to the entire system and the real economy. This is the systemic risk (Puri, 2022).

9.9 DeFi Valuation

Valuing decentralized finance (DeFi) projects can be a complex task due to the unique characteristics and evolving nature of the sector. A first approach to determine which assessment method is a priority can be as follows:

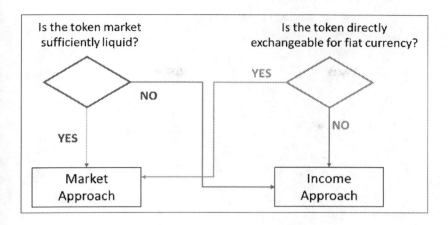

Market Approach

This approach consists of comparing the project to similar DeFi projects in terms of their market positioning, features, user base, and financial performance. Assess valuation metrics such as price-to-earnings (P/E) ratios, price-to-sales (P/S) ratios, or token price compared to TVL ratios. This comparative analysis can provide insights into the relative valuation of the project

1. The Total Value Locked (TVL): it is a metric used to measure the total value of digital assets that are locked or staked in a particular decentralized finance (DeFi) platform or distributed application, DApp (Dahlberg & Dabaja, 2021). A higher TVL means that more funds are locked into the DeFi protocol and that the protocol enjoys greater liquidity, popularity, and usability. Moreover, participants enjoy greater benefits and revenues. The market believes that projects with a TVL of more than 1 billion dollars are preferable as they are an indication of a professional team and greater usability of the protocol. Conversely, projects with low TVL, but with high reward promises for participants must raise a red flag as they can potentially be crypto Ponzi schemes (Fig. 9.11).
2. The market cap to TVL ratio: is calculated by dividing the market cap of crypto by its total value locked (TVL). It reflects the real

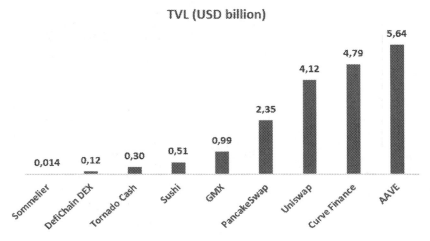

Fig. 9.11 TVL of 10 DeFi protocols on June 2, 2023 (*Source* DefiLlama.com)

appreciation of the market for the project itself: a ratio >1 means that the project is overvalued; if <1, the project is undervalued.

The comparison between the absolute TVL and the TVL ratio of individual projects can be a useful indicator of their quality and market appreciation as shown in Fig. 9.12.

3. The P/E Ratio: In traditional finance, it is the ratio of the price of a share of the company to the dividend per share. A high P/E ratio means that investors are willing to bet on the growth of the company and its ability to increase profits. Conversely, a low P/E may indicate a deterioration in the business or the fact that the company is undervalued. If profits remain constant, it gives the investor an indication of the years required to recover the capital.

In DeFi finance this index makes sense when the protocol remunerates those who provide liquidity (Eloise, 2020). Dex exchanges remunerate themselves by charging a small percentage fee on the aggregated volume ($) of transactions. When a liquidity provider burns their pool tokens to reclaim their stake of the total reserve, they receive a proportionally distributed amount of the total fees accumulated while they were staking. Table 9.2 shows the fees charged by four popular Dex exchanges.

9 DECENTRALIZED FINANCE (DEFI) 323

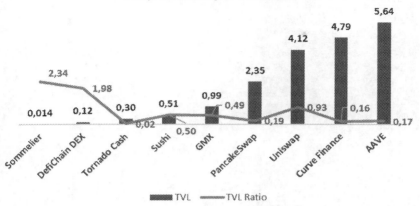

Fig. 9.12 Processing of data extracted from DefiLlama.com and Coinmarketcap.com on June 2, 2023

Table 9.2 Dex exchanges

DEX	FEE (%)
Sushi	0,30
AAVE	5,81
MakerDao	3,22
Uniswap	0,30

The P/E formula for Dexs is the following:

$$\frac{Price}{Earnings} = \frac{Price}{\frac{TotalEarnings}{NumberofShares}} = \frac{Price}{TotalEarnings} = \frac{1}{\frac{1}{\frac{MarketCap}{Price}}}$$

$$= \frac{MarketCap}{TotalEarnings}$$

where

$$TotalEarnings = 24hVolumeAnnualized \times Fee\%$$

The results are presented in Table 9.3 and Fig. 9.13.

Table 9.3 DEX statistics

DEX	Volume 24 h Annualized	FEE (%)	MKT Cap	P/E
Sushi	6.147.358.835	0.30	195.204.000	10.58
AAVE	14.430.640.000	5.81	916.216.880	1.09
MakerDao	863.590.000	3.22	165.345.000	5.95
Uniswap	274.461.750.000	0.30	2.915.757.000	3.54

Processing of data published by DefiLlama.com and CoinMarketCap.com on June 2, 2023

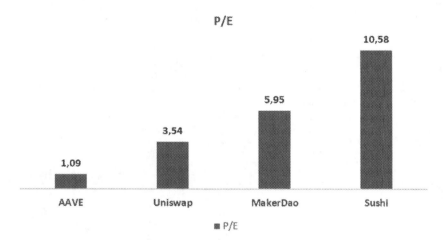

Fig. 9.13 Processing of data published by DefiLlama.com and CoinMarketCap.com on June 2, 2023

4. Additional benefits of the market approach. The comparative analysis inherent in the market approach involves comparing a particular DeFi protocol with its competitors or similar projects in the ecosystem. Here's how comparative analysis can be applied to the valuation of DeFi:

5.

(a) Market Share and Competitive Landscape: Comparative analysis helps assess a DeFi protocol's market share within its specific sector or industry. By comparing metrics such as total value

locked (TVL), transaction volume, or active user base, investors can gauge the project's position relative to its competitors. Understanding the competitive landscape is crucial in determining the project's valuation and growth potential.
(b) User Adoption and Activity: Comparative analysis allows for a comprehensive examination of user adoption and activity metrics. Evaluating the number of active users, user growth rates, user engagement, and retention rates of different projects provides insights into the popularity and adoption of a particular DeFi protocol. Projects with higher user adoption and activity levels often indicate a stronger value proposition and may be assigned a higher valuation.
(c) Revenue Generation: Comparative analysis enables the evaluation of revenue generation capabilities among similar DeFi projects. Assessing transaction fees, interest income, liquidity provider fees, or other sources of revenue can help determine the potential revenue streams of a project. Comparing revenue generation across similar projects can shed light on the competitiveness and valuation of the protocol.
(d) Tokenomics and Token Performance: Comparative analysis can be employed to evaluate the token economics and performance of different DeFi tokens. Comparing token supply, distribution models, token utility, market capitalization, trading volume, and price performance against similar projects can provide insights into the token's value and market perception. Understanding how a project's token compares to others in terms of market dynamics and investor sentiment is essential in valuation.
(e) Technology and Innovation: Comparative analysis allows for the assessment of technological advancements and innovation within the DeFi ecosystem. Examining the features, functionalities, scalability, security, and interoperability of different projects helps gauge the competitive advantages and potential valuation of a protocol. Projects that demonstrate technological leadership and innovation may be assigned a higher value.
(f) Regulatory Environment and Compliance: Comparative analysis includes considering the regulatory environment and compliance measures of DeFi projects. Evaluating how different protocols handle regulatory challenges and comply with relevant laws and regulations provides insights into the project's risk profile and

long-term sustainability. Comparing the compliance efforts and regulatory strategies among projects can impact their valuation.

Comparative analysis should be conducted carefully, considering various factors and considering the specific characteristics of each project. The competitive landscape and market conditions in the rapidly evolving DeFi space should be continuously monitored to ensure an accurate valuation.

Income Approach

An income approach is preferable when the token cannot be exchanged directly in fiat currency but requires an intermediate passage of exchange with other cryptocurrencies as well as if the liquidity is poor (e.g., in the early stage of a project).

Discounted cash flow (DCF) is a valuation method used to estimate the value of an investment based on its expected future cash flows. DCF analysis attempts to figure out the value of an investment today, based on projections of how much money it will generate in the future from the perspective of investors. In the case of the DeFi projects, the unlevered DCF formula shall be applied with the appropriate adaptations (Fig. 9.14).

The formula for calculating the value of a DeFi project based on the cash flows generated is as follows:

$$w = \sum_{t=1}^{n} \left(\frac{CF}{(1+c)t} + \frac{TV}{(1+c)n} \right),$$

where

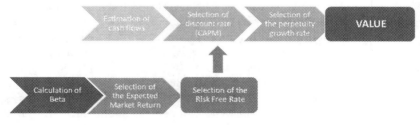

Fig. 9.14 Process of calculation of the value of a DeFi protocol with the DCF approach

w = value of the DeFi project
CF = Cash flow (dividends + rewards for active investors) at the year t

c = discount or required rate of return
$TV = Terminal Value = \frac{CF_n x (1+p)}{c-p}$
p = constant growth rate expected for dividends, in perpetuity
Here are some details on the model variables:

1. The perpetuity growth rate (p). It is typically between the historical inflation rate and the historical GDP growth rate (Gordon, 1959). Assuming a perpetuity growth rate above the GDP growth rate implies the idea that the growth of the project will exceed forever the growth of the economy. Recent world events show that indicators of GDP growth rate and inflation rate may undergo unexpected changes that make the choice of the perpetual growth rate even more difficult. The moment we write, the Organisation for Economic Co-operation and Development forecasts an inflation rate in the Euro area that ranges from 8.7% in the first quarter of 2023 to 4.9% in the fourth quarter of the same year (OECD, 2022) and the European Commission expects a GDP growth rate of 0.3% in the same area for the same year (European Commission, 2022). In consequence, a conservative rate of 2.0% seems to be appropriate.
2. The discount or required rate of return (c). There is currently no adequate risk rate in the digital asset market that can be used as a benchmark, therefore the expected annual returns in equity funding rounds for venture capital should be used. In those cases, the annual expected returns range from 25% (Cochrane, 2021) to 50% (Todaro, 2018a, 2018b); therefore, the discount rate should be chosen within this range depending on the estimated degree of risk of the project.
3. Criticism of the Total Value Locked (TVL) ratio entry in the formula. While the Gordon Growth Method to find a Terminal Value is the most suitable for DeFi projects (Gordon, 1959), the choice of growth rate is challenging because the DeFi sector is still young, and no historical indicators are available. Moreover, like all investment scenarios, the decision to contribute to decentralized finance is also influenced by factors such as inflation, interest rate levels, credit crunch, and, of course, more profitable investment opportunities making forecasting a constant presence of investors

difficult. Yet, the trend of crypto assets is influenced by the portfolio policies of institutional investors who make massive investments despite some formal aversion to the crypto world and then balance the portfolio at the end of the year creating spikes and collapses in the value of tokens that create doubts and perplexities in the retail market especially as observed between the end of 2021 and the beginning of 2022. Moreover, as said, the price variability of tokens is influenced by the level of the ownership concentration in the market and by the trading volume of the exchanges or exchange-like entities such as online wallets, OTC desks, and large institutional traders.

In effect, the DeFi Pulse Index (DPI) (a capitalization-weighted index that tracks the performance of decentralized financial assets across the market) gained 214.3% from January to November 2021 and then fell by 78.8% in November 2022. Also, the Total Value Locked (TVL) in the DeFi ecosystem lost 74.5% (from 160.99 billion dollars at the end of November 2021 to 41.09 billion dollars at the end of November 2022). Furthermore, the growth rate of a business is not uniform over time and should be modulated according to the different stages of development (startup, growth, maturity, renewal, or decline). Finally, platforms through which tokens can be pooled can suspend the right to put them in staking and to withdraw them at times when the market is unstable or hostile as well as for malfunctions or hacker attacks. All these circumstances, combined with the poor maturity of the DeFi sector, make us believe that it is not appropriate to include the Terminal Value in the formula or not.

Accordingly, the formula should be used in its simplified form:

$$w = \sum_{t=1}^{n} \left(\frac{CF}{(1+c)t} \right)$$

w = value of the DeFi project

CF = Cash flow (dividends + rewards for active investors) at the year t

c = discount or required rate of return

4. Challenges in the use of WACC and CAPM in the valuation of DeFi projects.

In the valuation of traditional companies, the discount rate normally used is the Weighted Average Cost of Capital (WACC) which blends the cost of risk capital with that of the company's debt. When the company has no debt, the discount rate used is equal to the cost of risk capital generally calculated using the Capital Asset Pricing Model (CAPM). It is difficult if not impossible to talk about equity or debt for a DeFi project. However, it is possible to remodel the CAPM formula to find the cost of a token (Todaro, 2018a). The formula is the following:

$$C_t = \beta \times (R_m - R_f) + R_f,$$

where
C_t = Cost of the token
β = Beta of the security
R_m = Expected Market Return
R_f = Risk-Free Rate

5. Challenges in the choice of Beta of the security in the valuation of DeFi projects.

Beta is a measure of the volatility, or systematic risk, of a security or portfolio in comparison to the market as a whole. A beta greater than 1.0 suggests that the stock is more volatile than the broader market, and a beta less than 1.0 indicates a stock with lower volatility.

Mathematically we can calculate the beta of a crypto asset by comparing how the asset Rp and an index/market Rb move relative to each other using a covariance formula and then we can divide that result by the variance of the index/market Rb alone (Todaro, 2018a).

$$\beta_p = \frac{Cov(R_p, R_b)}{Var(R_b)}$$

Using this formula by comparing Uniswap's historical prices with those of the TVL for the entire DeFi ecosystem in 2021–2022, we noted that the Beta of UNI is 0.58 meaning that UNI is less volatile than the TVL. The beta of the Polkadot token, DOT, is instead 1.24. Therefore, Polkadot was more volatile than TVL in the period considered (Fig. 9.15).

6. Empirical evidence.

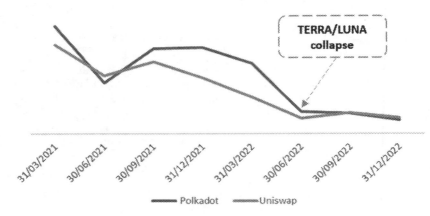

Fig. 9.15 Price variations of UNI and DOT, 2021–2022 (*Data source* Coinmarketcap.com)

Based on the assumptions and formulas presented in the previous paragraphs, the DCF of the investment in two DeFi protocols has been calculated in Table 9.4.

Table 9.4 DCF of DeFi protocols

	UNISWAP	POLKADOT
Beta	0.58	1.24
Expected Market Return	8.0%	8.0%
Risk-Free Rate	3.85%	3.85%
Cost of token/CAPM	6.26%	8.98%
Perpetuity growth rate	2.00%	2.00%
MKT Cap	$2,924,824,674	$6,291,570,290
Estimate Yields	18.48%	9.77%
Estimated Yields on MKT Cap	$540,507,600	$614,686,417
Circulating	577,501,036	1,190,594,233
Estimate Yields per token	$0.936	$0.516
Periods	5	5
DCF/Value	$4.61	$2.34
Price	$5.07	$5.29

The key features are the following:

(a) The beta of the tokens has been calculated concerning the TVL of the entire DeFi ecosystem in the period 2021–2022.
(b) The Expected Market Return was chosen as the approximate average of the data available at https://defillama.com/yields on June 3, 2023.
(c) The Risk-Free Rate is the United States 5-Year Bond Yield available at investing.com on the same date.
(d) The Cash Flows predictions are based on the Estimated Yields available at https://defillama.com/yields and https://www.coinbase.com/it/earn/staking/polkadot on June 3, 2023.
(e) The Market Capitalization and the Circulating Supply are based on the data available at https://www.coinbase.com/ on the same date.
(f) The Price of the tokens is based on the data available at https://www.coinbase.com/ on the same date.

7. Further considerations on the application of DCF in the DeFi projects.

Cash flow analysis in DeFi valuation can be complex and speculative due to the evolving nature of the industry. The accuracy of cash flow projections depends on the quality of data, assumptions, and the ability to anticipate market dynamics. Therefore, it's crucial to exercise caution and perform thorough due diligence when applying cash flow analysis in the valuation of DeFi protocols. Cash flow analysis plays an important role in the valuation of decentralized finance (DeFi) protocols. It involves assessing the cash flows generated by the protocol to estimate its intrinsic value. Here are some key aspects of cash flow analysis in DeFi valuation:

(a) Revenue Streams: DeFi protocols generate revenue through various streams such as transaction fees, interest income, liquidity provider fees, or other sources specific to the protocol. Cash flow analysis involves identifying and quantifying these revenue streams. For example, a lending protocol might generate income from interest payments made by borrowers.
(b) Future Cash Flow Projections: Estimating future cash flows is a crucial step in cash flow analysis. It involves making assumptions about the growth rate, user adoption, and market conditions.

For example, projecting transaction volumes, user activity, or the expansion of the protocol's ecosystem can help estimate future cash flows. These projections can be based on historical data, industry trends, or the protocol's development roadmap.

(c) Discounted Cash Flow (DCF) Analysis: DCF analysis is commonly used to determine the present value of future cash flows. It involves discounting projected cash flows to their present value using an appropriate discount rate. The discount rate reflects the risk and opportunity cost of investing in the DeFi protocol. Lower-risk protocols may have lower discount rates, while riskier protocols may require a higher discount rate.

(d) Sensitivity Analysis: Sensitivity analysis helps evaluate the impact of changing variables on the cash flow projections and valuation. By adjusting key assumptions, such as growth rates, transaction fees, or user adoption rates, analysts can assess the sensitivity of the valuation to different scenarios. This analysis helps identify the most critical factors driving the protocol's value and the potential risks involved.

(e) Risk Assessment: Cash flow analysis in DeFi valuation should also consider the risks associated with the protocol. Factors such as smart contract vulnerabilities, regulatory risks, market competition, and systemic risks within the DeFi ecosystem should be assessed and factored into the cash flow analysis. Evaluating the protocol's risk profile and incorporating risk-adjusted cash flows can lead to a more comprehensive valuation.

Further Elements to Be Analyzed in Any Valuation Approach of DeFi Projects

1. Token Market Performance in Deep: Token market performance is a significant aspect considered in the valuation of decentralized finance (DeFi) projects (Kampakis & Stankevičius, 2023). The performance of a token in the market provides insights into investor sentiment, demand, and the overall perception of the project's value. Here's how token market performance can be relevant in the valuation of DeFi:

(a) Price Appreciation: The price appreciation of a token over time is a key factor in its valuation. If a token's price has consistently increased, it suggests strong investor demand and market confidence in the project. Price appreciation can be driven by factors such as growing user adoption, increasing utility, positive news, or overall market trends. Higher price appreciation is often associated with a higher valuation.
(b) Market Capitalization: Market capitalization, calculated by multiplying the token's price by its circulating supply, is frequently used as an indicator of a project's valuation. Higher market capitalization generally implies a larger investor base, a more significant market presence, and potentially higher perceived value. However, it's important to consider that market capitalization alone may not provide a comprehensive view of a project's value, as it can be influenced by factors like token supply and distribution.
(c) Trading Volume: Trading volume reflects the liquidity and market activity of a token. Higher trading volume indicates increased interest, market participation, and potential trading opportunities. Analyzing trading volume can provide insights into the level of market engagement, the efficiency of trading, and the ease of buying and selling the token. Robust trading volume can contribute to a higher valuation by enhancing market dynamics and liquidity.
(d) Market Performance Relative to Peers: Comparing the token's market performance to its peers or similar projects within the DeFi ecosystem can be informative. Evaluating metrics such as price movements, market capitalization, trading volume, and other performance indicators relative to competitors allows for benchmarking analysis. Outperforming peers can suggest a stronger value proposition, leading to a potentially higher valuation.
(e) Price Volatility and Stability: The price volatility and stability of a token are considerations in its valuation. Lower price volatility may indicate a more stable and mature market, which can positively influence investor confidence and the token's value. Conversely, high price volatility may suggest higher risk and uncertainty, impacting the token's valuation negatively. The

ability of a token to maintain stable prices under varying market conditions is often valued by investors.
   (f) Investor Sentiment and Perception: Market sentiment and perception play a crucial role in token valuation. Positive sentiment, driven by factors such as positive news, endorsements from influential individuals or organizations, or community engagement, can drive up a token's value. Conversely, negative sentiment or skepticism can have an adverse effect. Monitoring investor sentiment and perception through social media, community forums, or sentiment analysis tools can provide insights into the token's valuation.
   (g) The competitive position. It includes the market potential for further development, the level of competition or lack thereof, and the market share of the project (Hancock, 2020).
2. Supply and Demand Dynamics: Evaluating the supply and demand dynamics of a token is critical for its valuation. Factors such as token issuance rate, maximum supply, token burn mechanisms, inflationary or deflationary features, and token distribution models can impact token scarcity and demand. Limited supply and increasing demand generally contribute to a higher token value.
3. Tokenomics and Incentive Structures: Examining the tokenomics and incentive structures within a DeFi project is essential. Tokens used to incentivize users, liquidity providers, or other participants can drive adoption and activity within the ecosystem. Understanding the alignment of incentives, reward mechanisms, and the impact on token demand and value is crucial for valuation.
4. Token Distribution and Allocation: The initial distribution and ongoing allocation of tokens can affect their value. Factors such as token vesting schedules, lock-up periods, founder/developer allocations, and token release mechanisms should be considered. A well-designed and fair token distribution model can enhance market confidence and positively impact the token's valuation.
5. Network Effects: Network effects occur when the value of a token and the associated DeFi protocol increase as more users and participants join the network. Factors such as the number of active users, the volume of transactions, and the ecosystem's growth can influence network effects. Positive network effects can drive up the demand for the token and, consequently, its valuation (Zao et al.,

2021). At the same time, it is necessary to evaluate if the protocol has connections with other protocols or with players of traditional finance and also the depth of the connections because the performance or even the defaults of these subjects can influence the value of the project.
6. The role of the token. The utility of a token within a DeFi ecosystem is a crucial factor in its valuation. Tokens may have various use cases, such as governance rights, staking for rewards, accessing specific features or services, or serving as a medium of exchange within the ecosystem. The more essential and diverse the utility of a token, the higher its potential value. It is an important point for any investor who directly influences the yield. The analysis must include the functional application of the token within the network and the changes in demand for the token over time.
7. Governance mechanisms. If the token gives voting rights, it is important to check whether a high concentration of decision-making power is in the hands of a selected few. Governance mechanisms can significantly impact the value of a token. Tokens that grant holders voting rights and influence over protocol decisions can be highly valued, as they enable token holders to shape the protocol's direction.
8. Qualitative Factors. In addition to quantitative factors, qualitative factors play a significant role in the valuation of decentralized finance (DeFi) projects. These qualitative factors provide insights into the project's potential, risks, and competitive advantages. Here are some key qualitative factors to consider in the valuation of DeFi:

   (a) Team and Expertise. Assessing the team behind a DeFi project is crucial. The factors to be considered are: the team's experience, expertise, and track record in the blockchain and financial industries; the team's ability to deliver on the project's roadmap, their knowledge of regulatory compliance, and their technical capabilities. A strong and experienced team increases the project's credibility and can positively impact its valuation.

   (b) Innovation and Unique Value Proposition. It is important to analyze the project's innovation and unique value proposition and to consider whether the project offers new and novel solutions, addresses existing pain points in the DeFi ecosystem, or introduces cutting-edge technologies. Projects that bring something unique to the table and differentiate themselves from competitors may have a higher valuation potential.

(c) User Experience and Interface. The user experience (UX) and interface design of a DeFi protocol can significantly impact its adoption and value. It must be evaluated how intuitive and user-friendly the protocol is for participants, including traders, lenders, borrowers, or liquidity providers. A well-designed and user-centric interface can enhance the protocol's adoption, liquidity, and overall valuation.

(d) Community and Ecosystem. It must be assessed the strength and engagement of the project's community and ecosystem, the level of community involvement, the size of the user base, and the level of participation in governance processes. A vibrant and active community can contribute to network effects, drive adoption, and positively impact the valuation of the project.

(e) Partnerships and Integrations. The project's partnerships and integrations with other platforms, protocols, or service providers should be also considered to evaluate the quality and significance of the partnerships and the potential impact on the project's valuation. Strategic collaborations can enhance the project's reach, expand its ecosystem, and unlock new growth opportunities.

(f) Regulatory Environment and Compliance. It must be evaluated the regulatory environment and the project's compliance efforts; the project's adherence to relevant regulations, its approach to Know Your Customer (KYC) and Anti-Money Laundering (AML) requirements, and its response to changing regulatory landscapes. A strong regulatory framework and compliance practices can mitigate risks and positively influence the project's valuation (Zetzsche et al., 2020).

(g) Market Perception and Sentiment. Monitoring market perception and sentiment surrounding the project is another key factor in the valuation of a DeFi project along with media coverage, social media sentiment, and community discussions to understand how the project is perceived by investors, analysts, and the broader DeFi community. Positive sentiment and market confidence can impact the project's valuation.

Qualitative factors should be considered alongside quantitative analysis and other valuation approaches, as shown above. Comprehensive due diligence, ongoing monitoring, and staying informed about the latest industry developments are crucial for a holistic evaluation of DeFi projects.

Risk Assessment

Risk assessment is a crucial component in the valuation of decentralized finance (DeFi) projects. Evaluating the risks associated with a DeFi protocol helps investors and analysts understand the potential vulnerabilities, challenges, and uncertainties that could impact the project's value. Here are some key aspects of risk assessment in the valuation of DeFi:

(a) Smart Contract Risks: DeFi protocols often rely on smart contracts to automate processes and execute transactions. Assessing the security and robustness of smart contracts is essential. Smart contract vulnerabilities, such as coding bugs, logic flaws, or potential attack vectors, can pose significant risks. Auditing the smart contract code, evaluating the security practices of the development team, and monitoring the protocol for potential security incidents are important in risk assessment.

(b) Market Risk: Market risk refers to the potential impact of broader market conditions on the valuation of a DeFi project. Fluctuations in cryptocurrency prices, changes in regulatory frameworks, macroeconomic factors, or shifts in investor sentiment can affect the valuation of DeFi tokens and the overall stability of the ecosystem. Analyzing market risk involves understanding the project's exposure to external factors and assessing the resilience of the protocol under different market scenarios.

(c) Liquidity Risk: Liquidity risk relates to the availability and stability of liquidity within a DeFi protocol. Illiquid markets can make it challenging for users to enter or exit positions, impacting the overall user experience and potentially affecting the valuation of the project. Assessing the depth of liquidity pools, monitoring trading volumes, and evaluating the risk of impermanent loss for liquidity providers are critical considerations in liquidity risk assessment.

(d) Regulatory and Compliance Risk: DeFi projects operate within a regulatory environment that is still evolving. Regulatory and compliance risks arise from potential legal challenges, regulatory scrutiny, or changes in regulatory frameworks that could impact the project's operations, market access, or overall viability. Understanding the regulatory landscape, monitoring compliance efforts, and assessing the project's risk mitigation measures are important in managing regulatory and compliance risk.

(e) Counterparty Risk: DeFi protocols often involve interacting with other participants, such as borrowers, lenders, or liquidity providers. Evaluating the counterparty risk associated with these interactions is crucial. Assessing the reputation, creditworthiness, and reliability of counterparties, as well as the protocol's mechanisms for managing default risk, can help gauge the potential impact on the project's valuation.

(f) Governance and Coordination Risk: Decentralized governance is a key feature of many DeFi projects, and assessing governance and coordination risk is important. Governance processes, decision-making mechanisms, and the level of community participation can impact the project's direction, adaptability, and long-term viability. Evaluating the effectiveness of governance models and the potential for conflicts or coordination challenges is essential in risk assessment.

Risk assessment in DeFi is an ongoing process due to the dynamic nature of the ecosystem. Continuous monitoring, staying informed about the latest developments, and conducting due diligence are essential for comprehensive risk assessment in the valuation of DeFi projects.

Valuing DeFi projects can be challenging due to the rapidly evolving nature of the sector and the uncertainties associated with regulatory frameworks, market conditions, and technological advancements. Therefore, a comprehensive valuation approach should incorporate a combination of quantitative and qualitative factors, as well as continuous monitoring and reassessment of the project's performance and market dynamics.

REFERENCES

Anoop, V., & Goldston, J. (2022). Decentralized finance to hybrid finance through blockchain: A case-study of actual and current. *Journal of Banking and Financial Technology*.

Bartoletti, M., Hsin-yu Chiang, J., Lluch-Lafuente, A. (2021). A theory of automated market makers in DeFi. In F. Damiani & O. Dardha (Eds.), *Coordination models and languages. COORDINATION 2021.* Lecture Notes in Computer Science (Vol. 12717). Springer. https://doi.org/10.1007/978-3-030-78142-2_11

Biais, B., Bisiere, C., Bouvard, M., & Casamatta, C. (2018, January 5). *The blockchain folk theorem* (Swiss Finance Institute Research Paper No. 17–75). https://ssrn.com/abstract=3108601

Brandinu, M. (2023). https://metlabs.io/ and https://maryjane.es/

Cochrane, J. H. (2021). *The risk and return of venture capital* (Working Paper 8066). https://www.nber.org/system/files/working_papers/w8066/w8066.pdf

Dahlberg, T., & Dabaja, F. (2021). *Decentralized finance and the crypto market: Indicators and correlations.* http://urn.kb.se/resolve?urn=urn:nbn:se:liu:diva-177960

Eloise. (2020). *P/E ratio for cryptocurrencies.* https://medium.com/coinmonks/p-e-ratio-for-cryptocurrencies-63dad08d26fc

European Commission. (2022). *Autumn 2022 economic forecast: The EU economy at a turning point.* https://ec.europa.eu/commission/presscorner/detail/en/ip_22_6782

Gordon, M. J. (1959). Dividends, earnings and stock prices. *Review of Economics and Statistics, 41*(2), 99–105.

Hancock, J. (2020). *How to choose an ICO for investment?* https://ethex-smm.medium.com/how-to-choose-an-ico-for-investment-5e777261c12f

Heimbach, L., Wang, Y., & Wattenhofer, R. (2021). *Behavior of liquidity providers in decentralized exchanges.* Cornell University. https://doi.org/10.48550/arXiv.2105.13822

Kampakis, S., & Stankevičius, L. (2023). *The Tokenomics audit checklist: Presentation and examples from the audit of a DeFi project, Terra/Luna and Ethereum 2.0.* University College London, Centre for Blockchain Technologies, London, UK. https://doi.org/10.31585/jbba-6-2-(1)2023

Kaufman, G. G., & Scott, K. E. (2003). What is systemic risk, and do bank regulators retard or contribute to it? *The Independent Review.*

Kim, P. (2022). *The Howey test: A set of rules that determine if an investment is a security.* https://www.businessinsider.com/personal-finance/howey-test?r=US&IR=T

Leloup, L. (2017). *Blockchain: La Révolution de la Confiance.* Editions Eyrolles.

Meshulam, D. (2022). *SEC Chair Gensler continues to push broad SEC authority over digital assets.* https://www.dlapiper.com/en/insights/publications/2022/09/sec-chair-gensler-continues-to-push-broad-sec-authority-over-digital-assets

Organisation for Economic Co-operation and Development. (2022). *Inflation forecast*. https://data.oecd.org/price/inflation-forecast.htm

Puri, V. (2022). *De-risking DeFi: Analyzing systemic risk in decentralized systems*. https://research.thetie.io/systemic-risk-in-defi/

Todaro, J. (2018a). *Valuing crypto assets using a DCF model*. https://medium.com/@john_19547/valuing-crypto-assets-using-a-dcf-model-bc6297b0bd25

Todaro, J. (2018b). *Finding an appropriate discount rate for crypto-currencies*, https://medium.com/@john_19547/finding-an-appropriate-discount-rate-for-crypto-currencies-14ff6190048b

Wilcox, B. (2001). *Names: Distributed, secure, human-readable: Choose two*. https://web.archive.org/web/20011020191610/http://zooko.com/distnames.html

Xuan, L. (2023). *The illusion of democracy? An empirical study of DAO governance and voting behavior*. https://ssrn.com/abstract=4441178 or https://doi.org/10.2139/ssrn.4441178

Zao, L., Khan, A., Gupta, S., & Luo, R. (2021). *Temporal analysis of the entire Ethereum blockchain network*. http://souravsengupta.com/publications/2021_www.pdf

Zetzsche, D., Arner, D., & Buckley, R. (2020, September 20). Decentralized finance. *Journal of Financial Regulation, 6*(2), 172–203.

CHAPTER 10

Cybersecurity

10.1 INTRODUCTION

Cybersecurity refers to the practice of protecting computer systems, networks, devices, and data from unauthorized access, attacks, damage, disruption, or theft. It encompasses a range of measures, technologies, processes, and best practices designed to safeguard digital assets and ensure the confidentiality, integrity, and availability of information and systems.

Key aspects and objectives of cybersecurity include:

1. Confidentiality: Safeguarding sensitive information and data by preventing unauthorized access or disclosure.
2. Integrity: Ensuring the accuracy, reliability, and consistency of data and systems by preventing unauthorized modifications or tampering.
3. Availability: Ensuring that computer systems, networks, and services are accessible and operational when needed, minimizing downtime and disruptions.
4. Authentication and access control: Verifying the identity of users and allowing access only to authorized individuals or entities based on appropriate privileges and permissions.
5. Threat detection and prevention: Identifying and mitigating potential threats and vulnerabilities in systems and networks, such as malware, viruses, hacking attempts, and unauthorized access.

6. Incident response and recovery: Developing plans and procedures to effectively respond to and recover from cybersecurity incidents, such as data breaches or system compromises.
7. Security awareness and training: Educating individuals about cybersecurity risks, best practices, and responsible use of technology to foster a culture of security and minimize human error.
8. Compliance and regulatory adherence: Following applicable laws, regulations, and industry standards related to data protection, privacy, and cybersecurity (Mohamed et al., 2021).

Cybersecurity measures include the implementation of firewalls, encryption, intrusion detection and prevention systems, antivirus software, secure coding practices, regular system updates and patches, secure network configurations, and user awareness training. Organizations and individuals employ cybersecurity strategies to protect sensitive information, financial assets, intellectual property, and critical infrastructure from cyber threats.

According to DefiLlama, the total value locked (TVL) in DeFi on May 1, 2022, was $158,945 billion. A year later, TVL had fallen to $58,257 billion.

The reduction in TVL in 2022 is mainly attributed to the collapse of the stablecoin Terra and its sister token, Luna, and the default of FTX. At the same time, the drop in TVL can be partially explained by financial losses due to token protocol vulnerabilities.

In fact, according to the REKT database, over the same period, over 957 million dollars were lost on the Ethereum network and over 849 million dollars on the Binance Smart Chain network (https://de.fi/rekt-database). Terra lost $40 billion on May 8, 2022, but other events and market factors came into play. In any case, those events introduce unique cybersecurity challenges.

DeFi platforms operate in a decentralized manner, relying on smart contracts and blockchain technology to facilitate financial transactions and provide various financial services. Since DeFi platforms handle significant amounts of value and often involve interactions with smart contracts and decentralized applications (DApps), they can be attractive targets for malicious actors seeking to exploit vulnerabilities.

Cybersecurity refers to the practice of protecting computer systems, networks, software, and data from digital threats, attacks, unauthorized access, and damage. It involves the implementation of measures and strategies to ensure the confidentiality, integrity, and availability of information in the digital realm.

Here are some key risks that organizations must address:

1. Unauthorized Access and Data Breaches: Attackers may attempt to gain unauthorized access to systems, networks, or sensitive data. This can lead to data breaches, unauthorized disclosure of information, identity theft, financial loss, or reputational damage.
2. Smart Contract Vulnerabilities: Smart contracts are susceptible to bugs and vulnerabilities that can be exploited to manipulate or steal funds. Developers must conduct thorough security audits and code reviews to identify and address potential vulnerabilities.
3. Economic Exploits: DeFi platforms rely on complex economic systems and incentive structures. Attackers can manipulate these systems to extract value or engage in arbitrage opportunities, causing financial losses for users.
4. Centralized Points of Failure: Although DeFi aims to be decentralized, some aspects of the ecosystem still have centralized components, such as oracles and off-chain infrastructure. These centralized elements can become points of vulnerability, as they can be targeted or compromised.
5. Malware and Ransomware Attacks: Malicious software, such as viruses, worms, and ransomware, can infect systems and disrupt operations, steal data, or encrypt files for ransom. Ransomware attacks, in particular, have become more prevalent and can cause significant financial and operational harm.
6. Phishing and Social Engineering: Cybercriminals employ various tactics, including phishing emails, deceptive websites, and social engineering techniques, to trick individuals into revealing sensitive information, such as passwords or financial details. These attacks can lead to unauthorized access, data breaches, or financial fraud.
7. Insider Threats: Insider threats arise when employees or authorized individuals misuse their access privileges to steal data, introduce malware, or cause intentional harm to systems or networks. Insider threats can be intentional or unintentional, highlighting the importance of proper access controls and monitoring.
8. Weak Authentication and Password Security: Inadequate authentication mechanisms, weak passwords, or password reuse across multiple accounts can make systems vulnerable to unauthorized

access. Multi-factor authentication (MFA) and strong password policies are essential to mitigate this risk.
9. Vulnerabilities in Software and Systems: Security flaws or vulnerabilities in software, operating systems, or network devices can be exploited by attackers to gain unauthorized access or disrupt services. Regular patching, vulnerability management, and secure coding practices are crucial for mitigating these risks.
10. Distributed Denial of Service (DDoS) Attacks: DDoS attacks involve overwhelming a network or system with a flood of traffic, rendering it unavailable to legitimate users. These attacks can disrupt services, cause financial losses, or act as a smokescreen for other malicious activities.
11. Third-Party Risks: Organizations often rely on third-party vendors, suppliers, or service providers, who may introduce cybersecurity risks. Inadequate security measures by third parties can lead to breaches, data loss, or supply chain disruptions. Thorough vendor risk assessments and contractual security requirements are important to manage this risk.
12. Lack of Security Awareness and Training: Human error remains a significant risk factor. Insufficient cybersecurity awareness and training can lead to employees falling victim to phishing attacks, inadvertently disclosing sensitive information, or failing to follow secure practices.
13. Regulatory and Compliance Risks: Organizations must comply with industry-specific regulations and data protection laws. Non-compliance can result in legal penalties, reputational damage, and loss of customer trust (Ramos et al., 2022).

To effectively manage these risks, organizations should implement a comprehensive cybersecurity framework that includes risk assessments, security policies and procedures, regular monitoring and detection mechanisms, incident response plans, employee training programs, and collaboration with relevant stakeholders (McKay, 2022). Additionally, users should take precautions such as using hardware wallets, practicing good password hygiene, and carefully evaluating the security measures of the platforms they interact with.

Strong cybersecurity measures are essential to maintain trust, protect user funds, and foster the long-term viability of the decentralized finance ecosystem.

To counter these challenges, it is important to have a comprehensive cybersecurity strategy in place that includes technological defenses, effective policies and procedures, and continuous staff training.

Cybersecurity concerns have a significant impact on decentralized finance (DeFi) due to the nature of the technology and the potential risks involved. Addressing cybersecurity concerns is vital for the long-term success and sustainability of the DeFi ecosystem. Robust security practices, thorough audits, continuous monitoring, and user education are essential to mitigate risks and build confidence in the security and reliability of DeFi platforms and protocols. Additionally, collaboration between developers, auditors, and the wider cybersecurity community can contribute to the ongoing improvement of DeFi security standards.

10.2 SWOT Analysis

The SWOT analysis (Strengths, Weaknesses, Opportunities, and Threats) is a strategic planning tool commonly used in business to assess the internal and external factors that may affect an organization's performance. While the SWOT analysis is not specifically tailored to cybersecurity, it can still have a significant impact on cybersecurity efforts. Here are some ways in which the SWOT analysis can influence cybersecurity:

1. Identification of Strengths and Weaknesses: Conducting a SWOT analysis helps identify an organization's strengths and weaknesses, including those related to cybersecurity. By assessing internal factors, such as existing security measures, infrastructure, employee awareness, and incident response capabilities, organizations can identify areas where they are well-prepared or vulnerable to cyber threats. This awareness can guide resource allocation and improvement initiatives.
2. Evaluation of Opportunities: The SWOT analysis allows organizations to identify potential opportunities in the cybersecurity landscape. This may involve emerging technologies, partnerships, or market trends that can be leveraged to enhance security posture. By recognizing these opportunities, organizations can align their cybersecurity strategies with emerging developments to stay ahead of threats.

3. Assessment of Threats: In the SWOT analysis, the "T" represents threats, which can include various cyber risks and vulnerabilities. This involves evaluating external factors such as evolving attack techniques, regulatory changes, industry-specific threats, and geopolitical influences that may impact the organization's security. By identifying and understanding these threats, organizations can proactively develop strategies to mitigate risks and strengthen their defenses.
4. Strategy Development: The insights gained from the SWOT analysis can inform the development of a robust cybersecurity strategy. By aligning the organization's strengths and opportunities with its weaknesses and threats, cybersecurity priorities can be defined. This includes determining investment areas, resource allocation, training programs, and incident response plans to address vulnerabilities and capitalize on opportunities.
5. Risk Management: The SWOT analysis can contribute to a more comprehensive risk management approach in cybersecurity. By understanding internal weaknesses and external threats, organizations can prioritize risks and allocate resources accordingly. This analysis helps organizations identify potential attack vectors, assess the likelihood and impact of various threats, and develop mitigation strategies to minimize potential damages.

The SWOT analysis can have a positive impact on cybersecurity by providing organizations with a holistic view of their internal capabilities and external factors. It aids in the development of proactive strategies, risk management, and the alignment of cybersecurity efforts with the organization's overall goals and objectives.

10.3 Digital Tokens and Cybersecurity

The link between cryptocurrencies, digital tokens, and cybersecurity is multifaceted and interconnected. Here are some key aspects of their relationship:

1. Blockchain Security: Cryptocurrencies and many digital tokens are built on blockchain technology, which relies on robust cybersecurity measures. Blockchain's decentralized and distributed nature,

along with cryptographic techniques, provides a secure and tamper-resistant infrastructure for transactions and data storage. Cybersecurity is crucial in protecting the integrity and confidentiality of blockchain networks, preventing unauthorized access, and ensuring the trustworthiness of cryptocurrency transactions.
2. Wallet Security: Cryptocurrencies and digital tokens are typically stored in digital wallets, which are software or hardware-based solutions. Wallet security is paramount in safeguarding private keys and access to funds. Strong security practices, such as using hardware wallets, implementing multi-factor authentication, and following best practices for password management, are essential to protect wallets from unauthorized access, theft, or loss.
3. Exchange Security: Cryptocurrency exchanges facilitate the buying, selling, and trading of digital assets. Ensuring the cybersecurity of these platforms is crucial to prevent unauthorized access, theft, or manipulation of funds and personal information. Exchange security includes measures such as robust authentication protocols, encryption of sensitive data, secure storage of assets, regular audits, and adherence to regulatory requirements.
4. Initial Coin Offerings (ICOs) and Token Sales: ICOs and token sales involve fundraising efforts where digital tokens are offered to investors in exchange for cryptocurrencies or traditional currencies. These events attract cybersecurity risks, as scammers may attempt to deceive investors or exploit vulnerabilities in smart contracts to steal funds. Conducting thorough due diligence on projects, verifying the legitimacy of token sales, and scrutinizing the security of smart contracts is crucial in mitigating risks.
5. Smart Contract Security: Smart contracts, which automate and execute predefined conditions on a blockchain, are used in various token-related transactions, such as ICOs, decentralized finance (DeFi) protocols, and token transfers. Ensuring the security and integrity of smart contracts is vital to prevent vulnerabilities or flaws that could be exploited by attackers. Formal code audits, vulnerability testing, and adherence to best practices in smart contract development help mitigate risks.
6. Phishing and Scams: The cryptocurrency space is prone to phishing attacks and scams, where malicious actors attempt to deceive users into revealing private keys, login credentials, or funds. These attacks

can occur through fake websites, phishing emails, or social engineering tactics. Raising awareness, implementing strong security practices, and using trusted sources for information and transactions are essential in protecting against these threats.
7. Regulatory and Compliance Considerations: The use of cryptocurrencies and digital tokens is subject to evolving regulatory frameworks in different jurisdictions. Compliance with relevant laws and regulations, such as Know Your Customer (KYC) and Anti-Money Laundering (AML) requirements, plays a crucial role in ensuring the security and legitimacy of cryptocurrency transactions.

Given the increasing popularity and value of cryptocurrencies and digital tokens, cybersecurity is paramount to protect users, their assets, and the integrity of the underlying blockchain infrastructure. Robust security practices, awareness of risks, and adherence to best practices are essential for individuals, organizations, and service providers involved in the cryptocurrency ecosystem.

Blockchains and cybersecurity have several interconnected links due to the nature of blockchain technology and its impact on security (Demirkan et al., 2020). Here are some key connections between blockchains and cybersecurity:

1. Data Integrity and Tamper Resistance: Blockchains are designed to maintain the integrity of data by providing a tamper-resistant and immutable record. The decentralized and distributed nature of blockchains ensures that once data is recorded on the blockchain, it is extremely difficult to alter or tamper with. This property enhances the security of data stored on the blockchain, making it valuable for applications where data integrity is critical.
2. Cryptographic Security: Cryptography is a fundamental component of blockchain technology. Cryptographic techniques, such as public-key cryptography and hashing algorithms, are used to secure transactions, validate identities, protect data privacy, and ensure the integrity of data stored on the blockchain. Robust cryptographic security mechanisms are essential to prevent unauthorized access, tampering, or manipulation of blockchain data.
3. Consensus Mechanisms: Blockchain networks rely on consensus mechanisms to reach an agreement on the validity of transactions

and the state of the blockchain. Consensus mechanisms, such as Proof of Work (PoW) or Proof-of-Stake (PoS), provide security by ensuring that the majority of network participants agree on the correctness of the blockchain's history. This consensus mechanism enhances the security of the blockchain network against malicious actors attempting to alter the transaction history.
4. Decentralization and Resilience: Blockchain's decentralized architecture improves cybersecurity by distributing data and computational resources across a network of nodes. This decentralization reduces the single point of failure and makes it more difficult for malicious actors to compromise the system. It enhances the resilience of the blockchain network against attacks, as the network can continue to operate even if some nodes are compromised or go offline.
5. Smart Contract Security: Smart contracts, which are self-executing contracts with predefined conditions on the blockchain, are susceptible to security vulnerabilities if not developed and audited properly. Issues such as coding errors, logic flaws, or improper input validation can lead to vulnerabilities that attackers may exploit. Ensuring the security of smart contracts is crucial to prevent unauthorized access, financial losses, or disruptions to blockchain applications.
6. Identity and Access Management: Blockchains can provide enhanced identity and access management (IAM) capabilities. By leveraging cryptographic techniques, blockchain-based identity solutions can offer secure and decentralized identity verification, reducing the reliance on centralized systems that may be susceptible to data breaches or identity theft. Blockchain-based IAM can improve cybersecurity by mitigating risks associated with compromised credentials or identity fraud.
7. Supply Chain Security: Blockchains can enhance supply chain security by providing transparency, traceability, and verification of goods and transactions. By recording supply chain data on a blockchain, stakeholders can ensure the integrity of the information, track the provenance of goods, and detect and prevent counterfeit or fraudulent activities.
8. Auditing and Compliance: Blockchain technology can facilitate auditing and compliance processes by providing an immutable and transparent record of transactions. This can simplify the verification of compliance with regulatory requirements and enable more

efficient auditing procedures, improving the security and trustworthiness of financial transactions and records.

It is important to note that while blockchains can enhance certain aspects of cybersecurity, they are not a panacea. Proper implementation, adherence to best practices, ongoing monitoring, and a holistic cybersecurity approach are still necessary to address the full range of cybersecurity challenges.

10.4 Valuation

Economic valuation approaches for cybersecurity products typically aim to assess the financial impact and cost-effectiveness of implementing such products. Here are a few commonly used economic valuation approaches in the cybersecurity domain:

1. **Cost–Benefit Analysis (CBA)**: Cost–benefit analysis evaluates the costs associated with implementing a cybersecurity product against the expected benefits and potential cost savings. It involves quantifying both tangible and intangible costs and benefits, such as direct financial investments, potential losses from security incidents, productivity gains, reduced downtime, reputational improvements, and regulatory compliance. By comparing the costs and benefits, organizations can determine the economic viability and potential return on investment (ROI) of deploying a specific cybersecurity product.

   Cost-benefit analysis is a crucial process in making strategic decisions about cybersecurity investments. It involves comparing the cost of implementing a security measure with the benefit or value it brings in reducing risk. Here's a simplified explanation of how to conduct a cost-benefit analysis in cybersecurity:

   a. Identify Costs: This includes direct costs associated with purchasing and implementing the cybersecurity technology or measure. Direct costs might include the price of the hardware or software, installation fees, and operational costs such as maintenance, updates, or upgrades. Don't forget to include indirect costs like training employees to use the new system or potential downtime during installation.

b. Estimate Benefits: The benefits of a cybersecurity investment are often more difficult to quantify, as they involve estimating the cost of potential future security incidents that the investment might prevent. Factors to consider might include:
- Risk Reduction: Calculate the cost of potential security breaches that could be avoided with the new measures. This can include financial losses, business interruption, regulatory fines, and reputation damage.
- Efficiency Gains: If the solution automates certain processes or reduces time spent on security tasks, these efficiency gains can be translated into financial terms.
- Compliance: If the solution helps the organization maintain compliance with laws and regulations, consider the potential fines and penalties avoided.
- Sensitivity Analysis: It is a good practice to conduct a sensitivity analysis, changing your assumptions to see how different scenarios affect the outcome. Cybersecurity is full of uncertainties, and it is important to understand how these can impact the cost–benefit analysis.

A cost–benefit analysis for cybersecurity investments can be complex. Not all benefits are easy to quantify, especially those related to brand reputation or customer trust. And not all costs are easy to predict, especially if you're trying to anticipate the myriad ways in which a cyber-attack could unfold. Therefore, while CBA is an important tool, it should be only one factor in the decision-making process.

2. **Return on Investment (ROI)**: ROI analysis focuses on measuring the financial return or value generated by investing in a cybersecurity product. It calculates the net gain or loss resulting from the investment and compares it to the initial investment cost. The ROI formula typically involves subtracting the total costs of implementing and maintaining the product from the total benefits achieved and then dividing the result by the investment cost.
3. **Total Cost of Ownership (TCO)**: TCO analysis assesses the comprehensive costs associated with acquiring, deploying, operating, and maintaining a cybersecurity product throughout its lifecycle. It considers not only the initial purchase cost but also factors like installation, training, maintenance, upgrades, support, and any associated indirect costs. TCO analysis helps organizations understand the long-term financial implications of implementing a

cybersecurity product and enables them to make informed decisions based on the total cost over time. Total Cost of Ownership (TCO) is a financial estimate that helps consumers and enterprise managers determine the direct and indirect costs of a product or system. In the context of cybersecurity, TCO can help an organization understand the true cost of its cybersecurity investments over time.

The TCO of cybersecurity includes a variety of costs:

a. Acquisition Costs: These are the upfront costs associated with purchasing cybersecurity solutions. This can include hardware, software, and the cost of licensing for various cybersecurity technologies.
b. Implementation Costs: These costs include the resources required to install and configure cybersecurity solutions. It might involve costs related to system integration, IT labor, or potential downtime during the implementation phase.
c. Operational Costs: These are the day-to-day costs of managing and maintaining cybersecurity solutions. It can include the costs of running a security operations center (SOC), employing cybersecurity professionals, conducting regular security audits, managing security updates and patches, and costs related to energy use or physical space.
d. Training Costs: These are the costs associated with training employees on the use of cybersecurity tools and general cybersecurity awareness. Training is an essential component of a successful cybersecurity strategy, as many breaches occur due to human error.
e. Upgrade and Expansion Costs: Over time, cybersecurity solutions may need to be upgraded or expanded to meet the growing needs of the organization and to keep up with evolving threats.
f. Costs of Downtime: In the event of a successful cyber-attack, the cost of downtime and business disruption can be substantial. While these costs are hopefully prevented or mitigated by the cybersecurity investment, they should be considered in the overall TCO as potential risks.
g. Incident Response and Recovery Costs: If a breach does occur, the organization will incur costs related to incident response and recovery. This might include the cost of investigating the breach,

recovering data, repairing damaged systems, communicating with customers, legal fees, and potential regulatory fines.

When calculating TCO, it is important to consider not just the visible costs, but also the hidden or less obvious costs. By taking a comprehensive view of the costs associated with cybersecurity, organizations can make more informed decisions and ensure they're investing their resources effectively.

4. **Risk Assessment and Risk Management**: Economic valuation of cybersecurity products can also involve assessing the potential risks and associated financial impacts that the products aim to mitigate. This approach focuses on estimating the potential losses or damages that could occur in the absence of adequate cybersecurity measures. By evaluating the probability and potential financial impact of security incidents, organizations can determine the value of investing in specific cybersecurity products to mitigate those risks.

5. **Cost-Effectiveness Analysis (CEA)**: Cost-effectiveness analysis compares different cybersecurity products or strategies to identify the most efficient and cost-effective option. It involves quantifying both the costs and the effectiveness of different solutions in achieving specific security objectives. The effectiveness can be measured in terms of risk reduction, incident response time, incident detection rate, or other relevant metrics. CEA helps organizations evaluate different cybersecurity products based on their cost-effectiveness ratio and select the option that offers the best balance between cost and effectiveness.

These economic valuation approaches assist organizations in making informed decisions regarding the implementation of cybersecurity products, considering their financial impact, cost-effectiveness, and return on investment. It is important to note that the specific approach chosen may depend on the organization's goals, requirements, and available data.

There are several valuation approaches consistent with the IVS 210 standards, described in paragraph 3.3 that can be used for cybersecurity, including:

1. **Cost-Based Approach**: This approach estimates the cost of replacing the cybersecurity measures that are in place. This can

include hardware, software, personnel training, and other costs associated with implementing and maintaining cybersecurity.
2. **Market-Based Approach**: This approach looks at the market value of similar cybersecurity measures. This can include looking at the prices of cybersecurity products and services offered by competitors or industry averages.
3. **Income-Based Approach**: This approach looks at the potential revenue that can be generated by the cybersecurity measures in place. This can include calculating the potential cost savings from avoiding cybersecurity incidents or the potential revenue growth from enhanced cybersecurity measures.

Each approach has its strengths and weaknesses, and the appropriate valuation approach will depend on the specific circumstances of the organization and its cybersecurity measures.

References

Demirkan, S., et al. (2020). Blockchain technology in the future of business cyber security and accounting. *Journal of Management Analytics, 7*, 189–208.

Mohamed, H., et al. (2021). *Finding solutions to cybersecurity challenges in the digital economy.* https://www.igi-global.com/chapter/finding-solutions-to-cybersecurity-challenges-in-the-digital-economy/264907

McKay, J. (2022). *DeFi-ing Cyber Attacks, A statistical analysis of cybersecurity attacks in decentralized finance.* https://tellingstorieswithdata.com/inputs/pdfs/final_paper-2022-jack_mckay.pdf

Ramos, S., et al. (2022). *Exploring blockchains cyber security techno-regulatory gap: An application to crypto-asset regulation in the EU.* https://papers.ssrn.com/sol3/papers.cfm?abstract_id=4148678

CHAPTER 11

Digital Token Valuation: Looking for a New Gold Standard?

11.1 The Digital Token Underlying as a Prerequisite for the Valuation

A digital token is a unit of value that exists in digital form and represents a certain asset, utility, or right. It is typically created and recorded on a blockchain or distributed ledger technology (DLT) and can be transferred, stored, and tracked electronically.

Here are some key characteristics of digital tokens:

1. Digital Representation: Digital tokens are purely digital assets that exist and can be accessed through digital platforms or networks. They do not have a physical form but are represented by unique data on a blockchain or DLT.
2. Blockchain or DLT Technology: Digital tokens are typically created, managed, and recorded on a blockchain or DLT. These decentralized systems ensure transparency, security, and immutability of token transactions and ownership.
3. Token Types: Digital tokens can serve different purposes depending on their underlying design and functionality. Some common types of digital tokens include:

a. Cryptocurrencies: These tokens, such as Bitcoin (BTC) (see Maesa et al., 2017) or Ethereum (ETH), are designed to function as a medium of exchange, store of value, or unit of account, similar to traditional currencies.
b. Utility Tokens: Utility tokens provide access to a specific product or service within a decentralized network or platform. They are used to pay for services, access certain features, or participate in a particular ecosystem.
c. Security Tokens: Security tokens represent ownership in an underlying asset or company and are subject to securities regulations. They can provide rights to dividends, profit sharing, or voting privileges.
d. Non-Fungible Tokens (NFTs): NFTs are unique digital tokens that represent ownership or proof of authenticity of a specific digital or physical asset. NFTs have gained popularity in the art and collectibles space.

4. Transferability and Ownership: Digital tokens can be transferred from one party to another through digital wallets or platforms. Ownership of a token is recorded on the blockchain or DLT, allowing for secure and transparent ownership tracking.
5. Smart Contract Functionality: Digital tokens can be programmed with smart contracts, which are self-executing contracts with predefined rules and conditions. Smart contracts enable automated and verifiable transactions and can add functionality to digital tokens, such as time-based restrictions or conditional transfers.
6. Interoperability: Digital tokens can be designed to be interoperable, allowing them to be exchanged or utilized across different blockchain networks or platforms. Interoperability enhances the liquidity and usability of digital tokens.

Digital tokens have gained significant attention and utility in various industries, including finance, gaming, supply chain, art, and more. They enable new forms of value exchange, ownership representation, and decentralized applications, providing opportunities for innovation and disruption in traditional systems.

When valuing a digital token, understanding the underlying factors and characteristics of the token is indeed a prerequisite. The specific features of the token and its underlying technology can significantly impact its valuation. Here are some key factors related to the digital token itself that are important for valuation (see Moro-Visconti, 2022):

1. Token Type: Consider the type of digital token you are valuing, such as a cryptocurrency, utility token, security token, or non-fungible token (NFT). Each type has distinct characteristics, use cases, and valuation considerations.
2. Tokenomics: Evaluate the token's tokenomics, which includes factors such as token supply, distribution mechanism, inflation rate, and token utility. Tokenomics can influence the token's scarcity, potential dilution, and economic dynamics within its ecosystem.
3. Token Utility and Use Cases: Understand the specific utility and use cases of the token. Assess how the token is used within its associated platform, ecosystem, or decentralized application (dApp). Consider its role in governance, staking, transactions, access to services, or other functions. The token's utility and demand for its use cases can affect its valuation.
4. Network Effects: Analyze the network effects generated by the token and its underlying platform. Network effects occur when the value of a network or ecosystem increases as more users or participants join. Strong network effects can drive user adoption, liquidity, and demand for the token, impacting its value.
5. Market Demand and Adoption: Assess the market demand for the token and its level of adoption. Factors such as user growth, partnerships, integrations, and market sentiment can impact the token's valuation. Consider the token's trading volume, liquidity, and market capitalization as indicators of market demand and adoption.
6. Token Governance: If the token has governance features, evaluate the influence and decision-making power granted to token holders. Understand the governance mechanisms, voting rights, and token holder participation in decision-making processes. The effectiveness and decentralization of token governance can impact the token's value.
7. Regulatory Considerations: Consider the regulatory landscape and legal compliance surrounding the token. Regulatory clarity or uncertainty can impact the token's valuation and market sentiment. Stay informed about legal and regulatory developments specific to the token's jurisdiction and the broader cryptocurrency industry.

8. Competitive Landscape: Analyze the competitive landscape and assess the token's unique value proposition compared to similar tokens or projects. Consider the project's differentiation, technological advancements, team expertise, partnerships, and competitive advantages.

Valuation of a digital token requires a comprehensive understanding of its underlying factors, use cases, market dynamics, and the broader ecosystem in which it operates. Conducting thorough research, staying updated on industry trends, and considering both quantitative and qualitative factors are crucial for a comprehensive token valuation.

The research question of this chapter is concerned with the evaluation of digital tokens, attempting to demonstrate which approaches could be used in analogy to traditional corporate finance appraisals. Much depends on the correct identification of what a digital token represents, especially considering its underlying asset, whenever it can be identified.

A digital token represents a specific amount of digital resources that can be owned, assigned to another, or redeemed later.

Digital tokens are either intrinsic or created by software and assigned a certain utility.

What follows is a macro classification of digital tokens.

1. Cryptocurrencies: these are tokens that have no counterparty and can be transferred via blockchain transactions. A cryptocurrency behaves like a currency even if it does not exist in physical form (like paper money). Generally, it is not issued by a central authority even if several countries are studying a national cryptocurrency. The cryptocurrency family includes:

   a. Non-backed Cryptocurrencies: these are digital tokens with an intrinsic value since their price is not anchored to assets with official values such as fiat coins, gold, or other exchange-traded commodities. Bitcoin, Ether, Litecoin, etc. belong to this category.
   b. Backed Stablecoins: these are tokens of the cryptocurrencies family where the price is pegged to fiat money or exchange-traded commodities (such as precious metals or industrial metals). Apart from the lower volatility, unlike other cryptocurrencies, stablecoins have one of the properties of the currency: the value reserve.

Examples of Stablecoins are USD Tether, designed to maintain a value equal to the US dollar, and Paxos Gold backed by gold.

   c. Crypto-Collateralized Stablecoins: these are digital tokens whose collateral is a cryptocurrency instead of a fiat or a commodity. An example of Crypto-Collateralized Stablecoins is DAI. DAI's price is pegged to the US dollar and is guaranteed by a mix of other cryptocurrencies that are deposited in smart contract safes every time a new DAI is minted.

   d. Algorithmic Stablecoins: in this case, the collateralization is done on the blockchain. Instead of supporting the currency with some resources, an "algorithmic central bank" is created that manages supply and demand based on rules encoded in a smart contract. Examples of Algorithmic Stablecoins are Frax and Ampleforth.

2. Utility Tokens: these are digital tokens that give the holder the right to receive a specific service or good from the issuer or from a third party who has signed a commercial agreement or where the holder has the right to participate actively in a DeFi project for example by placing the token in a liquidity pool. One of the most important utility tokens is ETH, considering that it is used to power smart contract agreements. Another example is the BNB token, which fuels the Binance Smart Chain and offers discounts to traders on the main Binance exchange.

3. Security Tokens: these are tokens that incorporate the right to receive a specific payment or a future payment or tokens. Examples of security tokens are Sia Funds, Bcap (Blockchain Capital), and Science Blockchain.

4. Governance Tokens: these are digital tokens that give the holder the right to vote by participating in a DAO. A decentralized autonomous organization (DAO) is an organization constructed by rules encoded as a computer program that is often transparent, controlled by the organization's members, and not influenced by a central government. In general terms, DAOs are member-owned communities without centralized leadership. A DAO's transaction records and program rules are maintained on a blockchain. Examples of governance tokens are Curve DAO, Uniswap DAO, and Aave.

The above classification of digital tokens should not be considered rigid because a digital token can belong to several categories simultaneously. For example, BNB token, as anticipated, is the fuel of the Binance Smart Chain and offers discounts to traders on the main Binance exchange. Therefore, it is classifiable as a utility token. However, it can be included in different online platforms allowing the holder to earn periodic percentage returns. In addition, an investor can buy a BNB token only in the expectation of its appreciation in the secondary market. In the latter two cases, the BNB token can be considered a security token since there is the co-existence of (i) capital use; (ii) a promise/expectation of the return of a financial nature; (iii) the assumption of a risk directly related to and related to capital use.

Like the BNB token, the ETH is classifiable in several categories. It is a Non-backed Cryptocurrency when required to buy thousands of ERC-20 tokens. It is a Utility Token when it is used to power smart contract agreements and it is a Security Token when the investor put it into staking or trades it in the secondary market. Finally, the ETH token can be classified as Backed Stablecoins. ETH is the fuel for the entire Ethereum ecosystem where most decentralized finance projects reside. Since it is only the decentralized finance that produces wealth within the Ethereum blockchain, we argue that decentralized finance is the underlying of the ETH. The further consideration is that, since ETH is the fuel of the Ethereum ecosystem, as the DeFi consolidates, the ETH will increasingly assume the function of utility token rather than cryptocurrency.

Consequently, the classification of most digital tokens does not depend on their nature, but on their use at the free choice of the holder.

This study will show that the two traditional approaches (Fazzini, 2018) used in corporate finance to estimate the value of a firm—Discounted Cash Flows, belonging to the family of the income approaches or market comparables—can be used even with digital tokens, even if many adaptations seem necessary.

The digital properties of the tokens, including their blockchain features, embody scalability potential that can be represented by power laws such as Metcalfe's. These features may influence the basic valuation parameters, starting from the EBITDA. Other traditional firm evaluation approaches (the balance sheet approach, the mixed equity/income approach, etc.) that are still used in Continental Europe, seem unable to capture—and express in market value terms—the peculiar feature of tokens.

To the extent that tokens, with their digital features, can be expressed considering even their underlying, they show some similarity with either derivatives or holding companies, even if these somewhat intriguing comparisons are too undefined to represent a real convergence.

Tokenomics

Tokenomics refers to the economic system and principles that govern the behavior and dynamics of a cryptocurrency or digital token. It encompasses various factors such as token distribution, supply, demand, utility, and incentives within a blockchain network or ecosystem. Tokenomics aims to create a sustainable and efficient economic model for the token and its associated platform.

Here are some key elements typically considered in tokenomics:

1. Token Distribution: Tokenomics addresses how tokens are initially distributed, whether through an initial coin offering (ICO), airdrops, or other means. The distribution method can impact token value and market perception.
2. Token Supply: Tokenomics also involves determining the total token supply and the mechanism for token issuance. The supply may be fixed or inflationary, depending on the token's purpose and goals.
3. Token Utility: Tokenomics considers the utility and functionality of the token within its ecosystem. Tokens can be used for various purposes such as payment for goods and services, access to platform features, staking, governance, or incentivizing network participants.
4. Token Governance: Many blockchain networks incorporate governance mechanisms that allow token holders to participate in decision-making processes. Tokenomics outlines how voting rights, proposals, and consensus mechanisms operate within the ecosystem.
5. Token Economics: Tokenomics examines the economic incentives provided to various participants within the ecosystem. This includes rewarding miners or validators for securing the network, offering staking rewards to token holders, or providing incentives for developers and users to contribute to the platform.
6. Token Burn or Buyback: Some tokenomic models include mechanisms for burning or buying back tokens from the market. Token burns reduce the total supply of tokens, potentially increasing their

scarcity and value. Buybacks involve using funds to repurchase tokens, which can also impact their price and market dynamics.
7. Market Demand: Tokenomics takes into account the factors that drive demand for the token. This includes factors such as the token's usefulness, adoption of the underlying platform, market speculation, and external factors like regulatory changes or industry trends.

By designing tokenomics that align with the goals of the project and its stakeholders, cryptocurrency projects aim to create a sustainable and thriving ecosystem that supports the growth and value of their tokens. However, tokenomics can vary significantly between different projects, and each project may have its unique approach based on its specific requirements and objectives.

All these features impact economic valuation.

Tokenomics has a significant impact on the economic, financial, and market valuation of digital tokens. Here are some key ways in which tokenomics influences these aspects:

1. Economic Impact: Tokenomics determines the economic dynamics of a digital token within its ecosystem. It defines how the token is used, its utility, and the incentives provided to participants. A well-designed tokenomics model can drive economic activity by encouraging token holders to actively participate in the network, contribute value, and drive adoption. This, in turn, can lead to increased transaction volumes, ecosystem growth, and overall economic prosperity.
2. Financial Impact: Tokenomics affects the financial aspects of digital tokens. The supply and demand dynamics, token issuance mechanisms, and utility value of the token influence its price and market capitalization. Tokenomics models that incorporate mechanisms such as scarcity, staking, burning, or buybacks can impact token scarcity and value. Moreover, tokenomics also defines how tokens are allocated, which can influence the wealth distribution and financial status of stakeholders.
3. Market Valuation: Tokenomics plays a crucial role in determining the market valuation of digital tokens. Factors such as token utility, adoption, project development progress, and market sentiment influence investor perception and demand. A strong tokenomics

model that effectively aligns incentives and provides tangible benefits to token holders can increase demand, liquidity, and market participation. On the other hand, poor tokenomics or lack of utility can result in decreased market interest and valuation.
4. Token Price Stability: Tokenomics can impact the stability of token prices. Well-designed tokenomics models often incorporate mechanisms to mitigate price volatility. For example, token burns or buybacks can reduce token supply and potentially increase price stability. Staking mechanisms or lock-up periods for tokens can also reduce short-term speculative trading and promote longer-term investment, which can contribute to price stability.
5. Investor Confidence: Tokenomics influences investor confidence in digital tokens. A transparent and well-thought-out tokenomics model provides clarity on the token's value proposition, utility, and potential returns on investment. It establishes trust and confidence in the project's long-term viability and growth prospects. Conversely, poorly designed tokenomics or lack of transparency can erode investor confidence, leading to decreased demand and valuation.

Tokenomics is just one aspect influencing the economic, financial, and market valuation of digital tokens. Other factors, such as overall market conditions, regulatory environment, competition, and technological advancements, also play significant roles in determining the success and valuation of tokens.

Tokenomics and SWOT analysis can have a significant impact on the market value of digital tokens:

1. Strengths: Tokenomics that highlight the strengths of a digital token, such as utility, scalability, and innovative features, can positively impact its market value. If a token offers unique functionality, solves real-world problems, or has a strong community, it may attract more demand and investor interest.
2. Weaknesses: Identifying and addressing weaknesses through tokenomics can improve market value. For example, if a token has limited utility or lacks a clear value proposition, adjusting the tokenomics to enhance its functionality or incentivize token adoption

can help overcome weaknesses and potentially increase its market value.
3. Opportunities: Tokenomics can leverage opportunities to drive market value. Identifying market trends, user needs, or potential partnerships can enable tokenomics to be designed to capture these opportunities. For instance, if a token can capitalize on emerging industries or technological advancements, it may experience increased demand and subsequently impact its market value.
4. Threats: Tokenomics can also mitigate threats that may impact market value. By considering potential threats, such as regulatory changes, competition, or market volatility, tokenomics can be structured to provide resilience or adaptability. This can help maintain market value in the face of challenges.

Market value is influenced by various factors beyond tokenomics and SWOT analysis. External factors such as overall market conditions, investor sentiment, industry developments, and regulatory decisions also play a role in determining the market value of digital tokens. Additionally, tokenomics should be designed with a long-term perspective and continuously adapted to meet evolving market demands and challenges.

11.2 Asset Class Valuation

Investors choose an asset class that refers to a set of items with some features in common. Historically there have been five main types of asset classes:

a. Stocks (equities)
b. Bonds
c. Cash equivalents (money market vehicles)
d. Real estate
e. Commodities

Cryptocurrencies are considered a further asset class, even if the question is still debated (see: https://www.wealthmanagement.com/opinions/opinion-crypto-not-asset-class), as many investors do not consider it a currency and realize that it has no independent value or inherent utility.

An asset class refers to a group of financial instruments that share similar characteristics and behave similarly within the financial markets. Cryptocurrencies, such as Bitcoin (BTC), Ethereum (ETH), and others, are digital assets that have gained recognition as a distinct asset class due to their unique features and market dynamics. Here's why cryptocurrencies are considered an asset class:

1. Unique Characteristics: Cryptocurrencies have distinct characteristics that set them apart from traditional asset classes. They are decentralized, digital, and often built on blockchain or distributed ledger technology. Cryptocurrencies provide a means of value exchange, store of value, or unit of account, similar to traditional currencies, but with unique properties.
2. Investment Potential: Cryptocurrencies have gained significant attention as investment vehicles. Investors are drawn to the potential for high returns, diversification benefits, and exposure to the growing blockchain and cryptocurrency industry. Cryptocurrencies offer opportunities for both short-term trading and long-term investment strategies.
3. Market Dynamics: Cryptocurrencies exhibit their market dynamics, including volatility, liquidity, and price movements. The cryptocurrency market operates 24/7, allowing for round-the-clock trading. Factors such as supply and demand, market sentiment, regulatory developments, and technological advancements can impact cryptocurrency prices.
4. Portfolio Diversification: Including cryptocurrencies in an investment portfolio can provide diversification benefits. Cryptocurrencies often have a low correlation with traditional asset classes like stocks, bonds, or commodities, meaning their price movements may not align with those of other asset classes. Adding cryptocurrencies to a diversified portfolio can potentially help reduce overall portfolio risk.
5. Growing Institutional Adoption: The increasing participation of institutional investors, hedge funds, and financial institutions in the cryptocurrency market further supports the recognition of cryptocurrencies as an asset class. Institutional adoption brings liquidity, infrastructure, and professional investment strategies to the market, enhancing its credibility and attractiveness.

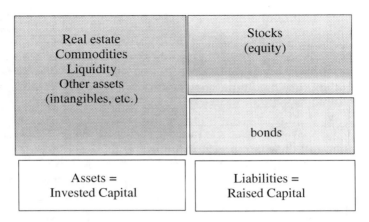

Fig. 11.1 From the balance sheet to the asset classes

The cryptocurrency market is relatively young and still evolving. Cryptocurrencies are subject to regulatory and legal considerations, technological risks, market volatility, and other factors that can impact their value and performance. As with any investment, thorough research, risk assessment, and understanding of the unique characteristics of cryptocurrencies are essential for making informed investment decisions.

Asset classes can be comprehensively considered within a balance sheet that expresses the assets and liabilities of a firm, as shown in Fig. 11.1.

The comprehensive valuation of a firm typically considers either the Enterprise Value (equity + bonds = financial debt) or the residual Equity Value, ultimately belonging to the shareholders.

Should cryptocurrencies be considered an asset class, they would be allocated within the assets (invested capital).

11.3 Digital Token Valuation

Digital token valuation refers to the process of determining the worth or value of a specific digital token within a given context. Valuing digital tokens can be challenging due to their unique characteristics and the evolving nature of the cryptocurrency and blockchain ecosystem. Here are some common approaches and factors to consider when valuing digital tokens:

1. Market Capitalization: Market capitalization is a commonly used method to gauge the value of a digital token. It is calculated by multiplying the token's current price by its circulating supply. Market capitalization provides a measure of the token's overall value within the market.
2. Token Utility and Adoption: The utility and adoption of a digital token play a significant role in its valuation. Evaluate the extent to which the token is being used within its associated platform or ecosystem. Consider factors such as the token's functionality, demand, user adoption, and the network effects it generates.
3. Tokenomics and Supply/Demand Dynamics: Assess the tokenomics of the digital token, which includes factors such as token issuance, token distribution, inflation rate, and scarcity. Evaluate the token's supply and demand dynamics, including factors like token burn mechanisms, token staking, and token locking periods, which can influence the token's value.
4. Revenue and Cash Flow Generation: Some digital tokens, particularly security tokens, provide rights to dividends, profit sharing, or other revenue streams. Evaluate the revenue generation potential of the underlying project or platform and assess the token's value based on expected cash flows or income streams.
5. Comparable Analysis: Conduct a comparative analysis by assessing similar digital tokens or projects in the market. Compare factors such as tokenomics, market adoption, team expertise, technological advancements, and competitive advantages. This analysis can provide insights into the relative value of the token concerning its peers.
6. Token Scarcity and Rarity: In the case of non-fungible tokens (NFTs) or unique digital assets, factors such as scarcity, rarity, and historical sales data can influence the token's value. Evaluate the uniqueness and demand for the specific digital asset represented by the token to gauge its valuation.
7. Regulatory and Legal Considerations: Regulatory and legal factors can impact the valuation of digital tokens. Assess the regulatory environment surrounding the token, including compliance with securities regulations, tax implications, and any legal restrictions or requirements. Regulatory clarity or uncertainty can affect the token's value and market sentiment.

Digital token valuation is a complex and dynamic process. The valuation methods and factors may vary depending on the specific token, its purpose, the underlying project or platform, and the prevailing market conditions. Conducting thorough research, analyzing multiple factors, and considering the unique characteristics of each digital token is crucial when attempting to determine its value.

The economic valuation of digital tokens cannot ignore the valuation and financial effects of their underlying (if and when it exists), synthesized in Table 11.1. Following the methodological premise of Sect. 11.2, whenever the underlying is missing, the digital token has to be appraised considering only "itself", as an empty shell/box.

A backed currency is a form of currency that comes with a guarantee that it can always be exchanged for a predetermined amount of another asset. The most common assets to back a currency with are gold and silver, but a currency can be backed by anything. Starting in 1879, the U.S. dollar was backed by gold, largely due to gold's fungibility and scarcity, important characteristics of money. Since President Richard Nixon decided to suspend US dollar convertibility to gold in 1971, a system of national fiat currencies has been used globally.

Fiat money can be:

- Any money that is not backed by a commodity.

Table 11.1 Digital tokens and their underlying

Digital token	Underlying
Non-backed Cryptocurrencies	None. However, the underlying of Ether could be the entire decentralized finance ecosystem managed in the Ethereum network on the observation that Ether is the gasoline of that network
Backed Stablecoins	Fiat money or exchange-traded commodities (such as precious metals or industrial metals)
Crypto-Collateralized Stablecoins	Reserves in cryptocurrencies
Algorithmic Stablecoins	Reserves in sisters' digital tokens are created in the same blockchain as the stablecoins
Digital Tokens linked to the DeFi projects	Market or income approach

- Money declared by a person, institution, or government to be legal tender, meaning that it must be accepted in payment of a debt in specific circumstances.
- State-issued money is neither convertible through a central bank to anything else nor fixed in value in terms of any objective standard.
- Money is used because of government decree.
- An otherwise non-valuable object that serves as a medium of exchange (also known as fiduciary money).

Backing a currency is done by the currency's issuer to ensure its value. Bitcoin and fiat currencies are not backed by any other asset. The big difference is that a fiat currency is a means of exchange to buy any possible physical asset, whereas bitcoins have different features. The difference between use value (utility) and exchange value (proportion at which a commodity can be exchanged with other commodities) matters in valuation and is difficult to adapt to cryptocurrencies (are they useful or exchangeable?).

Non-backed Cryptocurrencies have no underlying while, as anticipated, Backed Stablecoins are pegged to fiat money or exchange-traded commodities (such as precious or industrial metals). Crypto-Collateralized Stablecoins and Algorithmic Stablecoins are theoretically pegged to fiat currency.

As regards the latter cases (stablecoins pegged to fiat currency), their valuations should depend on forecasting the future value of money that, in turn, requires cross-estimates of many interacting economic variables. Stablecoins are backed by fiat currency that, as anticipated, ... is not backed. Even if fiat currencies are not backed anymore, after the end of the gold standard, they are entitled to be exchanged with real goods, and so are—indirectly—stablecoins.

As anticipated, Fiat money is not backed by a physical commodity, such as gold, recalling the "gold standard" system, abandoned in the Depression of the 1930s, by which the value of a currency was defined in terms of gold, for which the currency could be exchanged. Nowadays, fiat money is a government-issued currency, it is backed by the government that issued it. The value of fiat money is derived from several factors that can coexist like the relationship between supply and demand, inflation, possible devaluation, exchange rates, interest rates, money velocity, economic growth, political stability, and also from the trust that people have over the government. There is no utility to fiat money in itself. Fiat currencies only have value because the government maintains that value. Since fiat money is not a scarce or fixed resource like gold, central banks have much greater control over its supply, which gives them the power to manage many of the above-mentioned economic variables.

The bottom line is that all those cryptocurrencies cannot be valued. They can also be priced against other currencies (Damodaran, 2017).

The same conclusions can be drawn for the stablecoins pegged to gold. The price of gold is closely linked to some of the above-mentioned economic variables. Gold is a hedge against inflation and therefore its price reacts to changes in inflation. Interest rates are inversely correlated: generally, the price of gold falls when rates rise. Gold is considered a haven. Therefore, geopolitical crises have a positive impact on its price. Moreover, the price of gold is determined by the demand for industrial uses and the global production of jewelry.

Finally, the lack of liquidity in the stablecoins market should be stressed. At the time we write, the total value of the stablecoins locked in the DeFi is 137.03 billion dollars according to Defillama.com compared to the total marketable value of U.S. Treasury debt is 22,117.6 billion dollars.

11.4 Valuation of the Digital Tokens Linked to the DeFi Projects

Valuing digital tokens linked to decentralized finance (DeFi) projects can be challenging due to the unique characteristics and complexities of the DeFi ecosystem. Here are some considerations and approaches for valuing DeFi tokens:

1. Token Utility and Functionality: Evaluate the utility and functionality of the token within the specific DeFi project. Consider how the token is used within the project's ecosystem, such as for governance, staking, lending, borrowing, or liquidity provision. Assess the demand for the token based on its role and importance within the project's operations.
2. Cash Flow Generation: Some DeFi tokens provide revenue-sharing mechanisms or fee-generation capabilities. Assess the potential cash flows generated by the DeFi project, such as transaction fees, interest income, or protocol usage fees. Consider the sustainability and

growth potential of the project's revenue streams when valuing the token.
3. Total Value Locked (TVL): TVL is a common metric used in the DeFi space to gauge the value of assets locked within a particular DeFi protocol. It represents the value of assets, typically in cryptocurrency form, that users have deposited or staked in the protocol. Higher TVL can indicate higher adoption and potential value for the associated token.
4. Token Supply and Distribution: Analyze the token's supply and distribution. Factors to consider include the token issuance mechanism, inflation rate, token release schedules, and vesting periods. Assess the token's scarcity, potential dilution, and how the distribution model aligns with the project's goals and long-term value proposition.
5. Governance and Voting Rights: If the DeFi token provides governance or voting rights within the project, evaluate the influence and decision-making power granted to token holders. Consider the level of decentralization and community involvement in decision-making processes, as it can impact the perceived value of the token.
6. Project Fundamentals and Team Expertise: Assess the fundamentals of the DeFi project, including the team's expertise, track record, partnerships, technology stack, and security measures. Strong project fundamentals and a reputable team can contribute to the token's value and market perception.
7. Market Sentiment and User Adoption: Consider market sentiment and user adoption of the DeFi project and its associated token. Monitor community engagement, social media discussions, user feedback, and partnerships to gauge market sentiment. Higher user adoption and positive sentiment can impact the token's valuation.
8. Comparative Analysis: Conduct a comparative analysis by evaluating similar DeFi projects and their associated tokens. Compare factors such as TVL, tokenomics, project fundamentals, revenue models, and community dynamics to assess the relative value proposition of the token.

Valuing DeFi tokens is subject to market dynamics, regulatory considerations, technological risks, and other factors. The valuation of DeFi tokens may require a combination of quantitative and qualitative analysis, as well as ongoing monitoring of the project's performance and market trends.

Thorough research and understanding of the specific DeFi project and its token economics are crucial when assessing its value.

Before proceeding further, a clarification about the cryptocurrency ether (ETH) is necessary. ETH is the fuel for the entire Ethereum ecosystem, in particular for smart contracts. Consequently, the ecosystem of decentralized finance can be considered its underlying because it produces wealth within the Ethereum blockchain. The quality of ether as fuel for the network can make this cryptocurrency observed as a commodity (Damodaran, 2017). In any case, this does not solve the problem of the difficulty of its valuation. In addition to what has already been said about gold, including the law of supply and demand, prices can also be influenced by speculation. Investors in commodities purchase or sell them according to their expectations about future price trends.

While the above factors make market valuation of cryptocurrencies difficult if not impossible, the situation changes concerning digital tokens related to decentralized finance projects.

Identification of a methodology for the evaluation of digital tokens related to decentralized finance projects (in particular, utility tokens and security tokens) allows for expressing a judgment also on the total value of such projects providing useful indications of investment.

The DeFi world has introduced new paradigms in traditional finance and in all areas where parametric protocols can be applied. For these new technologies to bring real value, it is necessary to evaluate and select the most effective purpose appraisal techniques, avoiding the illusory methodologies applied to the Dotcoms at the end of the last century. For this reason, the most effective evaluation techniques remain those of traditional finance suitably adapted to the DeFi. A security token includes the right to future returns and, this feature allows to use of evaluation techniques of traditional finance suitably adapted to the DeFi.

More specifically, the choice of market or income approach depends on the token's liquidity and the project's stage of development. An additional parameter that influences the choice of one of the two approaches, is whether the token is directly exchangeable with fiat currency or not.

If the token market is sufficiently liquid and the token is directly exchangeable for fiat currency, it is reasonable to apply the market approach. On the contrary, when the token cannot be exchanged directly in fiat currency but requires an intermediate passage of exchange with other cryptocurrencies as well as if the liquidity is poor (e.g., in the early stage of a project), then it is certainly preferable to use an income approach.

As anticipated in a DeFi project, the investors in the token are divided into two categories. The ones in the first category take an active role because they use the protocol while the ones in the second category take a passive role by investing in the token only in the expectation of its appreciation without having a real interest in the project. This classification is a further discriminating factor in the choice of method as passive investors certainly consider it more useful (because it is faster) to use a market method.

Interestingly, the property rights (right to rewards and dividends) do not depend on the category of tokens, but on their use (in stake or not) at the free choice of the holder. These tokens are utility tokens because they contribute to the operation of the DeFi protocol, but they can assume the character of security tokens, for example, when the investor put them in a liquidity pool in exchange for a reward and/or dividends.

In the US to qualify a token as a security, it must pass the Howey Test based on 4 points: (a) A party invests money, (b) In a common enterprise, (c) With the expectation of profiting, and (d) Based on the efforts of a third party. The "Howey Test" is a test created by the Supreme Court for determining whether certain transactions qualify as "investment contracts". If so, then under the Securities Act of 1933 and the Securities Exchange Act of 1934, those transactions are considered securities and therefore subject to certain disclosure and registration requirements.

For the sake of completeness, however, it should be remembered that some authors argue that the tokens of decentralized finance do not pass the Howey Test (and, therefore, are not secure) because their value isn't generated by the efforts of others (Kim, 2022).

In some DeFi models, the token also gives the holder who participates in a DAO administrative rights (to cash in dividends, etc.) and voting rights. In this case, the token also assumes the function of a *governance token*.

Tokens in passive investors' wallets do not have property rights because they do not entitle to staking rewards and dividends. We wondered whether this difference affects the valuation criteria and/or whether the value of tokens is different depending on the type of investor. We have observed, however, that the difference between the tokens of the (active) investors participating in the project and those of the passive investors is not comparable to the difference between company shares of different categories where some types of shares have fewer rights and their price is discounted (as in the case of non-voting shares to which a discount for lack of those rights—DLVR—must be applied) (Much & Fagan, 2005; Smith & Amoako-Adu, 1995). As said, the property rights do not depend on the category of tokens, but on their use (in stake or not) at the free choice of the holder. Consequently, the evaluation criteria for tokens should be the same for both categories of investors. A further consideration confirming this conclusion is that the price of the token is equally influenced by the level of demand, the level of the ownership concentration in the market, and the trading volume of the exchanges or exchange-like entities such as online wallets, OTC desks, and large institutional traders whether the subsequent use of the token is staking or pure portfolio investment (Moro-Visconti & Cesaretti, 2022a).

The DeFi ecosystem is represented by a distributed network whose architectural design replicates a blockchain, with no hub (central/hierarchical) nodes. Network analysis may be ideally used to consider the scalability properties of evolving networks.

11.5 Income approach

As anticipated, an income approach is preferable when the token cannot be exchanged directly in fiat currency but requires an intermediate passage of exchange with other cryptocurrencies as well as if the liquidity is limited (e.g., in the early stage of a project).

The income (economic margin) that refers to the token can, however, undergo several passages, referring to different underlying. This value chain represents these steps, along which the economic margins eventually accrue. The appraisal is uneasy, especially when the chain is long and its nodes incorporate information asymmetries that increase overall risk.

Income approaches are based on the discounting of future revenue streams. They include both economic and financial margins, starting from their common denominator (the EBITDA, which represents the economic/financial marginality derived from the income statement). Most income valuations are based on cash flow forecasts, remembering that liquidity is an ideal proxy for value ("cash is king").

Discounted cash flow (DCF) valuation is used to estimate the value of an investment based on its expected future cash flows. DCF analysis attempts to figure out the value of an investment today, based on projections of how much money it will generate in the future from the perspective of investors. In the case of the digital token, the unlevered DCF formula shall be applied with the appropriate adaptations. The following core question arises: what is the real liquidity created by the token?

The formula for calculating the value (also) of a DeFi project based on the cash flows generated is as follows:

$$w = \sum_{t=1}^{n} \left(\frac{CF}{(1+c)t} + \frac{TV}{(1+c)n} \right)$$

w = value of the digital token
CF = Cash flow (dividends + rewards for active investors) at the year t
c = discount or required rate of return
TV = TerminalValue = $\frac{CF_n \times (1+p)}{c-p}$
p = constant growth rate expected for dividends, in perpetuity.

The DCF formulation is expressed by the Operating Cash Flow (Free Cash Flow to the Firm—FCFF), before financial debt service, discounted using the Weighted Average Cost of Capital (WACC). This brings us to the estimate of the Enterprise Value.

The alternative between FCFF and FCFE depends on the structure of the token: should we consider a "levered" case where the token represents an asset counterbalanced by equity + financial debt, then we should refer to operating cash flows.

Alternatively, Net Cash Flows (Free Cash Flow to Equity—FCFE) can be discounted at the cost of equity (traditionally proxied by the Dividend Discount Model or the Capital Asset Pricing Model) to estimate the Equity Value. This latter alternative is possibly more useful in the evaluation of tokens since they do not represent a comprehensive firm, but possibly an asset class that is not levered.

The perpetuity growth rate

Following classical literature, the perpetuity growth rate (p) typically lies between the historical inflation rate and the historical GDP growth rate. Assuming a perpetuity growth rate more than GDP growth implies that the project's growth will forever exceed the economy's growth.

Recent world events show that indicators of GDP growth rate and inflation rate may undergo unexpected changes that make the choice of the perpetual growth rate even more difficult.

The moment we write, OECD forecasts an inflation rate in the Euro area which ranges from 8.7% in the first quarter of 2023 to 4.9% in the fourth quarter of the same year and the European Commission expects a GDP growth rate of 0.3% in the same area for the same year. Consequently, a conservative rate of 2.0% seems to be appropriate.

The perpetuity growth rate is a concept commonly used in finance and valuation to estimate the long-term growth rate of cash flows. However, when it comes to the valuation of digital tokens, such as cryptocurrencies or utility tokens, estimating a perpetuity growth rate can be challenging due to several factors:

1. Volatility: Digital tokens are known for their high volatility, often experiencing significant price fluctuations in short periods. This makes it difficult to predict and estimate a stable long-term growth rate.
2. Lack of Cash Flow: Unlike traditional assets or businesses, digital tokens may not generate cash flows in the same way. Their value often depends on factors such as supply and demand dynamics, market sentiment, adoption, and utility within a specific ecosystem. As a result, applying traditional valuation models based on cash flows may not be straightforward.
3. Market Maturity: The digital token market is relatively new and still evolving. Many tokens are associated with emerging technologies or decentralized platforms, making it challenging to assess their long-term growth prospects accurately.
4. Regulatory and Legal Considerations: The regulatory environment surrounding digital tokens varies across jurisdictions. Regulatory changes or uncertainties can significantly impact the valuation and growth potential of tokens.

Given these challenges, estimating a perpetuity growth rate for digital tokens is not commonly practiced. Valuation approaches for digital tokens often involve considerations such as network effects, adoption rates, token utility, competitive landscape, and the overall potential of the underlying technology or platform. It is crucial to approach the valuation of digital tokens with careful analysis, understanding of the token's unique characteristics, and awareness of the specific market dynamics impacting its value.

The Discount or Required Rate of Return

There is currently no adequate risk rate in the digital asset market that can be used as a benchmark, therefore the expected annual returns in equity funding rounds for venture capital should be used as a tentative proxy. In those cases, the annual expected returns range from 25 to 50% (Cochrane, 2001; Todaro, 2018) therefore the discount rate should be chosen within this range depending on the estimated degree of risk of the project.

The discount or required rate of return in the valuation of digital tokens is a key factor used to determine the present value of future cash flows or expected returns associated with the token. However, estimating an appropriate discount rate for digital tokens can be challenging due to their unique characteristics. Here are some considerations:

1. Risk Factors: Digital tokens can be highly volatile and subject to various risks, including regulatory changes, technological obsolescence, security vulnerabilities, and market volatility. The discount rate should reflect these risks appropriately.
2. Market Risk Premium: The discount rate often includes a market risk premium, which compensates investors for taking on the risk associated with the overall market. The size of the market risk premium depends on factors such as the token's correlation with the broader market and the level of systemic risk.
3. Token-specific Factors: The discount rate may be influenced by token-specific factors, such as the stage of the project, the underlying technology, the token's utility, and the competitive landscape. Early-stage tokens or those associated with emerging technologies may have a higher required rate of return due to higher risks and uncertainties.
4. Opportunity Cost of Capital: The discount rate should also consider the opportunity cost of capital, which represents the return that investors could earn by investing in alternative assets with similar risk profiles.
5. Investor Preferences: Different investors may have varying risk preferences and required rates of return. The discount rate used in the

valuation should align with the target investor's risk tolerance and investment objectives.

It is important to note that determining the appropriate discount rate for digital tokens involves subjective judgment and may vary depending on the specific token and the context of the valuation. Financial models and valuation methodologies, such as the discounted cash flow (DCF) method or comparable analysis, can be used to estimate the present value of future cash flows or expected returns, incorporating the discount rate. However, due to the unique and evolving nature of digital tokens, valuation approaches should be applied with caution, and multiple scenarios or sensitivity analyses may be necessary to account for different risk factors and market conditions.

11.6 MARKET APPROACH

The market approach is one of the commonly used methods for valuing digital tokens. This approach relies on comparing the token being valued to similar tokens that have been traded in the market or have comparable characteristics. Here's how the market approach can be applied to the valuation of a digital token:

1. Identify Comparable Tokens: Start by identifying other digital tokens that are similar to the ones being valued. Similarity can be based on factors such as the underlying technology, token utility, target market, stage of development, or the ecosystem in which the token operates.
2. Gather Market Data: Collect data on recent transactions or trading activity of comparable tokens. This can include information on token prices, trading volumes, market capitalization, and any other relevant market data.
3. Analyze Pricing Patterns: Analyze the pricing patterns and trends of the comparable tokens. Look for factors that may influence their prices, such as news events, market sentiment, adoption rates, and changes in the overall cryptocurrency market.

4. Determine Valuation Metrics: Identify appropriate valuation metrics that are commonly used in the market for digital tokens. These can include price-to-earnings ratios, price-to-sales ratios, price-to-book ratios, or market capitalization multiples.
5. Apply Valuation Metrics: Once the valuation metrics are determined, apply them to the financial or operational data of the digital token being valued. This can involve multiplying relevant financial or operational metrics of the comparable tokens by the corresponding valuation multiples.
6. Adjust for Differences: Adjust the valuation multiples to account for any differences between the digital token being valued and the comparable tokens. Factors to consider may include variations in token utility, competitive advantages, growth prospects, or risk factors.
7. Calculate the Valuation: Finally, calculate the estimated value of the digital token by applying the adjusted valuation multiples to the relevant financial or operational data of the token being valued.

The market approach for valuing digital tokens has limitations. The market data may be limited or not available for some tokens, and the valuation multiples used may not capture the token's unique characteristics or future potential accurately. Additionally, market prices can be highly volatile and influenced by speculative factors, which may not reflect the fundamental value of the token. Therefore, the market approach should be used in conjunction with other valuation methods and qualitative analysis to arrive at a comprehensive and well-rounded valuation of a digital token.

If the token market is sufficiently liquid and the token is directly exchangeable for fiat currency, it is reasonable to apply the market approach, referring to comparable transactions.

While the previous methodology allows us to calculate the value of a DeFi project at present, the following formulas allow us to compare its relative value with its competitors or its previous performance.

In the case of comparable companies, the approach estimates multiples by observing similar firms (Fernandez, 2001). The problem is to determine what is meant by similar companies. In theory, the analyst should check all the variables that influence the multiple. These classic considerations have to be adapted to the digital token context.

In practice, companies should estimate the most likely price for a non-listed company, taking as a reference some listed companies, operating in the same sector, and considered homogeneous. Two companies can be defined as homogeneous when they present, the same risk, similar characteristics, and expectations.

The calculation is:

- A company whose price is known (P_1),
- A variable closely related to its value (X_1)

the ratio $P_1)/(X_1)$ is assumed to apply to the company to be valued, for which the size of the reference variable (X_2) is known.

Therefore:

$$(P_1)/(X_1) = (P_2)/(X_2)$$

so that the desired value P_2 will be:

$$P_2 = X_2[(P_1)/(X_1)]$$

According to widespread estimates, the main factors to establish whether a company is comparable are:

- Size;
- Belonging to the same sector (see, for instance, the Statistical Classification of Economic Activities in the European Community, commonly referred to as NACE);
- Financial risks (leverage);
- Historical trends and prospects for the development of results and markets;
- Geographical diversification;
- Degree of reputation and credibility;
- Management skills;
- Ability to pay dividends.

Founded on comparable transactions, the basis of valuation is information about actual negotiations (or mergers) of similar—i.e., comparable—companies.

The use of profitability parameters is usually considered to be the most representative of company dynamics.

Among the empirical criteria, the approach of the multiplier of the EBITDA (Earnings Before Interest, Taxes, Depreciation, and Amortization) is widely diffused, to which the net financial position must be added algebraically, to pass from the estimate of the enterprise value (total value of the company) to that of the equity value (value of the net assets). The formulation is:

$$W = \text{average perspective EBITDA} \times \text{Enterprise Value/sector EBITDA}$$
$$= \text{Enterprise Value of the company}$$

And then:

$$\text{Equity Value} = \text{Enterprise Value} \pm \text{Net Financial Position}$$

11.7 The Total Value Locked ratio

The Total Value Locked (TVL) ratio is a metric commonly used in the valuation and analysis of decentralized finance (DeFi) protocols and platforms that operate on blockchain networks. It measures the total value of assets (usually in the form of digital tokens) locked or held within a specific protocol or platform. The TVL ratio provides insights into the popularity, usage, and potential value of a DeFi platform. However, it is important to note that the TVL ratio itself is not a direct valuation method for individual digital tokens. Let's understand its significance in the valuation context:

1. TVL as a Proxy: The TVL ratio is often used as a proxy for the potential value or economic activity occurring within a DeFi protocol or platform. Higher TVL figures generally indicate greater adoption, usage, and potential revenue generation, which can contribute to the overall valuation of the platform.
2. Revenue Generation: Some DeFi platforms generate revenue through various mechanisms such as transaction fees, lending interest, liquidity provision incentives, or staking rewards. The TVL ratio can provide insights into the revenue-generating potential of a platform, which, in turn, may influence its valuation.

3. User Base and Network Effects: A higher TVL ratio suggests a larger user base and network effects within a DeFi platform. This can contribute to the platform's valuation, as a strong user base and network effects often result in increased liquidity, improved user experience, and a higher likelihood of platform sustainability and growth.
4. Comparison and Analysis: The TVL ratio can be used to compare different DeFi platforms within the same sector or market. Investors and analysts may assess the TVL ratio of different platforms to gain insights into their relative value, adoption, and growth potential. However, the TVL ratio alone does not provide a comprehensive valuation of individual tokens within those platforms.

When valuing individual digital tokens within a DeFi platform, it is crucial to consider additional factors, such as the token's utility, governance rights, revenue generation potential, market demand, and tokenomics. Token-specific valuation methodologies, such as discounted cash flow (DCF) analysis, comparables analysis, or token utility models, are typically employed to assess the intrinsic value of the token itself, taking into account both the underlying platform dynamics and broader market conditions.

Total value locked is a metric that is used to measure the overall health of a DeFi protocol. Three main factors are taken into consideration when calculating and looking at a decentralized financial services' market cap TVL ratio: calculating the supply, the maximum supply as well as the current price.

While the Gordon Growth Method (Gordon, 1959) to find a Terminal Value is the most suitable metric for DeFi projects, the choice of growth rate is challenging because the DeFi sector is still young, and no historical indicators are available.

Moreover, like all investment scenarios, the decision to contribute to decentralized finance is also influenced by factors such as inflation, interest rate levels, credit crunch, and, of course, more profitable investment opportunities making forecasting a constant presence of investors difficult.

Yet, the trend of crypto assets is influenced by the portfolio policies of institutional investors who make massive investments (despite some formal aversion to the crypto world) and then balance the portfolio at the end of the year creating spikes and collapses in the value of tokens that create doubts and perplexities in the retail market especially as observed between the end of 2021 and the beginning of 2022. Moreover, as said, the price variability of tokens is influenced by the level of the ownership concentration in the market and by the trading volume of the exchanges or exchange-like entities such as online wallets, OTC desks, and large institutional traders (Moro-Visconti & Cesaretti, 2022b).

In effect, according to coinmarketcap.com, the DeFi Pulse Index (DPI) (a capitalization-weighted index that tracks the performance of decentralized financial assets across the market) gained 214.3% from January to November 2021 and then fell by 78.8% in November 2022. Also, according to defillama.com. the Total Value Locked (TVL) in the DeFi ecosystem lost 74,5% (from 160.99 billion dollars at the end of November 2021 to 41.09 billion dollars at the end of November 2022).

Furthermore, the growth rate of a business is not uniform over time and should be modulated according to the different stages of development (startup, growth, maturity, renewal, or decline).

Finally, as it happened with the DeFi trading platforms Bancor in June 2022, platforms through which tokens can be pooled can suspend the right to put them in staking (and to withdraw them) at times when the market is unstable or hostile as well as for malfunctions or hacker attacks.

All these circumstances, combined with the poor maturity of the DeFi sector, make us believe that it is not appropriate to include the Terminal Value in the formula or not.

Accordingly, the formula of the DCF_{equity} should be used in its simplified form:

$$w = \sum_{t=1}^{n} \left(\frac{CF}{(1+c)t}\right)$$

w = value of the DeFi project
CF = Cash flow (dividends + rewards for active investors) at the year t
c = discount or required rate of return

Once the present value of the cash flows has been determined, the calculation of the market value (W) of the company may correspond to the:

a. Unlevered cash flow approach (to estimate the Enterprise Value):

$$W = \sum \frac{CF_0}{WACC} + TV - D$$

b. Levered cash flow approach (to estimate the Equity Value):

$$W = \sum \frac{CF_n}{K_e} + TV$$

where:

$\sum CF_0/WACC$ = present value of operating cash flows (FCFF)
$\sum CF_n/K_e$ = present value of net cash flows (FCFE)
TV = terminal (residual) value
D = initial net financial position (financial debt—liquidity)
WACC = average after-tax cost of a company's various capital sources (cost of collecting external capital), including common stock, preferred stock, bonds, and any other long-term financial debt.

Applying this index to two popular tokens (Sushi and Uniswap) and assuming the following data taken from coinmarketcap.com:

- $t = 10$
- CF = reward per token in stake on the assumption that they remain constant
- Sushi's CF per token = $ 0.9554 × 0.045 = $ 0.043
- Uniswap's CF per token = $ 4.99 × 0.07 = $ 0.349
- $c = 38\%$ (average between 0.25 and 0.50)

one gets:

- Value of the Sushi project per token: $ 0.11
- Value of the Uniswap project per token: $ 0.89.

As said, in DeFi projects, investors can take an active role (they use the protocol) or passive (they invest in the token only in the expectation of its appreciation without having a real interest in the project and this leads to an increase in market capitalization).

The TVL, therefore, reflects the real appreciation of the market for the project itself and, for this reason, is an important indicator of its value.

The TVL ratio, in its turn, is an indicator of whether a particular DeFi project is overvalued (ratio > 1) or undervalued (ratio < 1).

$$\text{TVL ratio} = \frac{\text{Market Capitalization}}{\text{Maximum Circulating Supply}}$$

where:

- Market Capitalization = Current Price × Circulating Supply.
- Market Capitalization is analogous to the free-float capitalization in the stock market.
- Maximum Circulating Supply is the number of tokens that will ever exist in the lifetime of the project. It is analogous to the fully diluted shares in the stock market.

Applying this index to two popular tokens on December 29, 2022, gives the following results applied to data taken from coinmarketcap.com:

$$\text{Sushi Token's TVL ratio} = \frac{\$212.315.366}{250.000.000} = 0.85 = \text{undervaluated}$$

$$\text{Uniswap Token's TVL ratio} = \frac{\$3.795.124.717}{1.000.000.000} = 3.80 = \text{overvalued}$$

Consequently, the Sushi token is more attractive to investors.

11.8 THE MARKET CAP TO TOTAL VALUE LOCKED RATIO

The Market Cap to Total Value Locked (MC/TVL) ratio is a metric used to assess the valuation and relative attractiveness of decentralized finance (DeFi) projects. It compares the market capitalization of a DeFi project's native token to the total value locked (TVL) within the associated protocols or smart contracts.

The formula for calculating the MC/TVL ratio is:

MC/TVL = Market Capitalization/Total Value Locked

Here are some key points to understand about the MC/TVL ratio:

a. Market Capitalization (MC): Market capitalization represents the total value of a token in circulation and is calculated by multiplying the token's price by its circulating supply. It provides a measure of the overall market value of a token.
b. Total Value Locked (TVL): Total Value Locked refers to the total value of assets, typically in the form of cryptocurrencies, locked within a specific DeFi protocol or smart contract. It represents the amount of capital invested or committed to the protocol.
c. Valuation Comparison: The MC/TVL ratio is used to compare the market capitalization of a DeFi project to the TVL it has attracted. A higher MC/TVL ratio may indicate that the market has priced the project's token at a higher valuation relative to the value of assets locked within its protocol.
d. Relative Attractiveness: The MC/TVL ratio can provide insights into the relative attractiveness of different DeFi projects. A lower ratio may indicate that the token's valuation is relatively lower compared to the value of assets locked, suggesting potential undervaluation. Conversely, a higher ratio may indicate that the token's valuation is relatively higher compared to the value of assets locked, suggesting potential overvaluation.
e. Interpretation: The interpretation of the MC/TVL ratio may vary depending on market conditions, project fundamentals, and industry trends. It is important to consider other factors, such as project growth, revenue generation, token utility, governance, and market sentiment when assessing the value and potential investment opportunities of a DeFi project.

The MC/TVL ratio should be used in conjunction with other fundamental and technical analyses to form a comprehensive evaluation of a DeFi project. This ratio can provide a high-level perspective on the relative valuation of projects but should not be the sole determinant of investment decisions.

The market capitalization expresses the market value of a listed stock. It can be used as an ideal proxy for the estimate of the market value of a digital token.

Total value locked is a metric that is used to measure the overall health of a DeFi protocol. Three main factors are taken into consideration when calculating and looking at a decentralized financial services' market cap TVL ratio: calculating the supply, the maximum supply, as well as the current price.

The market cap to TVL ratio is calculated by dividing the market cap of crypto by its total value locked (TVL). While many beginner crypto investors get dazzled by a high market cap, it is this ratio that shows whether it has good investment potential.

Even the Market Cap to TVL ratio is an indicator of whether a particular DeFi project is overvalued (ratio > 1) or undervalued (ratio < 1).

The TVL and the market cap of a project are both indicators of market value. However, they are not the same even if it is advisable to look at both indicators. While a market cap is a simple way to show the value of one company, based on its one stock type or cryptocurrency, a TVL can show the value of a project, based on its inner workings across different locked assets.

$$\text{Market Cap to TVL ratio} = \frac{\text{Market Capitalization (\$)}}{\text{Total Value Locked (\$)}}$$

Applying this index to the same two popular tokens on December 29, 2022, gives the following results also applied to data taken from coinmarketcap.com:

$$\text{Sushi Market Cap to TVL ratio} = \frac{\$212.315.366}{\$2.287.403.208} = 0.09 = \text{undervaluated}$$

$$\text{Uniswap Market Cap to TVL ratio} = \frac{\$3.795.124.717}{\$3.336.088.430} = 1.14 = \text{overvaluated}$$

This index confirms that the Sushi token is more attractive to investors.

11.9 THE PRICE TO EARNINGS RATIO (P/E)

The Price to Earnings ratio (P/E ratio) is a commonly used valuation metric in traditional finance that compares a company's stock price to its earnings per share (EPS). However, when it comes to digital tokens, which often operate in decentralized ecosystems and may not have traditional earnings in the same sense as companies, applying the P/E ratio directly may not be appropriate. Here are some considerations regarding the use of the P/E ratio in the valuation of digital tokens:

a. Earnings Definition: Digital tokens may not generate traditional earnings like profits or dividends. Their value often relies on factors such as utility within a specific platform or ecosystem, supply and demand dynamics, and market sentiment. As a result, determining earnings for digital tokens can be challenging.
b. Token Utility and Cash Flows: Instead of focusing on earnings, the valuation of digital tokens often revolves around token utility and potential cash flows. The utility of the token within the platform or ecosystem, such as transaction fees, staking rewards, or governance rights, can be assessed to estimate potential cash flows.
c. Tokenomics and Token Metrics: Tokenomics refers to the economic model and characteristics of a digital token. Understanding token metrics, such as total supply, circulating supply, inflation rates, and token distribution mechanisms, can provide insights into the token's potential value and growth prospects.
d. Valuation Models: To value digital tokens, alternative valuation models specific to the token and its ecosystem are often employed. These models can include discounted cash flow (DCF) analysis, which estimates the present value of expected future cash flows, or token utility models that factor in token usage and adoption rates.

It is crucial to tailor the valuation approach to the unique characteristics and dynamics of digital tokens. While the P/E ratio may not be directly applicable, other token-specific valuation methods can provide insights into the intrinsic value and growth potential of digital tokens within their respective ecosystems.

A P/E (price-to-earnings) ratio is, in general terms, a metric that compares a company's share price to its annual net profits. This ratio can be used to compare companies of similar size and industry to help determine which company is a better investment. This ratio is commonly used for listed securities and represents an investment benchmark.

A high P/E ratio indicates a growth forecast in the value of tokens according to operators. In contrast, investors prefer lower P/E ratios because they indicate that the price of the token is affordable. In the case of decentralized finance, the formula must be adapted as follows:

P/E raito = Current Token Price/Dividend + Rewards per Token

Applying this index to the same two popular tokens on December 29, 2022, gives the following results also applied to data taken from *coinmarketcap.com*:

$$\text{Sushi Token's P/E ratio} = 0.9554/0.045 = 21.23$$

$$\text{Uniswap Token's P/E ratio} = 4.99/0.07 = 71.29$$

Consequently, at the date, it seems that the market predicts a higher growth of the value of the Uniswap token than that of Sushi.

11.10 Valuation of Non-backed Cryptocurrencies Locked Up in Staking on a Proof-of-Stake Network

Valuing non-backed cryptocurrencies that are locked up in staking on a Proof-of-Stake (PoS) network involves assessing various factors related to the staking process, network dynamics, and market conditions. Here are some considerations for valuing such cryptocurrencies:

1. Staking Rewards: Evaluate the staking rewards offered by the PoS network. Stakers earn rewards for participating in the network by locking up their tokens and contributing to network security and consensus. Assess the reward rate, inflation rate, and the potential long-term value of the staking rewards when valuing the locked-up tokens.
2. Token Supply and Inflation: Consider the token supply dynamics and the inflation rate of the cryptocurrency. Staking often involves a lock-up period during which tokens are inaccessible. Analyze the impact of token lock-up and inflation on the overall token supply and its potential effect on the token's value.
3. Staking Participation Rate: Assess the participation rate of stakes within the PoS network. Higher staking participation generally indicates stronger network security and confidence in the project. Evaluate the level of engagement from token holders and their

commitment to staking as it impacts the network's overall stability and token valuation.
4. Network Security and Consensus: Analyze the security and consensus mechanisms of the PoS network. A robust and secure network is essential for the token's long-term value. Assess factors such as the quality of the underlying technology, the strength of the consensus algorithm, and the reputation of the network validators.
5. Market Demand and Liquidity: Consider the market demand and liquidity for the cryptocurrency. Evaluate factors such as trading volume, liquidity across different exchanges, and the level of market activity. Higher liquidity and trading activity can indicate increased market demand and potentially impact the token's valuation.
6. Token Utility and Governance: Evaluate the utility and governance features of the cryptocurrency. Assess the role of the token within the PoS network, such as its use for transaction fees, voting rights, or access to network services. Token utility and governance mechanisms can impact the token's value and desirability for stakes.
7. Market Sentiment and Investor Confidence: Monitor market sentiment and investor confidence in the PoS network and the locked-up cryptocurrency. Positive market sentiment, community engagement, and confidence in the project's long-term prospects can influence the valuation of the locked-up tokens.
8. Risk Factors and Market Conditions: Consider the risks associated with staking, including potential slashing risks, network vulnerabilities, and regulatory factors. Assess market conditions and factors that may affect the overall cryptocurrency market, such as regulatory changes, technological advancements, or market volatility.

Valuing non-backed cryptocurrencies locked up in staking requires a thorough understanding of the specific PoS network, its dynamics, and the broader cryptocurrency ecosystem. It's important to consider both the inherent risks and the potential rewards associated with staking, as well as the market conditions and the long-term sustainability of the network when assessing the valuation of locked-up tokens.

Crypto staking is the process of locking up crypto holdings to obtain rewards or earn interest. Cryptocurrencies are built with blockchain technology, in which crypto transactions are verified, and the resulting data is stored on the blockchain. The purpose of blocking tokens on a Proof-of-Stake (PoS) network is to propose, attest, and add blocks to the blockchain. It is a revenue-generating task for the benefit of the validators chosen by the protocol to submit a new block to the chain. The staking yield can be calculated as follows:

$$\text{Validator Staking Yield} = \frac{\text{Validator Staking Rewards}}{\text{Validator Staking Balance}} - \% \text{ Loss due to Slashing}$$

where:

$$\text{Validator Staking Rewards} = \text{Annual Network Staking Rewards} \times \frac{\text{Validator Staking Balance}}{\text{Total Network Amount Staked}}$$

And

$$\text{Annual Network Staking Rewards} = (\text{Issuance per block} + \text{Transaction fees per block}) \times \text{Blocks per hour} \times 24 \text{ hours} \times 365 \text{ days}$$

As anticipated, such staking is a revenue-generating task and, consequently, the valuation of the token could be based on yield flows. The problem is that much of the information needed to apply the model is uncertain or unknown:

- The transaction fees are usually voluntary payments by the users,
- It is particularly difficult to predict the number of new tokens issued because this measure is based on the total stake in the network,
- Variables like "Blocks per hour", "Validator Staking Balance" and "% Loss due to Slashing" are necessarily unknown (Slashing is a mechanism to give penalties for breaking protocol rules. They result in the reduction of the validator's locked tokens or its rewards.

11.11 Conclusion

The main approaches to evaluating companies commonly used in practice are:

- The balance sheet-based approach—simple and complex;
- The income approach;
- The mixed capital-income approach;

- The financial approach;
- Market approaches and valuation through multiples.

The balance sheet-based approach and the mixed approach do not apply to digital tokens that represent an asset class, not a firm with a comprehensive balance sheet, composed of assets versus liabilities and equity.

The central element in determining the value of a firm is the estimate of its future ability to generate an income or financial flow capable of adequately rewarding its shareholders after debt service.

Among the approaches used by operators to identify the market value of the firm, the financial and income approaches are the most appropriate to represent the expected fair remuneration of shareholders. This also holds for digital tokens, as shown above.

The economic valuation of digital tokens cannot ignore the valuation and financial effects of their underlying. The consequence is that, despite various proposed approaches, the valuation of tokens that do not have an underlying (such as bitcoin) and of tokens pegged to fiat money, precious metals, or cryptocurrencies is almost impossible. Alternatively, it is possible to make economic valuations of digital tokens linked to decentralized finance projects that incorporate rights to financial returns. In those cases, an income approach is preferable when the token cannot be exchanged directly in fiat currency but requires an intermediate passage of exchange with other cryptocurrencies as well as if the liquidity is poor (e.g., in the early stage of a project).

Various circumstances, combined with the poor maturity of the DeFi sector, make us state that it is not appropriate to include the Terminal Value in the formula. On the contrary, if the token market is sufficiently liquid and the token is directly exchangeable for fiat currency, it is reasonable to apply the market approach. Two methods can be applied. The Total Value Locked (TVL) ratio reflects the real appreciation of the market for a DeFi project and, for this reason, is an important indicator of its value. Usually, investors prefer to adopt the method of the Price to Earnings Ratio (P/E). They prefer the lower P/E ratios because they indicate that the price of the token is affordable. However, in the case of the DeFi projects, the traditional formula must be adapted.

REFERENCES

Cochrane, J. H. (2001). *The risk and return of venture capital* (NBER Working Paper 8066). https://www.nber.org/system/files/working_papers/w8066/w8066.pdf

Damodaran, A. (2017). The bitcoin boom: Asset, currency, commodity or collectible? https://aswathdamodaran.blogspot.com/2017/10/the-bitcoin-boom-asset-currency.html

Fazzini, M. (2018). *Business valuation: Theory and practice.* Palgrave Macmillan.

Fernandez, P. (2001). *Valuation using multiples. How do analysts reach their conclusions?* IESE Business School.

Gordon, M. J. (1959). Dividends, earnings, and stock prices. *Review of Economics and Statistics, 41*(2), 99–105.

Kim. (2022). *The Howey test: A set of rules that determine if an investment is a security.* https://www.businessinsider.com/personal-finance/howey-test?r=US&IR=T

Maesa, D. D. F., Marino, A., & Ricci, L. (2017). Data-driven analysis of bitcoin properties: Exploiting the users' graph. *International Journal of Data Science and Analytics, 61*(1), 63–80.

Moro-Visconti, R. (2022). *Augmented corporate valuation. From digital networking to ESG compliance.* Palgrave Macmillan.

Moro-Visconti, R., & Cesaretti, A. (2022a). *Variability of cryptocurrencies: Causes and consequences.* https://doi.org/10.13140/RG.2.2.14873.70240

Moro-Visconti, R., & Cesaretti, A. (2022b). *DeFi protocols in the insurance industry.* https://doi.org/10.13140/RG.2.2.32573.54241

Much, P. J., & Fagan, T. J. (2005). *The value of voting rights, financial valuation* (pp. 1–7).

Smith, B. F., & Amoako-Adu, B. (1995). Relative prices of dual class shares. *Journal of Financial and Quantitative Analysis, 30*, 223–239.

Todaro, J. (2018). *Valuing crypto assets using a DCF model.* https://medium.com/@john_19547/valuing-crypto-assets-using-a-dcf-model-bc6297b0bd25

CHAPTER 12

The Cryptocurrency Crash of 2022: Which Lessons for the Future?

12.1 Annus horribilis

Year 2022 was certainly the *annus horribilis* for crypto finance. Bitcoin lost 63.29%, the Total Value Locked (TVL) in the DeFi ecosystem collapsed by 78.18%, and TERRA's default burned $40 billion. In the collapse of FTX, customers lost $8 billion. These just to name a few because in 2022 the sector burned 2 trillion dollars in capitalization.

The causes of this disaster are varied. Sometimes these are fraudulent behavior of platform managers, other times the default was the consequence of utopian business models. Macroeconomic factors also played a role. Among others, the increase in interest rates reduces investment in crypto finance as much as traditional ones. To all this was added the contagion effect supported by user behavior based only on panic and/or information asymmetries and/or misinterpretation of some phenomena (Boran, 2010).

Is it therefore possible to learn lessons for the future from these events?

12.2 The Cryptocurrency Bubble

As it can be seen in Fig. 12.1, in March 2021, the price of Bitcoin peaked and then collapsed to a low in June. That peak is "a bubble", a "cryptocurrency bubble".

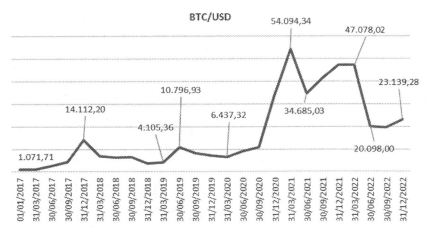

Fig. 12.1 Prices of BTC. 6 years

The "cryptocurrency bubble" is a phenomenon where the prices of cryptocurrencies experience a rapid and unsustainable increase, followed by a significant decline. During a bubble, the value of cryptocurrencies can skyrocket due to speculation and investor hype, often driven by the fear of missing out on potential gains. However, the bubble eventually bursts, causing prices to plummet, often leading to significant financial losses for investors.

Several factors can contribute to the formation of a cryptocurrency bubble:

1. Speculation: Speculators enter the market to make quick profits, driving up demand and prices. This speculative behavior can lead to an unsustainable increase in prices (Mayer, 2021).
2. Investor psychology: Investor sentiment plays a crucial role in the formation of a bubble. When investors witness others making significant profits, they may feel the fear of missing out and joining the market, further driving up prices. This herd mentality can contribute to the rapid growth and subsequent collapse of a bubble.
3. Lack of intrinsic value: Cryptocurrencies often lack intrinsic value or tangible assets backing their worth. Their value primarily relies

on market demand and investor sentiment. This lack of underlying value can make the market more susceptible to speculative bubbles.
4. Regulatory uncertainties: Cryptocurrencies operate in a relatively new and evolving regulatory landscape. Uncertainty or unfavorable regulations can create a volatile environment and contribute to market instability.

It's important to note that not all increases in cryptocurrency prices signify a bubble. Some price surges can be driven by genuine market demand, technological advancements, or other fundamental factors. In other words, not all bubbles come from speculative phenomena, and not all market crashes come from bubbles. These crashes can be triggered by various factors, including:

1. Speculative bubbles. As mentioned earlier, when prices rise rapidly due to speculation and investor hype, a bubble can form. When the bubble bursts, it often leads to a market crash as prices plummet and investors rush to sell their holdings.
2. Regulatory actions. Government regulations or actions can have a significant impact on cryptocurrency prices. Negative regulatory decisions, such as bans or restrictions on cryptocurrencies, can create panic among investors, leading to a market crash.
3. Security breaches. High-profile security breaches, such as hacks on cryptocurrency exchanges or vulnerabilities in blockchain networks, can erode investor confidence and trigger a sell-off, resulting in a market crash.
4. Market manipulation. Manipulative practices, such as pump-and-dump schemes or coordinated selling, can cause sudden price declines and market crashes.

12.3 Which Lessons for the Future?

Returning to the disasters of crypto finance that occurred in 2022 and the question posed in the premises, is it therefore possible to learn lessons for the future from these events? We should have learned some lessons from similar events in traditional finance. Some catastrophic events that happened in crypto finance have common points with the Tulip Bubble in 1637 (the Dutch tulipmania was one of the most famous market bubbles and crashes of all time. It occurred in Holland when speculation drove the value of tulip bulbs to extremes) or Charles Ponzi's Postal Coupons in 1920 and the failure of the Lehman Brothers in September 2008 among others. New lessons are, however, imposed by the fact that crypto finance uses new technologies that it is not yet fully subject to central authority controls, and that, consequently, there are no investor protection systems.

An important preliminary consideration is that the world's major cryptocurrency defaults occurred in the field of cryptocurrencies and, most importantly, cryptocurrency exchanges.

Take, for example, the default of Terra-Luna. The Terra blockchain was presented as a fully functional ecosystem of decentralized applications but, it was only a complex platform for the issuance and exchange of the two cryptocurrencies Terra (UST) and Luna (LUNA).

12.4 Volatility Does Not Give Guarantees

TerraUSD (UST) was a stablecoin not backed by U.S. dollars; instead, it was designed to maintain its peg through a complex model called a "burn and mint equilibrium". This method uses a two-token system, whereby one token is supposed to remain stable (UST) while the other token (LUNA) is meant to absorb volatility. USTs were minted by burning LUNA. The idea was that, if the UST value went above $1, the equivalent value of LUNA would be burned, which minted more UST, making it less valuable. Whereas, if the UST price dropped below $1, they were swapped for LUNA, which in turn made UST more valuable. UST could also be swapped for LUNA (right of token holders contributing to default).

The Anchor Protocol was a lending and borrowing protocol built on the Terra chain. Investors who deposited UST in the Anchor Protocol were receiving a 19.45% yield that was paid out from Terra's reserves.

In May 2022, however, the faults in Terra's ecosystem were exposed, and LUNA saw a massive crash in its price (Fig. 12.2).

This came against the backdrop of a bearish wider crypto market, with Bitcoin hitting a 10-month low on 10 May 2022. The same day, LUNA saw its value plummet below $40. The cryptocurrency then plunged to its all-time low of $0.00001675 on 13 May.

Subsequently, Terra's stablecoin, which is algorithmically supported by LUNA, lost its $1 peg. According to CoinMarketCap, the price fell to $0.29 on 11 May (Fig. 12.3).

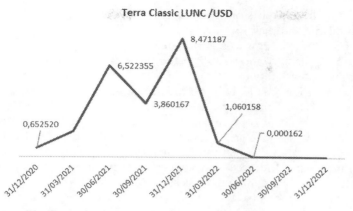

Fig. 12.2 Prices of LUNC token 2021–2022

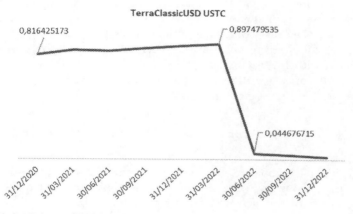

Fig. 12.3 Prices of USTC 2021–2022

Likely causes of the collapse included mass withdrawals from the Anchor Protocol days before the collapse, investor concerns about cryptocurrencies more generally, and a drop in the price of bitcoin.

During the collapse, holders converted Terra into Luna via the mint-and-burn system, which caused the price of Luna to collapse due to its increased supply. This in turn destabilized the balancing mechanism between the currencies.

The first lesson this story teaches is that the cryptocurrency market is highly volatile and that assuming that the stability of a currency (UST) is guaranteed by an asset whose price is determined by supply and demand is pure utopia. Stability and volatility cannot coexist, and no business model can upset this certainty.

Even fiat money (the U.S. dollar, the euro, and other major global currencies) is not backed by a physical commodity, such as gold or silver but, since it is a government-issued currency, it is backed by the government that issued it. The value of fiat money is derived from the relationship between supply and demand, the stability of the issuing government, and the trust that people have in the government, rather than the worth of a commodity backing it.

The fiat currencies have value because the government maintains that value. Since fiat money is not a scarce or fixed resource like gold, central banks have much greater control over its supply, which gives them the power to manage economic variables such as credit supply, liquidity, interest rates, and money velocity.

This last aspect is completely absent in cryptocurrencies being, by nature, decentralized tools. That is, no central banks are governing their circulation with the consequence that their price is determined only by supply and demand. Irrational bubbles are mainly driven by psychological factors, herd instincts, etc. (Hafner, 2020).

The Role of the Exchanges in the Volatility of the Cryptocurrencies

Stating that the price of cryptocurrencies is determined only by supply and demand is simplistic, however, two other important elements of the market strongly affect the price, and that have frustrated the original promises of this new architecture to democratize financial services. The first one is the role of the cryptocurrency exchanges inside the cryptocurrency network.

Starting from 2015, 75% of the real Bitcoin volume has been linked to exchanges or exchange-like entities such as online wallets, OTC desks, and large institutional traders. In contrast, other known entities are only responsible for a minor part of the total volume. Different from traditional, regulated exchanges, cryptocurrency markets consist of many non-integrated and independent exchanges without any provisions to ensure that investors receive the best price when executing trades. As a result, the consistency of the Bitcoin price across exchanges depends on arbitrageurs and speculators who trade across them (Makarov & Schoar, 2022).

Ownership Concentration

The further cause of cryptocurrency variability is the concentration of ownership.

The analysis of this phenomenon is important because, not only those who hold large amounts of cryptocurrency can benefit more than others from their appreciation, but above all because a great concentration means a great depreciation of the currency when these holders make mass sales.

Many analyses of the concentration of bitcoins have been conducted which have led to different results. "About 2% of bitcoin accounts hold 95% of the available coins" (Bloomberg, November 18th, 2020, and The Economist, December 7th, 2021); "1,000 people own 40% of all Bitcoins" (Business Insider, February 27th, 2021); "the top 40pc of all Bitcoin, roughly $240bn, is held by just under 2,500 known accounts out of roughly 100 m overall" (The Telegraph, January 22nd, 2021); "the top 10,000 holders make about 0.014% of Bitcoin holders. As of January 2021, these top 10,000 addresses were holding 4.8 million of the 18.5 million bitcoins that were in circulation at that point, which is 26% of all the Bitcoin wealth" (Makarov & Schoar, 2022).

The reality is that it is very difficult to conclude the real concentration because one should take into account factors and subjects that cannot be analyzed such as custodians, lost coins (where the owners lost their private key or passed away without passing on this necessary information beforehand), wrapped bitcoin (tokenized representation of bitcoin that enables their use on blockchains to which they are not native, e.g., the Ethereum ecosystem), OTC (Over the Counter) brokers, mining pools, and institutional miners (Weimans, 2022).

The lesson that we should take is that stability and/or certainty of returns cannot coexist with volatility and no business model can upset this certainty.

The Ghost of Charles Ponzi is Still Among Us

In the 1970s, Bernie Madoff placed invested funds in convertible arbitrage positions in large-cap stocks, with promised investment returns of 18–20%. In 1920, Charles Ponzi promised investors a 50% return within a few months (in effect, Ponzi, being a good Italian, tended to exaggerate). In 2022, Do Kwon and Daniel Shin, founders of Terra, granted a 19.45% yield on staking UDT in the Anchor protocol. In the same period of the high yield of the UDT staking, an investor in a ten-year US Treasury note was receiving a yield between 1.5% and 3%.

This lesson, despite the examples of history, is never learned. The promise of high short-term earnings is one of the pillars of Ponzi schemes.

In addition, the payment of Terra's yield was made with Terra's reserves which means that the returns were paid either with coins invested by other investors or minting other USTs. Gold coins do not grow in the field of miracles (Collodi, 1883). In other words, if the returns do not arise from the difference between revenues and costs (and the business model must explain it clearly), they are paid with Ponzi money which, sooner rather than later, ends.

12.5 Due Diligence is Still in Fashion

Samuel Benjamin Bankman-Fried, founder and CEO of the cryptocurrency exchange FTX and associated trading firm Alameda Research, both collapsed in late 2022, is the son of two professors at Stanford Law School and nephew of the dean of Columbia University Mailman School of Public Health. He graduated from the Massachusetts Institute of Technology in 2014 with a bachelor's degree in physics and a minor in mathematics. Do Kwon, one of the founders of Terra, received his BS in computer science from Stanford University. How not to trust people with pedigrees like these? (Fig. 12.4).

The PEPE coin opened at $0.00000006036401729083 on the day of its market launch in mid-April 2023 and it gained 6.779.32% in 20 days since its market launch reaching a market cap of $666,621,832. But who created it? Nobody knows. Are all those who have made top dollars interested in knowing? Did those investors engage themselves in due diligence to evaluate everything about the company's social media activity, from the founders' credentials to their level of transparency to what others say about it on social media forums to the competition? (Fig. 12.5).

Since many cryptocurrencies, from bitcoin to PEPE, from means of payment have been used for speculative purposes, investors often prefer to trust rumors about other people that have become millionaires overnight rather than engage in due diligence. But good old-fashioned due diligence will never go out of style even in the crypto world. For example:

Fig. 12.4 Prices of FTT token 2021–2022

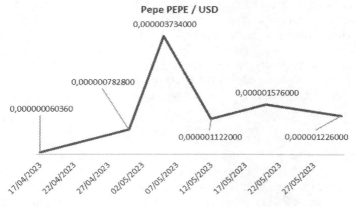

Fig. 12.5 Prices of PEPE token April 2023–May 2023

1. What are the credentials of the founders and the CEO? (the experience with Samuel Benjamin Bankman-Fried and Do Kwon must not demotivate).
2. Is the business model rational and, above all, understandable, or is it expressed in smoky terms with complex or incomprehensible mechanisms? Have you noticed that behind every crypto scandal, there

is a mysterious algorithm that generates returns through arbitrage equally unlikely?
3. Has the offer of tokens and their trading been authorized by any market control authority?
4. If the company acts as a custodian, does it have appropriate security safeguards that are independently audited and tested regularly, adequate balance sheets and reserves as commercial entities, transparent and accountable customer disclosures, and clear policies to not use customer assets for proprietary trading or margin loans in leveraged trading?
5. Is the platform domiciled in a jurisdiction that allows to appeal to a court or arbitration in case of wrongdoing?

Regulators, central banks, and other intermediaries, with the formalities and controls they impose, are certainly not consistent with the speed of decentralized finance but it is a fact that they play a risk-reducing role in traditional finance. Crypto finance is based on decentralization and disintermediation and, therefore, on the absence of these players even if regulators in many countries begin to take an interest in the subject. In other words, in the crypto world, there are no entities that play the risk control role, and this confirms the need to conduct in-depth due diligence before investing in cryptocurrencies or decentralized finance projects.

12.6 Pump and dump

25 days after the peak of its price, the PEPE coin lost 68.38% (even if it remained higher than the launch price). One of the positive aspects of blockchain is transparency so we all know that six wallets hold over $1 million worth of PEPE tokens, raising questions about the token's decentralization and the risk of market manipulation by a select few holders. This concentration of wealth in a few hands has the potential to affect the token's price and make it vulnerable to market volatility.

The lesson to be drawn from the history of the PEPE token, as from that of other tokens, is that one can test the concentration of wealth in the blockchain. A high concentration is a wake-up call about possible sudden price collapses aimed at enriching only those who have concentrated a large number of tokens in their hands rather than in their wallet (Weimans, 2022).

12.7 The Crypto Assets Are of This World

Experience has shown that the price of cryptocurrencies is influenced by the trend of interest rates such as the stock market index, albeit with variability of different amplitudes which means that it is used as a financial investment instrument (Fig. 12.6).

A rise in interest rates leads investors to assume that companies will be less profitable because of rising debt costs and falling revenues. Moreover, a higher interest rate means a lower present value of their cash flow. All these factors reduce the market value of companies and, consequently, less attention from investors who will prefer shorter-term bonds or shorter-life alternative assets because they believe that investing in equity is too risky.

The connection with the crypto market lies in the fact that higher interest rates can increase borrowing costs, which can make it more expensive for investors to borrow money to invest in cryptocurrencies. Moreover, the same consideration made for the traditional market applies to that crypto assets. Cryptocurrencies are high-risk/high-return assets. In periods of rising interest rates investing in cryptocurrencies is considered too risky.

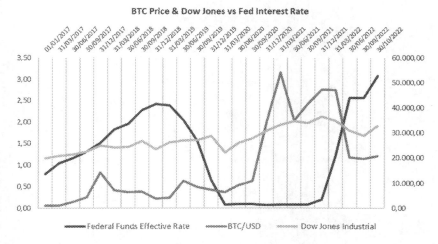

Fig. 12.6 Correlation between BTC and Fed's interest rates

Finally, the increase in the interest rate leads to a lower present value of cash flow from the rewards paid by the DeFi projects and, therefore, less interest in investments in the DeFi ecosystem (Fig. 12.7).

Several studies have been conducted on the correlation between bitcoin uncertainty, prices, and volatility in the cryptocurrency market. The result of these studies is a guide to forecasting the market for crypto assets. They show that:

- Cryptocurrency markets experience an increase in volatility when investors' fears are increased (Akyildirim et al., 2020),
- The News-based Implied Volatility index (NVIX) affects long-term cryptocurrency volatility (Fang et al., 2020),
- The Trade Policy Uncertainty (TPU) in the US negatively affects bitcoin returns (Gozgor et al., 2019),
- Uncertainty harms the Bitcoin market in the US and Japan whereas in China it has a positive effect (Shaikh, 2020),
- Chinese Economic Policy Uncertainty (EPU) index affects bitcoin returns positively (Chen et al., 2021),
- The twitter-based EPU positively affects the returns of cryptocurrencies,

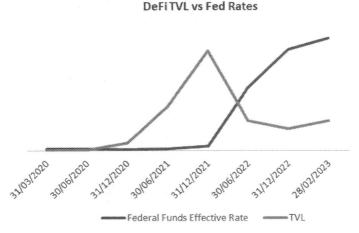

Fig. 12.7 Correlation between DeFi TVL and Fed's interest rates

- The uncertainty of cryptocurrency policy (UCRY Policy) negatively impacts Bitcoin (Lucey et al., 2021),
- The BC (Bitcoin in circulation) has a significant, positive relationship with the Bitcoin's price (BTC) in the long run; the EX (exchange rate) has a significant, negative relationship with the BTC, and the PO (popularity) has a significant, positive relationship with the BTC in the short run (Karaömer, 2022),
- There is a positive relation between the volatility of liquidity and expected returns. The volatility of liquidity is a currency-specific characteristic that measures the uncertainty associated with the level of liquidity of the currency at the time of the trade (Leirvik, 2021),
- Since investors are exposed to not only the risk of the level of liquidity but also the variation in the level of liquidity, risk-averse investors require a risk premium for holding currencies with high variation in liquidity (Leirvik, 2021).

12.8 "Too Big to Fail" Doesn't Work in the Crypto World

The crisis of 2008 has taught us that banks, insurance, and certain financial market infrastructures can be so large, complex in their operational activity, and interconnected with other market participants that their bankruptcy could undermine financial stability and damage the economic system as a whole. Therefore, various states and governments are often forced to bail out these struggling companies even at the expense of taxpayers and at the risk of unintended market distortions and potential false incentives.

At its height, FTX was valued at $32 billion. At its peak, TerraUSD was worth $18 billion and firmly in the top ten in market ranking. Despite their size and the losses that would have caused their default, no white knight, private or public, came to their rescue.

Whatever the reason why central authorities have no interest in saving crypto finance companies despite the damage their defaults prove to savers, the fact is that those who invest in crypto assets do not have life belts regardless of the size of the subjects in which they invested. The crypto world is mostly unregulated, and even for that very reason the Central Authorities do not intervene.

12.9 Contagion is Real

The collapse of FTX and TERRA has shown that decentralized finance is also subject to contagion risks. Contagion is fueled by the intrinsic volatility of each currency, and its correlation with other nodes (cryptoassets and their underlying investors …), within a network ecosystem. Digitalization is a strong catalyzer of contagion, even due to the immediacy of computerized reactions. Contagion is, however, traditionally softened by information asymmetries that prevent arbitrage.

FTX and TERRA may seem like two different episodes, however, blockchain analytics firm Nansen conducted on-chain research that suggests that the events leading up to FTX's collapse were originally triggered by the Terraform Labs collapse.

Then, crypto exchange and stablecoin issuer Gemini had exposure to Genesis and the lending partner for Gemini Earn and Genesis had exposure to FTX. In consequence, on the same day when FTX filed for bankruptcy, Gemini announced withdrawals from its Earn product may be delayed.

After this announcement, traders on decentralized finance lending protocol Aave started short-selling Gemini Dollar, GUSD, in anticipation that Gemini might become another victim of the FTX contagion. This side effect is an example of how the contagion spreads through an information channel due to information asymmetries and/or misinterpretation of some phenomena (Boran, 2010) or by psychological factors, herd instincts, etc. (Hafner, 2018).

The FTX default has quickly infected other crypto companies. The asset management firm Galaxy Digital, the venture capital firm Sequoia Capital, the hedge fund Galois Capital, the crypto lending company BlockFi, the exchange Crypto.com, the crypto market maker Wintermute, the investment firm Multicoin Capital, the trading company CoinShares, the investment firm Pantera Capital, the exchange Nexo, all had FTX exposures.

After TerraUSD collapsed, the resulting contagion led to hedge fund Three Arrows Capital, lender Celsius Network, and crypto broker Voyager Digital filing for bankruptcy over the next two months.

In the introduction, we stressed that the world's major cryptocurrency defaults occurred in the field of cryptocurrencies and, most importantly, cryptocurrency exchanges. The reason is that exchange platforms often provide several services like lending, brokerage, clearing, custody, and exchanges that, in traditional finance, are separated by regulation. There are still no crypto finance regulations or laws that impose such separation. This leads to a strong interconnection between crypto ecosystem entities that increase the risk of contagion.

This risk is nonexistent or, at least, reduced in DeFi projects that use digital tokens for fuel purposes and, above all, if those tokens are not listed for trading. To see if there is a risk of infection from other entities, the project's white paper should be analyzed to assess the degree of its "closure" to the entire ecosystem.

12.10 Let's Get Physical

8.9 billion dollars of customers were lost only in the collapse of FTX.

History has also taught us that leaving money on centralized or DeFi exchange is not safe. As in traditional finance, even crypto platform managers may be tempted to use client funds for unauthorized purposes. In addition, platforms are subject to hacker attacks. 2022 was the most successful year for hackers with over 100 protocol breaches.

Therefore, money should be stored in hardware wallets and transferred to exchanges only when one decides to make transactions. Hardware wallets are safer than online wallets because they are immune to hacker and malware attacks.

References

Akyildirim, E., Corbet, S., Lucey, B., Sensoy, A., & Yarovaya, L. (2020). The relationship between implied volatility and cryptocurrency returns. *Finance Research Letters, 33*(101212), 1–10.

Boran, M. (2010). Market dynamics & systemic risk. 23rd Australasian Finance and Banking Conference 2010 Paper.

Chen, T., Lau, C. K. M., Cheema, S., & Koo, C. K. (2021). Economic policy uncertainty in China and bitcoin returns: Evidence from the COVID-19 period. *Frontiers in Public Health, 9*(140), 1–7.

Collodi, C. (1883). *The adventures of Pinocchio. Story of a puppet.* Paggi (Ed.).

Fang, T., Su, Z., & Yin, L. (2020). Economic fundamentals or investor perceptions? The role of uncertainty in predicting long-term cryptocurrency volatility. *International Review of Financial Analysis, 71*(101566), 1–12.

Gozgor, G., Tiwari, A. K., Demir, E., & Akron, S. (2019). The relationship between bitcoin returns and trade policy uncertainty. *Finance Research Letters, 29*, 75–82.

Hafner, C. M. (2018). *Testing for bubbles in cryptocurrencies with time-varying volatility*. Institut de statistique, biostatistique et sciences actuarielles, and CORE, Université Catholique de Louvain.

Hafner, C. M. (2020, Spring). Testing for bubbles in cryptocurrencies with time-varying volatility. *Journal of Financial Econometrics, 18*(2), 233–249.

Karaömer, Y. (2022). Is the cryptocurrency policy uncertainty a determinant of bitcoin's price? *Pamukkale University Journal of Social Sciences Institute*, (50), 369–378, Denizli.

Leirvik, T. (2021, January). Cryptocurrency returns and the volatility of liquidity. *Finance Research Letters, 44*, 102031.

Lucey, B. M., Vigne, S. A., Yarovaya, L., & Wang, Y. (2021). The cryptocurrency uncertainty index. *Finance Research Letters, 102147*, 1–14.

Makarov, I., & Schoar, A. (2022). Cryptocurrencies and decentralized finance (DeFi). https://papers.ssrn.com/sol3/papers.cfm?abstract_id=4104550

Mayer, S. (2021). *Token-based platforms and speculators*. University of Chicago, Booth School of Business, and HEC.

Shaikh, I. (2020). Policy uncertainty and bitcoin returns. *Borsa Istanbul Review, 20*(3), 257–268.

Weimans, M. (2022). Widespread estimates of individual bitcoin ownership concentration are oversimplified and irrelevant. Available at https://ecommerceinstitut.de/bitcoin-wealth/

CHAPTER 13

FinTech and Digital Payment Systems Valuation

13.1 Introduction

Fintech is a combination of two words: finance and technology. It refers to the use of digital technology to improve and automate financial services. This can include things like online banking, mobile payment services, digital currencies, and peer-to-peer lending platforms. Fintech is all about making financial services more accessible, efficient, and affordable for everyone. This tentative definition highlights the growing importance of cryptoassets within the FinTech landscape. Cryptocurrencies are reshaping the FinTech ecosystem by introducing new financial instruments, decentralization, and innovative technology solutions. While these trends offer opportunities for efficiency and inclusion, they also raise regulatory and security challenges that the FinTech industry and governments must address as the space continues to evolve.

Financial technology companies (FinTechs) are gaining momentum, fueled by drivers such as the sharing economy, and include peer-to-peer lending platforms (even for crowdfunding activities) that have opened marketplaces for multiple economic actors and enabled the co-creation of value as Uber has for cars (Hommel & Bican, 2020).

Technological startups include companies operating in the FinTech segment, providing services and financial products with ICT technologies. FinTechs reformulate business models (Gomber et al., 2018; Schallmo & Williams, 2018), making use of innovative software and algorithms, value chains based on interactive computer platforms, artificial intelligence, and big data.

Financial services, which focus on the transmission of information on digital platforms, rely on innovative activities (Sironi, 2016) concerning the processing of data and their interpretation in real-time with automated descriptive, prescriptive, and predictive technologies.

FinTech (Fatás, 2019) has become a hot term due to many driven forces, which include technical development, business innovation expectations (market), cost-saving requirements, and customer demands (Gai et al., 2018). Other factors concern the regulatory framework and the macroeconomic scenario characterized by low-interest rates, leading to a reduction of the institutions' profitability, and promoting investments aimed to increase the organizations' efficiency (Piobbici et al., 2019).

Fintech refers to a vast and diverse industry that disrupts the industry (Vives, 2019), solving friction points for consumers and businesses.

The banking industry is facing radical transformation and restructuring, as well as a move toward a customer-centric platform-based model. The competition will increase as new players enter the industry, but the long-term impact is more open. The regulation will decisively influence to what extent BigTech will enter the industry and who the dominant players will be. The challenge for regulators will be to keep a level playing field that strikes the right balance between fostering innovation (Chen et al., 2019) and preserving financial stability. Consumer protection concerns rise to the forefront (Vives, 2019).

The main areas of activity are (Gai et al., 2018; Haddad & Hornuf, 2019; Sarhan, 2020):

- Financial technologies applied to blockchains (Skinner, 2016) and distributed ledger technology based on data archives, whose records are public on a computer network and without the need for a central register;
- Digital Payments: Fintech companies are revolutionizing the way payments are made by offering digital payment solutions. This includes mobile wallets, peer-to-peer payment platforms, contactless payments, and cryptocurrency payments.
- Online Lending: Fintech platforms enable individuals and businesses to obtain loans online, often bypassing traditional banks. These platforms use algorithms and alternative data sources to

assess creditworthiness and offer faster and more accessible lending options.
- Personal Finance and Wealth Management: Fintech companies provide tools and platforms to help individuals manage their finances, budgeting, savings, and investments. This includes robo-advisors, automated investment platforms, expense-tracking apps, and financial planning tools.
- Crowdfunding: Fintech has popularized crowdfunding platforms, allowing individuals and businesses to raise funds from many people through online platforms. Crowdfunding can be used for various purposes, such as startup funding, charitable causes, or creative projects.
- Insurtech: Fintech innovations have also impacted the insurance industry. Insurtech companies offer digital insurance solutions, streamlined claims processing, personalized policies based on data analytics, and improved customer experience through online platforms and mobile apps.
- Blockchain and Cryptocurrency: Fintech has embraced blockchain technology and cryptocurrencies. Blockchain provides secure and transparent transaction processing, while cryptocurrencies like Bitcoin and Ethereum offer decentralized digital currencies and investment opportunities.
- Regtech: Regulatory technology, or regtech, involves using technology to facilitate compliance with financial regulations. Fintech companies develop tools for risk management, fraud detection, customer due diligence, and reporting to ensure compliance with regulatory requirements.
- Open Banking: Fintech has driven the concept of open banking, which involves opening banking systems and data to third-party developers. This allows for the development of innovative financial services and the integration of multiple financial accounts and services into a single platform.
- Financial Inclusion: Fintech activities aim to improve financial inclusion by providing services to underbanked and underserved populations. This includes mobile banking solutions, microfinance platforms, and digital wallets that enable access to financial services for individuals who lack traditional banking options.

- Data Analytics and Artificial Intelligence: Fintech leverages data analytics and artificial intelligence to analyze vast amounts of financial data, detect patterns, make predictions, and enhance decision-making processes. These technologies are used in risk assessment, fraud detection, credit scoring, and personalized financial recommendations.

These activities represent some of the main areas where fintech has made significant advancements, but the field is constantly evolving as new technologies and ideas emerge.

- Crypto and digital money;
- Peer-to-peer loans (P2P);
- Smart contracts (using the blockchain) that automatically execute contracts between buyers and sellers;
- Open banking is supported by blockchain applications that create a service through a connected network of financial institutions and third-party providers.
- IT security, through or decentralized storage of data, and anti-fraud systems;
- Applications in the insurance field (InsurTech) or regulation (RegTech);
- Asset management (robo-advice, social trading, wealth management, personal financial management apps, or software).

Figure 13.1 contains a complementary taxonomy of the main FinTech areas (Eickhoff et al., 2017; Gimpel et al., 2018; Lee & Shin, 2018).

While crypto currencies raise several ethical concerns, including the lack of market transparency, controls, and money laundering, other blockchain applications are based on more solid perspectives.

The valuation issues of FinTech companies must be adapted to often young companies, given the novelty of the sector, which have all the prerogatives of startups (in terms of expected growth, survival rate, volatility, etc. ...). The valuation methodologies must consider first the underlying business model.

13 FINTECH AND DIGITAL PAYMENT SYSTEMS VALUATION

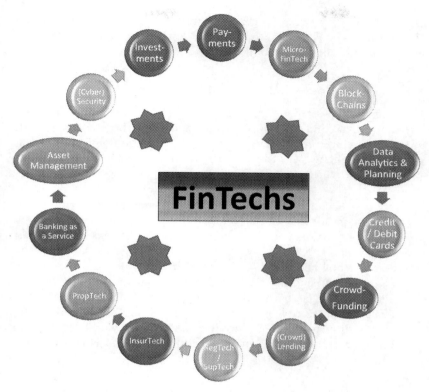

Fig. 13.1 Main FinTech activities

According to Accenture (2016), there are two types of FinTech companies: competitive and collaborative.[1] Competitive companies are mature firms, not necessarily specializing in FinTech, looking to squeeze out new competitors by applying lower prices. In this case, it would be any of

---

[1] The MSCI ACWI Banks Index is composed of large and mid-cap stocks across 23 Developed Markets (DM) countries and 26 Emerging Markets (EM) countries*. All securities in the index are classified in the Banks industry group (within the Financials sector) according to the Global Industry Classification Standard (GICS®). The top 5 constituents are: JPMORGAN CHASE & CO US; BANK OF AMERICA CORP US; WELLS FARGO & CO US; HSBC HOLDINGS (GB) GB, and CITIGROUP US. See https://www.msci.com/documents/10199/1b714b5e-5e20-405d-acfa-cb18ae63f669.

the previously mentioned larger companies, as they make up the bulk of investments in FinTech. Collaborative companies are those who offer services to enhance the position of competitors.

13.2 The Digital Ecosystem

The digital ecosystem (Drummer et al., 2016) is a prerequisite for the evaluation of any FinTech, and may be consistent with the DeFi architecture. Political-Economic-Sociocultural-Technological-Legal-Environmental (PESTLE) analysis may help in this preliminary activity. In particular:

- Political factors concern governmental policies to control the banking industry;
- Economic factors are influenced by expected savings and competitivity gains;
- Sociocultural influences concern the changing attitudes and necessities of consumers who look for a seamless banking experience;
- Technological factors are the engines behind FinTech;
- Legal issues are concerned with the regulation of the industry and the consistency of FinTech products and services with banking rules;
- Environmental concerns may be softened with paperless digital choices.

Platforms are digital enablers and facilitators of exchange (of goods, services, and information) between different types of stakeholders that could not otherwise interact with each other. Transactions are mediated through complementary players that share a network ecosystem (Armstrong, 2006; Rochet & Tirole, 2003). Due to their digital characteristics, they have a global outreach that gives them the potential to scale.

FinTechs find their rationale and natural habitat in a digital ecosystem where they act as an intermediating platform among networked stakeholders. Incumbents in the financial industry (e.g., established banks, traditional financial intermediaries, etc.) are threatened by iconic Big Techs and startups that innovate the business models and may erode market shares.

Digital platforms are at the basis of technology-enabled business models that facilitate exchanges between multiple groups—such as end-users and producers—who do not necessarily know each other.

The continuous upgrade of the technological environment creates new possibilities and reshapes the value and supply chain of financial intermediation, disrupting the existing business models.

Whereas traditional firms create value within the boundaries of a company or a supply chain, digital platforms utilize an ecosystem of autonomous agents to co-create value (Hein et al., 2019).

Digital platforms can be represented by FinTechs, and they act as a bridging node that connects digital clients to traditional or innovative financial intermediaries. Whenever platforms connect different layers (each representing a network sub-system), they can increase the systemic value. Digital platforms are multisided digital frameworks that shape the terms on which participants interact.

Digitalization is defined as the concept of "going paperless", namely as the technical process of transforming analog information or physical products into digital form. The term 'digital transformation' refers, therefore, to the application of digital technology as an alternative to solve traditional problems. As a result of digital solutions, new forms of innovation and creativity are conceived, while conventional methods are revised and enhanced.

Digitally born startups or similar tech businesses are not the only ones interested in adopting digital processes. Traditional businesses may be digitalized as well (e.g., a simple farmer willing to increase exponentially his/her production of tomatoes may digitalize the production activities through new systems or machines). In practice, with digitalization, traditional firms improve their key economic and financial parameters, as the EBITDA, increases, while the WACC reduces, so improving the DCF and the enterprise value (EV):

$$\text{DCF(unlevered)} = \Sigma \frac{O_{\text{CF}} \uparrow}{\text{WACC} \downarrow} \cong \text{Enterprise Value} \uparrow\uparrow \qquad (13.1)$$

In synthesis, digitalization brings speed and quality at a low cost, thus representing a key driver for scalability itself. Digitalization pushes up Operating Cash Flows (FCFF) and, consequently, enables a business process reengineering of traditional firms, which may presuppose incremental production growth. Digitalization normally brings to an increase in sales, accompanied by a decrease in OPEX (monetary operating expenses). This process increases the EBITDA, with a consequential improvement of operating cash flows.

Network theory (see, Barabási, 2016) is the study of graphs as a representation of either symmetric or asymmetric relations between discrete objects. In computer science and network science, network theory is a part of graph theory: a network can be defined as a graph in which nodes and/or edges have attributes (e.g., names). Digital platforms are made scalable by their networking properties, since new and bigger nodes get increasingly connected with value-adding additional links. Artificial intelligence complements this value co-creating process, for instance getting additional data (nodes) in the Web (with ChatBots, etc.) and interpreting them (so establishing new links).

Digital platforms are intrinsically networked, as anticipated, and within networks, they represent a bridging node that connects preexistent and additional users (stakeholders) with stronger links.

The properties of networked platforms are intrinsically consistent with the FinTech evolving ecosystem. Evolutionary trends are also consistent with "self-learning" artificial intelligence processes. Digital platform analysis can give an interpretation of FinTechs that consider from an unconventional perspective their properties and potential.

13.3 Financial Bottlenecks: Inefficiencies and Friction Points

An analysis of the main bottlenecks of the supply and value chain of the financial industry goes beyond the narrow scope of this chapter. It might, however, be mentioned that frictions increase the costs charged to the consumers, burdening the intermediation process with undue inefficiencies and longer passages that fuel rigidity.

Challenges and opportunities facing the financial services industry (Burlakov, 2019) concern:

- Cybercrime threats;
- Regulatory compliance;
- Customer and employee retention;
- Blockchain integration;
- Artificial intelligence and big data applications.

13 FINTECH AND DIGITAL PAYMENT SYSTEMS VALUATION

Two main value drivers are represented:

a. Savings due to disintermediation and efficiency gains;
b. Improved availability and fungibility of access to the services.

Cheaper and always available financial services substantially increase the perceived Value for Money for the consumers and the other stakeholders that form the financial ecosystem, fostering its long-term sustainability. The joint impact of savings and improved fungibility is likely to have a scalable impact in terms of client outreach. Higher volumes (due to more frequent negotiations and a wider set of products) may partially offset lower margins for traditional banking intermediaries (Fig. 13.2).

Bottlenecks determine the throughput of a supply chain. Recognizing this fact and making improvements will increase cash flow. A bottleneck (or constraint) in a supply chain is the resource that requires the longest time in operations of the supply chain for certain demands.

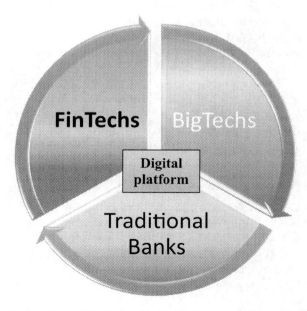

Fig. 13.2 Interaction of FinTech with BigTechs and traditional banks

Financial bottlenecks are intrinsic in the supply chain design, where intermediation is a long labor-intensive process. Each additional chain increases the marginal costs eventually charged to the final user and makes the whole supply chain more rigid. Digital applications contribute to shortening the supply chain that also become more resilient. Positive economic marginality derives from this reengineering process and should be shared among the supply chain stakeholders that include consumers.

13.4 The Accounting Background for Valuation

The evaluation is sensitive to forward-looking data that can be used to build up a sound business plan with a time horizon coherent with the average life cycle of the products and services of FinTech.

As shown in Chapter 2, a business plan is a formal accounting statement that numerically describes a set of business goals, the reasons why they are believed attainable, and the strategic plan and managerial steps for reaching those goals. Hypotheses and visionary ideas of game-changers must be transformed into numbers and need to be backed by reasonable and verifiable assumptions about future events and milestones (Moro Visconti, 2019b).

The accounting background is composed of pro forma balance sheets (of some 3–5 years) and perspective income statements. The matching of these two documents produces expected cash flow statements. Economic and financial margins are the key accounting parameters for valuation that are represented by the EBITDA, the EBIT, the operating and Net Cash Flows, and the Net Financial Position, as will be shown in the formulation of the appraisal approaches.

13.5 FinTech Business Models

FinTech is an elastic business that can concentrate on market niches and specific customer segments, leveraging an innovative use of (big) data, and proposing new disruptive products and services.

Osterwalder et al. (2005, p. 12) identify nine common business model elements: value proposition, target customer, distribution channel, relationship, value configuration, core competency, partner network, cost structure, and revenue model.

FinTechs can complementarily be a:

a. A catalyzer/upgrader (digital enabler) of traditional business models, bringing efficiency gains and pollinating the activity of ordinary banks or other financial intermediaries; FinTech providers use technology to disrupt these services by offering consumers a more compelling offering such as enhanced capabilities, convenience, or lower prices and fees (EY, 2019).
b. A pioneer of innovative products and services, normally through a B2B channel. An invented service is one that did not exist before but is now possible through technology and alternative business models, such as peer-to-peer lending and mobile-phone payments. Some invented services fill niches in the market, and others have the potential to redefine and transform entire financial subsectors (EY, 2019).

Innovation may, for instance, concern:

- Digital platform economy: handling of third parties: improving existing processes—co-opetition as a new business model;
- Open architectures and cloud: open vision—biometric and geolocalization to improve security standards;
- Change management—new legacies;
- Frictionless processes for client onboarding.

Table 13.1 synthesizes the FinTechs' main typologies and business models (see also Das, 2019; Tanda & Schena, 2019).

The appraisal methodology may conveniently start from a strategic interpretation of the business model (that derives from accounting data) to extract the key evaluation parameters to insert in the model, as shown in Fig. 13.3.

An analysis of the business model may conveniently consider:

1. The revenue model;
2. The strategic goals;
3. The growth drivers;
4. The expected investments;
5. The market trends (Fig. 13.4).

Table 13.1 FinTech typologies and business models

Typology	Business model
Financing solutions	Pure equity crowdfunding (retail); club deals; and funding from institutional investors
Blockchain	The blockchain is a decentralized and distributed digital ledger that corresponds to an open database with a pattern of shareable and unmodifiable data that are sequenced in chronological order. The main applications are cryptocurrencies; banking and payments; cybersecurity; supply chain management; forecasting; networking and IoT; insurance; private transport and ride-sharing; cloud storage; charity; voting; healthcare; and crowdfunding
Payment systems and processing (PayTech)	Credit cards; mobile payments through apps; virtual POS; online wallet; money transfers. Payment innovations throughout the year have been largely all about mobile e-wallets and contactless payments. PayTech firms also focused on ensuring the security of transactions leveraging artificial intelligence and machine learning technologies Global consumers have grown less reliant on cash, enhancing the growth profile of mobile payments firms
P2P loans	Peer-to-peer (P2P) lending is the practice of lending money to individuals or businesses through online services that match lenders with borrowers. Peer-to-peer lending companies often offer their services online and attempt to operate with lower overhead and provide their services more cheaply than traditional financial institutions
Open banking	In October 2015, the European Parliament adopted a revised Payment Services Directive, known as PSD2. The new rules included aims to promote the development of neo-banks or challenger banks' use of innovative online and mobile payments through open banking

(continued)

Table 13.1 (continued)

Typology	Business model
Big data & analytics	Big data analytics is the often-complex process of examining large and varied data sets, or big data, to uncover information—such as hidden patterns, unknown correlations, market trends, and customer preferences—that can help organizations make informed business decisions. Big data based on payment transaction data provides insight into customer retention, identification of criminal activities, or future customer behavior
Insurtech	Insurtech refers to the use of technology innovations designed to squeeze out savings and efficiency from the current insurance industry model
RegTech	Regulatory technology, in short, RegTech, is a new technology that uses information technology to enhance regulatory processes. With its main application in the financial sector, it is expanding into any regulated business with an appeal to the Consumer Goods Industry. Regtech, post-financial crisis—with MiFiD II, Basel III, and GDPR—may have been the initial external driver to ensure full compliance, and this has ensured a dramatic rise in technological solutions, and crucial in increasing efficiency, for example, by reducing gap-analysis time
SupTech	Use of innovative technology (big data, artificial intelligence, blockchains, etc.) by supervisory agencies to support supervision. Suptech will help authorities to become more data-driven (Di Castri et al., 2019)
Micro-FinTech	FinTech applications to microfinance activities (microcredit; microdeposits; microinsurance; micro-consulting). M-banking boosts volumes and fosters marginality gains (Moro Visconti, 2019a)

(continued)

Table 13.1 (continued)

Typology	Business model
Banking-as-a-service	End-to-end process ensuring the execution of a financial service provided over the web
Artificial intelligence	AI will transform nearly every aspect of the financial service industry. Automated wealth management, customer verification, and open banking all provide opportunities for AI solution providers
PropTech	Property technology, short called Proptech, sometimes also called Real estate technology, is a term that encompasses the application of information technology and platform economics to real estate markets

Fig. 13.3 Evaluation methodology

FinTechs cooperate with banks (Dorfleitner & Hornuf, 2019). Cooperation is primarily geared toward the integration or use of a FinTech application (product-related cooperation).

An interpretation of the business model of each FinTech can be given using the SWOT analysis.

A further issue to be considered in the strategic analysis of the business model is the patentability of the algorithm that is behind FinTech's formulation. Software applications may be protected by patent law (in the US) or copyright law (in the EU).

The potential of FinTechs (in terms of products and services offered, strategic goals, etc.) concerns:

1. Problem-solving capacity (disruptive solutions to existing problems);

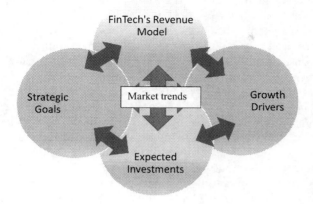

Fig. 13.4 Business model and value drivers

2. Total Addressable/Available Market;
3. New applications/Products/Services enabled by technology;
4. Lower Distribution/Intermediation and Operational costs (efficiency gains);
5. Revenue Model (market traction);
6. Cross-selling opportunities.

13.6　Digital Payment Systems

Digital payments represent the most important FinTech activity, and they are fully consistent with digital tokens and cryptocurrencies.

Digitization, propelled by the advent of smartphones and the internet, has brought about significant changes to payment systems. Here are some ways in which this transformation has occurred:

1. Mobile Payments: The widespread adoption of smartphones has facilitated the rise of mobile payment solutions. Mobile wallets, such as Apple Pay, Google Pay, and Samsung Pay, enable users to make payments using their smartphones at physical point-of-sale terminals or online. This has made payments more convenient and streamlined, reducing the reliance on physical cards or cash.

2. Online Payments: The internet has revolutionized online payments. E-commerce platforms and online marketplaces have integrated secure payment gateways, allowing customers to make purchases electronically. This shift has expanded global commerce and opened new business opportunities, making it easier for merchants to accept payments from customers around the world.
3. Peer-to-Peer Payments: Digital platforms have facilitated peer-to-peer (P2P) payments, enabling individuals to transfer funds directly to one another. Services like PayPal, Venmo, and Zelle provide seamless P2P payment options, simplifying the process of splitting bills, repaying friends, or conducting small-scale transactions.
4. Contactless Payments: The digitization of payment systems has led to the proliferation of contactless payment technologies. Near Field Communication (NFC) and Radio Frequency Identification (RFID) enable users to make payments by simply tapping or waving their smartphones or contactless cards at payment terminals. This method offers convenience, speed, and enhanced security compared to traditional payment methods.
5. QR Code Payments: QR code-based payments have gained popularity, particularly in emerging markets. Users can scan QR codes displayed by merchants using their smartphone cameras, linking to a payment app or digital wallet, and complete the transaction. QR code payments are cost-effective, easy to use, and can be deployed in various environments, including small businesses and street vendors.
6. Blockchain and Cryptocurrencies: The emergence of blockchain technology and cryptocurrencies has disrupted traditional payment systems. Blockchain-based payment networks offer secure, transparent, and decentralized transactions, eliminating the need for intermediaries. Cryptocurrencies, such as Bitcoin and Ethereum, provide alternative digital currencies that can be used for online transactions, further expanding payment options.
7. Data and Analytics: Digitization has enabled the collection and analysis of vast amounts of payment data. Payment service providers can leverage this data to gain insights into consumer behavior, preferences, and trends. Such analytics help businesses optimize their payment processes, personalize user experiences, and detect and prevent fraudulent activities.

The arrival of smartphones and the internet has transformed payment systems by enabling mobile payments, online transactions, P2P transfers, contactless payments, and the adoption of innovative technologies like blockchain and cryptocurrencies. This digital revolution has made payments faster, more convenient, and accessible to a broader range of users, reshaping the way we conduct financial transactions.

A digital payment system, also known as an electronic payment system or e-payment system, is a method of making financial transactions electronically, without the use of physical currency or traditional banking instruments like checks. It allows individuals and businesses to send and receive money digitally using various electronic devices such as computers, smartphones, or other connected devices.

There are several types of digital payment systems available today, including:

1. Online Banking: Many banks offer online banking services that allow customers to transfer funds, pay bills, and manage their accounts through internet banking platforms.
2. Mobile Payments: With the proliferation of smartphones, mobile payment systems have become increasingly popular. These systems enable users to make payments using their mobile devices by linking their bank accounts, credit cards, or digital wallets to mobile payment apps such as Apple Pay, Google Pay, or Samsung Pay.
3. Digital Wallets: Digital wallets are applications that store payment card information securely, allowing users to make purchases online or in physical stores by scanning QR codes or using near-field communication (NFC) technology. Examples of digital wallets include PayPal, Venmo, and Alipay.
4. Peer-to-Peer (P2P) Payments: P2P payment systems enable individuals to transfer funds directly to one another using mobile apps or online platforms. These systems often utilize bank transfers or digital wallets to facilitate transactions. Popular P2P payment services include Zelle, PayPal, and Square Cash.
5. Cryptocurrencies: Cryptocurrencies, such as Bitcoin and Ethereum, provide a decentralized digital payment system based on blockchain technology. Transactions are recorded on a public ledger, and users can send and receive digital currencies directly without intermediaries like banks.

Digital payment systems offer several advantages, including convenience, speed, and enhanced security compared to traditional payment methods. They allow for seamless transactions, reduce the need for cash handling, and enable faster processing times.

It's worth noting that the availability and adoption of digital payment systems may vary by country and region, as different regions may have their own preferred platforms or regulatory frameworks in place.

Cryptocurrencies have had a significant impact on the digital payment system. Here are some key effects:

1. Decentralization and peer-to-peer transactions: Cryptocurrencies operate on decentralized networks, such as blockchain, which enables direct transactions between users without the need for intermediaries like banks or payment processors. This eliminates the need for centralized authorities to verify and facilitate transactions, allowing for faster and cheaper peer-to-peer transactions.
2. Increased accessibility: Cryptocurrencies have made digital payments accessible to individuals who may not have access to traditional banking services. People in underbanked or unbanked regions can use cryptocurrencies to send and receive funds, opening up new economic opportunities.
3. Global transactions and remittances: Cryptocurrencies enable cross-border transactions without the need for traditional currency exchange systems. This can significantly reduce the time and cost associated with international remittances, benefiting individuals and businesses involved in global trade.
4. Security and privacy: Cryptocurrencies use advanced cryptographic techniques to secure transactions and user identities. The use of public and private keys enhances security and reduces the risk of fraud or identity theft. Additionally, some cryptocurrencies offer enhanced privacy features, allowing users to have more control over their financial information.
5. Innovation in financial services: The rise of cryptocurrencies has sparked innovation in the financial sector. Blockchain technology, which underlies most cryptocurrencies, has the potential to revolutionize various aspects of the digital payment system, including smart contracts, supply chain management, and transparent auditing.

6. Volatility and risk: Cryptocurrencies, such as Bitcoin, have been known for their price volatility. This can introduce risk and uncertainty for users and businesses that rely on cryptocurrencies for payments. However, the development of stablecoins, which are cryptocurrencies pegged to stable assets like fiat currencies, aims to mitigate this volatility issue.
7. Regulatory challenges: The emergence of cryptocurrencies has posed regulatory challenges for governments worldwide. Authorities are grappling with how to regulate and supervise these digital assets while ensuring consumer protection, preventing money laundering, and addressing other potential risks.

Cryptocurrencies have brought significant changes to the digital payment system, promoting decentralization, accessibility, security, and innovation. However, challenges related to volatility and regulation still need to be addressed for cryptocurrencies to achieve wider adoption and integration into mainstream digital payments.

Fintechs have had a profound impact on the digital payment system. Here are some key effects:

1. Enhanced user experience: Fintech companies have revolutionized the user experience in digital payments. They have developed intuitive mobile apps and online platforms that offer streamlined and user-friendly interfaces, making it easier for individuals and businesses to make payments, manage their finances, and track transactions in real time.
2. Increased convenience and accessibility: Fintech solutions have made digital payments more convenient and accessible to a broader range of users. With the proliferation of smartphones and internet connectivity, fintechs have developed mobile payment apps, digital wallets, and payment gateways that allow users to make payments anytime, anywhere, using their mobile devices.
3. Innovation in payment methods: Fintech companies have introduced new payment methods and technologies that go beyond traditional payment systems. These include contactless payments, biometric authentication, QR codes, and peer-to-peer payment platforms. These innovations have facilitated faster, more secure, and frictionless transactions.

4. Integration of multiple financial services: Fintechs have integrated various financial services into their digital payment platforms. Users can now access services like budgeting tools, personal finance management, investment options, and loan applications within a single app or platform. This consolidation of services provides users with a holistic financial management experience.
5. Lower costs and increased efficiency: Fintech solutions have disrupted the traditional payment system by offering cost-effective alternatives. They often have lower transaction fees compared to traditional banking systems, enabling businesses to save money on payment processing. Moreover, fintechs leverage automation, data analytics, and artificial intelligence to streamline processes, reduce manual errors, and increase the efficiency of digital payments.
6. Financial inclusion: Fintechs have played a vital role in promoting financial inclusion by reaching underserved populations. They have developed solutions that cater to individuals who have limited access to traditional banking services. Through digital payments, fintechs have provided opportunities for these individuals to participate in the digital economy, receive payments, and manage their finances.
7. Collaboration and competition with traditional players: Fintech companies have spurred competition and collaboration within the financial industry. Traditional financial institutions are adapting to the changing landscape by partnering with or acquiring fintech startups to integrate innovative payment solutions into their offerings. This collaboration benefits consumers by providing a wider range of digital payment options.

Fintechs have brought significant advancements to the digital payment system, enhancing user experience, convenience, and accessibility. They have introduced innovative technologies, increased efficiency, and promoted financial inclusion. As fintech continues to evolve, it is likely to further reshape the digital payment landscape and drive further innovation in the financial industry.

The digitization of payment systems can serve as a foundation for the provision of broader financial services, particularly in countries with underdeveloped financial systems. This transformation can be especially significant in poorer countries:

1. Financial Inclusion: Digitized payment systems provide an opportunity to extend financial services to unbanked and underbanked populations. With the widespread adoption of smartphones and internet connectivity, individuals in poorer countries can access mobile wallets and payment apps, allowing them to receive and make digital payments. This inclusion in the formal financial system opens doors to a range of other services like savings accounts, loans, insurance, and investment opportunities.
2. Access to Credit: Traditional banking systems often have strict requirements for accessing credit, making it challenging for individuals in poorer countries to secure loans. However, with the digitization of payment systems, alternative credit assessment models can be developed. By analyzing digital transaction data, fintech companies can assess creditworthiness and offer microloans or small-scale credit to individuals who were previously excluded from formal lending channels.
3. Remittances: Many individuals in poorer countries rely on remittances from family members working abroad. Traditional remittance channels can be slow, expensive, and prone to intermediaries taking significant fees. Digitized payment systems, coupled with the use of cryptocurrencies or stablecoins, can facilitate faster, more secure, and cost-effective cross-border transactions, enabling individuals to receive remittances directly into their digital wallets.
4. Microfinance and Savings: In countries with less developed financial systems, microfinance institutions play a crucial role in providing small-scale loans and financial services to entrepreneurs and low-income individuals. Digitized payment systems can support microfinance by enabling efficient loan disbursements, repayments, and savings mobilization. Mobile wallets can serve as a platform for individuals to save and accumulate funds, improving their financial stability and enabling them to access larger financial services in the future.
5. Insurance and Risk Management: Digitized payment systems can also facilitate the provision of insurance products to individuals in poorer countries. By leveraging transaction data and digital identities, insurers can develop affordable and customized insurance plans tailored to the specific needs of these populations. This can help individuals mitigate risks associated with health, crop failure, natural disasters, and other unforeseen events.

6. Financial Education and Empowerment: Digitized payment systems can be coupled with financial education initiatives to empower individuals in poorer countries with financial literacy. Mobile apps and digital platforms can offer resources, tools, and educational content to help individuals understand basic financial concepts, manage their finances, and make informed decisions.

By leveraging digitized payment systems, poorer countries can leapfrog traditional financial infrastructure and embrace innovative financial services. This can contribute to poverty reduction, economic growth, and improved livelihoods by providing access to credit, savings, insurance, and other essential financial tools.

Payments through apps that utilize QR codes, fast payment networks, and high-speed internet connections have transformed the way transactions are conducted. Here are some key benefits of these technologies:

1. Speed and Convenience: QR code-based payments offer a fast and convenient way to make transactions. Users can simply scan the QR code displayed by the merchant or recipient, enter the payment amount, and authorize the transaction. This process is typically faster than traditional payment methods, such as cash or card payments, reducing waiting times and improving overall efficiency.
2. Enhanced Security: QR code payments enhance security compared to traditional payment methods. The use of encrypted QR codes ensures that sensitive payment information is securely transmitted. Additionally, some QR code payment apps utilize tokenization, which replaces the actual card or account details with unique tokens, further protecting users from potential fraud or data breaches.
3. Cost-effectiveness: QR code payments can be cost-effective for both merchants and consumers. Merchants can reduce the costs associated with cash handling and traditional point-of-sale systems. For consumers, there may be no additional fees or minimal transaction charges, making it an affordable payment option.
4. Wide Acceptance: QR code payments are widely accepted across various merchants, including small businesses and street vendors. This acceptance is especially valuable in regions where cash remains dominant, as QR codes can bridge the gap between digital payments and the cash-based economy.

5. Accessibility and Financial Inclusion: QR code payments can improve financial inclusion by providing access to digital payment options to individuals who may not have access to traditional banking services. If users have a smartphone and a reliable internet connection, they can participate in the digital economy and make transactions using QR code payment apps.
6. Integration with Existing Infrastructure: QR code payments can be seamlessly integrated with existing payment infrastructure. Merchants can generate QR codes that link to their bank accounts or payment processors, enabling easy reconciliation and settlement. This integration facilitates the adoption of QR code payments without requiring significant changes to existing systems.
7. Analytics and Personalization: QR code payment apps can collect valuable transaction data, providing insights into consumer behavior and preferences. This data can be leveraged to offer personalized recommendations, loyalty rewards, and targeted marketing campaigns. Such analytics enable businesses to better understand their customers and tailor their offerings accordingly.

Payments through apps that utilize QR codes, fast payment networks, and high-speed internet connections offer speed, convenience, security, and cost-effectiveness. These technologies have the potential to accelerate the shift toward a cashless society, drive financial inclusion, and foster economic growth by providing efficient and accessible payment solutions.

Some countries are establishing multilateral payment linkages that enable their citizens to use their domestic payment systems or favorite payment apps when traveling or making transactions abroad. Here are a few examples and benefits of such initiatives:

1. Unified Payment Platforms: Certain countries have developed unified payment platforms that integrate various domestic payment systems, such as mobile wallets or digital payment apps, into a single platform. These platforms facilitate cross-border payments, allowing citizens to use their preferred domestic payment methods when traveling internationally. This simplifies transactions for users and promotes seamless payment experiences across borders.
2. International Interoperability: Multilateral payment linkages aim to establish interoperability between different countries' payment

systems. This means that individuals can use their domestic payment apps or cards in partner countries, enabling them to make transactions abroad without the need for currency exchange or relying solely on international payment methods. This can enhance convenience, reduce costs, and provide familiarity for users.
3. Enhanced Financial Inclusion: Multilateral payment linkages can promote financial inclusion by extending access to digital payment systems beyond national borders. Individuals who have limited access to traditional banking services in their home countries can still utilize their preferred domestic payment methods when traveling or working abroad, facilitating their participation in the digital economy.
4. Tourism and Business Facilitation: Simplifying cross-border payments through multilateral linkages can boost tourism and business activities. Visitors or international business travelers can seamlessly use their domestic payment apps or cards to make payments, eliminating the need for currency conversion or dealing with unfamiliar payment systems. This can enhance the overall experience for travelers and promote economic interactions between countries.
5. Collaboration between Countries: Building multilateral payment linkages requires collaboration and agreements between participating countries. Such collaborations foster closer relationships and cooperation in the financial and economic sectors. It allows countries to align their regulatory frameworks, develop common standards, and share best practices in payment systems, ultimately enhancing cross-border financial integration.
6. Innovation and Technological Exchange: Establishing multilateral payment linkages encourages the exchange of technological advancements and innovations between countries. Participating countries can learn from each other's experiences and leverage successful domestic payment systems to improve their offerings. This can spur innovation, drive the adoption of advanced technologies, and foster healthy competition in the global payments landscape.

Multilateral payment linkages that enable citizens to use their domestic payment systems or favorite payment apps abroad promote convenience, financial inclusion, tourism, and business facilitation. These initiatives reflect a growing trend toward seamless cross-border payments and collaborative efforts to enhance the overall payment experience for individuals across different countries.

Cryptocurrencies are having a significant impact on the business models of FinTech companies in several ways:

1. New Payment Methods: Cryptocurrencies offer an alternative to traditional fiat currencies for transactions. They allow for fast, borderless transactions, which can be particularly beneficial for international payments. Many FinTech companies are integrating cryptocurrencies into their platforms to provide more payment options to their customers.
2. Decentralized Finance (DeFi): DeFi refers to the shift from traditional, centralized financial systems to peer-to-peer finance enabled by decentralized technologies built on blockchain, the technology behind cryptocurrencies. DeFi platforms allow for borrowing, lending, earning interest, and more, all without a traditional financial institution acting as an intermediary. This opens new business models for FinTechs that are leveraging these capabilities.
3. Blockchain Services: Blockchain, the technology that underpins cryptocurrencies, has uses beyond just supporting digital currencies. It offers increased transparency, security, and efficiency, and many FinTechs are developing blockchain-based services. These can include anything from smart contracts to secure supply chain management solutions.
4. Tokenization: Tokenization, particularly through Non-Fungible Tokens (NFTs), is another avenue opened up by cryptocurrency technology. Tokenization allows for digital ownership of a unique piece of content on the blockchain. FinTechs can use this for a variety of purposes, such as tokenizing real-world assets or intellectual property.
5. Fundraising: Initial Coin Offerings (ICOs) and Security Token Offerings (STOs) have emerged as alternatives to traditional fundraising methods. FinTech startups can issue their tokens to raise capital, often with fewer regulations and lower costs than traditional financing.
6. Remittances: Cryptocurrencies are being used to streamline and lower the cost of remittance services, a significant market for many FinTech companies.

7. Cryptocurrency Trading Platforms: Some FinTechs have made cryptocurrencies the core of their business model by offering cryptocurrency trading platforms. These platforms may offer features such as spot trading, futures contracts, margin trading, and more.

While cryptocurrencies present many opportunities, they also come with challenges. Regulatory uncertainty, scalability issues, security risks, and volatility are all factors that FinTechs need to consider when integrating cryptocurrencies into their business model.

13.7 Banks Versus FinTechs: Cross-Pollination and Scalability

Traditional banks and FinTech companies represent different ends of the financial services spectrum. Banks offer stability, trust, and extensive customer bases, but are often hindered by legacy systems and slower decision-making processes. Conversely, FinTechs are known for their agility, innovation, and technological prowess but often struggle with customer trust and scaling their operations. There has been a growing trend toward cross-pollination and collaboration between banks and FinTechs, each adopting strengths from the other to scale up and provide better services.

Cross-Pollination

Cross-pollination refers to the exchange of ideas, technologies, and practices between different sectors or entities. In the case of banks and FinTechs, this could involve:

- Banks adopting FinTech innovations: Traditional banks are increasingly recognizing the need to modernize and digitize their services. They are adopting FinTech innovations such as mobile banking, AI-driven customer service, and blockchain technology. Some banks have even created innovation labs or partnered with FinTech startups to accelerate this process.
- FinTechs leveraging bank infrastructure: FinTechs are often more agile and innovative than banks, but they lack the established infrastructure and customer trust that banks have. As such, many

FinTechs partner with banks to offer their services on top of the bank's existing infrastructure, which can provide a more secure environment and instill more customer trust.

Scalability

Scalability refers to the ability of a system to handle a growing amount of work, or its potential to be enlarged to accommodate growth. For both banks and FinTechs, scalability is a critical factor:

- For banks: Adopting FinTech innovations can help banks scale their services, reach more customers, and improve efficiency. For instance, utilizing AI and machine learning can help banks automate routine tasks, provide personalized services, and make more accurate risk assessments, all of which can help them serve more customers more effectively.
- For FinTechs: Partnering with banks can help FinTechs scale their operations by giving them access to a larger customer base and more resources. At the same time, FinTechs need to ensure that their solutions can handle increased demand and larger volumes of transactions as they grow.

In conclusion, the relationship between banks and FinTechs is increasingly symbiotic, with both sides recognizing the value that the other brings. Through cross-pollination and collaboration, banks and FinTechs can improve scalability, reach more customers, and provide better financial services.

The business model of a bank is vastly different from that of a typical FinTech and this difference reflects in the balance sheet and the income statement.

The balance sheet of a bank is characterized by a binding structure, due to the presence of the supervisory capital and bank deposits (in the liabilities) and loans to customers (within the assets). The assets and liabilities structure of a typical FinTech is much "lighter", being represented by net working capital and some capitalized assets (tangible and intangible), against equity and financial debt in the liabilities.

The income statement reflects these differences:

- The bank has economic margins represented by the interest rate differential and the net contribution of commissions;
- FinTech has a more standard EBITDA and EBIT, sourced by the difference between operating revenues (from services) and monetary OPEX (to get to the EBITDA) or comprehensive OPEX, including depreciation and amortization, to determine the EBIT.

The different income statements, driven by the respective business models of either the bank or the FinTech, reflect a completely different attitude toward (digital) scalability.

FinTechs have a revenue model that is much more scalable than that of a typical bank. Whereas a bank is limited in its growth potential by constraints such as the supervisory capital (a percentage of its loans, weighted for risk), huge fixed costs for personnel, and difficult upside in a mature market, FinTechs incorporate a digital potential in an intrinsically scalable business model.

Even if FinTechs have a higher marginality potential, they still need the volumes (client base, etc.) and the market caption bound to traditional banks.

13.8 Insights from Listed FinTechs

FinTechs have a hybrid business model, as they operate in the financial (banking) sector deploying their technological attitudes. Evaluators may wonder if FinTechs follow the typical evaluation patterns of bank/financial intermediaries or those of technological firms. Preliminary empirical evidence—reported below—shows that the latter interpretation is consistent with the stock market mood.

This indication is important for the assessment of the best evaluation criteria.

The following graph (with data sourced from Bloomberg) contains the comparative stock market price (from August 1, 2015, to June 2023) of:

a. IFINXNT—Indxx Global Fintech Thematic Index
b. MXW00BK—MSCI World Banks Weighted Equity Index[2]

[2] See footnote 1.

c. MXW00IT—MSCI World (ex-Australia) Information Technology Index (Fig. 13.5)

Despite the young age of FinTechs, many of these firms are experiencing significantly faster growth than their traditional financial services peers. This reflects in the performance of FinTech companies tracked by the Indxx Global Fintech Thematic Index,[3] the underlying index for the Global X FinTech ETF (FINX), relative to the Financial Select Sector Index.

The differences in the stock prices reflect not only a different market mood but also a cost of capital (cost of equity) that is not the same and influences the valuation of each firm.

FinTechs seem far from the banks even because they have a different model, as they do not collect deposits and lend money, intermediating financial resources; FinTechs are not hyper-regulated deposit-taking institutions, and they just provide financial service and do not intermediate "money" as a product, and they do not need a supervisory capital like banks.

The preliminary conclusion that FinTechs follow the evaluation parameters of technological firms has, however, some caveats that may tentatively be summarized as follows:

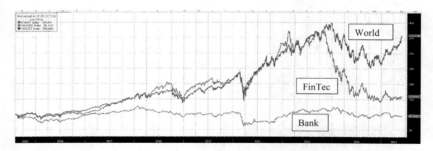

Fig. 13.5 FinTech versus technological and banking stock market index

---

[3] The Indxx Global Fintech Thematic Index is designed to track the performance of companies listed in developed markets that are offering technology-driven financial services which are disrupting existing business models in the financial services and banking sectors. The index has been backtested to June 30, 2015, and has a live calculation date of August 29, 2016. https://www.indxx.com/indxx-global-fintech-thematic-index-tr.

a. If FinTech firms are the purchase target of (much bigger and consolidated) ordinary banks/financial intermediaries, then the valuation criteria of the latter predominate, at least after the acquisition (and especially if FinTechs are merged into traditional banks);
b. The underlying market and business model of maturing FinTechs may become less technological and more "client-based";
c. Some established criteria used in the evaluation of traditional banks are, however, hardly applicable even in perspective (e.g., consideration of "physical" banking branches as a positive element).

13.9 Valuation Methods

Valuing fintech companies can be challenging due to their unique business models and reliance on technology. Several valuation approaches are commonly used for fintech. Here are some of the main approaches:

1. Comparable Company Analysis (CCA): This approach involves comparing the financial and operational metrics of the fintech company with similar publicly traded or recently acquired companies in the same industry. Key factors considered include revenue growth rates, profitability, customer base, market share, and valuation multiples (such as price-to-sales or price-to-earnings ratios).
2. Discounted Cash Flow (DCF) Analysis: DCF analysis estimates the present value of a fintech company's expected future cash flows. This approach involves forecasting future cash flows, applying a discount rate to account for the time value of money and risk, and calculating the net present value (NPV) of the cash flows. DCF analysis requires making assumptions about revenue growth, profitability, capital expenditure, and cost of capital.
3. Venture Capital (VC) Method: The VC method is often used to value early-stage fintech startups. This approach considers the potential exit value of the company through future rounds of funding or acquisition. Valuation is determined by estimating the company's future funding rounds, assuming dilution of ownership, and applying appropriate valuation multiples based on the startup's growth potential and industry benchmarks.

4. Market Capitalization: For fintech companies that are publicly traded, market capitalization (market cap) can be used as a valuation measure. Market cap is calculated by multiplying the company's share price by the total number of outstanding shares. However, it's important to consider other factors like financial performance and growth prospects alongside market cap when assessing the value of a fintech company.
5. Transaction-Based Approach: This approach looks at recent transactions and acquisitions in the fintech sector to determine valuation. By analyzing the purchase price of comparable companies and considering deal multiples, investor interest, and market trends, an estimated valuation can be derived for the fintech company in question.
6. Revenue and User-Based Models: Some fintech companies are valued based on their revenue generation potential or the number of users/customers they have. This approach involves estimating the company's future revenue growth, market share, and monetization strategies, and applying appropriate multiples or benchmarks based on industry standards or comparable companies.

Valuing fintech companies can be subjective and requires careful consideration of various factors. Different valuation approaches may be used in combination, depending on the stage of the fintech company, the availability of data, and the specific circumstances of the valuation. Consulting with financial professionals experienced in valuing technology companies or fintech specialists can provide valuable insights and expertise in the valuation process.

The evaluation criteria typically follow the (actual and prospective) business model of the target company.

The technological value driver seems, at least in this historical phase, prevalent over the banking/financial activity, as shown in Fig. 13.6. A preliminary consideration may, however, indicate that the business model is slightly more "bank-centric" than the evaluation criteria.

The reasons for this divergence are manifold: banks are capital- and labor-intensive institutions and are strictly supervised (not only since they are financial institutions but also because they collect deposits and are so regulated by Central Bank authorities).

FinTechs are quite different, although they share with banks a common underlying framework.

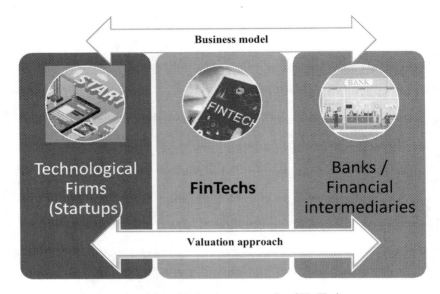

Fig. 13.6 Business model and valuation approach of FinTechs

Banking and financial activities (Damodaran, 2009) follow peculiar valuation patterns that often concentrate on parameters like adjusted equity or dividends. These parameters are, however, not particularly meaningful with FinTechs since they are not capital-intensive firms, and their capacity to pay-out dividends is absent in the startup phase.

If the FinTech activity is developed within a banking group by a captive company, its strategic meaning may be that of a catalyzer of (traditional) banking activity. In this case, what mostly matters is not the value of FinTech (Yao, 2018) as a stand-alone reality, but rather its contribution to the incremental marginality of the (traditional) banking group to which it belongs. FinTechs naturally tend to cooperate with banks, as in most cases they represent their customers. (Product-related) cooperation is primarily geared toward the integration or use of a FinTech application cooperation (Brandl & Hornuf, 2017).

In this case, the value may be inferred even with differential income methodologies, traditionally used in the evaluation of intangible assets (within the income approaches).

According to the International Valuation Standard IVS 210, § 80:

80. Premium Profit Method or With-and-Without Method
80.1 The premium profit method, sometimes referred to as the with-and-without method, indicates the value of an intangible asset by comparing two scenarios: one in which the business uses the subject intangible asset and one in which the business does not use the subject intangible asset (but all other factors are kept constant). (…)
80.2 The comparison of the two scenarios can be done in two ways:
a) calculating the value of the business under each scenario with the difference in the business values being the value of the subject intangible asset, and
b) calculating for each future period the difference between the profits in the two scenarios. The present value of those amounts is then used to reach the value of the subject intangible asset.

In this case, what matters for the evaluation is the with-and-without availability of the FinTech business that can be considered as the "intangible" asset indicated in IVS 210.

Demyanova (2018) considers several methodologies that, in most cases, are hardly applicable to FinTechs. For example, the liquidation value or book-value method is not consistent with the innovative nature of startups that become valueless if wound up and derive most of their potential value from intangible assets. The Berkus method appears too undetermined, and real options may be embedded in the estimate of future cash flows with multiple scenarios. A synthesis is reported in Table 13.3.

According to Moro Visconti et al. (2020), in an equity valuation theory and practice, there are generally two valuation approaches—discounted cash flows (DCF) and comparables.

A comparison of the primary evaluation criteria in traditional (non-financial) firms, high-tech firms (startups), and banks/financial intermediaries is reported in Table 13.2.

Table 13.2 is complementary to Table 13.3.

The Financial Approach

The financial approach is based on the principle that the market value of the company is equal to the discounted value of the cash flows that the company can generate ("cash is king"). The determination of the cash

Table 13.2 Comparison of the main evaluation approaches of traditional firms, technological startups, and banks

Traditional firm	Technological startup (IPEV, 2018; other methods)	Bank (financial intermediary)
Balance sheet-based (Fernandez, 2001)	Venture Capital method	Expected dividends per share/Dividend Discount Models
Income	Binomial trees	Adjusted book value of equity (to proxy Market value)
Mixed capital-income	Net Asset Value	Excess Return Models
Financial (DCF)		
Market multiples (comparable firms) (IPEV, 2018)		

Table 13.3 FinTech valuation approaches

Method	Description
Liquidation value	Break-up value of tangible assets
Book value	The accounting value of tangible assets
Discounted cash flows	Discount of Operating Cash Flows to get Enterprise Value or Net Cash Flows to get Equity Value
First Chicago	Situation-specific business valuation approach used by venture capital and private equity investors for early-stage companies. This model combines elements of market-oriented and fundamental analytical methods
Payne scoring	Weighted average value compared to similar firms
Berkus	Considers five key success factors: (1) Basic value, (2) Technology, (3) Execution, (4) Strategic relationships in its core market, and (5) Production, and consequent sales
Real options	An economically valuable right to make or else abandon some choice that is available to the managers of a company, often concerning business projects or investment opportunities

flows is of primary importance in the application of the approach, as is the consistency of the discount rates adopted.

The doctrine (especially the Anglo-Saxon one) believes that the financial approach is the "ideal" solution for estimating the market value for limited periods. It is not possible to make reliable estimates of cash flows for longer periods. "*The conceptually correct methods are those based* on cash flow discounting. *I briefly comment on other methods since—even though they are conceptually incorrect—they continue to be used frequently*" (Fernandez, 2001).

This approach is of practical importance if the individual investor or company with high cash flows (leasing companies, retail trade, public, and motorway services, financial trading, project financing SPVs, etc.) is valued.

Financial evaluation can be particularly appropriate when the company's ability to generate cash flow for investors is significantly different from its ability to generate income, and forecasts can be formulated with a sufficient degree of credibility and are demonstrable.

There are two complementary criteria for determining the cash flows:

The Cash Flow Available to the Company (Free Cash Flow to the Firm)

This configuration of expected flows is the one most used in the practice of company valuations, given its greater simplicity of application compared to the methodology based on flows to partners. It is a measure of cash flows independent of the financial structure of the company (unlevered cash flows) that is particularly suitable to evaluate companies with high levels of indebtedness, or that do not have a debt plan. In these cases, the calculation of the cash flow available to shareholders is more difficult because of the volatility resulting from the forecast of how to repay debts.

This methodology is based on the operating flows generated by the typical management of the company, based on the operating income available for the remuneration of own and third-party means net of the relative tax effect. Unlevered cash flows are determined by using operating income before taxes and financial charges.

The cash flow available to the company is, therefore, determined as the cash flow available to shareholders, plus financial charges after tax, plus loan repayments and equity repayments, minus new borrowings and flows arising from equity increases.

The difference between the two approaches is, therefore, given by the different meanings of cash flows associated with debt and equity repayments.

Cash flows from operating activities are discounted to present value at the weighted average cost of capital.

This configuration of flows offers an evaluation of the whole company, independently from its financial structure. The value of the debt must be subtracted from the value of the company to rejoin the value of the market value, obtained through the cash flows for the shareholders.

The relationship between the two concepts of cash flow is as follows:

cash flow available to the company = cash flow available to shareholders
+ financial charges (net of taxes)
+ loan repayments − new loans

(13.2)

The (Residual) Cash Flow Available to Shareholders
This configuration considers the only expected flow available for members' remuneration. It is a measure of cash flow that considers the financial structure of the company (levered cash flow). It is the cash flow that remains after the payment of interest and the repayment of equity shares and after the coverage of equity expenditures necessary to maintain existing assets and to create the conditions for business growth.

In M&A operations, the Free Cash Flow to the Firm (operating cash flow) is normally calculated to estimate the Enterprise Value (comprehensive of debt). The residual Equity Value is then derived by subtracting the Net Financial Position.

The discounting of the free cash flow for the shareholders takes place at a rate equal to the cost of the shareholders' equity. This flow identifies the theoretical measure of the company's ability to distribute dividends, even if it does not coincide with the dividend paid.

Cash flow estimates can be applied to any type of asset. The differential element is represented by its duration. Many assets have a defined time horizon, while others assume a perpetual time horizon, such as shares.

Cash flows (CF) can, therefore, be estimated using a normalized projection of cash flows that it uses, alternatively:

- Unlimited capitalization:

$$W_1 = \mathrm{CF}/i \qquad (13.3)$$

- Limited capitalization:

$$W_2 = \text{CF}\, a\, n - i \quad (13.4)$$

where W_1 and W_2 represent the present value of future cash flows.

The discount rate to be applied to expected cash flows is determined as the sum of the cost of equity and the cost of debt, appropriately weighted according to the leverage of the company (the ratio between financial debt and equity). This produces the Weighted Average Cost of Capital (WACC):

$$\text{WACC} = k_i(1-t)\frac{D}{D+E} + k_e\frac{E}{D+E} \quad (13.5)$$

where:

k_i = cost of debt;
t = corporate tax rate;
D = market value of debt;
E = market value of equity;
$D + E$ = raised capital;
k_e = cost of equity (to be estimated with the Capital Asset Pricing Model—CAPM or the Dividend Discount Model).

The cost of debt capital is easy to determine, as it can be inferred from the financial statements of the company. The cost of equity or share capital, which represents the minimum rate of return required by investors for equity investments, is instead more complex and may use the CAPM or the Dividend Discount Model (a method of valuing a company's stock price considering the sum of all its future dividend payments, discounted back to their present value. It is used to value stocks based on the net present value of future dividends).

The formula of the CAPM is the following:

$$E(r)_{\text{FinTech}} = r_{\text{free}} + \beta_{\text{FinTech}}[(E(r)_{\text{market}} - r_{\text{free}}] \quad (13.6)$$

where:

$E(r)_{\text{FinTech}}$ = expected return of the FinTech listed stock
r_{free} = risk − free rate of return (e.g., of a long − term Government bond)

β_{FinTech} = sensitivity of the FinTech's stock to the market price
$(E(r))_{\text{market}}$ = expected return of the (benchmark) Stock market

A central element is represented by the beta (b) of the FinTech to be evaluated which consists of the ratio between the covariance of the FinTech security with its stock market, divided by the variance of the market. Market betas, subdivided by industry, may be detected from the dataset of A. Damodaran (see, for instance, http://pages.stern.nyu.edu/~adamodar/New_Home_Page/datafile/Betas.html).

Once the present value of the cash flows has been determined, the calculation of the market value W of the company may correspond to:

a. The unlevered cash flow approach:

$$W = \sum \frac{CF_0}{WACC} + VR - D \qquad (13.7)$$

b. The levered cash flow approach:

$$W = \sum \frac{CF_n}{K_e} + VR \qquad (13.8)$$

where:

$\sum CF_0/WACC$ = present value of operating cash flows
$\sum CF_n/K_e$ = present value of net cash flows
VR = terminal (residual) value
D = initial net financial position (financial debt—liquidity)

The residual value is the result of discounting the value at the time n (before which the cash flows are estimated analytically). It is often the greatest component of the global value W (above all in intangible-intensive companies) and tends to zero if the time horizon of the capitalization is infinite (VR/∞ = 0).

The two variants (levered versus unlevered) give the same result if the value of the firm, determined through the cash flows available to the lenders, is deducted from the value of the net financial debts.

13 FINTECH AND DIGITAL PAYMENT SYSTEMS VALUATION

Operating cash flows (unlevered) and net cash flows for shareholders (levered) are determined by comparing the last two balance sheets (to dispose of changes in operating Net Working Capital, fixed assets, financial liabilities, and shareholders' equity) with the income statement of the last year.

The accounting derivation of the cash flow and its link to the cost of capital (to get DCF—Discounted Cash Flows) is illustrated in Table 13.4.

The net cash flow for the shareholders coincides with the free cash flow to equity and, therefore, with the dividends that can be paid out, once it

Table 13.4 Cash flow statement of a FinTech and link with the cost of capital

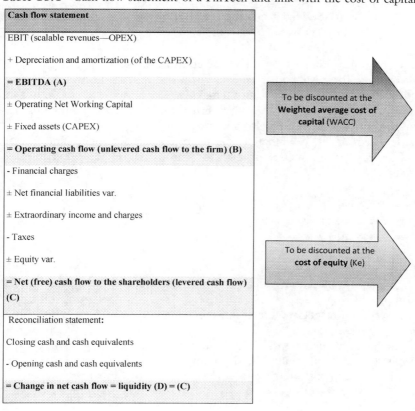

has been verified that enough internal liquidity resources remain in the company.

Empirical Approaches (Market Multipliers)

The market value identifies:

a. The value attributable to a share of the equity expressed at stock exchange prices;
b. The price of the controlling interest or the entire share equity;
c. The traded value for the controlling equity of comparable undertakings;
d. The value derived from the stock exchange quotations of comparable undertakings.

Sometimes comparable trades of companies belonging to the same product sector with similar characteristics (in terms of cash flows, sales, costs, etc.) are used. Innovative FinTechs, like other startups, are often difficult to compare with "similar" firms, due to their complex business model, and lack of historical track record.

In practice, an examination of the prices used in negotiations with companies in the same sector leads to quantifying average parameters:

- *Price/EBIT*
- *Price/cash flow*
- *Price/book-value*
- *Price/earnings*
- *Price/dividend*

These ratios seek to estimate the average rate to be applied to the company being assessed. However, there may be distorting effects of prices based on special interest rates, in a historical context, on difficulties of comparison, etc.

In financial market practice, the multiples methodology is frequently applied. Based on multiples, the company's value is derived from the market price profit referring to comparable listed companies, such as net profit, before tax or operating profit, cash flow, equity, or turnover.

The attractiveness of the multiples approach stems from its ease of use: multiples can be used to obtain quick but dirty estimates of the company's value and are useful when there are many comparable companies listed on the financial markets and the market sets correct prices for them on average.

Because of the simplicity of the calculation, these indicators are easily manipulated and susceptible to misuse, especially if they refer to companies that are not entirely similar. Since there are no identical companies in terms of entrepreneurial risk and growth rate, the assumption of multiples for the processing of the valuation can be misleading, bringing "fake multipliers".

The use of multiples can be implemented through:

a. Use of fundamentals;
b. Use of comparable data:

   i. Comparable companies;
   ii. Comparable transactions.

Comparables may be looked for consulting databases like Orbis (https://www.bvdinfo.com/en-gb/our-products/data/international/orbis).

Among the empirical criteria, the approach of the multiplier of the EBITDA (Earnings Before Interest, Taxes, Depreciation, and Amortization) is widely diffused. The net financial position must be added algebraically to the EBITDA, to pass from the estimate of the enterprise value (total value of the company) to that of the equity value (value of the net assets). The formulation is as follows:

$$W = \text{average perspective EBITDA} * \text{Enterprise Value/sector EBITDA}$$
$$= \text{Enterprise Value of the Company} \qquad (13.9)$$

And then:

$$\text{Equity Value} = \text{Enterprise Value} \pm \text{Net Financial Position} \qquad (13.10)$$

The DCF approach can be linked to the market approach since they both share as a starting parameter the EBITDA.

13.10 Market Stress Tests and Business Model Sensitivity

Market stress tests are now routine for banks, especially after the big crisis of 2008. The impact of market crises on FinTechs is mixed and may be quite different from other industries, as shown for example in Fig. 13.5.

The relationship between the business model and its surrounding environment is evident, and it is normally the latter that influences the former.

The sensitivity of a (listed) FinTech over its stock market can be measured by the beta (b) coefficient that is given by the covariance between the listed FinTech and its market of listing, divided by the variance of the market:

$$\beta_{\text{FinTech}} = \frac{\text{Cov}(\text{FinTech}, \text{Market})}{\text{Variance Market}} \quad (13.11)$$

FinTech's sensitivity to crises is uneasy to assess since its historical track record is limited. They were nonexistent during the big Internet/NASDAQ bubble of March 2000 and hardly present during the double-dip recession of 2008–2011.

Early indications from the Covid-19 pandemic crisis, which started in January 2020, show a sharp decline followed by a recovery, with a pattern again similar to that of the technological firms, and much more volatile than that of the bank index.

In broader terms, the business model sensitivity impacts the valuation since this appraisal process should carefully consider different scenarios.

Whereas sensitivity analysis analyzes the impact of one change at a time on a valuation parameter, more comprehensive scenario analysis incorporates several parameters that are simultaneously changing.

The total Net Present Value of the three projects, which are considered not mutually exclusive (since venture capital can take over all of them), nor with synergistic effects between them (which is possible, especially if the sectors and business models intersect), is positive if the rate at which they are discounted is less than 13.93%. This rate represents the watershed, which expresses the break-even point at which the Net Present Value of the project portfolio is zero, calculated through the iterative search for the Internal Rate of Return (which is the rate that makes the NPV = 0).

Venture capital (Cumming & Schwienbacher, 2018) must make a comparison between its cost of raising financial resources (weighted average cost of capital, which coincides with the cost of equity capital if the venture capital has not resorted to debt) and the return that the investments offer. In all cases where the expected return is lower than the cost of capital (IRR < WACC), it will not be convenient to undertake the investment.

Binomial networks (traditionally used as decision trees or to determine the pricing of options) are flexible: by adapting the parameters of the expected variance of the value and the probability that the value increases (upside potential) or decreases (downside risk), it is possible to estimate, with basically unlimited ramifications, a wide range of scenarios. The possibility of correcting the estimates along the way, refining them based on what happened in the portion of time passed (which declines a chronological process of time decay), represents a further element to improve the forecasts. Timely big data may conveniently be introduced in the model.

13.11 Challenges and Failures: Why FinTechs Burn Out

Startup failures are so common that they cannot refrain from influencing valuation, for instance, increasing the risk embedded in the discount rate of expected cash flows.

Failures have common features among the different startups but are industry-specific. And the financial sector has its own rules.

While the fintech industry offers great potential for innovation and growth, many fintech startups face challenges and, in some cases, fail. Here are some reasons why fintech may burn out or struggle:

1. Funding and Capital Constraints: Fintech startups often require substantial investments in technology development, talent acquisition, regulatory compliance, and market expansion. Limited access to funding or difficulties in securing additional capital can hinder their growth and sustainability.
2. Regulatory and Compliance Burdens: Fintech companies operate in a highly regulated industry that requires compliance with various financial, data privacy, and consumer protection regulations.

Adhering to these regulations can be complex, time-consuming, and costly, particularly for startups with limited resources and expertise.
3. Trust and Security Concerns: Fintech companies handle sensitive financial information and transactions, which requires establishing trust with customers. Any breach in security or privacy can damage their reputation and erode customer confidence. Implementing robust security measures and addressing cybersecurity threats is crucial but can be challenging for startups.
4. Competitive Landscape: The fintech industry has become increasingly crowded, with a growing number of startups and established financial institutions entering the market. Fintech companies need to differentiate themselves and offer unique value propositions to stand out. Competing against well-established incumbents with larger customer bases and resources can be challenging.
5. Scalability and Customer Acquisition: Fintech startups often face difficulties in scaling their operations and acquiring a large customer base. Building trust, attracting customers, and achieving profitability can take time and significant marketing efforts. Scaling operations to handle increasing transaction volumes and maintaining quality customer service can be demanding.
6. Technological Challenges: Fintech companies rely heavily on technology infrastructure, and issues such as system failures, downtime, or data breaches can significantly impact their operations. Staying up-to-date with evolving technologies, maintaining robust systems, and addressing technical challenges can be demanding, especially for startups with limited technical expertise.
7. Limited Industry Experience: Founders and team members of fintech startups may lack deep industry knowledge and experience in finance, banking, or regulatory compliance. Understanding the complexities of the financial industry and navigating regulatory frameworks is crucial for success in the fintech space.
8. Resistance to Change: Traditional financial institutions may be resistant to adopting fintech innovations, which can slow down market adoption and partnership opportunities. Overcoming the inertia of established players and convincing them of the value proposition of fintech solutions can be a challenge.
9. Economic and Market Volatility: Fintech companies can be vulnerable to economic downturns and market volatility, which can impact consumer behavior, investment activity, and funding availability.

Uncertain economic conditions can affect fintech startups' ability to raise capital and grow their business.

It's important to note that while these challenges exist, many fintech startups successfully navigate them and thrive. Overcoming these hurdles often requires a combination of strategic planning, strong execution, continuous innovation, partnerships with established players, and adaptability to the evolving market conditions.

Among the reasons that may cause the default of Fintech startups, the following are worth mentioning[4]:

- **Underfunding.**
- **Choosing an inexperienced Venture Capital.**
- **Overlooking compliance.** Regulatory complexity is often underestimated.
- **Thinking a fintech startup is the same as any other tech startup.** Psychological behaviors around money, credit, savings, and payments are different from those concerning IT, biotechnologies, etc.
- **Competing solely on cost.** Banks have massive (traditional) scale advantages.
- *Going digital, FinTechs may reengineer traditional business models but the task is uneasy and risky.*
- **Overconfidence.** Creating a new market is no easy task. Many Fintechs think that their business model is so innovative that they have no competitors. Whenever there is competition, geographical segmentation may represent a weak barrier, due to increasing financial globalization. Innovation may become increasingly challenging in a crowded and over-competitive market.
- **Underestimation of the length of the sales cycle.** Financial institutions are notoriously slow purchasers of anything new.
- **Missing sales strategy.** Fintech startups are often the brainchild of software experts who have limited sales and marketing skills.
- **Lack of understanding of the financial market.** Fintech startups pursuing a B2C business model often overestimate the extent to which consumers will: (1) change their behavior and (2) pay for a

---

[4] See https://www.forbes.com/sites/ronshevlin/2019/07/29/why-fintech-startups-fail/#30c33e6a6440.

new product or service in addition to all the things they already pay for. While a B2B model may be a better path for some fintech startups, some fail by not understanding that they are a vendor—not a partner—which may require a completely different set of skills and capabilities from those they already have.

13.12 Concluding Remarks

FinTechs are reshaping the banking industry, proposing innovative technological solutions that foster customer-centricity.

The main thesis of this chapter is that the evaluation of FinTechs follows appraisal approaches that are (unsurprisingly) like those of technological startups. Even if the underlying industry is represented by bank activities, FinTechs are innovators/facilitators of financial activities and are not personally involved in the borrowing/lending intermediation business. Due to their nature as technological providers of financial services, FinTechs can be assimilated into innovative startups (or more mature companies).

Evaluation methodologies are important to assess and refine not only to ease the M&A activity but also to foster value recognition for all the stakeholders that are involved in the value co-creation paradigm. The customer's experience (and the big data continuously fueled by feedback) is a central factor in the digital economy as it adds value to the whole process. Fair remuneration of the clients remains, however, a hot issue.

FinTechs and, in particular, digital payment systems are reshaping the crypto industry, providing the main tools and services to make it work.

References

Accenture. (2016). *FinTech and the evolving landscape.* Available at https://www.accenture.com/us-en/insightFinTech-evolving-landscape

Armstrong, M. (2006). Competition in two-sided markets. *Rand Journal of Economics, 37*(3), 668–691.

Barabási, A. (2016). *Network science.* Cambridge University Press.

Brandl, B., & Hornuf, L. (2017). *Where did FinTechs come from, and where do they go? The transformation of the financial industry in Germany after digitalization.* Available at https://ssrn.com/abstract=3036555.

Burlakov, G. (2019). *10 Challenges for the financial services industry in 2019.* Available at https://technorely.com/blog/financial-industry-challenges/.

Chen, M. A., Wu, Q., & Yang, B. (2019). How valuable is FinTech innovation? *The Review of Financial Studies, 32*(5), 2062–2106.
Cumming, D. J., & Schwienbacher, A. (2018). Fintech venture capital. *Corporate Governance. An International Review, 26*(5), 374–389.
Damodaran, A. (2009). *Valuing financial service firms.* Available at http://people.stern.nyu.edu/adamodar/pdfiles/papers/finfirm09.pdf
Das, S. R. (2019). The future of fintech. *Financial Management, 48*, 981–1007.
Demyanova, E. A. (2018). The topical issues of valuation of companies under the conditions of Fintech. *Strategic Decisions and Risk Management, 1*, 88–103.
Di Castri, S., Hohl, S., Kulenkampff, A., & Prenio, J. (2019). The SupTech generations. *FSI Insights on policy implementation, 19.*
Dorfleitner, G., & Hornuf, L. (2019). FinTech business Models. In *FinTech and data privacy in Germany.* Springer Nature.
Drummer, D., Jerenz, A., Siebelt, P., & Thaten, M. (2016). *FinTech—Challenges and opportunities: How digitization is transforming the financial sector.* McKinsey & Co.
Eickhoff, M., Muntermann, J., & Weinrich, T. (2017). What do FinTechs actually do? A Taxonomy of FinTech Business Models. *ICIS Proceedings, 22.*
EY. (2019). *Global FinTech adoption index 2019.* Available at https://www.ey.com/en_gl/ey-global-fintech-adoption-index
Fatás, A. (Ed.). (2019). *The economics of Fintech and digital currencies.* Available at https://voxeu.org/content/economics-fintech-and-digital-currencies
Fernandez, P. (2001). *Valuation using multiples. How do analysts reach their conclusions?* IESE Business School.
Gai, K., Qiu, M., & Sun, X. (2018). A survey on Fintech. *Journal of Network and Computer Applications, 103*, 262–273.
Gimpel, H., Rau, D., & Röglinger, M. (2018). Understanding FinTech start-ups—A taxonomy of consumer-oriented service offerings. *Electronic Markets, 28*, 245–264.
Gomber, P., Kauffman, C., & Weber, B. W. (2018). On the Fintech revolution: Interpreting the forces of innovation, disruption, and transformation in financial services. *Journal of Management Information Systems, 35*(1), 220–265.
Haddad, C., & Hornuf, L. (2019). The emergence of the global fintech market: Economic and technological determinants. *Small Business Economics, 53*, 81–105.
Hein, A., Schreieck, M., Riasanow, T., Setzke, M., Wiesche, M., Bohm, M., & Krcmar, H. (2019, November). Digital platform ecosystems. *Electronic Markets.*
Hommel, K., & Bican, P. M. (2020). Digital entrepreneurship in finance: Fintechs and funding decision criteria. *Sustainability, 12*, 8035.

IPEV. (2018). *Valuation guidelines*. Available at http://www.privateequityvalua tion.com/Valuation-Guidelines

Lee, I., & Shin, Y. J. (2018). Fintech: Ecosystem, business models, investment decisions, and challenges. *Business Horizons, 61*(1), 35–46.

Moro Visconti, R. (2019a). *Microfintech: Outreaching financial inclusion with cost-cutting innovation*. Available at https://www.researchgate.net/public ation/332818363_microfintech_outreaching_financial_inclusion_with_cost-cutting_innovation

Moro Visconti, R. (2019b). *How to prepare a business plan with excel*. Available at https://www.researchgate.net/publication/255728204_How_to_Prepare_a_Business_Plan_with_Excel

Moro-Visconti, R., Cruz Rambaud, S., & López Pascual, J. (2020). Sustainability in FinTechs: An explanation through business model scalability and market valuation. *Sustainability, 12*, 10316.

Osterwalder, A., Pigneur, Y., & Tucci, C. L. (2005). Clarifying business models: Origins, present, and future of the concept. *Communications of the Association for Information Systems, 16*(1).

Piobbici, F., Rajola, F., & Frigerio, C. (2019). Open innovation effectiveness in the financial services sector. In N. Mehandjiev, & B. Saadouni (Eds.), *Enterprise applications, markets, and services in the finance industry* (Vol. 345). FinanceCom 2018. Lecture Notes in Business Information Processing. Springer.

Rochet, J. C., & Tirole, J. (2003). Platform competition in two-sided markets. *Journal of the European Economic Association, 1*(4), 990–1029.

Sarhan, H. (2020, July). *Fintech: An overview*. Available at https://www.resear chgate.net/publication/342832269

Schallmo, D. R. A., & Williams, C. A. (2018). Digital transformation of business models, digital transformation now! In *SpringerBriefs in business*. Springer.

Skinner, C. (2016). *ValueWeb: How fintech firms are using mobile and blockchain technologies to create the Internet of Value*. Marshall Cavendish.

Sironi, P. (2016). *FinTech innovation*. Wiley.

Tanda, A., & Schena, C. (2019). *FinTech, BigTech and banks. Digitalisation and its impact on banking business models*. Palgrave Macmillan.

Vives, X. (2019). Digital disruption in banking. *Annual Review of Financial Economics, 11*(1), 243–272.

Yao, J. (2018). *Valuation of a Fintech company*. Available at https://repositorio.iscte-iul.pt/bitstream/10071/18806/1/Master_Jiayu_Yao.pdf

CHAPTER 14

Digitalization and ESG-Driven Valuation

14.1 INTRODUCTION

Digitalization and ESG-driven valuation are two important concepts that have gained significant attention in recent years, particularly in the business and investment sectors. Concerns about the environmental sustainability of energy-eating cryptocurrencies (due to their validating blockchains) are growing, and require increasing attention. The environmental sustainability of cryptocurrencies, particularly those using Proof of Work, is a growing concern that is gaining attention from investors, regulators, and the cryptocurrency community itself. As a result, there is a push for more sustainable practices within the cryptocurrency space to align with ESG principles and reduce the environmental footprint of blockchain technology.

Digitalization (as shown in Chapter 3) refers to the process of adopting and integrating digital technologies, tools, and strategies into various aspects of business operations and processes. It involves leveraging technologies such as artificial intelligence, big data analytics, cloud computing, the Internet of Things (IoT), and automation to enhance efficiency, productivity, and innovation.

Digitalization has transformed industries across the globe by enabling new business models, improving customer experiences, optimizing supply chains, and unlocking new revenue streams. It allows companies to gather and analyze vast amounts of data, leading to better decision-making,

© The Author(s), under exclusive license to Springer Nature Switzerland AG 2023
R. Moro-Visconti and A. Cesaretti, *Digital Token Valuation*,
https://doi.org/10.1007/978-3-031-42971-2_14

personalized marketing, and improved performance. Additionally, digitalization facilitates connectivity and collaboration, both internally and externally, by enabling remote work, virtual meetings, and online platforms.

ESG stands for Environmental, Social, and Governance, representing a set of criteria used to assess the sustainability and societal impact of a company's operations. ESG factors have become crucial considerations for investors and stakeholders, beyond traditional financial metrics, in evaluating the long-term value and risk profile of an investment.

ESG-driven valuation involves assessing a company's performance and potential based on its environmental practices, social responsibility initiatives, and corporate governance standards. This evaluation framework considers factors such as carbon emissions, resource consumption, waste management, employee welfare, diversity and inclusion, community engagement, ethical business practices, board composition, executive compensation, and transparency in reporting.

Investors are increasingly recognizing that companies with robust ESG practices tend to outperform their peers in the long run. They are focused not only on financial returns but also on aligning their investments with sustainable and responsible business practices.

Digitalization and ESG-driven valuation are interconnected in several ways:

1. Digitalization enables ESG data collection and analysis: Digital technologies play a vital role in gathering, managing, and analyzing ESG-related data. Through digital tools, companies can track their environmental impact, monitor social initiatives, and report on governance practices. This data is crucial for assessing ESG performance and informing investment decisions.
2. Digitalization supports ESG reporting and transparency: Digital platforms and technologies facilitate improved transparency and reporting mechanisms for ESG data. Companies can use digital channels to communicate their ESG initiatives and progress to investors, stakeholders, and the wider public. This transparency enhances trust and accountability.
3. Digital solutions enable ESG-driven efficiencies: Digitalization can help companies optimize their operations to reduce resource consumption, minimize waste, and mitigate environmental impact.

For example, smart energy management systems, supply chain digitization, and remote work solutions contribute to environmental sustainability and social welfare.
4. ESG considerations drive digital transformation: Increasing investor and consumer demand for ESG-aligned companies has driven businesses to incorporate ESG principles into their digital transformation strategies. Companies are leveraging digitalization to enhance their ESG performance, such as adopting renewable energy sources, reducing carbon footprint, and improving labor standards.

In summary, digitalization and ESG-driven valuation are intertwined, with digital technologies playing a crucial role in enabling ESG data collection, reporting, and performance improvements. As sustainability and responsible investing continue to gain momentum, businesses will increasingly leverage digitalization to support their ESG initiatives and align their operations with environmental and social goals.

Cornell and Shapiro (2021) front a core cost–benefit issue: "In addition to explicit contracts, corporations issue their stakeholders' implicit claims, including fair treatment of employees and the promise of continuing service to customers. Corporate value is created by selling these implicit claims for more than it costs to honor them. Recently, a new class of non-investor stakeholders, related to environmental, social, and governance (ESG) issues, has arisen. Although many ESG advocates stress their role in creating shareholder value, they do not explain how this value creation occurs".

The world we live in is characterized by growing complexity and disruptive events, starting from climatic changes. ESG protocols tackle these issues, even if their effectiveness is still questionable.

According to Milton Friedman, the main responsibility of a company is the maximization of the shareholders' returns. For decades, environmental, social, and governance (ESG) responsibilities were not considered relevant by most of the companies that have been focusing on profit maximization. Not only were ESG responsibilities believed to merely have no incidence on financial performance, but they were also perceived as a potential burden to the latter, being related to cost increases. Nevertheless, in the last twenty years, environmental, social, and governance issues revealed their influence not only on profitability but also on the financial viability of several firms. As a natural consequence, the process of asset allocation started evolving. Furthermore, a raising environmental, social, and governance consciousness has been observed worldwide (Billio et al., 2021).

14.2 Sustainable Business Planning

Sustainable business planning involves incorporating environmental, social, and economic considerations into the strategic planning and decision-making processes of an organization. It aims to create a business model that is environmentally responsible, socially conscious, and financially viable in the long term.

Here are some key elements and principles of sustainable business planning:

1. Environmental Sustainability:

    a. Assessing and minimizing the environmental impact of business operations, products, and services.
    b. Adopting sustainable practices, such as energy and resource efficiency, waste reduction, and pollution prevention.
    c. Embracing renewable energy sources and reducing greenhouse gas emissions.
    d. Incorporating circular economy principles, including recycling, reusing, and reducing waste throughout the value chain.

2. Social Responsibility:

    a. Promoting fair labor practices, including safe working conditions, fair wages, and employee well-being.
    b. Respecting human rights and ensuring diversity, equity, and inclusion within the organization and its supply chain.
    c. Engaging with local communities and stakeholders, supporting social initiatives, and contributing to the well-being of society.
    d. Ensuring responsible sourcing and ethical procurement practices.

3. Economic Viability:

    a. Integrating sustainability into the core business strategy to create long-term value.
    b. Identifying new market opportunities and revenue streams through sustainable products and services.

c. Managing risks associated with environmental, social, and governance (ESG) factors that can impact business performance.
d. Engaging with investors and stakeholders who prioritize sustainable practices.

4. Stakeholder Engagement:

   a. Engaging with employees, customers, suppliers, investors, and local communities to understand their sustainability expectations and concerns.
   b. Collaborating with stakeholders to develop shared goals, strategies, and initiatives.
   c. Establishing transparent communication channels and reporting mechanisms to provide information on sustainability performance.

5. Lifecycle Thinking:

   a. Considering the entire lifecycle of products and services, from design and production to use and disposal.
   b. Integrating concepts such as eco-design, product stewardship, and extended producer responsibility.
   c. Implementing strategies to promote product longevity, repairability, and recycling.

6. Regulatory Compliance and Standards:

   a. Complying with relevant environmental, labor, and social regulations and standards.
   b. Seeking certifications and labels that demonstrate commitment to sustainability, such as LEED, B Corp, or ISO standards.

7. Continuous Improvement:

   a. Setting clear sustainability goals and targets, regularly monitoring progress, and reporting on performance.
   b. Conducting regular assessments and audits to identify areas for improvement.
   c. Encouraging innovation and embracing emerging technologies and practices that contribute to sustainability.

Sustainable business planning requires a shift in mindset from a short-term profit orientation to a long-term perspective that considers the triple bottom line: people, planet, and profit. It involves aligning business objectives with societal and environmental needs, integrating sustainability into core operations, and fostering collaboration and transparency with stakeholders.

Business planning is a core pillar of dynamic sustainability, as it represents a formal document that envisages long-term economic and financial perspectives. Appropriate business planning, with continuous fine-tuning, backs sustainability strategies and so fosters ESG compliance. ESG targets may well be embodied in business planning key factors, for instance, envisaging:

a. A periodical check-up of the business continuity (capacity for the firm to keep a going concern for at least the next 6–12 months);
b. A consequential consideration of the perspective of economic and financial equilibrium (capacity of the firm to generate positive economic and financial margins, respectively represented by EBITDA, EBIT, pre-tax/net profit, or operating and net cash flows).
c. A sensitivity analysis, conducted with a deterministic or stochastic approach that embodies stress tests, to assess the break-even point, with appropriate strategies to avoid or bypass a disaster case;
d. A continuous reengineering and reformulation of the business plan hypotheses, exploiting bottom-up evidence from the external market and customers;
e. A prompt reaction to equity or cashflow burnouts, should these criticalities occur.

Business planning is a well-known tool for strategic formulation and execution (Lasher, 2010; Sahlman, 1997). The value of planning is driven by the possibility of evaluating alternative actions and being able to improve strategies. Before market entry, the main purpose of the evaluation is to pursue good and terminate bad business ideas (Chwolka & Raith, 2012). Planning is beneficial for performance (Brinckmann et al., 2010). Decision-making, however, remains a challenging task in the current age of forecasting (Asaduzzaman et al., 2015). As Razgaitis (2003) shows, prognosticators apply Monte Carlo Analysis to determine the likelihood and significance of a complete range of future outcomes; Real Options Analysis can then be employed to develop pricing structures, or options, for such outcomes. The forecasting effectiveness of traditional financial risk measures can be improved by integrating financial risk with an ESG risk measure that considers ESG entropy (Ielasi et al., 2021).

Designing and creating a business model is crucial for a successful firm's operation in today's market in a complex and changing environment. A business model is a factor that differentiates one firm from another—it defines the distinctions of the firm, how the firm deals with the competition, the firm's partnerships, and customer relations (Koprivnjak & Peterka, 2020). Business modeling is increasingly focused on sustainability orientation, extended value creation, systemic thinking, and stakeholder integration (Breuer et al., 2018).

Business planning follows a typical managerial top-down approach where management-prepared forecasts and projections are conceived within the firm and occasionally compared with market returns. The increasing availability of timely big data, sometimes fueled by the Internet of Things (IoT) devices, allows for receiving continuous feedback that can be conveniently used to refresh assumptions and forecasts, using a complementary bottom-up approach. Top-down and bottom-up are both strategies for information processing and knowledge ordering.

Forecasting accuracy can be substantially improved by incorporating timely empirical evidence, with a consequent reduction of both information asymmetries and the risk of facing unexpected events, concerning the magnitude of their impact. Since risk is represented by the difference between expected and real events, if occurrences are timely incorporated into expectations, this differential is minimized. This intuitive concept is well-known, but its practical implications are amplified by the unprecedented presence of big data.

Valuation criteria of the project or investment are typically linked to business planning metrics, especially if they are based on Discounted Cash Flows (DCF). DCF forecasting can be greatly improved by timely big data feedback that positively affects the numerator, represented by growing cash flows (that incorporate real option flexibility), and decreasing discount rates (cost of capital) that reflect reduced risk. Value-adding strategies can conveniently reshape supply and value chains that embed information-driven resilience.

Network theory may constitute a further interpretation tool, considering the interaction of nodes represented by IoT and big data, mastering digital platforms, and physical stakeholders (shareholders, managers, clients, suppliers, lenders, etc.). Artificial intelligence, database interoperability, and blockchain applications are consistent with the networking interpretation of the interaction of physical and virtual nodes.

The interaction of big data with traditional budgeting patterns creates flexible (real) options nurtured by a networked digital ecosystem, eventually bringing augmented business planning.

14.3 The Cost of Collecting Capital: A Comparison between Traditional and ESG-Firms

The cost of capital refers to the required rate of return or the cost incurred by a company to raise funds from investors and financiers. When comparing the cost of capital between traditional firms and ESG (Environmental, Social, and Governance) firms, there are several factors to consider:

1. Risk Perception: ESG firms typically place greater emphasis on sustainability, responsible business practices, and long-term value creation. As a result, they may be perceived as having lower environmental and social risks compared to traditional firms that may not prioritize these factors. This perception can potentially reduce the risk premium demanded by investors and lenders for investing in ESG firms, thereby lowering their cost of capital.
2. Investor Demand: There is growing investor demand for sustainable and socially responsible investments. As a result, ESG firms may have access to a larger pool of investors who specifically seek out companies with strong ESG performance. This increased demand can lead to more favorable terms for ESG firms when raising capital, potentially reducing their cost of capital compared to traditional firms.
3. Reputation and Brand Value: ESG firms that have established a strong reputation for sustainability and responsible practices may benefit from the enhanced brand value and customer loyalty. This can positively impact their financial performance and reduce the perceived risk, resulting in a potentially lower cost of capital compared to traditional firms.

4. Regulatory Environment: The regulatory landscape is evolving to incorporate ESG considerations, with an increasing number of jurisdictions implementing regulations related to ESG disclosures and reporting. ESG firms that proactively meet these requirements may be seen as more transparent and compliant, which can positively influence their cost of capital.
5. Access to Funding Sources: ESG firms may have access to a wider range of funding sources, including impact investors, green bonds, and sustainability-focused funds. These specialized funding sources may offer more favorable terms and lower costs of capital, contributing to a cost advantage for ESG firms compared to traditional firms.

While ESG firms may experience potential cost advantages in terms of their cost of capital, this does not imply that all ESG firms will have lower costs of capital compared to traditional firms. The cost of capital is influenced by numerous factors, including industry-specific risks, company size, financial performance, and market conditions.

Additionally, as ESG considerations become more mainstream, the gap in the cost of capital between ESG and traditional firms may diminish over time. It is expected that both the perceived risks and investor demand associated with ESG factors will continue to evolve, potentially impacting the cost of capital for ESG firms.

The cost of capital for ESG firms may be influenced by factors such as risk perception, investor demand, reputation, regulatory environment, and access to specialized funding sources. However, it is essential to conduct a comprehensive analysis on a case-by-case basis to assess the specific cost of capital dynamics for individual firms within different industries and markets.

The cost of capital for a firm represents the economic-financial expenditure to collect equity and financial debt from shareholders or, respectively, debtholders. Whereas traditional—often "polluting"—firms collect ordinary capital/equity from shareholders and issue standard debt (underwritten by banks, bondholders, etc.), ESG-compliant firms issue capital for targeted equity-holders and green bonds or other sustainable debt.

A comparison is represented in Fig. 14.1.

Giese et al. (2019) show that companies' ESG information is transmitted to their valuation and performance, both through their systematic risk profile (lower costs of capital and higher valuations) and their

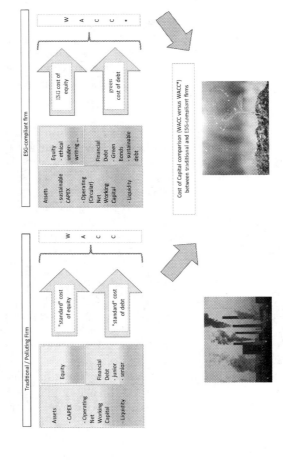

Fig. 14.1 Cost of capital: comparison between traditional and ESG-firms

idiosyncratic risk profile (higher profitability and lower exposures to tail risk).

The cost of capital represents, as shown above, the denominator of the DCF, since the cost of equity is used to discount net cash flows, and the WACC to discount operating (unlevered) cash flows.

ESG factors can contribute to changing DCF in two ways—modifying either the cash flows in the numerator and/or the corresponding cost of capital in the denominator. The standard DCF formula is:

$$\text{DCFoperating} = \sum_{i=1}^{n} \frac{CF_1 + CF_2 + \ldots + CF_n}{(1 + \text{WACC})} \quad (14.1)$$

where CF is the operating cash flow and WACC is the weighted average cost of capital.

Should ESG parameters have a positive impact on both cash flows and WACC, the formula would be:

$$\text{DCFoperating*} \uparrow\uparrow = \sum_{i=1}^{n} \frac{CF_1 \uparrow + CF_2 \uparrow + \ldots + CF_n \uparrow}{(1 + \text{WACC}) \downarrow} \quad (14.2)$$

The rationale behind this multiplying improvement that affects both the numerator and the denominator, boosting the DCF*, may be found in the ability to improve cash flows, thanks to savings or revenue increases, and to minimize the risk embedded in the WACC, lowering the cost for collecting sustainable capital. This proves an uneasy but highly rewarding target.

Should the cost of capital increase and/or the cash flows decrease, stakeholders (both debtholders and shareholders, if operating cash flow is the selected parameter) would face a deteriorating situation. This may be the case in the first years of the environmental investment when the payoff is still far and the startup costs increase.

14.4 Sustainability Patterns

Sustainability patterns refer to recurring trends and practices that contribute to sustainable development and address environmental, social, and economic challenges. Economic sustainability also matters (no money, no party ...). These patterns emerge as societies and organizations strive to create a more sustainable future. Here are some common sustainability patterns:

1. Circular Economy: The circular economy pattern aims to minimize waste and maximize resource efficiency. It promotes the concept of a closed-loop system where products and materials are reused, repaired, or recycled rather than disposed of after use. This pattern reduces resource consumption, decreases waste generation, and promotes sustainable production and consumption.
2. Renewable Energy Transition: The shift toward renewable energy sources, such as solar, wind, and hydroelectric power, is a prominent sustainability pattern. This transition aims to reduce dependence on fossil fuels, mitigate climate change, and promote cleaner and more sustainable energy generation.
3. Sustainable Agriculture: Sustainable agriculture focuses on environmentally friendly and socially responsible farming practices. This pattern emphasizes organic farming methods, biodiversity conservation, soil health improvement, water conservation, and reducing the use of synthetic inputs. It aims to ensure long-term food security while minimizing environmental impacts.
4. Green Building and Infrastructure: The adoption of green building and infrastructure practices is another sustainability pattern. This includes constructing energy-efficient buildings, using sustainable construction materials, implementing renewable energy systems, incorporating green spaces, and promoting water and waste management strategies that minimize environmental impact.
5. Eco-Mobility and Transportation: The promotion of eco-mobility and sustainable transportation is a growing sustainability pattern. This involves encouraging the use of public transportation, cycling, walking, and electric vehicles. It aims to reduce greenhouse gas emissions, air pollution, and congestion while improving accessibility and promoting healthier lifestyles.
6. Responsible Consumption and Production: Responsible consumption and production patterns emphasize sustainable and ethical consumer choices. This includes reducing waste generation, promoting sustainable and fair-trade products, embracing minimalism, adopting sharing and collaborative consumption models,

and supporting businesses with transparent and responsible supply chains.
7. Social Equity and Inclusion: The sustainability pattern of social equity and inclusion emphasizes the importance of addressing social inequalities and promoting equal access to resources and opportunities. This includes initiatives focused on poverty reduction, gender equality, inclusive education, healthcare access, and promoting diversity and social cohesion.
8. Sustainable Supply Chains: Sustainable supply chain patterns focus on integrating sustainable practices across the entire supply chain. This includes responsible sourcing, ethical labor practices, waste reduction, carbon footprint reduction, and fostering collaboration with suppliers and stakeholders to ensure sustainable and resilient supply networks.
9. Awareness and Education: The sustainability pattern of awareness and education emphasizes the importance of raising awareness and promoting education about sustainability issues. This includes educational programs, campaigns, and initiatives that aim to inform individuals, communities, and organizations about sustainable practices, climate change, biodiversity conservation, and social responsibility.

These sustainability patterns illustrate the diverse approaches and strategies employed to create a more sustainable world. By adopting and implementing these patterns, societies, and organizations can contribute to long-term environmental preservation, social well-being, and economic prosperity.

The forecast of future cash flows is possibly the main criticality of DCF metrics, and the risk that effective cash flows may (greatly) differ from expected ones needs to be incorporated into the cost of capital. This well-known consideration is difficult to put into practice, especially when projections are long-termed or when they concern volatile businesses, such as startups or technological industries.

Sustainability concerns so affect estimates, and the cost of capital discount factor included in expected cash flows may conveniently incorporate heterogeneous functions that, as anticipated, refer to:

a. Circular economy patterns;

b. Sharing economy
c. The resilience of supply and value chains;
d. Digital platforms and networks;
e. Intangible-driven scalability potential and real options.

Sustainability factors are expected to lower the cost of capital, improving the occurrence and stability of expected cash flows and attracting ESG-sensitive investors. Both costs of debt and cost of equity are lower for firms that disclose sustainability performance information when compared to firms that do not disclose similar information (Ng & Rezaee, 2012).

Sustainability impacts the firm's value, expected cash flows, and systematic risk of an overall market portfolio. Figure 14.2 recalls the main sustainability patterns.

Sustainability patterns may affect both the systematic and the specific cost of capital components of a firm. As anticipated, the systematic component relates to the market (risk-free interest rates, then summed up with the firm-specific spread to determine the cost of debt; firm's beta, to express its sensitivity toward the stock market premium, as a proxy of the cost of equity).

Sustainability strategies impact both the ecosystem and the individual firm. The ecosystem, eventually related to the stock markets, benefits from the impact of sustainability factors, especially if they are coordinated and synergistic, and is sensitive to ESG achievements that improve the overall wealth. At the firm level, a better ecosystem may lower the overall cost of capital, making the capital markets more efficient and resilient.

Digital platforms improve the architectural frame-working of the ecosystems and catalyze their functioning, operating as an orchestra director that coordinates and fine-tunes the market players.

Scalability is both market- and firm-driven, as it benefits from an overall ecosystem functioning that creates the market conditions for individual firm achievements.

Jiménez and Grima (2020) point out that the link between the cost of equity and sustainability is extremely timely as it can have great potential in reinforcing good practices regarding sustainable engagement among listed companies, which can also be regarded as trendsetters by other types of companies and institutions.

14 DIGITALIZATION AND ESG-DRIVEN VALUATION 473

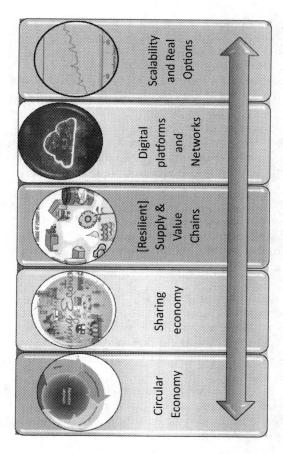

Fig. 14.2 Sustainability patterns

Circular Economy

The circular economy is an economic model that aims to minimize waste, maximize resource efficiency, and promote sustainable production and consumption. It is a departure from the traditional linear economy, which follows a "take-make-dispose" approach, where resources are extracted, transformed into products, and eventually discarded as waste. "Brick-and-mortar" traditional firms are the main players of "physical" circular economy. The influence of cryptocurrencies comes later, adding up further intricacies.

In a circular economy, the focus is on keeping products, materials, and resources in use for as long as possible through strategies such as:

1. Design for Durability and Reuse: Products are designed with a focus on durability, repairability, and ease of disassembly to enable components and materials to be reused or recycled at the end of their life cycle. This includes using standardized components and considering modular design principles.
2. Resource Recovery and Recycling: The circular economy emphasizes the recovery and recycling of materials from products at the end of their life cycle. This involves establishing efficient collection, sorting, and recycling systems to extract valuable materials and reintroduce them into the production process.
3. Remanufacturing and Refurbishment: Remanufacturing involves restoring used products to their original condition, often with upgraded components, extending their lifespan and reducing the need for new production. Refurbishment focuses on repairing and rejuvenating products to extend their usability and value.
4. Waste-to-Energy and Biomass: In situations where materials cannot be recycled or reused, the circular economy promotes the use of waste-to-energy technologies to convert waste into energy or heat. Biomass, such as organic waste, can be used to generate bioenergy through processes like anaerobic digestion or composting.
5. Collaborative Consumption and Sharing Economy: The circular economy encourages collaborative consumption models, such as sharing, renting, or pooling resources. This reduces the need for individual ownership and promotes the more efficient use of products, minimizing waste and resource consumption.

6. Product as a Service: The concept of "product as a service" involves shifting from a focus on selling products to providing services. Instead of owning products, consumers access them through a service-based model. This incentivizes manufacturers to design products that are durable, easily repairable, and recyclable, as they retain ownership and responsibility for the product's life cycle.
7. Closing Material Loops in Industries: Industries are encouraged to adopt circular practices by establishing closed-loop systems within their operations. This involves recycling and reusing waste generated during production processes, reducing the extraction of virgin resources, and minimizing waste sent to landfills.

Benefits of the circular economy include:

- Reduction in resource consumption and waste generation
- Conservation of natural resources and ecosystems
- Lower greenhouse gas emissions and reduced environmental impact
- Enhanced resource security and resilience to supply chain disruptions
- Creation of new business opportunities and job creation in circular economy sectors
- Cost savings through improved resource efficiency and reduced waste management expenses

The circular economy offers a sustainable and regenerative approach to economic activity, shifting from the current linear model to a more resource-efficient and environmentally friendly system. It requires collaboration among businesses, governments, consumers, and other stakeholders to implement circular practices and drive the transition toward a more sustainable future.

The impact of the circular economy model on the cost of capital is still largely undetected. Initial green investments may have long-term payback but should eventually become sustainable. The cost of capital of these investments may increase in the first years but then gradually decrease, especially if there are incentives to carry on green investments (and restrictions for polluting ones). What matters is, more than the individual cost of capital (within each firm), the overall collective cost (of capital) borne by a comprehensive ecosystem.

Circular systems employ reuse, sharing, repair, refurbishment, remanufacturing, and recycling to create a closed-loop system, minimizing the use of resource inputs and the creation of waste, pollution, and carbon emissions.

Combining sustainable consumption with the circular economy concept could help tackle challenges, such as resource scarcity and climate change by reducing resource throughput and increasing the cycling of products and materials within the economic system, thereby reducing emissions and virgin material use (Tunn et al., 2019).

According to the Center for Economic Development & Social Change, global economic growth is facing increasing challenges in terms of sustainability. Under this assumption, the new model of Circular Economy takes place: it promises economic growth with low or zero costs in terms of materials, energy, and environmental impact. As the Industrial Revolution promised benefits from an excess availability of resources, the Circular Economy takes advantage of resource constraints. Increasing efficiency means improving the ratio between input (environmental impact) and output (return) through behavior, technology, and planning. The reasons to achieve better efficiency are many: the scarcity of resources, the increasing environmental impact, and the promised economic return. The challenges are also many. First, incentives are low. That is because of the low cost of some resources, too low to encourage recycling and efficiency. Moreover, investments in efficiency require payback periods longer than the industrial standard, beyond a large financial capital.

Figure 14.3 shows an example of a circular economy flowchart.

The circular economy can have a significant impact on the economic and financial valuation of cryptocurrencies and digital tokens. The circular economy is an economic model that aims to maximize resource efficiency, minimize waste generation, and promote sustainable practices throughout the value chain. Here's how the circular economy can influence the valuation of cryptocurrencies and digital tokens:

a. Sustainability and Environmental Impact: The circular economy emphasizes sustainable resource management, reducing environmental impact, and promoting recycling and reuse. Cryptocurrencies and digital tokens associated with projects that embrace

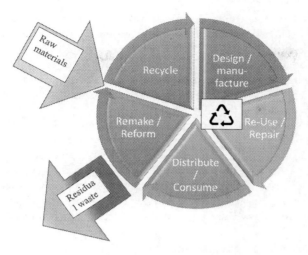

Fig. 14.3 Circular economy FlowChart

circular economy principles can enhance their sustainability credentials, attracting investors and users who value eco-friendly practices. This increased demand can positively impact the valuation of tokens.

b. Token Utility and Use Cases: The circular economy often entails designing products and services for durability, repairability, and resource efficiency. Cryptocurrencies and digital tokens can facilitate transactions and incentives within circular economy platforms that promote sustainable consumption and resource management. Tokens that enable circular economy use cases, such as incentivizing recycling, peer-to-peer sharing, or sustainable supply chain management, can gain value as their utility aligns with the circular economy objectives.

c. Stakeholder Engagement: The circular economy encourages collaboration among stakeholders, including businesses, consumers, and regulators, to drive sustainability goals. Cryptocurrencies and digital tokens that enable transparent and efficient stakeholder engagement can support circular economy initiatives. Projects that facilitate traceability, accountability, and incentive mechanisms for participants along the value chain can enhance their value proposition, attracting stakeholders and positively influencing token valuation.

d. Market Opportunities and Innovation: The circular economy presents opportunities for innovative business models and disruptive technologies. Cryptocurrencies and digital tokens that leverage blockchain technology to enable circular economy solutions can benefit from market opportunities and drive innovation. Such projects may attract investment and partnership opportunities, positively impacting their financial valuation.
e. Regulatory Environment: Governments and regulatory bodies are increasingly recognizing the importance of the circular economy and enacting policies to promote sustainable practices. Tokens associated with circular economy projects that comply with regulatory requirements and demonstrate commitment to sustainability may gain regulatory support and have a favorable position in compliance-driven markets. This can contribute to their financial valuation.

The impact of the circular economy on the valuation of cryptocurrencies and digital tokens can vary based on factors such as market demand, investor sentiment, and the specific use cases and value proposition of the tokens. However, embracing circular economy principles and aligning token utility with sustainable practices can enhance the economic and financial valuation of cryptocurrencies and digital tokens by attracting investors, fostering innovation, and addressing societal and environmental challenges.

Resilient Supply and Value Chains

Resilient supply and value chains refer to systems that are designed to withstand and adapt to disruptions, uncertainties, and shocks while maintaining continuous operations and delivering value to customers. Resilience is essential for businesses to navigate challenges such as natural disasters, geopolitical conflicts, economic downturns, and pandemics. These "physical" challenges may be increasingly related to a rapidly evolving crypto world. Here are key aspects of resilient supply and value chains:

1. Redundancy and Flexibility: Resilient supply chains incorporate redundancy by diversifying suppliers, production sites, and distribution channels. This reduces the risk of disruptions caused by

a single point of failure. Flexibility allows for agile responses to changing conditions, such as quickly shifting production, reallocating resources, or adjusting distribution strategies.
2. Risk Assessment and Management: Resilient supply chains conduct comprehensive risk assessments to identify vulnerabilities and potential disruptions. This involves analyzing risks related to suppliers, logistics, geopolitical factors, natural disasters, and other factors. Risk management strategies are then developed to mitigate identified risks through contingency plans, insurance coverage, and strategic partnerships.
3. Collaboration and Communication: Resilient supply chains prioritize collaboration and communication among supply chain partners. Effective communication channels and information sharing facilitate rapid response to disruptions and enable proactive decision-making. Collaboration also allows for shared resources, joint problem-solving, and coordinated recovery efforts.
4. Technology and Data Integration: Resilient supply chains leverage technology and data integration to enhance visibility, traceability, and real-time information exchange. Advanced analytics, Internet of Things (IoT) devices, and supply chain management systems enable better demand forecasting, inventory management, and proactive risk monitoring. Technology also supports remote work capabilities and digital collaboration, enabling operational continuity during crises.
5. Supplier Relationship Management: Resilient supply chains establish strong relationships with suppliers based on trust, transparency, and cooperation. Close collaboration with key suppliers fosters a better understanding of their capabilities, vulnerabilities, and contingency plans. This enables proactive risk mitigation, effective problem-solving, and shared recovery strategies.
6. Scenario Planning and Business Continuity: Resilient supply chains engage in scenario planning to assess potential disruptions and develop corresponding contingency plans. This involves simulating various scenarios and evaluating the impact on operations, identifying critical functions, and establishing alternative strategies to ensure business continuity. Continual testing, reviewing, and updating of business continuity plans is crucial.
7. Sustainable Practices: Resilient supply chains often integrate sustainable practices as part of their strategy. This includes considering

environmental impact, social responsibility, and ethical considerations in supplier selection, material sourcing, production processes, and logistics. Sustainable practices contribute to long-term resilience by minimizing risks associated with resource scarcity, regulatory changes, and reputational damage.
8. Continuous Improvement and Learning: Resilient supply chains embrace a culture of continuous improvement and learning. Regular evaluations and assessments of supply chain performance, feedback mechanisms, and post-disruption analyses help identify areas for improvement. Lessons learned from past disruptions are incorporated into strategies, processes, and training programs to enhance future resilience.

By implementing these practices, businesses can enhance the resilience of their supply and value chains, better adapt to disruptions, and ensure the continued delivery of value to customers. Resilient supply chains are better equipped to navigate uncertainties and position themselves for long-term success.

Supply and value chains are becoming more resilient, thanks to digitalization and networking. This impacts the cost of capital, softening overall risk. Resilience is also embedded in real options and may be estimated with a differential approach, comparing a standard (and somewhat rigid) supply chain with a resilient one (which is the added value?).

Resilient networks (e.g., digital supply chains) are elastic to external shocks, for instance, given by a node deletion (what happens if a physical or digital bridging node is deleted? Railway systems are more vulnerable than aviation systems since it is easier to replace a missing airport than a central station. Node deletion is, however, useful during pandemics).

Upson and Wei (2019) examine the impact of supply chain concentration on a firm's financing costs, showing that purchasing firms engaging in multiple supplier relationships are subject to higher firm risk and cost of equity.

Sharing Economy and Collaborative Commons

The sharing economy and collaborative commons are two related concepts that emphasize sharing resources, assets, and services among individuals and communities. The impact of the sharing economy on cryptocurrencies can be complex and multifaceted, as both of these trends have been reshaping traditional economic and financial models in their own right. Cryptocurrencies offer benefits like reduced transaction costs and increased security, making them appealing to participants in the sharing economy. However, regulatory challenges and the volatility of cryptocurrencies can also present risks. As both trends continue to evolve, their interactions will likely become more pronounced, and their impact on the broader economy will become clearer. While they share some similarities, there are distinct differences between the two:

Sharing Economy: The sharing economy refers to an economic system in which individuals or organizations share access to goods, services, or resources, often facilitated through digital platforms. It enables individuals to monetize their underutilized assets and allows others to access those assets on a temporary or on demand basis. Key characteristics of the sharing economy include:

1. Peer-to-Peer Transactions: The sharing economy facilitates direct transactions between individuals, bypassing traditional intermediaries. This enables individuals to monetize their assets, such as spare rooms (e.g., Airbnb), vehicles (e.g., Uber, Lyft), or personal skills (e.g., TaskRabbit).
2. Access over Ownership: Rather than owning goods or assets, participants in the sharing economy prioritize access and usage. They share resources, such as homes, cars, or tools, for a specific duration or purpose, reducing the need for individual ownership.
3. Platform Facilitation: Digital platforms play a crucial role in connecting individuals who want to share resources or services. These platforms provide a marketplace, facilitate transactions, and often include reputation systems and reviews to build trust among participants.
4. Efficiency and Sustainability: The sharing economy can promote resource efficiency and environmental sustainability by maximizing the use of existing resources and reducing waste. By sharing assets, there is a potential reduction in overall consumption and a more efficient allocation of resources.

Collaborative Commons: The collaborative commons refer to a socio-economic system in which individuals and organizations collaboratively create, share, and manage resources for the collective benefit. It involves the open sharing of knowledge, ideas, and innovations to foster collaboration and co-creation. Key characteristics of the collaborative commons include:

1. Open Collaboration: The collaborative commons emphasize collaboration, cooperation, and collective action. It involves individuals and organizations contributing their knowledge, expertise, and resources to create shared value and solve common challenges.
2. Open Source and Open Access: The collaborative commons often embrace the principles of open source and open access, allowing for the unrestricted sharing of information, data, and intellectual property. This promotes innovation, knowledge dissemination, and the democratization of resources.
3. Commons-Based Peer Production: The collaborative commons is characterized by commons-based peer production, where individuals collectively contribute their efforts and resources to create and maintain shared resources. This can be seen in projects like Wikipedia, open-source software development, and citizen science initiatives.
4. Non-Monetary Exchange: The collaborative commons emphasize non-monetary forms of exchange, such as sharing, gifting, and mutual aid. It focuses on social capital, reputation, and reciprocity as motivating factors for participation and contribution.
5. Long-Term Sustainability: The collaborative commons often align with sustainable practices and the preservation of common resources. It seeks to foster resilience, inclusivity, and long-term well-being by ensuring equitable access to resources and addressing environmental and social challenges.

While the sharing economy and collaborative commons share a focus on sharing and collaboration, the sharing economy is primarily driven by market transactions and the temporary utilization of underutilized assets, while the collaborative commons emphasize open collaboration, knowledge sharing, and the collective creation and management of resources for the common good.

The sharing economy (Mallinson et al., 2020) is an economic model defined as a peer-to-peer (P2P) based activity of acquiring, providing, or sharing access to goods and services that is often facilitated by a community-based online platform.

The capitalist sharing economy is a socio-economic system built around the sharing of resources. It often involves a way of purchasing goods and services that differs from the traditional business model of companies hiring employees to produce products to sell to consumers. It includes the shared creation, production, distribution, trade, and consumption of goods and services by different people and organizations (https://en.wikipedia.org/wiki/Sharing_economy).

The key assumptions of the sharing economy are consistent with the sustainability of the supply chain (Banaszyk & Łupicka, 2020).

In *The Zero Marginal Cost Society*, Rifkin (2014) describes how the emerging Internet of Things is speeding us to an era of nearly free goods and services, precipitating the meteoric rise of a global Collaborative Commons and the eclipse of capitalism. These visionary theories are consistent with sharing economy patterns.

The impact on the cost of capital is still debated.

Scalability and Real Options

Scalability pertains to the ability of a system or business model to handle growth and increased demand efficiently, while real options involve the evaluation of strategic choices and flexibility in decision-making based on changing market conditions or new information. Both concepts play important roles in business strategy, growth, and adaptation to market dynamics. Scalability is critical for the practical usability and adoption of cryptocurrencies, while real options provide a framework for making strategic decisions in a rapidly evolving and uncertain market. Both factors play a crucial role in shaping the cryptocurrency ecosystem and influencing the success and value proposition of individual cryptocurrencies and blockchain projects.

Scalability positively impacts the expected cash flows, sometimes to a great extent. It may also have an impact on the cost of capital that is, however, more difficult to ascertain. Scalable cash flows reported in the numerator of the DCF formulation may be more volatile than normal ones, so demanding a higher discount rate. On the other side, scalability may have a positive impact on resilience and sustainability.

Scalability first impacts the EBIT and sterilizes the impact of non-monetary operating costs (depreciation and amortization), on the EBITDA representing the real engine behind value creation and economic-financial growth.

Based on these premises, further consideration concerns the impact of the intangible investments on the EBITDA's components, represented by the difference between the operating (monetary) revenues and the (monetary) OPEX.

The representation may be synthesized in Fig. 14.4.

1. Intangible-driven growth in monetary revenues may be given by:

    a. Their contribution to the approach of new markets,
    b. The sales-driving digital platforms,
    c. The incremental/differential role of brands, patents
    d. Revenue and market share protection, with entry barriers
    e. Digital scalability, driven by Metcalfe or Moore law externalities
    f. Real options (to expand, contract out ...)

2. Intangible-driven savings in monetary OPEX may be given by:

    a. Productivity and efficiency gains
    b. (Digital) supply chain savings

3. Risk reduction:

    a. Affects the denominator of DCF (discount factor incorporating the cost of capital)
    b. Reduces the difference between expected and real outcomes, even thanks to timely reengineering of the business planning incorporating big data
    c. Improves the resilience and flexibility of the supply and value chain.

Flexibility (resilience) represents a key characteristic of scalability and can be enhanced using real options, concerned with the right—but not the obligation—to undertake certain business initiatives. In particular, the options available can concern the expansion, the deferral, or the abandonment of a capital investment project, such as described in Table 14.1.

Real options create the right, but not the obligation, to purchase the underlying asset at a defined exercise price. A case of real options application is the use of patents; in fact, patents allow their owners to choose between exclusively commercializing the patented invention sometimes during the patent term, or foregoing commercialization altogether. So, real options affect the valuation of potential investments and may be

14 DIGITALIZATION AND ESG-DRIVEN VALUATION 485

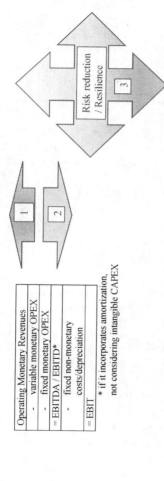

Fig. 14.4 The Impact of the Intangible Investments on the EBITDA

Table 14.1 Real options

Real option	Main features
Option to expand	To undertake a project to expand the business operations (e.g., a sushi chain considering opening new restaurants)
Option to defer or wait or suspend	Option of deferring the business decision to the future (e.g., a food chain considering opening new restaurants this year or in the next year) or suspending an unprofitable activity
Option to abandon	Option to cease a project to realize its scrap value (e.g., a manufacturing company decides to sell old equipment)

incorporated in discount models as the Net Present Value, in the sense that when investments or assets, like patents, are evaluated through NPV techniques, real options can be used to make forecasts more flexible (Iazzolino & Migliano, 2015).

ESG features that embed real options (e.g., to expand an environmental-friendly business, or to suspend and reconvert a polluting activity) can improve the resilience of capital budgeting forecasts, potentially adding value. The extent of this gain is, however, still largely undetected, as is the cost of capital savings.

Impact of ESG Parameters on the Valuation of Digital Tokens and Cryptocurrencies

ESG parameters have a growing influence on the valuation of digital tokens and cryptocurrencies. ESG factors assess the sustainability and ethical practices of an entity, including its environmental impact, social responsibility, and governance practices. ESG parameters impact the valuation of digital tokens and cryptocurrencies:

1. **Investor Preference**: ESG considerations are increasingly important to investors, including those in the cryptocurrency market. Many investors prioritize projects that demonstrate a commitment to sustainable practices, social responsibility, and strong governance. Tokens associated with projects that align with ESG principles may

attract greater investor interest and demand, potentially leading to increased valuation.

ESG considerations are increasingly relevant to cryptocurrency investors:

a. Sustainable Investing: Many investors are embracing sustainable investing principles, seeking to align their investments with their values and contribute to positive social and environmental outcomes. As cryptocurrencies gain mainstream adoption, investors are extending ESG considerations to this asset class as well, evaluating the sustainability and impact of digital tokens and blockchain projects.

b. Environmental Impact: Cryptocurrencies, particularly those that rely on proof of work (PoW) consensus algorithms like Bitcoin, have faced criticism for their environmental footprint due to high energy consumption. Investors are increasingly conscious of the carbon footprint and energy efficiency of cryptocurrencies. They seek projects that incorporate sustainable practices, such as using renewable energy sources or implementing more energy-efficient consensus mechanisms like proof-of-stake (PoS). Tokens associated with environmentally friendly projects may be viewed more favorably by ESG-focused investors.

c. Social Responsibility: ESG considerations also encompass social responsibility factors. Investors look for projects that demonstrate a commitment to social impact, ethical practices, and inclusivity. Cryptocurrencies and blockchain projects that prioritize financial inclusion, empower underserved communities, or support social initiatives tend to attract investors who value social responsibility.

d. Governance and Transparency: The governance practices of blockchain projects are another key aspect of ESG considerations. Investors assess the transparency, accountability, and decision-making structures within projects. They favor projects with robust governance frameworks, clear roadmaps, and effective community engagement. Transparent reporting, adherence to regulatory compliance, and measures to combat fraud and illicit activities are also vital considerations for ESG-focused investors.

e. Regulatory Compliance: As the cryptocurrency market continues to evolve, regulatory scrutiny and compliance requirements are increasing. ESG-focused investors seek projects that proactively address regulatory compliance, including anti-money laundering (AML) and know-your-customer (KYC) standards. Projects that navigate regulatory challenges effectively and demonstrate a commitment to compliance are likely to attract investors who prioritize ESG considerations.

Overall, ESG considerations are becoming an integral part of investment decisions in the cryptocurrency market. Investors are recognizing the importance of sustainability, social responsibility, and strong governance in evaluating the long-term viability and value of digital tokens and blockchain projects. As a result, projects that effectively address ESG factors are likely to gain a competitive edge in attracting ESG-focused investors.

2. **Risk Mitigation**: ESG parameters can be used to evaluate the risk profile of digital tokens and cryptocurrencies. Investors are becoming more aware of potential risks associated with projects that have poor environmental practices, weak social responsibility, or inadequate governance structures. Tokens that demonstrate a focus on mitigating these risks through transparent reporting, compliance, and sustainable practices may be viewed as less risky and more valuable in the long term.

    ESG factors contribute to risk mitigation:

    a. Environmental Risk: ESG considerations assess the environmental impact of digital tokens and cryptocurrencies. Projects that consume excessive energy or contribute to carbon emissions can face environmental risks, including regulatory scrutiny, reputational damage, or potential restrictions on their operations. By evaluating and addressing environmental risks, projects can mitigate the potential negative impact on their operations and market value.

    b. Social Risk: ESG factors also evaluate social risks associated with digital tokens and cryptocurrencies. These risks can include issues related to data privacy, user protection, social inclusivity, or support for unethical practices. Projects that proactively address these risks by implementing robust data protection measures, fostering community engagement, and promoting inclusivity can mitigate social risks and enhance their reputation.

c. **Governance Risk**: ESG parameters assess the governance practices of projects, including transparency, accountability, and decision-making structures. Weak governance practices can lead to governance risks, such as mismanagement, fraud, or lack of regulatory compliance. By establishing strong governance frameworks and ensuring transparency and accountability, projects can mitigate governance-related risks and build investor trust.
d. **Regulatory Risk**: Regulatory scrutiny is a significant risk factor for digital tokens and cryptocurrencies. ESG considerations encompass compliance with regulatory requirements, such as anti-money laundering (AML) and know-your-customer (KYC) regulations. Projects that prioritize regulatory compliance and demonstrate adherence to applicable laws and regulations can mitigate regulatory risks and reduce the potential for legal challenges or regulatory sanctions.

By incorporating ESG considerations into risk assessments, investors can gain a comprehensive understanding of the risk profile associated with digital tokens and cryptocurrencies. Evaluating and addressing environmental, social, and governance risks helps projects anticipate and mitigate potential challenges, enhancing their resilience and long-term viability. Moreover, projects that effectively manage ESG risks may attract ESG-focused investors who prioritize sustainability, social responsibility, and strong governance, thus positively influencing market demand and valuation.

3. **Regulatory Environment**: ESG considerations are increasingly being integrated into regulatory frameworks worldwide. Governments and regulatory bodies are exploring ways to ensure that digital tokens and cryptocurrencies comply with ESG standards. Failure to meet these standards may result in regulatory hurdles or reputational damage. Tokens that proactively address ESG parameters and align with evolving regulations may have a competitive advantage in terms of valuation. The policy system concerns:

   a. **Regulatory Frameworks**: Governments and regulatory bodies worldwide are working to establish regulatory frameworks for digital assets, including cryptocurrencies. These frameworks aim to address various aspects, including investor protection, market integrity, anti-money laundering (AML) measures, and compliance with ESG principles. Regulatory initiatives, such as licensing requirements, disclosure standards, and mandatory reporting, can help enforce ESG standards within the cryptocurrency industry.

b. Sustainability Initiatives: Some governments and regulatory bodies are actively promoting sustainability within the cryptocurrency sector. They are encouraging the use of renewable energy sources for mining operations and incentivizing projects that adopt energy-efficient consensus algorithms. For example, initiatives like the Crypto Climate Accord aim to make the cryptocurrency industry 100% renewable by 2025, highlighting the importance of sustainability and environmental considerations.

c. ESG Reporting and Disclosure: Governments and regulatory bodies may introduce requirements for ESG reporting and disclosure by digital asset issuers and service providers. Similar to traditional financial reporting, these regulations would mandate the disclosure of ESG-related information, such as environmental impact, social initiatives, and governance practices. Enhanced transparency and standardized reporting can help investors make informed decisions and foster accountability within the cryptocurrency market.

d. Investor Protection: Investor protection is a key consideration for governments and regulators. They are focused on ensuring that investors in digital tokens and cryptocurrencies are adequately informed about the risks and ESG-related factors associated with their investments. Regulatory measures, such as investor education initiatives, risk disclosure requirements, and combating fraudulent activities, aim to safeguard investor interests and promote responsible investing within the cryptocurrency ecosystem.

e. Collaborations and International Standards: Governments and regulatory bodies are also collaborating with industry stakeholders, standard-setting organizations, and international bodies to develop ESG standards specific to digital assets. Collaborative efforts can lead to the establishment of industry best practices, ESG frameworks, and international standards that promote sustainability, social responsibility, and sound governance practices across the cryptocurrency market.

Regulatory approaches and progress in ESG compliance within the cryptocurrency industry can vary between jurisdictions. The regulatory landscape is evolving, and governments are continually assessing the best approaches to balance innovation, investor protection, and ESG considerations within the digital asset space.

4. **Market Access and Partnerships**: ESG parameters can impact the ability of digital tokens and cryptocurrencies to access certain markets or form partnerships. Some exchanges, investment funds, and institutional investors have specific ESG criteria for listing or investment. Tokens that meet these criteria may gain easier market access and attract partnerships, potentially increasing their liquidity and valuation.

ESG considerations influence market access and partnerships:
 a. Exchange Listings: Many cryptocurrency exchanges are starting to incorporate ESG criteria into their listing requirements. Exchanges may evaluate projects based on their commitment to environmental sustainability, social impact, and governance practices. Tokens that align with ESG standards are more likely to meet the listing criteria of exchanges that prioritize sustainability and responsible investing. Meeting these criteria can provide increased market access and liquidity for tokens.
 b. Institutional Investment: Institutional investors, such as investment funds, pension funds, and endowments, are increasingly considering ESG factors when making investment decisions. These investors often have their own ESG guidelines or mandates, and they may prioritize investments that align with their sustainability and responsible investing goals. Digital tokens and cryptocurrencies that demonstrate strong ESG practices may attract institutional investment, leading to increased liquidity and valuation.
 c. Partnerships and Collaboration: ESG considerations can influence partnership opportunities for digital tokens and cryptocurrencies. Businesses and organizations that prioritize ESG values may prefer to collaborate with projects that share similar commitments. For instance, companies focused on sustainability or social impact may seek partnerships with tokens that align with their values and have a positive ESG track record. Collaborations with reputable partners can enhance the credibility and adoption potential of tokens.

d. Regulatory Compliance: ESG compliance is becoming increasingly relevant in regulatory frameworks. Governments and regulatory bodies may require digital tokens and cryptocurrencies to adhere to ESG standards to ensure compliance and protect investors. Projects that demonstrate a commitment to ESG principles are more likely to gain regulatory approval and meet compliance requirements, enabling access to regulated markets and broader investor participation.
e. Investor Demand and Sentiment: ESG considerations are driving investor demand and sentiment in the cryptocurrency market. Investors, particularly those focused on sustainable investing, are actively seeking projects that prioritize ESG principles. Tokens that meet ESG standards can attract a broader investor base, create positive sentiment, and potentially experience increased demand, leading to higher market value.

By incorporating ESG parameters into their operations and demonstrating a commitment to sustainability, social responsibility, and strong governance, digital tokens, and cryptocurrencies can enhance their market positioning, attract partnerships with like-minded organizations, and gain access to regulated markets and institutional investors. ESG considerations have the potential to contribute to the long-term success and valuation of tokens in an increasingly ESG-conscious investment landscape.

5. **Reputation and Brand Image**: ESG considerations contribute to the reputation and brand image of digital tokens and cryptocurrencies. Projects that prioritize sustainability, social impact, and responsible governance tend to build a positive reputation within the crypto community and beyond. A strong reputation can attract a larger user base, developer community, and strategic collaborations, which can positively impact valuation.

ESG factors influence reputation and brand image:

a. Sustainability and Environmental Responsibility: ESG considerations evaluate the environmental impact of digital tokens and cryptocurrencies. Projects that demonstrate a commitment to sustainability, energy efficiency, and minimizing carbon footprints are viewed more favorably by stakeholders. By adopting environmentally responsible practices, tokens can enhance their reputation as environmentally conscious and attract investors and users who value sustainability.

b. Social Responsibility and Impact: ESG factors encompass social responsibility and the impact of projects on society. Digital tokens and cryptocurrencies that prioritize social initiatives, promote financial inclusion, or support charitable causes can enhance their brand image as socially responsible entities. This fosters a positive reputation and attracts users and investors who value projects with a positive societal impact.
c. Governance and Transparency: ESG considerations evaluate the governance practices and transparency of projects. By adopting strong governance frameworks, ensuring transparent decision-making processes, and providing clear information to stakeholders, tokens can build a reputation for good governance. This establishes trust and confidence among investors, users, and the broader community, positively impacting their brand image.
d. Investor Trust and Confidence: ESG considerations are important factors for investors who prioritize sustainable and responsible investing. Tokens that demonstrate a commitment to ESG principles can gain the trust and confidence of these investors, who see the alignment of values as a key driver for investment decisions. Building investor trust enhances the reputation and brand image of tokens, attracting more investors and potentially increasing market demand.
e. Differentiation in the Market: ESG considerations provide an opportunity for tokens to differentiate themselves in a crowded market. By emphasizing their commitment to sustainability, social responsibility, and strong governance, tokens can set themselves apart from competitors and carve a unique brand identity. This differentiation can attract users, investors, and partners who value ESG-focused projects, contributing to a positive brand image.

A strong reputation and brand image as an ESG-conscious project can lead to increased market recognition, user adoption, and investor interest. It can also help tokens withstand potential challenges and regulatory scrutiny, as ESG-focused projects are often seen as more trustworthy and resilient. Therefore, incorporating ESG considerations and communicating ESG efforts effectively can be instrumental in shaping the reputation and brand image of digital tokens and cryptocurrencies.

The impact of ESG parameters on the valuation of digital tokens and cryptocurrencies is still evolving, and industry standards are being developed. As the focus on sustainability and responsible investing grows, ESG factors are likely to become even more influential in shaping the market value of tokens and the overall cryptocurrency ecosystem.

REFERENCES

Asaduzzaman, M., Shahjahan, M., & Murase, K. (2015). Real-time decision-making forecasting using data mining and decision tree. *International Journal on Information, 18*(7), 3027–3047.

Banaszyk, P., & Łupicka, A. (2020). Sustainable supply chain management in the perspective of sharing economy. In K. Grzybowska, A. Awasthi, & R. Sawhney (Eds.), *Sustainable logistics and production in industry 4.0. EcoProduction (environmental issues in logistics and manufacturing)*. Springer.

Billio, M., Costola, M., Hristova, I., Latino, C., & Pelizzon, L. (2021). Inside the ESG ratings: (Dis)agreement and performance. *Corporate Social Responsibility and Environmental Management, 28*(5), 1426–1445.

Breuer, H., Fichter, K., Lüdeke-Freund, F., & Tiemann, I. (2018). Sustainability-oriented business model development: Principles, criteria and tools. *International Journal of Entrepreneurial Venturing, 10*(2), 256–286.

Brinckmann, J., Grichnik, D., & Kapsa, D. (2010). Should entrepreneurs plan or just storm the castle? A meta-analysis on contextual factors impacting the business planning–performance relationship in small firms. *Journal of Business Venturing, 25*(1), 24–40.

Chwolka, A., & Raith, M. A. (2012). The value of business planning before start-up—A decision-theoretical perspective. *Journal of Business Venturing, 27*(3), 385–399.

Cornell, B., & Shapiro, A. C. (2021). Corporate stakeholders, corporate valuation and ESG. *European Financial Management, 27*(2), 196–207.

Giese, G., Lee, L., Melas, D., Nagy, Z., & Nishikawa, L. (2019). Foundations of ESG investing: How ESG affects equity valuation, risk, and performance. *The Journal of Portfolio Management, 45*(5), 69–83.

Grossman, S. J., & Stiglitz, J. E. (1977). On value maximization and alternative objectives of the firm. *The Journal of Finance, 32*(2), 389–402.

Iazzolino, G., & Migliano, G. (2015). The valuation of a patent through the real options approach: A tutorial. *Journal of Business Valuation and Economic Loss Analysis, 10*(1).

Ielasi, F., Capelli, P., & Russo, A. (2021). Forecasting volatility by integrating financial risk with environmental, social, and governance risk. *Corporate Social Responsibility and Environmental Management, 28*(5), 1483–1495.

Jiménez, R. G., & Grima, A. Z. (2020). Corporate social responsibility and cost of equity: Literature review and suggestions for future research. *Journal of Business, Accounting and Finance Perspectives, 2*(3), 15.

Koprivnjak, T., & Peterka, S. O. (2020). Business model as a base for building firms' competitiveness. *Sustainability, 12*(21), 1–18.

Lasher, W. (2010). *The perfect business plan made simple: The best guide to writing a plan that will secure financial backing for your business.* Broadway Books.

Mallinson, D. J., Morçöl, G., Yoo, E., Azim, S. F., Levine, E., & Shafi, S. (2020). Sharing economy: A systematic thematic analysis of the literature. *Information Polity, 25*(2), 143–158.

Ng, A. C., & Rezaee, Z. (2012). Sustainability disclosures and cost of capital. Available at https://ssrn.com/abstract=2038654

Razgaitis, R. (2003). *Dealmaking using real options and monte Carlo analysis.* Wiley Finance.

Rifkin, J. (2014). *The zero marginal cost society: The internet of things, the collaborative commons, and the eclipse of capitalism.* Palgrave Macmillan.

Sahlman, W. A. (1997). How to write a great business plan. *Harvard Business Review, 75*(4), 98–109.

Tunn, V. S. C., Bocken, N. M. P., van den Hende, E. A., & Schoormans, J. P. L. (2019). Business models for sustainable consumption in the circular economy: An expert study. *Journal of Cleaner Production, 212,* 324–333.

Upson, J., & Wei, C. (2019). Supply chain concentration and cost of capital. Available at https://ssrn.com/abstract=3532089

Index

A
Accounting background, 420
Algorithmic stablecoins, 111, 122, 123, 359, 369
Asset class, 3, 4, 35
Augmented business planning, 466

B
Backed stablecoins, 111, 112, 120, 121, 358, 360, 369
Balance-sheet-based approach, 38, 41
Banking-as-a-Service (Baas), 424
Bitcoin, 2, 7, 9, 20, 107–111, 113, 115, 117, 127, 130, 131, 133, 163, 167, 168, 172, 177, 178, 186, 194, 284, 358, 369, 392, 395, 398–402, 406, 407, 413, 426, 427, 429, 487
Break-even point, 452, 464
Bubble, 35, 124, 126, 127, 175, 395–397, 400, 452
Burn out, 453
Business model, 4, 32, 38, 49, 87, 95, 96, 155, 161, 165, 169, 173, 175, 178, 187, 188, 218, 229–233, 235, 244, 247–249, 253, 259, 263, 267, 270, 271, 275, 277, 278, 282, 293, 307, 395, 400–403, 411, 414, 416, 417, 420, 421, 424, 435–441, 452, 455, 459, 462, 465, 478, 483
business plan, 31, 32, 52, 316, 317, 420, 464

C
CAPEX, 38, 41, 46, 58, 66, 88, 96, 101, 485
Capitalization, 3, 6, 20, 32, 36, 47, 48, 51–53, 63, 65, 69, 85, 87, 109, 114, 118, 127, 304, 325, 328, 331, 333, 357, 362, 367, 378, 379, 383, 385, 386, 395, 441, 446–448
Circular economy, 462, 470, 471, 474–478
Comparables, 37, 119, 279, 360, 382, 443, 451

Contagion, 395, 408, 409
Corporate valuation, 27, 42
Cost approach, 85, 91, 93, 158, 274, 280
Cost of capital, 25, 51, 52, 65, 377, 439, 440, 445, 449, 453, 465–469, 471, 472, 475, 480, 483, 484, 486
Crypto art, 142
Crypto assets, 112, 117, 304, 382, 405–407
Crypto collateralized stablecoins, 121, 122
Crypto exchanges, 114, 287, 408
Cybersecurity, 18–20, 24, 280, 341, 342, 344–354, 454

D

Damages, 18, 28, 125, 341–344, 346, 351, 353, 407, 454, 480, 488, 489
Decentralization, 2, 5, 17, 109, 128, 167, 169, 171, 175, 176, 178, 180, 183, 186, 188, 189, 194–196, 204, 253, 284, 290, 292, 293, 295–297, 299, 309, 349, 357, 371, 404, 428, 429
Decentralized Finance (De.Fi.), 16, 112, 114, 129, 179, 195, 222, 237, 287–289, 306, 307, 309, 313, 320, 321, 327, 331, 332, 335, 337, 344, 345, 347, 360, 368, 370, 372–374, 381, 382, 385, 392, 404, 408, 435
Digital art, 7, 9, 136, 138, 141–145, 147–149, 158, 163, 284
Digital ledger, 165, 167, 422
Digital money, 414
Digital museums, 143
Digital payment, 1, 22–24, 412, 425, 427–434, 456

Digital platforms, 15, 16, 100, 102–104, 144, 145, 148, 160, 179, 215, 218, 225, 241, 243–245, 247–255, 259–270, 275–281, 355, 412, 417, 418, 426, 432, 460, 465, 472, 481, 484
Digital scalability, 162, 267, 484
Digital supply chain, 256, 259–262, 480
Discounted cash flows, 32, 47, 276, 360, 443, 444, 449, 465
Distributed networks, 298, 299
Due diligence, 308, 331, 337, 338, 347, 402, 404, 413

E

E-commerce, 16, 105, 173, 179, 187, 218, 226, 229, 248–251, 262, 267, 271, 275, 426
Economic marginality, 47, 50, 100, 102, 420
Enterprise value, 29–32, 36, 58, 60, 63–65, 69, 73, 77, 88, 94, 276, 279, 366, 375, 381, 383, 417, 444, 446, 451
Environmental, social, and governance (ESG), 24, 25, 230, 460, 461, 463–467, 469, 472, 486–493
Ethereum, 2, 7, 9, 20, 109, 112, 113, 115, 130, 133, 163, 165, 168, 177, 178, 186, 194, 195, 284, 287, 290, 291, 302, 303, 310, 342, 356, 360, 365, 368, 372, 401, 413, 426, 427

F

Financial approach, 29, 30, 49, 58, 158, 274, 392, 443, 444
Financial capacity, 27
Firm evaluation, 360

Functional analysis, 31, 32

G
Geolocalization, 421
Gold standard, 369
Goodwill, 29, 45, 50, 81, 83, 87, 90, 92, 93, 95, 101, 102, 150

H
Hash, 167, 169, 303

I
Income approach, 29, 47, 48, 86, 91, 93, 97, 270, 279, 326, 360, 368, 372–374, 391, 392, 442
Insurtech, 173, 413, 414, 423
Interactive art, 142–144, 152
Interest rates, 69, 123, 320, 369, 370, 395, 400, 405, 412, 450, 472
Internet of value, 10–12, 176–184

L
Learning curves, 248
Liquidity, 16, 17, 20, 36, 41, 44, 46, 60, 65, 66, 69, 93, 95, 96, 114, 117, 121, 122, 125, 128, 132–134, 138, 165, 191, 195, 237, 276, 288, 289, 306, 315, 318, 321, 322, 325, 331, 333, 334, 336–338, 356, 357, 363, 365, 370, 372, 374, 375, 381, 382, 384, 390, 400, 407, 450, 491
liquidity pools, 111, 287–290, 294, 296, 304, 309, 311, 313–316, 337, 359, 373

M
Malware, 341, 343, 409

Market approach, 29, 31, 69, 85, 91, 95, 275, 276, 324, 372, 378, 379, 392, 451
Market valuation, 77, 94, 127, 128, 165, 362, 363, 372
Monetary equity, 45–47
Multilayer networks, 99, 212–216, 218

N
Net cash flows, 31, 32, 38, 59, 65, 66, 76, 95, 96, 101, 375, 384, 420, 444, 448, 449, 464, 469
Network Theory, 98, 202, 204, 245, 249, 261, 264, 418, 465
New media art, 143
Non-Fungible Tokens (NFT), 7–10, 16, 133–138, 163–166, 229, 357
Normalized income, 48–52

O
Operating cash flows, 30, 32, 59, 65, 66, 76, 88, 94–96, 101, 375, 384, 444, 448, 449
Ownership concentration, 115, 116, 328, 374, 383, 401

P
P2P lending, 173
P2P networks, 298
Platform-as-a-Service (PaaS), 272, 273
Ponzi, 321, 398, 401, 402
Price to Earnings ratio (P/E ratio), 322, 387, 388, 392
Proof-of-Stake (PoS) network, 318, 389, 390

R

Real options, 67, 85, 96, 162, 261, 443, 444, 464, 472, 480, 483, 484, 486
Risk management, 17, 18, 24, 122, 126, 133, 317, 318, 346, 413, 431, 479

S

Scalability, 4, 12, 13, 15, 22, 23, 88, 91, 95, 103, 114, 125, 128, 145, 161, 168, 180–182, 189–191, 193, 195, 196, 205, 206, 208, 211, 213, 238, 263–265, 272, 273, 275, 280, 282, 283, 299, 319, 325, 360, 363, 374, 417, 436–438, 454, 472, 483, 484
Sharing economy, 179, 180, 218, 230, 248, 249, 411, 472, 474, 480–483
Smart contract, 7, 9–11, 16, 17, 109–113, 122, 128, 129, 134, 164, 167–169, 172–178, 184, 186, 193–196, 205, 238, 287, 288, 290, 294–297, 299, 303, 305–310, 314–319, 332, 337, 342, 343, 347, 349, 356, 359, 360, 372, 385, 386, 414, 428, 435
Smart transactions, 10–12, 174, 175, 193
Social network, 148, 161, 179, 188, 205, 208, 209, 213, 214, 220, 230, 264
Supply and value chains, 201, 248, 262, 263, 418, 465, 472, 478, 480, 484

Sustainable capital, 469
SWOT, 127, 345, 346, 363, 364, 424

T

Timestamp, 146, 167, 172, 303
Tokenomics, 6, 37, 119, 325, 334, 357, 361–364, 367, 371, 382, 388
Total Value Locked (TVL) ratio, 327, 381, 392
Tracking, 146, 173, 223, 278, 356, 413

V

Value added, 53, 211
Value chains, 215, 262, 263, 412
Value co-creation, 100, 102, 180, 187, 188, 229, 230, 245, 456
Venture capital, 293, 294, 302, 307, 309, 327, 377, 408, 440, 444, 452, 453
Virtual marketplaces, 14–16, 241–244, 281–284
Volatility, 7, 17, 21, 22, 53, 110, 111, 115–118, 121–124, 128, 130–133, 195, 275, 280, 284, 289, 304, 317–319, 329, 333, 358, 363–366, 376, 377, 390, 398, 400, 401, 404, 406, 407, 414, 429, 436, 445, 454
Voting pool, 296, 309, 311, 313–316

W

With or without, 96, 153, 269, 270, 274

Printed in the United States
by Baker & Taylor Publisher Services